Frederick F. Lighthall received his AB degree from Oberlin College in History and his AM and PhD degrees from Yale University in Educational Psychology. Before joining the faculty of the University of Chicago in 1960 he was employed as a farmer, an internal auditor in a ball bearings factory, and a public school teacher. His early research interests related to education focused on emotional and cognitive aspects of the learner—he co-authored *Test Anxiety in Elementary School Children* (New York, Wiley, 1960) with Sarason and others—but gradually gave way to social and organizational aspects of schooling, particularly on how members of school staffs succeed or fail in their efforts to work together productively. Professor Lighthall is currently extending the ideas worked out in this book to analyses of the decision processes of NASA and Morton-Thiokol engineers and managers just prior to the fatal launch of the Space Shuttle Challenger in 1986. He produced *Local Realities, Local Adaptations* in collaboration with **Susan D. Allan** of Falls Church, Virginia Public Schools, USA.

Local Realities, Local Adaptations

Problem, Process and Person in a School's Governance

Frederick F. Lighthall
University of Chicago

In Collaboration with

Susan D. Allan
Falls Church, Virginia
Public Schools

 The Falmer Press

(A member of the Taylor & Francis Group)
London • New York • Philadelphia

UK   The Falmer Press, Falmer House, Barcombe, Lewes, East Sussex. BN8
            5DL

USA   The Falmer Press, Taylor & Francis Inc., 1900 Frost Road, Suite 101,
            Bristol, PA 19007

© Frederick F. Lighthall 1989

First published 1989

British Library Cataloguing in Publication Data
Lighthall, Frederick F.
    Local realities, local adaptations:
    problem, process, and person in a school's governance.
    1. United States. Schools. Management
    I. Title II. Allan, Susan D.
    371.2′00973

    ISBN 1-85000-587-7
    ISBN 1-85000-588-5 pbk

Library of Congress Cataloging-in-Publication Data
Lighthall, Frederick F.
    Local realities, local adaptations: problem, process, and person in a
school's governance/Frederick F. Lighthall in collaboration with Susan D.
Allan.
        p.   cm.
    Bibliography: p.
    Includes index.
    ISBN 1-85000-587-7. — ISBN   1-85000-588-5 (pbk.)
    1. High schools — Administration — Case studies. 2 Conflict man-
agement — Case studies. I. Allan, Susan D. II. Title. LB2822.L48
1989
373. 12—dc20

Jacket design by Caroline Archer

Typeset in 10½/12pt Caledonia
by Graphicraft Typesetters Ltd., Hong Kong
Printed and bound by Taylor and Franeis (Printers) Ltd, Basingstoke

Contents

Contents

List of Tables

List of Figures

Preface

At every turn humans are confronted with a particular set of realities at once familiar and strange, understandable and confusing, confirming and threatening, safe and dangerous: the realities of other humans. Our need for others in our organization — our university or factory or police department — to cooperate in joint work leads to various kinds of trouble as soon as regular policies and procedures fail. We usually muddle through, but often we waste more dear energy and good will than we bargained for, and sometimes we end in absurdity or disaster, bewildered by others' pigheaded recalcitrance or, more often, by the sheer otherness of others, the apparent narrowness of their attachments or fears, preventing them from seeing the wider benefits of our favored action.

When we agree with each other, we savor the warmth of confirmation. We try at virtually every turn, as we go about our work with others, to make and maintain agreements — agreements in principles, procedures, concepts, perspectives, goals, and values. But when we clearly disagree, we often — too often for our peace of mind or actual security — see others' otherness as less aware, narrower in perspective, or shadier morally than our own tested reality. We mentally gird our loins to overcome those others' limitations and to establish as dominant the agreement we see as more aware of complexities, broader in perspective, loftier in ideal. But our internal girding is accomplished by our own categories of thought and assessments of reality, all of which gives more protection to our own ways of doing things than to others' ways of doing things. And to the extent that our emotions are aroused or we become threatened by the others' different goals and outlooks, we tend to stop inquiring and to slide into projecting our own fears and suspicions onto the other. The process of casting the others' differentness into categories of lesser, narrower, and suspect is accomplished imperceptibly: we focus on handling the differentness, not on the process of doing so.

Between these two extremes of confirming agreement and clear, cold difference lies most of daily life in organizations. It is in this mixed, normal state of hearing others' plans and views as not entirely expected but not entirely unexpected either, that something between warm confirmation and cold rejection occurs which we need to understand in its mixed, in-between nature. We need that understanding in order to get better, individually and collectively, at applying intelligent minding to the ways we can contribute to, or unwittingly subvert, cumulative action. In particular, we need to understand this mixed condition in order to understand why apparently good plans and innovations, thought up by learned, sensitive, moral people, so often become the occasion for overt and covert resistance and for wasted, emotionally draining effort in all kinds of organizations. Such efforts consume not only participants' energies, but also their good will and optimism, leaving them increasingly suspect of any change that does not come from themselves for their own good.

This book is about that world of normal human interchange where participants take in each others' differences oscillating between denigrating rejection and enthusiastic endorsement, where they want and try to understand each other up to a point. That point is crucial. It marks the end of willingness to listen and learn and the beginning of the urge just to tell and to do; the end of openness to others' realities and the beginning of closure to those realities. This is the domain where getting things done tends so often to pre-empt achieving a shared, coherent and integrated understanding of who the central participants are, what they are up to and why, and where we legitimately fit into the effort. That gap in shared understanding tends to be filled by each participant, separately, out of his or her own minding — thus achieving a private coherence at the expense of a shared understanding, a cognitive schema that makes merely personal sense instead of a common purpose that engenders coherent, coordinated action.

This book examines mundane efforts in a setting familiar to all, a secondary school, efforts of healthy, intelligent, productive persons in a thriving institution to make its schooling better from within by changing its 'governance'. While the substantive vehicle is a school and improvements in governance, the focus of interest is in the generic social psychological and organizational processes of people trying to get something done together in an organization — in ways that honor the collective enterprise while retaining coherence and opportunity for each separate participant. Think of it as an empirical essay on the struggle and relations between local realities and collective order, an essay on the emergence or failure of community among participants in action.

But think of it, too, as an attempt to break new ground in social science method. I offer three exemplars of a new unit of analysis, the problem-solving episode. This unit offers, I think, a new window from which can be seen some new aspects of organizational life and some familiar aspects in a new light. That 'light' is adaptation in a more or less Darwinian sense, where response is made to conditions that at least some participants judge to have taken a turn for the worse.

Part I of the book lays out the argument, basic concepts, background, and participants. Parts II, III, and IV trace three unfolding adaptations. Each part offers analytical commentaries interjected into the narrative, ending with a table of variables which seem to explain main outcomes. The last table of variables integrates those of the first two. Part V concludes with contributions of the whole project to data, theory, method, and practice.

I gratefully acknowledge support in the early phases of this project from Jack Glidewell, whose ideas, experience, and friendship were essential; and from the National Institutes of Health (NIMH Grant 5-T21-MH-11217) which supported the training program that spawned this project. Susan D. Allan's influence and contributions are only partially visible in the narratives and on the title page; I am grateful to her not only for her substantive and editorial critiques but also for her partnership at Trinity and stimulating friendship beyond. My wife, Maureen, gave devotedly her editorial talents and insightful wisdom in every phase and mood of this long project.

A number of colleagues have contributed well beyond the call of duty or friendship. Sr. Claudia has read every page and conferred at length; hers was a singular and unique contribution of openness, authenticity, and courageous self-examination. Larry V. Hedges, too, has read every page and provided perspective, challenge, and much clarification; his has been an unparalleled collegial gift. Philip Runkel, Bruce McPherson, Barry Schwartz, Donald Fiske, and Richard Shweder each commented on all or extensive parts of the manuscript in illuminating detail. John Lofland gave a helpful reading to Parts I and II, and Dean Pruitt offered especially helpful advice on the ideas and presentation of Part III.

Other colleagues, students, and friends whose special insights on parts of the manuscript I am happy to acknowledge gratefully are Clayton Alderfer, Chris Argyris, Joe Braun, Anthony Bryk, Thomas Chockley, Mihaly Csikszentmihalyi, Joyce DeHaan, James Dillon, Morton Deutsch, Harold Dunkel, Donald Erickson, Michael Fullan, Jacob Getzels, Egon Guba, Suzanne Kobasa, Nancy Lighthall, Susan Lourenco, Richard Magjuka, Eugene McDowell, Seymour Sarason, Richard Schmuck, Daniel Solomon, Nancy Stein, Herbert Thelen, Sveinung Vaage, Ellen Wentland, and Victor Yngve. All shortcomings of book are mine and remain despite their best efforts.

An intensive project like this combines with a mind like mine to turn writing into years. Sons and daughter have grown up and grandchildren have come on the scene since this project began. The ups and downs over that span could not have been managed without the warm encouragement of my mother, Helen F. Lighthall, and of Maureen, Alison, David, Paul, Dick, Mary, Bill and Steve. I thank them for their familial love and encouragement.

Frederick F. Lighthall
Chicago, IL

Part I
Introduction

Chapter 1

Purposes, Argument, and Concepts

At one level of analysis this book is about some innovations in school governance having to do with the sharing of power and responsibility. At that level, the book traces one school administrator's attempts to solve some important organizational problems and to resolve a deeply frustrating conflict with a co-administrator. The book does illuminate important aspects of school administrators' organizational lives. But the chief intent and focus of the book is at a deeper level, one where schools and other formal organizations produce collective action whose forms and dynamics are indistinguishable from one kind of organization to another. At this more generic level the book focuses on the ways in which the local organizational realities of an organization's members trigger and constrain their local adaptations. By 'local adaptation' I mean simply the adjustments people make, individually and in their organizational groupings, to upsetting changes in their circumstances, in their aspirations, their hopes and fears, their revised outlooks — in short, adaptations to disturbing changes in their local realities.

While we do participate in organized concerted action with others, we do so always with a first commitment to meeting our own necessities. These 'necessities' may be moral or sensual, intellectual or emotional, short-term or long-term. But they are always local: particular to our own immediate realities. I want to write a good book. But just now I must write this sentence — and return to it after answering the telephone. We all have larger commitments to citizenship and justice, but the boss has more work and we stay overtime. Then the house repairs need attention, the baby is crying, and it is lunchtime. We do commit ourselves to participate with others in lofty goals and big plans, but we do so in the midst of daily adaptations to life's mundane and circumstantial demands. Our ideas and ideals are translocal, even universal, but our lives are lived minute to minute, hour to hour, day by day immersed in the chronic task of fashioning particular solutions to our own problems.

This circumstantial localism is exacerbated by the fractionated division of labor of modern society. Everyone is familiar with the secondary school but perhaps few of us think of it as afflicted with the same specialization in its roles as is found in hospitals, businesses, and government. Consider: teachers teach but do not do the work or have the problems of the school administrator, the school counselor, the school nurse, the school psychologist, the school social worker, or the school secretary. Each of these roles carries with it not only special daily duties but also its own special training and frequently specialized professional certification. To be an adequate teacher or administrator, one must give careful attention and energy to the immediate, mundane, locally situated and distinctive demands of teaching or administering.

This role-specific localism implies much for how we are able to cooperate with others — and how we refuse to cooperate with others — in their lofty plans and ideals. The story of much of what is labeled, 'resistance to change' is captured in a little verse by Lucille Clifton:[1]

> why some people be mad at me sometimes
> they ask me to remember
> but they want me to remember
> their memories
> and i keep on remembering mine.

The Argument in Six Paragraphs

1.   All complex organizations — schools, law firms, police departments, churches, or manufacturing companies — have primary unifying purposes or missions. Schools engender certain knowledge, attitudes, habits, and skills in students. Law firms offer legal services for clients. Actions in different kinds of organization tend to be constrained by their primary, unifying purposes. But in order to carry out their respective unitary purposes, the regular tasks necessary to do so are *divided* up into separately identified, specialized roles and different levels of authority. A coherent achievement of purpose is accomplished only through diverse functions: functions carried out by restricting members' actions to relatively circumscribed, specialized segments of the organization's overall mission. Specialized functions are separated out from the overall purpose; in the case of schooling, choosing curricula, instruction, managing students' emotional and career problems, handling written communications, monitoring and organizing the adults to carry out the mission, and maintaining the physical plant in which the mission is carried out.

2.   These circumscribed functions become regularized and routinized as 'roles', 'procedures', 'policies', 'levels of authority' and the like. The roles of curriculum coordinator, teacher, guidance counselor, secretary, administrator, and custodian are created. And members who carry out each of these functions try to reduce their work to routinized procedures for dealing

with repeated events and demands. But organizations face constant disruptions in routine, from without and from within: organizational routines are under constant repair. Curriculum is always changing, as are specific outlooks and techniques of teaching, of offering guidance services, administering a school, and so on.

3. Disturbances in organizational functioning, however, become identified by members carrying out specific functions, and tend to be identified by them as impediments to their own functioning. The organization itself, as a total entity, has no capacity to identify, construe, or respond to disturbances except through its role-situated and hierarchically placed members. Contrary to popular belief, the chief leaders of any organization do not possess 'the big picture' of their organization, if by this is meant how the entire organization is functioning. They possess their own big picture, which is constrained like all others by their particular position, by the information that comes to it, and by their position-specific attachments and goals. Thus, specialized roles and levels not only carry out separately identified functions but also create and maintain *local frames of reference*, local subjective realities, by which members interpret smooth and disturbed functioning. The child's scraped knee on the playground becomes, for the teacher a normal event, a problem whose routine solution is clear: send the child to the school nurse. The school nurse regards the abrasion as simply a technical problem for which she has standard technical skill: she simply cleans and bandages the abrasion. For the principal, however, the abrasion may constitute a source of questions whether the teacher was exercising proper supervision and whether parents might complain. But these local frames of reference do more than organize diagnoses of disturbances; they also motivate and shape repairs. Members repair disturbances in ways favorable to their own local performance and with resources locally available. Repairs, being construed and accomplished locally, tend to be guided only secondarily by reference to a central mission and are only secondarily responsive to how local functions, once repaired, participate integratively, coherently, or cumulatively toward fulfilling the organization's overall purpose. Thus, the school administrator who receives news of another playground accident may worry about parental complaints and possible vulnerability to litigation. She may decide this disturbance is serious enough to attend to more closely, and to ask the school nurse to keep a new kind of record, one that lists all accidents in sequence by name of victim, nature of injury, treatment, time and place of occurrence, and teacher(s) in supervision at the time. The same event becomes diagnosed, so to speak, differently across different roles: normal for some, a disturbance that threatens smooth functioning for another.

4. Adaptations responsive to local disturbances tend, however, to require coordinated action across different roles and levels of authority. The school administrator cannot obtain data herself directly, so requires the cooperation of the school nurse. But the school nurse, whose activities may

5

well be already full, experiences disturbances of her own, one of which may be the administrator's request, which the nurse may easily agree to before realizing the implications, a request for what she soon may regard as unnecessary paper work to be delayed and resisted. The information the nurse is asked to obtain and record may not in any way she can see facilitate her own nursing function; indeed, she may regard it as an impediment. Not only does it take time away from other work that is *organizationally required*; it also puts her in what she may regard as a spying relation to the teachers, her fellow union members. Thus may local adaptations become vulnerable to local realities. Partial and particular adaptations to particular, local disturbances (or threats of disturbances) are more easily accomplished than are adaptations that integrate the local realities of all participants whose normal functioning is affected by the adaptations.

5.   Thus, the very strength of complex organizations, their specialized roles and levels of authority, engender local commitments and frames of interpretation which set in motion actions addressed to locally diagnosed disturbances. But those actions normally involve trans-local participation by members whose local realities do not fit with or are actually antagonistic to the 'correction' or 'repair' contemplated. Add to the localism created by separate roles and levels of authority another powerful source of localism: the idiosyncratic outlooks and adjustments of each *individual* member of the organization. Each person tends to attend selectively to not only his or her work-related demands and routines but also to his or her personal aspirations and outlooks. The new school administrator who was not renewed in his last administrative position because he was insensitive to parental criticism brings to the special role of school administrator a special personal agenda within that role: a local sensitivity within the circumscribed realities of the special role. Person and role combine to render the localism of members' subjective realities a chronic and intensely defended source of challenge to integrative functioning among persons across roles. The challenge is more than met by many organizations, of course. But many organizations fail, many function only marginally, and many that succeed commit expensive blunders. The question about cohesion Emil Durkheim (1964/1893) raised about society is thus confronted at the level of each daily adaptation in organizations: how do organizations overcome their own deeply embedded and functional localism and thereby fulfill their unifying, primary purposes? And in what specific ways does this localism weaken or prevent that fulfillment or actually lead to absurdity or disaster?

6.   Examining local disturbances in organizational functioning and local adaptations to them is a needed new agenda for social scientists.[2] By examining instances of trans-local participation, that is, cross-role, cross-level action, in local adaptations *as they unfold* we see a picture of organizational functioning that (1) speaks directly to practitioners' interests in getting things done with others to make their organization more effective; (2) contrasts sharply both with views of organizational function-

ing suggested by rational choice models or by the current most prominent model offered in refutation of the rational choice model, the 'garbage can' model of James March and his associates, a new picture that contests the validity of the garbage can metaphor (Cohen, March, and Olsen, 1972; March and Olsen, 1979); (3) shows psychological and social psychological functioning to be more illuminated by the pragmatists' concepts of acts and problems (Mead, 1938; Dewey, 1938) than by concepts of 'problem' employed by cognitive theorists like Greeno (1978) or Simon (1976, 1979, 1981) or Wertheimer (1959), whose concepts of problem must be sharply distinguished from that of the pragmatists; (4) calls for integrating pragmatist views of problem and problem solving with theories of conflict and conflict management (e.g., Deutsch, 1973), two traditions heretofore separate; and (5) places research on organizational change and innovation implementation (e.g., Pressman and Wildavsky, 1979; Corbett, Dawson, and Firestone, 1984; Fullan, 1982; Huberman and Miles, 1984) in a more encompassing framework, showing an incapacity of previous conceptual or empirical research to address crucial questions of origins, adaptation, and effectiveness.

Organizational Adaptation

I begin by borrowing a basic idea from clinical and ego psychology, that an effective person is one who integrates realities of given situations into action in those situations. 'Realities', in that context is designedly plural: it includes not only the person's environment, which includes other persons and their subjective minding, but also the person's situationally relevant ideals, purposes, and fears. By 'integrates' is meant attention to, and synthetic taking account of, a process that leads to a set of fitting, stable relations among internal, subjective elements of the person's world and external, observable elements in the given situation.[3] Extrapolate from the idea of a person's effectiveness as reality integration to the level of the organization and it becomes: organizational action regarding X is effective to the extent that the action integrates (attends to, takes account of, and shapes itself according to) accessible organizational realities regarding X. This leads us immediately to explicate and delimit 'accessible organizational realities' regarding some matter, X.

Organizational Realities

Most readers will imagine organizational realities to refer to perceivable conditions of some organization — the size of its budget, its available resources, its profitability and indebtedness, its market or appeal to a public — in short, to conditions 'out there' in the organization. Those images are not so much incorrect as merely incomplete. They leave out of account two crucial matters related to organizational reality. The first omission from this realist, materialist, or objectivist conception of organizational reality is the empirical manner in which those budgetary and market factors 'out there' in the organization become identified and responded to by the on-going organization. The second omission is another kind of organizational content, every bit as powerful in shaping organizational action and success as budget, resources, or market: the *subjective commitments about the organization that operate in the minds of organization members* — commitments about their role, their opportunity for personal advancement, about proper functioning and obligations, about their own skills and resources, about norms of conduct and the division of labor.

Consider the second matter first. The contents of a member's minding about organizational life relate that person to the rest of the organization by means of immediate, binding, and forceful constraints that are inside the member's skin, so to speak. They are often not at all visible or otherwise easily sensed. But what a person feels about the justness of criticism received, for example, or about recognition of his or her worth or about what is required for effective completion of a task — these are organizational realities that command energetic attention from members and that can easily pre-empt other, more visible organizational realities in shaping the member's behavior. Many instances of the forceful operation of this more psychological, less tangible or visible reality[4] will appear in the narratives and analyses of Parts II, III, and IV.

The point here is that these subjective organizational commitments to which members respond, often with high and relentless energy, *are at once potent and diffused throughout the organizational membership.* If some organizational change is to be made, say a new curriculum for a school or a new procedure for a sales office, it inevitably meets and must come to terms with the already existing social psychological order. That order consists in the sum total of organizational commitments already subjectively operating in the teachers or office personnel. So, first: organizational realities exist in important measure as subjectively operating commitments and as contents of minding *in* members. Second: those realities are distributed across the organization's separate roles and levels of authority.

Now consider the first matter, above, the matter of how those environmental conditions which exist 'out there' in the point-at-able site and records of the organization come to be known and acted upon by individuals or groups in the organization. Clearly they become known through the perceptions and communications of the members, i.e., through the (effective or ineffective) operations of individual and collective human intelligence. Just as clearly, this mechanism by which organizational matters 'out there' become known is a capacity of the same psyches of the same members in whom those 'organizational commitments' of the previous paragraph 'subjectively operate'. That is, objective (i.e., methodically observable) organizational realities become collected and fused with subjective organizational realities in the only apparatus an organization has for doing so, the psyches of its members. To be sure, these psyches operate in a socially communicating and a culturally symbolizing context, but it is in them and through them that organizational realities are synthesized and communicated — from objective conditions to subjective minding and from subjective mind to subjective mind. Organizational realities, therefore, become sensed, retrieved, and synthesized in the on-going functioning of the organization via members' psyches alone — psyches interacting, psyches reflecting roles and sub-cultures, but psyches.

Are all operating realities regarding some organizational disturbance or corrective action equally important, equally necessary to integrate into the action? If we think of everyday functioning and everyday changes, not all members are affected by or care about or are needed to act on any given event or proposed change. But in saying as much, I have identified three very usable criteria for judging whether a given organizational reality (operating psychologically in a given member) needs to be integrated into a proposed organizational action to solve an organizational problem: (1) the extent to which the person *cares* about the change; (2) the extent to which the person's normal organizational functioning will *be affected by* the change; and (3) the extent to which the change *depends on the person's participation*. These three criteria identify members I shall call 'constituents' of any given problem or proposed solution.[5] In respect to a given problem or proposal, X, some persons will be zero on all three of these criteria, i.e., will be non-constituents (simply members) regarding X; others will be heavily implicated by all three criteria, crucial constituents of X.

In following organizational action, I shall be watching for how organizational realities that are implicated in the action — in its hoped for outcomes and in its emergent effects — how these constituent realities become integrated with the action (and vice versa) and how some constituent realities come to be excluded from the action. I shall be working on the hypothesis that constituent realities that are excluded will undermine the coherence and cumulative force of the action, tending in specific ways to nullify its thrust and to dissipate its energy.[6]

In general, each person in an organization constructs his or her own reality of the organization with respect to each matter they might attend to. Since 'realities', here, refers to 'that to which a person actually responds', that is, perceptions, thoughts, feelings, and commitments that actually arise psychologically and shape a person's action, each person's comparisons, contrasts, and syntheses of what he or she sees with what he or she fears or desires or values also is part of his or her reality. A person's fears, desires, and values may be responses, in some broad sense, but they are also responded to by that person and as such constitute part of that person's operating reality. Since a host of such subjective contents can enter any member's constructions regarding any matter, including those subjective contents we would call assessments of objective reality, the realities of an organization's members have much room for individuality as well as for commonality.

For example, consider the simple matter of a test to be given by a teacher to students. The teacher's realities with respect to the giving of the test will be in many ways very different from the students' realities. But the realities of those students who are well prepared will be different in important regards from those of students who are ill prepared. Among the well prepared, those who must be absent from class on the day of the test will, again, have a different reality about the giving of the test than well prepared students able to be present. Each person whose functioning is impinged on by the giving of the test has local situations and subjective assessments into which the test must be integrated, local adaptations that must be made regarding the test.

Organizational reality with respect to any given matter, then, is plural, not singular, is distributed across members and observers, and includes for each member and observer local contents which motivate and shape local adaptations.

Criteria of Effectiveness

Many scholars of organizations prefer to avoid altogether questions of organizational effectiveness. To make judgments about effectiveness is to leave the realm of science, they feel, to enter the realm of values where science should be neutral. In any case, they feel, since there can be no agreement on effectiveness it is a quagmire of confusion that research should avoid. My view is that those attempts to be neutral actually bootleg values and evaluation into research, camouflaged in the very concepts they employ — 'organization', 'communication', 'solution', 'cooperation', 'productive', and other concepts that carry implicit evaluations of effectiveness. While I recognize the plurality of values, I prefer to deal with the question of effectiveness directly, as other organizational theorists do (e.g., Cameron and Whetten, 1983a), by applying pluralistic criteria explicitly. If it is important to discover those processes that lead to effective organizational functioning, I can see no way out of being explicit about criteria for effective and ineffective functioning. I set out five criteria of effective organizational action below, in discussing the concept of 'problem'. In the view of the constructivist theory of organizational reality and adaptation offered in this book, no organizational action is generated except as it is generated by and addressed to some subjectively construed organizational problem. Once 'organizational problem' is clarified, the criteria can be fully set forth. These ideas will be expanded below when I provide a specific definition of 'problem' and then consider 'organizational problem' and the 'constituents' of an organizational problem.

The first contribution this book attempts, then, is an exploration of the integration and non-integration of organizational realities as sources of effective and ineffective organized action. Consider, now, a second contribution this exploration hopes to make: a contribution to the theory of problems and problem solving.

Two Kinds of Problem

If we take adaptation as a central orientation and motivation of human life, then the psychological condition I call 'problem' is a proper starting point for shifts in organized action. The condition of minding I will refer to as 'problem' captures the essential elements of a recognized disturbance in one's adaptation. The most energizing and shaping form of a person's operating reality at any given moment is the problem that person is engaged in solving. An underlying and frequently explicit argument of this book is that we cannot understand organized behavior without understanding the problems operating in the participants. Because problems are starting points and continuing forces, it is essential to be clear about the meaning of 'problem'.

I distinguish two traditions of problem solving in psychology: the materialist or objectivist and the idealist. Studies in the objectivist tradition, in which problems are located in an external cultural or material world, typically use the terms 'problem' and 'problem-solving' with no awareness of the other, subjectivist, tradition or that there might be any fundamental difficulties in conceptualizing 'problem' itself. Studies in this first, objectivist tradition interchange terms like 'problem', 'task', 'puzzle', and 'question'. All of these are seen as events, objects, or conditions of the external world. The common, core meaning of 'problem' in this tradition is a culturally defined gap or contradiction in a culturally defined pattern of elements such that, when the gap is filled or the contradiction resolved, a culturally defined whole is achieved. The defining culture may be Western culture, defining a 'problem' such as 'x + 2 = 9; solve for x,' or the subculture of cognitive psychologists, defining the following 'problem':

Replace the letters in the following array by numerals from 0 to 9. The resulting array should be a correct arithmetical sum:	DONALD + GERALD ——————— ROBERT (Hint: D = 5)[7]

Each problem of this type is external to the individual who is to solve it. It is provided by a culture in which all of the elements, even the missing ones, are known. To solve a problem of this kind, the individual must put aside his or her own uniqueness and instead, internalize the rules and assumptions of the culture and manipulate the elements relevant to the culturally defined problem in a manner consistent with cultural rules.

Moving the knight in a straight line across the chessboard simply will not do: no culturally approved solution of a chess problem can be achieved in that way. To solve this kind of problem the individual must be properly and thoroughly acculturated because the problem is set up by, and organized in terms of, the surrounding culture.[8]

Studies in the second, idealist or subjectivist tradition typically neither refer to studies of the first kind nor use the term 'problem', using instead terms like 'dissonance', or 'conflict'. This tradition focuses not on cultural forms but on psychological states. Dewey, whose conception of problem attempts a synthesis of the two traditions (Dewey, 1938), provides nonetheless a rich vocabulary for this second tradition. A problem is a condition of 'indeterminacy', of 'doubt', 'confusion', of being 'unsettled' (Dewey, 1938, pp. 105–107). Festinger's (1957) definition and characterizations of dissonance are important in this subjectivist tradition:

> the relation between two elements [of thought, feeling, or belief] is dissonant if, disregarding the others, the one does not, or would not be expected to, follow from the other (p. 15).

> The existence of dissonance, being psychologically uncomfortable, will motivate the person to try to reduce the dissonance and achieve consonance (p. 3).

> ... dissonance, ... the existence of nonfitting relations among cognitions, is a motivating factor in its own right (p. 3).

> If two elements are dissonant with one another, the magnitude of the dissonance will be a function of the importance of the elements (p. 16).

The close connection between this stream of thought, which Festinger traces back to the work of Myrdal (1944) and Heider (1958), can be seen simply by translating Festinger's words, above, into parallel statements in the language of adaptive problem-solving:

> The relation between two elements of a person's subjective reality (thought, feeling, belief) is incompatible, and therefore constitutes a problem, if, disregarding other realities, the one element does not follow from the other *in the subjective assessment of the person.*

> A problem, rising from a sense of incompatibility between elements in mind and being psychologically uncomfortable, will motivate the person to try to reduce the incompatibilities and achieve a solution to the problem.[9]

> A problem, consisting of the existence in subjective reality of nonfitting relations among cognitions, sentiments, values, and beliefs, is a motivating factor in its own right.

If two elements of minding are incompatible with one another, the magnitude of the problem will be a function of the importance of the elements.

For example, suppose it is winter, that I want to go back home after a day's work and I find my car has a flat tire. I am frustrated, but the solution is routine if cold: use the spare. Then I find that the spare, too, is without air. My desire to return home is strong but I also sense an obdurate barrier that I cannot just wish away. Focally, my intention to use my car as transportation and my perception that my car cannot make the trip constitutes a strong incompatibility. The incompatibility is in my minding, not out there in the world. The world allows flat tires and people who want to go home to exist, side by side, without any incompatibility or disturbance. This incompatibility constitutes a pressing problem *of mine* whose pressure for solution is proportional to (1) my desire to get home and (2) the degree to which the absence of transportation is irreversible.

Now suppose that I come upon my car with the flat tire on a hot summer day, that my car's air conditioning does not work, and that I really didn't want to drive home in the summer heat anyway. Suppose, that is, that along with a habitual tendency to drive home when I have driven in to the university, I wish, today, to take the air conditioned rapid transit and have my wife meet me at the other end. In that case, a case of different perceptions and intentions, incompatibilities, too, differ. On the one hand I have the car to drive home, but on the other hand I do not want to go through the heat of driving it home.

Finding the flat tire and the airless spare in the face of that problem becomes not an element in a problem but, rather, a solution: a condition now blocks me from doing what I did not want to do but felt obliged to do. The direction and strength of our commitments largely shape and constrain our demanding problems. If I get to the rapid transit station and find I do not have enough money for a ticket, I will have yet another problem.

Note how different this kind of problem is from the first, culturally defined, 'objective' kind. This second kind depends utterly on my own personal commitments and local situation, my own evaluations and perceptions. My problem of the flat tire has no culturally right answer because it is in the domain of individual adaptation in emergent circumstances and under the constraint of individual resources. Problem in this sense is internal and personal, particular and emergent. It is neither culturally shared nor a condition of the external, objective world.

Being internal and psychological rather than external and cultural, this kind of problem possesses a property wholly absent in the cultural kind, a property of crucial importance in understanding emergent individual or organizational behavior. This second, individual and psychological kind of problem tends regularly and strongly to *pre-empt its possessor's attention and to arouse its possessor's motivation.* Whatever I may be thinking about on that wintry day as I approach my car, desiring strongly to drive home, that train of thought is upset, sidetracked by the image of the flat tire. The incompatibility between desire and means triggers motivation and attention. They are deployed in the service of reducing the incompatibility to some tolerable level.

Culturally defined 'problems', in contrast, have no such attentional or motivational demand in the person who is confronted with them. For one who cares nothing about chess no configuration of pieces on the chessboard can constitute a problem in the psychologically adapting sense. For the student indifferent to math, $x + 24 = 16$ is something just as easily left ignored, left printed at the back of the assigned chapter, out there in the culture, not inside where motivation, attention, and thoughts operate. Thus, problems of the first, objectivist kind must somehow be internalized to become problems of the second, psychologically arresting kind. They must first be possessed in order to command the possessor's attention and other resources.

In contrast, problems of the second kind originate from within. They have no distance to travel from an outside culture to reach the psyche. They are produced by the psyche. Cultural problems, as all teachers know, must often travel great and hard distances before their culturally defined gaps and contradictions become internalized and felt psychologically as important, as something worth responding to. Often the distances are simply not traversed and the culturally defined problems, so important to the teacher as agent of culture, remain external, never taking possession of the student the way problems of the second kind do every day.

This book is about problems of the second kind only: adaptational problems. The book concentrates on emergent adaptations to organizational conditions conceived by some member to be incompatible with some value or perception or some other commitment of the member.

Organizational Problems

Because organizational problems, considered not culturally but as elements in adaptation, involve a judgment about something wrong or weak about an organization, they are not 'out there' in the organization. Being particular evaluative judgments about what is out there, organizational problems are in the realm of judgment. An organizational condition that is synthesized as a problem by one member is a 'fact of life' for another — as in our earlier example of the scraped knee. It is not the conditions themselves which inherently carry problematic qualities — not, at least, in the second, psychologically operating sense of problem.

An organizational problem (in the second sense, and the only sense I shall use from here on), then, is some particular person's perception or conception of some organizational condition which is incompatible, in that person's judgment, with some value or goal or other conception held by that person. Two contents of a person's minding have thus come into opposition, contents that refer in some way to an organizational matter.

The contents of any member's problem (the elements in opposition) ordinarily implicate only some, not all, aspects of the problem solver's organization. Among those implicated aspects ordinarily are other people, people whose ways of thinking and acting (and current problems) would have to change or whose cooperation would be necessary for the problem in question to be solved for the problem solver in question. Those other people's operating realities regarding the problem in question vary, and ordinarily will include among them realities opposed to changes implied by the problem solver's solutions — as with the nurse's reaction to the administrator's new scheme for collecting information about accidents. These *constituent realities* — both those consonant and those dissonant with the problem solver's — constitute the organizational realities that will shape any solution. Beyond a problem's constituent realities are the realities of all the other organizational members who are not implicated in the problem or its solution, the realities of any observers regarding the problem in question, and that objective, inaccessible reality known only through omniscience — the 'real' organization. All these together constitute Organizational Reality regarding the problem in question. My fundamental working hypothesis, very globally, is that organizational action regarding any problem, x, will be effective to the extent that it integrates Organizational Reality regarding x. Functionally, this means the integration of members' and observers' realities; practically it often means the integration of the most influential constituent realities, those operating in persons with formal authority and status regarding x, those operating in persons informally situated to influence x, those organized specifically to deal with x, and especially the realities of members who belong to two or all three of these categories.

Of course, problems of this second, adaptive kind can be shared by two or two thousand people. But they are still conditions of those persons' minding, not conditions of the world 'out there'. Problems that arrest people's attention and trigger action are always relative to psyches; they are often not related to objective (i.e., systematically observable) conditions. Since this relentlessly subjective, self-constructed nature of problem runs counter to wide usage (but not all usage) in the natural language, and since many who are interested in organizations tend to reify organizational conditions 'out there' as that to which members respond, it is important to press home this point with an example.

Before the example, however, it is important to point up, in an organizational conext, the necessity for distinguishing between problems of the two types — the external, objectivist, culturally shared problem with a culturally correct solution, on the one hand, and, on the other, the internal, personally felt, psychologically impinging and motivating problem oriented to a local adaptation. Our project is to explain why people actually do what they do, not what culturally they should do. The fact that we also, in separate analyses, compare what members actually do with explicit standards of effectiveness does not nullify in the least that we are examining their behavior in terms of operating realities irrespective of the cultural correctness of those realities. The point to be kept in mind is that only problems of the second, locally adaptive kind refer to what the individual is actually responding to, not what he or she is supposed, culturally, to respond to. It is only problems of the second kind that have any bearing on action at the level of the acting person or group in a concrete organizational setting.

The Challenger's 'Temperature Problem'

Now to the example, illustrating the point that problems are conditions of minding, produced by subjective judgments. Problems of adaptation are not, as we tend often to think they are, conditions 'out there' in the organization. Consider the recent fatal accident of the space shuttle, *Challenger*, where all seven crew members perished because, according to extensive investigations since the accident,[10] a joint around the circumference of the outer shell of the right solid rocket booster failed to seal properly under the temperature conditions obtaining at the time of launching.

The cylindrical shell of these rocket booster motors, about 150 feet in length, was constructed by joining several segments of cylinders about 25 feet in length. Each joint of these smaller cylindrical segments was achieved by machining a split in the upper lip of the lower segment, forming a deep groove around the edge that would face upward, and by fitting into that grooved or split lip the lower (unsplitted) lip of the next higher segment. The joint was similar to the tongue and groove joint in cabinets, where the lower segment's split lip provided the groove and the upper segment's single lower lip provided the tongue. The joint was crucial in containing the pressurized gas fuel.

If the burning gas did escape in more than minute quantities for more than a few hundredths of a second, it would melt away the shell around the hole through which it was leaking, expanding the hole and thus the volume both of the escaping gas and of the mass and intensity of burning, a self-accelerating burn-through. Since the solid rocket boosters were immediately adjacent to the huge external fuel tank positioned between the two boosters, any burning gas escaping from either booster on the side next to the external fuel tank would inevitably burn into and breach the shell of that fuel tank, igniting its hydrogen and oxygen propellents. The resulting intensity of heat and thrust would engulf and destroy the relatively small space shuttle attached. However small a malfunction in the sealing skin or joints of either booster, therefore, it would, in the language of several of the pre-accident memoranda, accelerate 'catastrophically' unless countered in its very earliest milliseconds.

In order to seal this joint so that the volatile fuel gases would not leak out, two vulcanized rubber rings (O-rings), whose circumference matched that of the rocket segment but whose width and height was slightly more than a quarter of an inch, were positioned between the inside lip of the lower segment and the tongue of the upper segment, in two grooves cut into the inside lip. These O-rings were designed to be sucked into the joints between sections of the boosters where gases might begin to escape. The pressure created by the escaping gas itself would be, and on many occasions was, sufficient to pull the pliable O-rings into the small space through which any gas escaped, thus damming the flow.

At certain temperatures the cushioning material of the O-rings was sufficiently pliable to fill the gap; at certain colder temperatures it was not pliable and responded only slowly to the gas pressure. On the day of the *Challenger* shuttle launch the temperature was at least 15 degrees below the lowest temperature on any previous launch and the material evidently did not respond quickly enough to prevent gas leakage too great to be reversed, resulting in the fatal explosion.

Of course, as soon as the malfunction killed the seven astronauts, everyone was appalled and the managers involved immediately felt the tension that direct implication in a fatality brings. Here and for the moment, cultural problem and adaptational problem largely coincided. But just where had the failure occurred and what organizational conditions were implicated in producing the failing part? Investigation of these questions led to conclusions that help illustrate the psychological relativity of organizational problems.

In brief, the booster rocket joints, and the O-rings in particular, had been regarded with suspicion for some years. That suspicion crystallized and became explicitly associated with low temperatures after anomalies of erosion and burning had been discovered in the booster joints of flight 51C on January 24, 1985, a year before the fatal launch. The temperature for that flight was 53 degrees, which was characterized in an official report shortly thereafter as the 'worst case temperature change in Florida history.'[11] Warnings were issued in writing by Thiokol engineers and were known and understood by the NASA and Thiokol managers well before the accident.

The basic conditions that led to the disaster — low temperature interacting with O-rings — were (1) reflected in empirical observations known by NASA and Thiokol engineers, (2) felt to be problematical by persons in authoritative positions, and (3) communicated in forceful language to managers empowered to postpone the launching. But the conditions of temperature and O-ring performance themselves were not *taken* as problematical before the accident itself by the key officials at Thiokol and NASA.

In the final pre-launch conference of managers and engineers at Morton Thiokol, interrupting a telephone conference to deal specifically with the question of whether temperatures at the launch site were suitable for a launch, interchanges among managers and engineers rather dramatically revealed the subjective, psychological relativity of organizational problems. Roger Biosjoly, one of Thiokol's engineers closest to the development, testing, and evaluation of the booster rockets, gave this version of the interchanges between himself and the company managers and between another engineer, Arnold Thompson, and the company managers:

> Those of us who opposed the launch [to take place the following day] continued to speak out, and I am specifically speaking of Mr. Thompson and myself because in my recollection he and I were the only ones that vigorously continued to oppose the launch.... So we spoke out and tried to explain once again the effects of low temperature. Arnie [Thompson] actually got up from his position which was down the table, and walked up the table and put a quarter pad down in front of the table, in front of the management folks, and tried to sketch out once again what his concern was with the joint, and when he realized he wasn't getting through, he just stopped.
>
> I tried one more time with the photos. I grabbed the photos, and I went up and discussed the photos once again and tried to make the point that it was my opinion from actual observations that temperature was indeed a discriminator and we should not ignore the physical evidence that we had observed ... I also stopped when it was apparent that I couldn't get anybody to listen.... After Arnie and I had our last say, Mr. Mason [Senior Vice President of Morton Thiokol and ranking manager present] said we have to make a management decision. He turned to Bob Lund and asked him to take off his engineering hat and put on his management hat. From this point on, management formulated the points to base their decision on. There never was one comment in favor, as I have said, of launching by any engineer or other non-management person in the room.[12]

The participants all had reviewed the same data about joints and O-rings of the solid rocket boosters. Biosjoly and Thompson had both felt a problem regarding temperatures in relation to a successful launch. They could not solve that organizational problem themselves: they were not the managers authorized to make the decisions, so their role was to induce their problem in the managers. Their efforts failed. The managers, holding different responsibilities, responding to different local realities, had different problems.

To understand the actions of each participant we must understand the problems they were responding to, not the problem they should have been responding to, from some cultural or value standpoint. Clearly illustrated here is that problems of adaptation do not exist 'out there' in physical or chemical reality. Problems of adaptation originate psychologically, and vary from psyche to psyche. This book addresses the kinds of process, both reality-integrating and reality-blocking, that arise in attempts to accumulate individual action into a complex collective product, a local, intra-organizational adaptation. The episode of abortive problem solving narrated and analyzed in Part II, producing an organizational absurdity (culturally speaking), suggests several new ways to look at the kind of maladaptive organizational problem solving evident in the *Challenger* shuttle accident.

Again, the point to be kept in focus, the point dramatically illustrated in the decision to launch *Challenger* despite warnings about cold temperatures, is that even empirically demonstrated conditions of vital importance to the organization, conditions that can be fatal, are not problematical unless and until they are *possessed by psyches that synthesize them as problems*. I use the word, 'synthesize', to emphasize the organismically produced nature of problems. The incompatibilities that arise in the minding that each of us accomplishes are not discovered in our environments; adaptational problems, thus, are not 'discovered', or 'seen', or 'perceived'. We might say that such problems are 'constructed', but that implies too conscious and planned a process. Just as our bodies synthesize cholesterol and hormones biochemically, our minding synthesizes problems psychologically. *Organizational problems, thus, are the products of individual, psychological synthesis.*

The Problem-Solving Episode: The Basic Unit of Data

All organizational problems, while they are incompatibilities in particular minds, that is, incompatible cognitive-affective contents of particular persons' psyches, refer to organizational conditions. While there are basically two kinds of organizational problem, we are interested in only one kind: the incompatibility whose possessor (the person with the problem in question) has concluded that he or she cannot solve the problem autonomously but must have the active help or at least passive permission of others whose participation in bringing about a solution is necessary. The kind of organizational problem I do not deal with in this book, and which poses much greater methodological difficulties, is the autonomous problem, that which a person can solve alone.

Because this book focuses on collective functioning in organizations, not merely individual functioning, it deals only with interdependent problem solving between the problem synthesizer and others. Once an organizational problem of this interdependent kind has been synthesized by someone, we still have no observable evidence of it as a problem. It is internal until the person who first 'has' it communicates about it in some fashion to someone else. The communication will, of course, not ordinarily be in the technical terms I have been using, like 'synthesize' or 'problem'. Because problems contain incompatibilities among the contents of minding and because such incompatibilities are felt as threats to cognitive and emotional equilibrium, they generate prompt cognitive search for resolution. Thus, the form in which a problem is communicated first is often not a problem at all but a problem that has already been transformed — into a question or even more frequently, a proposal for action.

The first person to synthesize and communicate about an organizational problem, the 'problem originator' in my terms, initiates activities that involve other members. Those activities ramify among still other members until, at some point, all participants who have been involved in the problem or its transformations stop taking action on the problem's transformation. For them it is finished, either 'solved' (meaning, for them, solved satisfactorily) or not worth working on any longer. When all action ceases on a problem's transformation (into solution, plan, implementation or routinization), a solution has, in a social psychological sense, been implemented. That is, incompatibilities that were once operating in participants are reduced to the point where the now weakened or fully resolved incompatibilities no longer demand action.

The problem-solving episode[13] consists of all action stemming from the organizational problem and concerned with its solution that takes place between the first communication of a problem (or its solution) by the problem originator, on one hand, and the implemented solution (cessation of problem-connected action), on the other. The action may take a day or years; it may involve two persons or scores; it may take place within a single level in the organization or across many levels. But the episode constitutes a social psychological whole in that it begins with the first communication of a problem and ends as participants recruited into solving the problem experience closure (not necessarily success).

If one imagines problematic content moving from an originator to others, and from them to still others, ramifying outward in a process tending toward action that reduces the original incompatibilities by attempts to change organizational conditions, then it should be clear that problem solving tends to recruit into itself specific, problem-related participants. The membership of this emergent form of action can be known in advance only in part; it, too, is largely emergent. But in the end it is definitive: some members have been recruited into this problem's episode, some have not. Whether a problem's logical constituents — those members and groups logically implicated in any solution to the problem, or substantially affected by its solution — have been recruited into the action and, if so, the extent to which their problem-relevant realities have been integrated into the action, are important empirical questions.

Problem Hierarchy and Selection for Study

Students early in the study of adaptive problem solving often ask whether a particular problem of a problem originator was *really* the problem that the originator had, whether it wasn't this *other* problem instead. Their confusion is common. It is based on the erroneous assumption that a person 'has' only one problem at a time and that our task is to find *it* and follow its solution. Too bad for the student that matters are more complicated: we all work on many problems almost simultaneously. While some problems are in the early stages of work, others are in the final stages of implementation, with many others in stages in between. While one problem holds our focal attention, others are still very much in mind.

In sum, each of us (and any collectivity, as well) at any moment is working on a hierarchy of problems, problems ordered by priority, priority determined (usually tacitly, not deliberately) by some mixture of importance, urgency, and opportunity. There are, therefore, two questions of interest to researchers. The first is not whether X problem is or is not *'the'* problem that a member of an organization is working on so much as whether a given set of incompatibilities is *one* problem that he or she is working on. The second question is whether a problem, once identified with an organizational member as originator, involves commitments sufficiently intense, organizational ramifications sufficiently wide, and constituents sufficiently varied to render its investigation theoretically or practically useful to the researcher. The synthesis of organizational problems is ubiquitous; selection of problems to follow is up to us, and rests on our criteria.

One criterion of great importance to researchers is observability. When an organizatonal problem can be solved by its originator alone, as in changing his or her own mode of behavior with others, the problem and process are rather hidden. But organizational problems that require others' cooperation, as in the institution of new policies or roles or procedures, also ordinarily require the originator to communicate important elements of the problem and, just as important, provide occasions — and usually repeated occasions — for others to inquire about and to clarify reasons, causes, and problems lying behind solution attempts. Thus, an originator's dependence on others for solution becomes an important criterion for selection: it provides occasions for participants' overt interchanges about the problem itself, thus providing an observer with data about the problem's contents.

The three problems selected for study in this book (1) were synthesized by the most powerful executive in the school, (2) involved intense (if sometimes ambivalent) commitments, (3) were not solvable by the originator alone, and (4) ramified extensively across roles and levels of the organization. Following them required travel over many parts of the organization, outward, downward, and upward.

Problem-Solving Effectiveness

We are now in a position to set forth the criteria promised earlier for the effectiveness of organizational action. I assess the effectiveness of action, considered always in relation to the particular problem initiating, fueling, and guiding the action, in five dimensions. The five dimensions of effectiveness, or five criteria, divide into two groupings. The first two dimensions reflect participants' local realities while the last three represent observations, that is, one or more observers' local realities. Thus, both idealist-conceptualist criteria and realist-materialist criteria are employed. The first two criteria concern the participants' subjective satisfaction or closure regarding the implemented solution: (1) satisfaction or closure for the problem originator and (2) satisfaction or closure for the other participants, assessed individually or in clusters of participants with similar reactions. 'Satisfaction' denotes a favorable evaluation of the implemented solution, while 'closure' simply means that a participant considers the problem finished with, not worth working on any longer. A third criterion is the extent to which conditions originally felt to be problematic were observably changed as a direct result of the problem-solving process. A fourth criterion is the extent to which confusions or cross purposes previously leading to wasted resources or to substantial dissatisfaction were reduced or eliminated as a result of the problem-solving process. The fifth criterion is the extent to which new resources were released or recruited into the organization as a result of the process.[14]

Assessing effectiveness along any of these dimensions requires collecting data after the solution has been implemented, i.e., after action on the focal problem has ceased. How long that post-episode data gathering should continue is a basic methodological question. It is central to questions of reversibility and of evaluation generally, which I address in Part V.

Toward Generalizations

One drawback of combining narrative history with participant observational study of an organization's problem solving is that the specific and detailed tends to crowd out the generic and generalizable. To mitigate this difficulty I interrupt the narrative regularly to make analytical comments, to point up what I consider to be the important parts of the process. This 'pointing up' stems always from one vantage point, a vantage point supplied by the writings of Martin Buber (1965), who emphasized the 'elemental otherness of the other.' It is the vantage point of multiple realities and it suggests the proposition from which virtually all of my analysis of the narratives derives, namely, that organizational action regarding problem X will be effective to the extent that it integrates into action the constituent parties' different organizational realities regarding X.

The meaning of 'integrates' in this context will become clear in the many analyses of particulars that are provided in Parts II, III, and IV. For the moment, synonyms will have to suffice: 'take mutual account of', 'include', 'mutually respond to', and 'modify mutually according to'. Mutuality here does not refer to a feeling of fellowship. It refers to the often coldly calculated, impersonal matter of taking the other's functioning, on which one depends, into account in one's own actions. It may also include, of course, the accommodations that friends or lovers make to each other's realities. Mutuality here has the flavor of 'negotiation', but may and may not entail any conscious process of negotiation as described, for example, by Pruitt (1981).

The narratives of Parts II, III and IV, as I say, alternate every several pages with analytical commentary. The material in these analytical commentaries is the basis, for the most part, of my attempt at the end of each part to pull together those variables that are suggested by the data and my analyses, variables affecting the degree of effectiveness of the implemented solution.

The Overall Project of Episodic Analysis.

My overall project has four parts. First, to trace all problem transforming events from the originator's first communication of it to others to the point where the last active participant has stopped activity on the problem. That is the narrative part. Narratives of different episodes from many settings will be needed to test the variables I extract from this book's three narratives.

The second part is analysis of the narrative. Analysis is of several kinds, within the overall rubric of the integration of multiple realities into on-going problem solving. One kind of analysis examines communication, another the cumulativity vs. discontinuity of the transforming process, another the sequential structure of participations. The reader will find these and other analyses identifiable as they are encountered. More kinds of analysis are needed.

These analyses, included among the analytical commentaries, are then pulled together in the form of tables of variables. At the end of Part III I accumulate not only those variables suggested by the conflict pursued in Part III but also those of Part II, with an attempt to keep a kind of box score on which variables from Part II show up again in Part III. I accumulate variables in the same way at the end of Part IV, finally ending with a list of twenty-two component variables. These I synthesize into five major variables that I hypothesize to be general and to account for substantial variation in problem-solving effectiveness and ineffectiveness. These five major variables, with their 22 components, are collected into a table that cites page numbers where the narrative suggests the operation of each component variable. Variables are thus grounded in the narratives and explained in the alternating analytical commentaries. That constitutes the second part of the overall project.

The third part, rather separate, involves examining the outcomes and effects of the problem-solving process in terms of the five criteria set forth above. These criteria and their use in evaluation are independent of the analyses of the narrative. Students' analyses of their own episodes in seminars suggest that these five criteria are useful and generally communicable and that such evaluations, if made carefully, can speak persuasively and with authority.

The fourth and culminating part of the overall project is to link characteristics of process with degrees and dimensions of effectiveness. Once an episode of problem solving has been evaluated for its effectiveness, hypotheses can be drawn connecting aspects of the problem-solving process, particularly in terms of the variables, on the one hand, and the outcomes, on the other. Thus, as the project goes forward, we will connect protocols of process with given degrees and dimensions of effectiveness, noting which variables tend to turn up repeatedly, which occasionally, and which only in isolated instances. Different kinds of setting (e.g., in the different kinds of organization proposed by Etzioni, 1961) are expected, of course, to exert theoretically and practically interesting influences on the pattern of relations between process and outcome.

This book takes a first step in this project. It provides a first attempt to carry out each of the four parts. It is, like all first attempts, rough. Gaps in data and problems of method will be pointed out as the reader moves through the narrative and analyses. Nonetheless, I believe the study makes contributions to data, theory, method, and practice as set forth in Part V.

Enough of the concepts and vocabulary have now been introduced to carry the reader into the first episode. The episodic data will supply further specification and will provide the context needed for more abstract concepts regarding process, cumulativity, reversibility and the like. Chapter 2 introduces the setting, some administrative history, and the roles that Susan Allan and I began to establish and then modified. It ends by introducing the major participants in the book's episodes.

Notes

1. 'why some people be mad at me sometimes' by Lucille Clifton, reprinted from *Next: New Poems*, Copyright © 1987 by Lucille Clifton, with the permission of BOA Editions, Ltd. and brought to my attention by Arnold Levin.

2. This agenda is not addressed by studies in laboratories because that behavior addresses experimenters' purposes, not those of the participants, and samples behavior over durations of only minutes or, rarely, hours. This agenda is not well addressed by interview studies of organization members, because participants have only dim awareness of their psychological or social *processes* and because, without direct observations of the phenomena investigators can hardly know what interview questions to ask. Finally, this agenda is not addressed so far by ethnographic studies of organizational life because they have not been informed by a pragmatic perspective, therefore do not conceive of changes as adaptations, and therefore cannot follow unfolding adaptations over time.

3. The methodological and conceptual difficulties accompanying such a reality-integration concept of effectiveness seem amply outweighed by the recurrent guidance provided by the basic formulation that a person's or group's situational effectiveness depends upon an integration of situational realities into situated action. The reader will be able to judge for herself or himself the extent to which such difficulties are overcome as he or she follows the three narratives and analysis of reality-integrating or -excluding action presented in Parts II, III, and IV.

4. I provide one list of the kinds of contents of operating reality in Appendix I. Other investigators would provide their own lists, but while theirs would differ, their list would also be finite and all of our lists would have much overlap. Crucial for the present theory is not definitiveness of the kinds of contents that can be synthesized into problems, but the functional presence and power of problems themselves in daily mindings as cognitive-perceptual guides and as sources and organizers of motivation.

5. This concept of a *problem's* constituency is not to be confused with Cameron and Whetten's (1983) concept of constituency. Their constituency is an organization's constituency, made up of persons and groups outside the organization, the organization's publics or markets, on which the organization as a whole depends. It is normally possible to identify from the problem alone, even before considering solutions, some problem constituents. From the perspective of any solution, much more definitive identification can be made of the problem-solving constituents. One does not have to solve a problem, therefore, before knowing whose realities must be integrated for an effective solution. For further discussion see p. 384 ff. in Part V.

6. A note can provide only the outlines of a social constructivist theory of organizational reality. A basic distinction is made between 'complete and objective' reality, 'out there', as if known by an omniscience, and reality that is accessible to human actors and responded to by them. So we begin with a formulation of organizational reality with respect to some matter, x:

OR(x)	IS MADE UP OF	H(x):	AND	G(x):
organizational reality (x)		human constructions with respect to x		complete and objective reality with respect to x

Human constructions, H(x) — concepts *and* commitments, interpretations *and* evaluations, perceptions *and* dilemmas — regarding any matter, x, break into two kinds: (1) the constructions of organizational participants (students, teachers, workers, bosses, privates, generals) whose ongoing action is informed by their ongoing constructions and vice versa, and (2) the constructions of observers of the organization, e.g., scientists and outside consultants. Participants sometimes take on the role of observers, and vice versa, but the content and context of action makes it generally clear what role, participant or observer, a person is taking at any given time. Since we have n participants in an organization and o observers, our formulation of accessible and inaccessible organizational reality becomes:

OR(x)	IS MADE UP OF	n(x), o(x)	AND	G(x):
		Available, accessible universe regarding x as it is responded to by persons in the organization		(regarding x) 'as it is'; both as it is responded to and as it is not responded to by persons in the organization.

What we posit as an existing universe 'out there' regarding any issue or event, x, is approximated by observers' perceptions and other subjective realities regarding x — o(x) — and is observed and responded to in action by members, n(x). Observers in organizations concerned with some matter, x, often collect data about n(x), organizational realities about x constructed by the organization's members.

With respect to any given organizational matter, x, only a subset of n members, in general, will be touched by it or will be implicated in action regarding it. Those members whose normal organizational functioning will be impinged on by x, who care about x, or whose action is necessary to x can be considered as 'constituents' of x, a sub-set of n who are implicated somehow in x, whom we can conveniently label c, for constituents of x. Thus our formulation of accessible organizational reality regarding x becomes:

OR(x)	IS MADE UP OF	c(x), nc(x), and o(x)

where c(x) are the realities of constituent members implicated in the matter or issue at hand, x; nc(x) are the realities of members who are not constituents of x, who are not implicated in x; and o(x) are observers' realities regarding x.

The constituent realities regarding any matter, x, that is, the operating, subjective realities of members whose functioning is somehow impinged upon by x, can be further usefully subdivided into three categories as follows:

Operating realities of participants who hold *formal status* in the organization, positions whose authority gives them some decision-making power to influence x — fs(x);

operating realities of participants who hold *informal status* in the organization, positioned in social networks in such a way as to have power to influence x by virtue of friendship relations — is(x); and

operating realities of participants who are members of an *organized group* one of whose purposes is to deal explicitly with x, in support or opposition — g(x).

Combinations of formal and informal status and degrees of organization are possible, of course, and the more status and organization a constituent participates in, the more problem-solving effectiveness requires that his or her realities on the matter be integrated into action on the matter. The greater, also, will be his or her capacity to communicate his or her reality on the matter to others.

Thus, finally, accessible organizational reality regarding x can be seen as distributed across the organization among the following categories of participants: observers, non-constituent (unimplicated) members, constituent members holding formal status regarding x, members holding informal status regarding x, members organized to deal with x, and combinations of these.

7. Simon, H. A., 'Is thinking uniquely human?', *University of Chicago Magazine*, Fall, 1981, 12-21. Other examples of this kind of culturally shared problem are arrays of pieces of chess on a chessboard and a favorite of the Gestalt psychologists,

the 'pendulum problem' (Maier, 1970, pp. 179–189). More recent efforts by Newell and his associates using the State, Operator, And Result (SOAR) computer system also use the culturally shared problem and do not deal with adaptive problem solving. Indeed, they cannot: to give up winning a game or achieving a culturally shared goal is frequently adaptive but never can count as a solution in such systems. For an accessible account of these recent advances in artificial intelligence, see the recent series of articles in *Science* (e.g., Waldrop, 1988).

8. It is no accident that psychologists have chosen this kind of problem as the means of studying human thought and creativity: it places the problem under the control of the experimenter, among the independent variables. That is, the problem of this type can be varied systematically or held constant, independent of the subject's psychological functioning. The 'solution,' being known beforehand, allows the investigator to compare the subject's solution with the limited set of 'correct' solutions provided by culture. It is this cultural externality that makes the meanings of 'task,' 'question,' 'puzzle,' and 'problem' so easily interchangeable in this first tradition: each of these refers to a culturally defined form.

9. Compare these descriptions of problem or dissonance to the one described by March and Olsen (1979) as 'familiar' and 'useful' but as inapplicable to decision processes where ambiguity is high: 'At a certain point in time some participants see a discrepancy between what they think the world ought to be (given present possibilities and constraints) and what the world actually is. This discrepancy produces individual behavior, which is aggregated into collective (organizational) action or choices' (p. 13).

10. *Report of the Presidential Commission on the Space Shuttle Challenger Accident*, June 6, 1986.

11. *Report of the Presidential Commission on the Space Shuttle Challenger Accident*, June 6, 1986, Vol. I, p. 147.

12. *Report of the Presidential Commission on the Space Shuttle Challenger Accident*, June 6, 1986, Vol. I, pp. 92–93.

13. The term 'episode' crops up frequently in current social science writing (e.g., Harré and Secord, 1972). The three distinctive characteristics of the episode conceptualized and investigated here are that each episode (1) possesses a definable beginning and end, (2) is associated with a single agenda of transforming action — a problem and its solution, and (3) is related substantively to organizational conditions.

14. A sixth criterion, suggested by seminar students Bill Michalak and Tom Chockley, is the extent to which the functioning of non-participants benefits or suffers from the effects of episodic action. This criterion is not employed here because observations were limited primarily to participants.

Chapter 2

Trinity: Setting, Background, First Contacts, and Participants

Holy Trinity High School is run by the Blessed Sisters of Trinity for young women who plan to go on to college. The Blessed Sisters of Trinity (B.S.T.) is a large, comparatively well endowed religious order with a long history of service through schools and hospitals. Trinity High is, of its kind, a large school: with more than 1,200 students and more than 100 faculty members.[1] The school is situated in a community that is middle to upper middle-class, ethnically Eastern European and Irish, predominantly Roman Catholic, and virtually all white. At the time of the study, competition to enter Trinity was stiff, sometimes fierce. For the most part this stemmed from its excellent academic reputation. Some 90 per cent of Trinity's student body went on to higher education. But in part the competition among Catholic parents to enroll their daughters at Trinity also arose from parents' feelings that public schools were not only academically inferior but also had student bodies that were racially mixed or largely black. Trinity was 98 per cent white, the small minority of black girls coming mostly from upper middle-class families. The faculty was all white, predominantly female, and about 60 per cent lay, 40 per cent religious. Most of the teaching nuns were from the Blessed Sisters of Trinity; all of Trinity's administrators or, as they were called, 'executives', were sisters from that parent religious order.

The school building itself was connected to the religious order's local convent, with definite boundaries between the two, and sprawled over acreage that included a large north parking lot connected by a roadway to a large south parking lot. The building's six main wings extended in an irregular pattern in roughly a north-south direction, with a cluster of gym and separate cafeteria attached at the northwest, the front office approximately north-center, and another cafeteria at the far south. A seventh wing, an auditorium building, extended to the west. The two cafeterias, north and south, were necessary to accommodate the four daily luncheon shifts.

Innovations in the Religious Order and at the University of Chicago

The problem solving examined in Parts II, III, and IV can be adequately understood only in the context of more sweeping changes at the time. One was ramifying through the Catholic Church: implementations of the Second Vatican Council (Vatican II). These, in turn, were affecting the B.S.T. as a religious order within the Church. Trinity, a single school run by the order, came under these influences. The background to be described, then, figures importantly in later interpretations of specific problem solving within Trinity.

In the five years just preceding our entry, the religious order had undergone substantial reorganization in response to the democratizing and ecumenical influence of Vatican II. In particular, the rigid hierarchical concentration of powers in mothers superior had been eliminated, replacing it with elected councils and teams of executives. The order had succeeded in infusing into its national, regional, and local governance the principle of elected leadership. The order had also done away with the titles 'Superior' and 'Mother Superior' and 'Regional Mother'. At every point where it had existed, the language of 'Mother' and 'Superior', carrying the image of parental authority and parent-child relationships, was replaced with more neutrally bureaucratic language: 'executive', 'administrator', 'coordinator', 'director', 'council', and 'team'.

School administrations, however, were appointed by the elected leadership of the religious order's regional office. The team of regional executives having jurisdiction over Trinity, responsible for administering all regional schools and hospitals, had been experimenting with new forms of school administration. In the year just prior to our entry, for example, Trinity was administered by a 'team' of four 'executives', two co-directors and two associate directors. Such forms were intended to increase participation in decision making and to counter the old forms, and the old norms that had grown up around them, which emphasized a concentration of power and of valid judgment in a single Superior and a dependence on the part of all nuns under the Superior's charge.

Sr. Claudia, the co-director of Trinity with Sr. Norma during the year that we carried out our observations (the year, 01–02), had been heavily involved at both the national and regional levels in bringing about these democratizing changes. She also had been at Trinity for a dozen years, first as teacher and then chairman (the term used at that time) of English. Three years before we arrived at Trinity, Sr. Claudia became assistant principal under Sr. Jeanine, who at the time of our observations, chaired the religious order's team of regional executives. Sr. Norma had taught mathematics for most of the twelve years she had been at Trinity, and had become chair of the mathematics department before being appointed as co-director of Trinity with Sr. Claudia. Sr. Claudia, in addition to being chair of the

English department, had been appointed director of curriculum. Both Sr. Claudia and Sr. Norma had been nuns for more than 20 years, having entered in the same novitiate class.

The year after being assistant principals under Sr. Jeanine, Sr. Claudia and Sr. Norma became assistant principals under Sr. Mary Florentine Rose. The participatory decision-making arrangement among the three of them at that time was such, apparently, that the two assistants, Sr. Claudia and Sr. Norma, were delegated or assumed almost all of the weighty administrative burden, leaving Sr. Mary Florentine Rose with a relatively light role. This, at any rate, was Sr. Claudia's later testimony on the matter.

The following year (00–01), the year before we arrived at Trinity, Sr. Mary Florentine Rose assumed a post in another high school. Later testimony from Sr. Jeanine indicated that Sr. Mary Florentine Rose felt that she had been pushed out of the principalship at Trinity, and she blamed Sr. Claudia, Sr. Jeanine said. (Sr. Claudia later was aghast at such an interpretation.) Sr. Claudia herself later indicated that Sr. Mary Florentine Rose's position as principal had been untenable because the things Sr. Jeanine had previously done had been given over to or assumed by Sr. Claudia and Sr. Norma, who had been Sr. Jeanine's two assistant principals the year before.

After Sr. Mary Florentine Rose indicated she would leave Trinity, a four-sister team was appointed to administer Trinity during 00–01: Sr. Claudia and Sr. Norma were named co-directors, and Sr. Florence Ellen and Sr. Mary Catherine were named as associate directors in charge, respectively, of the business office and of publications and public relations. The co-directorship, in effect, legitimated the dual roles that Sr. Claudia and Sr. Norma had begun to work out under Sr. Jeanine and Sr. Florentine Rose. Having provided a bit of the Trinity administrative history, let me provide background on parallel developments at the University of Chicago, developments that brought us in contact with Sr. Claudia and Trinity.

While these innovations in team administration were being tried at Trinity, Jack Glidewell and I were trying something new of our own at the University of Chicago: preparing a new kind of specialist to enact a new kind of role in schools. We had developed a training program to prepare what we called 'social psychological specialists' to become internal organizational consultants in schools, staff persons who would collect data about organizational functioning and help members work through their implications for change. The second sentence in a brochure that we circulated widely at that time reads: 'A primary focus of this helping role is to assist the adult staff in a school to formulate and induce planned change together'.

The language of the rest of the brochure has much the same tone as the language that the Blessed Sisters of Trinity were then writing into post-Vatican II revisions of their *Fundamental Postulates* and of their *Vows, Virtues, and Disciplines*, documents used as curriculum for novitiate training and as guides in difficult decision making. These revisions used phrases like 'mutual respect and trust', 'generous concern shown in listening for another's truth', 'to raise up people who understand that the very humanness of their lives is a function of the communicative relationship', and 'maximize the possibility of value changes and needed renewal'. Compare the tone of these with the language from the brochure of our training program at the university:

> ... By helping groups stick to their problems, confront social factors that cause tension, or attend to a host of other such group problems, the specialist helps the group become more flexible, open, and productive in a way that makes all who are in the group feel a part of the decision-making and thereby committed to any particular decision.
>
> Purposes guiding cooperative action and planning in schools should be common purposes. Common purposes grow out of collective examination of those held separately by individuals in the group or organization. Common purposes stand in contrast to those that merely reflect one's own purposes, someone else's purposes, or someone's assumptions about what everyone's purposes are.

Students in the program carried out role functions in school settings in their second year, through a half-time internship. The training program and some of its successes and failures are described elsewhere (Lighthall and Braun, 1976), but one difficulty shared by all students immediately as they entered their internships was the overwhelming complexity of school life, their sense of being bombarded from all sides by events in the host schools that pulled them this way and that. In pro-seminar discussions among these interns a request was made for an initial 'game plan', some beginning project that would provide a simplifying focus enabling students to engage in useful activities immediately, while still leaving in the hands of regular school members control over which problems would be selected for work. I wrote out a number of 'game plans', each centered on a single concept — e.g., communication, conflict, problem solving, exchange — which would be drawn on by students in the next round of internships.

As the number of students in the program grew, and consequently the need for more internship sites, new means were required to recruit cooperating school districts. A conference of invited school administrators was decided on, where university students and faculty would describe the program, and where school faculty and administrators from previous internship sites would give testimony about the issues addressed and benefits resulting from the new role. After the conference, administrators who had attended indicated by correspondence their interest in exploring internships further. Among those who attended, and who indicated interest in pursuing an internship, were a Sr. Claudia and a Sr. Sabrina from Holy Trinity High School in Indiana, about an hour's drive from the university.

As we planned follow-up meetings to arrange internships, Trinity was relegated to the bottom of the list because of its distance. But one student who had already finished her internship gave glowing accounts of Trinity. Other schools nearer the university might not offer internships, and Trinity might be needed. So I arranged a meeting with Sr. Claudia and some of her colleagues at Trinity and traveled down there one day in May of the year 00–01, the school year before our observations.

The First Meeting at Trinity

In attendance besides myself were Sr. Claudia (Co-Director in charge of personnel and curriculum, and Chair, Department of English), Sr. Norma, (Co-Director in charge of student activities and discipline), Sr. Sabrina (Chair of the Guidance Department), Sr. Mary Lucille, (member of the Guidance Department), Sr. Catherine (Associate Director, publications and public relations), and Sr. Florence Ellen (Associate Director, business office).

After describing our program, the role for which we were training students, the importance of an advisory committee in the host school to which an intern would be attached, and some of our previous internship arrangements and activities,[2] I asked if they would say something about the kinds of problems of communication and cooperation they thought a person in such a role might help them deal with. After a silence of eight seconds, terminated by laughter, Sr. Claudia commented that the size of the faculty made for a 'huge' communication problem, that they did not all share the same goals, even within the executive group. This led to a discussion of the changes the administrative group had undergone the previous three years, and of the Academic Senate, composed of the chairs of the 14 academic departments. I then asked if they could put their finger on any problem currently being talked about.

Sr. Claudia spoke of 'difficulty' among the four-member executive group, of 'stepping on toes', and said, 'and I think it is something we have *not* worked through successfully'. She asked what the others thought. Sr. Florence Ellen indicated vaguely, and with Sr. Norma's help more clearly, that she had not been able to exercise her actual expertise, business and finance, that year because her time had been spent on other matters. She explained that she was new to the school, while both Sr. Norma and Sr. Claudia had been there a long time, and that she had little to contribute to executive group discussions of the other areas. Consequently she had resigned from the executive group as of June, to be simply the business manager reporting to the executives.

In the course of clarification, Sr. Norma explained that the job descriptions for the two associate directors had been written by herself and Sr. Claudia the year before. While their own roles had remained unchanged, she said, they had taken all of the duties of the principal and divided them up in their job descriptions of the two associate directors. This fitted with Sr. Claudia's later contention that the previous principal's position had been untenable.

Sr. Claudia came back to problems:

> Sr. Claudia: ... there are certainly very definite times when, you know, we can't communicate, at this point, just among ourselves and, um, and I think this is one of the communication problems among staff, in the sense that ... I'm sure that it's not articulated at any point to any staff, still they are aware of the fact that, you know, we are having our own tensions, and we're having our own disagreements, we're having our own differences on basic policy.
>
> Lighthall: Could you put your finger just on ... could you give me a little ... 'Basic policy'?
>
> Sr. Claudia: Yeah, well, you know, I ... I feel that I'm a source of, you know, a great problem in the sense that I come on so strong and that, you know, I just feel ... I think the rest of the team said this to me, that they resent the fact that ...
>
> Lighthall [interrupting]: If you have an idea you get it out there, is that it?
>
> Sr. Claudia: Well, I don't know the whole thing. ... I think this is a great source of tension within the group of four and I'm sure that, then, it's articulated in other ways, you know, to the staff as a whole. So that I know that I, personally, would be very grateful for, you know, the reaction of ... of process to see what it is that I'm doing that seems to be causing it, you know. (E:5/13/01; 1:432–460)

Discussion turned to the ways interns helped faculty and administration gather data about aspects of school life and functioning,[3] which led Sr. Sabrina to note the special problems created by a faculty's living together, on campus, in the same religious community. This led me to touch on, and led them to deny, the possibility of inter-group conflict between the lay and the religious faculty. Further discussion of internships prompted me to provide an example of internship activities:

> Lighthall: I can describe what the interns in one school have been doing where there was a race problem. There aren't very many black kids in that school and no black faculty. The black kids who are there feel discriminated against. And the white kids there feel that special treatment is being given to the black kids. And there are interchanges which are definitely hostile between the black and white kids.
>
> Well, okay, this is a touchy one for this all-white faculty. How do you begin to get a handle on whether there is or ... what the

nature of the race problem is? Well, what they did was to have all the faculty members sit down in an institute day with a little training in the gathering of what we call episodes, and then all the faculty members were paired to interview each other about an episode that had to do with some human relations problem [that they had observed during the following week].

Well, a whole raft of these came in. They were judged [by the interns]: Is this a race problem or isn't it? You got a look at the number of these that were judged 'race problem' or not by the black female intern and the white male intern together ... it was interesting to watch *their* interactions to decide whether this was a race problem or not and to come out with what the criteria were. That was really a learning experience for *them*. But then we said, 'Okay, it's been good for you. Why don't you have them [the faculty and administration] do it: talk about whether this incident, that you've all read, is a race problem, and then ... say what their criteria are for deciding.' Again, a consciousness building: what constitutes a race problem? So the faculty get involved by looking at data ... known to have been gathered by faculty.

So that's another thing that has been done. I don't know if it makes any sense at all for you. But you can see the analogues to that kind of thing. (E:5/13/01; rl:742–80)

After discussing the process by which interns might decide to select Trinity as an internship site, Sr. Norma re-raised the question of the composition of the intern's advisory committee, suggesting that students be included. She alluded to a problem of the relation between faculty and students, that she sensed some problem but didn't know how much of a problem existed. I pointed out one cost of having students, faculty and administration in the same advisory committee: 'the possibility of exploring mistakes that the executive group makes'[4] could be embarrassing to each of the adult groups.

After further discussion of an advisory committee for one or two interns and of the possibilities that one or two might select Trinity (during which I said that if I were one I would want to come to Trinity), I said that if no interns did select Trinity I would be interested in exploring the possibility of studying Trinity as an organization. This suggestion was greeted with a mixture of approving smiles and comments and non-committal reactions, after which I left.

As it turned out, no student elected an internship at Trinity. Over the summer I turned over the possibility that I myself might do a kind of half-time internship at Trinity. It seemed like a good idea for me to try to enact the role first hand, to discover the gaps and weaknesses of these initial role plans and, in general, to investigate the down-to-earth conditions into which we were sending our students. I would combine my interest in studying Trinity with my interest in testing out this new role for myself. By mid-August I decided to carry out at Trinity what I had begun to think of as a 'research and consultation role' or a 'consultation-research'.

Negotiations and Entry

In the initial May meeting at Trinity, described above, Sr. Norma had actively participated in the discussion, seeking to influence the composition of the advisory committee for the internship. Her active participation gave the strong appearance of support for the idea of interns of this new role at Trinity. After that meeting, however, Sr. Norma evidently expressed misgivings about interns coming to Trinity. A field note gives the flavor of the executives' respective responses to an internship being established at Trinity; it also reveals my own thinking at that time about the nature of an internship for myself at Trinity:

> 8/3/01 — Contact 7. Sr. Catherine called back . . . She said that Sr. Claudia [who was at a summer conference] had said to be completely frank about the situation re interns: namely, that most of them were very excited about the poss[ibility] of our being in Tr[inity] but that one person, Sr. Norma, had been reluctant. She had said that morale was so low that to bring in someone who would criticize would be damaging. Sr. Catherine said at this point that she hoped her own bias was doing justice to Sr. Norma's point of view but that she, Sr. Catherine, was very positive (not her word), very much for our coming out there with an intern position. . . .
>
> I explained that the students had elected not to come to Trinity, because of its size and distance from the university, but that I had thought that I would like to come out and try to understand what was happening there . . . and that I might be of some help. . . . We set a meeting tentatively for 8/25, when the other sisters would be on hand. (Bk.IV, p. 66)

Earlier in the summer, Susan Allan, then working on her doctorate at Michigan, had made arrangements to study with Jack Glidewell and me at Chicago for a year, and had expressed interest in the internship at Trinity. I told Sr. Catherine in that telephone conversation that I would 'have a research assistant along'.

An Ambivalence and a Shift

In just these few notes a duality and a tension are evident that are inherent in the kind of project reported in this book. On the one hand, it commits us to empirical research, to gathering data in the natural setting, to 'try to understand what [is] happening there', and it is appropriate to speak of 'a research assistant'. On the other hand, it commits us to being 'of some help', to 'helping people understand what [is] happening' in their organization.

While the ambivalence will be evident to the reader throughout, it must be said that we began our work at Trinity with ideas about 'intervention' that by November had shifted much more intensively toward research. I had four phases of work in mind at that time: (1) gathering and editing of observations and recordings (from meetings) of interactions among members that revealed important processes; (2) use of the edited observations and recordings in group discussions with participants, discussions designed to increase their awareness of organizational processes and to promote clarification of shared problems regarding those processes; (3) collaborative design with the participants and others of solutions for problems; and (4) further episodic data gathering to follow the problem-solving process thus set in motion. All of this was naively overambitious.

We attempted neither these grandiose interventions nor, with one exception at the end of the year (see Appendix II), the kind of episodic review I described above in connection with race relations. The demands involved in following a single substantial problem from its synthesis through to implemented solution were simply underestimated. While episodic data were in my mind at the outset mere means to the end of collaborative intervention and evaluation of intervention, it became apparent by about mid-November that it was most important, given the limits of time and resources, to concentrate on the centerpiece, still vague but coming by that time into clearer focus: the historical unfolding of organizational problems and their transformation.

Negotiation and Entry Proceed

On August 24 I telephoned Sr. Catherine to verify our meeting the following day. We talked about who would attend from Trinity (Susan Allan had not yet arrived). Besides Sr. Catherine, Sr. Claudia and Sr. Sabrina were expected. Sr. Norma had not yet returned from summer vacation. My field note regarding the conversation ends with the sentence, 'If Sister Norma is not present I see a problem there; but one that later inclusion should take care of'.

Two things are worth comment in this field note. First, I had not yet thoroughly distinguished problem in its psychological, adaptational sense from problem in its cultural, external sense. It is important to add that I had also not yet fully differentiated 'episode' from 'incident' and thus, had not linked its origin and termination with the synthesis and solution of a problem (in the second sense described in Chapter 1). The second point about this field note is that I had already begun to synthesize a problem of inclusion and exclusion of Sr. Norma, a problem that (1) paralleled a problem already operating in Sr. Claudia regarding Sr. Norma's absences and (2) had a counterpart in Sr. Norma's reality. Our respective problems regarding Sr. Norma's inclusion and exclusion would intensify for each of us.

On August 25 I met with Sr. Claudia and Sr. Catherine. While waiting a half hour for Sr. Norma to arrive, Sr. Claudia and Sr. Catherine described their current planning for opening the school. When it was clear that Sr. Norma would not be present,[5] Sr. Claudia said she was 'embarrassed'. Sr. Catherine said she was 'embarrassed and annoyed', expressing also some of Sr. Claudia's feelings. I described our training program and internship in much the same terms as I had used in the May 13 meeting, emphasizing that 'social processes' — e.g., communication, decision making, problem solving — were largely determined by what I called 'social reality', collective contents of minding to which people responded. (I had no conception, then, of 'constituent reality', as described in Chapter 1). I pointed out that 'episodes' (i.e., episodic data) were the chief means of both raising consciousness about organizational processes and the chief basis for thinking about improvements in organizational functioning.[6] The role of the interns was that of gathering these episodes and helping members of their advisory committee consider them with an eye toward improving organizational functioning — 'to help the people involved [in the episode's action] understand what they went through'.

Since organization members, in schools and elsewhere, normally possess neither the norms nor the vocabulary to talk about the social psychological processes through which they accomplish their work, the interns, in this case myself and Sue Allan, together with one or more advisory committees, would create local norms, occasions, and techniques for capturing and reviewing organizational processes.

To capture and review episodes[7] with others at Trinity, we needed to establish ourselves as observing and consulting members of one or two groups, preferably already on-going groups, that would not only do their normal work, but would also serve as our advisory committee in the collection and consideration of episodic data. Because the purpose for my being at Trinity was to 'try out' this new 'method' of organizational consultation, we would also, I said, need general permission, and the permission of these groups in particular, to obtain and quote from observations of members at work. Transcripts of interchanges would help describe particular concrete settings and interactions needed to convey an accurate sense of the method at work, to quote both for instructional purposes and for later publication — with all names kept anonymous.

It was possible, I said, to study organizational processes openly, with everyone knowing explicitly that we were doing just that, without substantial distortion in the processes themselves. While momentary distortions in the *contents* of communication would occur, I said, the processes of communication, having 'deeper roots', were much less 'reactive', far less under conscious control. The kind of role we were trying to develop would, over time, I said, bring such processes under more conscious control.[8]

Sr. Claudia and Sr. Catherine restated their understanding of Sr. Norma's reservations: that the faculty had already been rather shocked by student criticism of 'boring' teaching and that more discussion was needed before any decision was made to have our internship at Trinity. Sr. Claudia said that she did not agree that there was lowered morale among the staff. She said she saw a good deal of support among the department chairs for having interns at Trinity. I agreed that we needed further discussion with each successive group to which we might want to become attached for the year. Toward the end of the meeting Sr. Claudia said, 'I find it extremely exciting to be in on your research', a sentiment Sr. Catherine heartily seconded.

Three groups were candidates as settings within which Allan and I would carry out the consultation-research: (1) the executive team ('executive council') of three members, (2) the 25-member faculty-student council ('Trinity council'), and (3) the Academic Senate, composed of the chairs of all academic departments. I interpreted early support from Sr. Claudia and Sr. Catherine for our 'research' and 'internship' as a basis for meeting regularly with, and gathering data from, the executive council. This was later confirmed, with some qualifications, by Sr. Norma.

I met on September 15 with the Academic Senate and explained the idea of the internship and what it entailed. Sr. Norma was in attendance and, though she was one of the most active participants, voiced no concerns about an internship at Trinity. By this time, however, I was beginning to feel that two groups would be quite enough, and that the executives and the Trinity council would give us the full spread of 'levels' from the students through the top leadership of the school.

Trinity council's members' responses to our September 22 proposal — to study their functioning as a council and then help them function better — ranged from warmly receptive to indifferent. Sr. Norma's sentiments were not voiced because she was absent. After discussion a vote was taken on the proposal that the Trinity council be one of the groups to which we would be attached for our consultation-research. It passed unanimously.

On each of the occasions when the Trinity council discussed possibilities and directions for our consultation-research within the Trinity council — on September 22, October 20, and November 2 — Sr. Norma was absent. Thus, Sr. Norma was absent from important discussions about our entry by both of the groups — the executives and the Trinity council — which became our organizational 'homes', the legitimate settings, for the new role and its activities. It was soon thereafter decided, again in discussion between Sr. Claudia and me and again in the absence of Sr. Norma, that the Academic Senate would not be nearly as useful a 'window' into the workings of the school or as a consultation site as the two other groups would be.

As it turned out, our unintended exclusion of Sr. Norma from the process of legitimating our entry into Trinity resulted from exclusionary moves she had already begun on her own as part of a process of change within her: a process of cutting ties with the religious order and working out changes in self, in employment, and in life style, changes that drew her away fromTrinity, not only emotionally but also physically, thus causing her absences from decision-making processes. This private change on Sr. Norma's part, its impact on her functioning as an executive and on Sr. Claudia, and Sr. Claudia's attempts to manage her conflict with Sr. Norma are narrated and analyzed in the episode of Part III. The episode of abortive problem solving of Part II took place in the shadowy context of that on-going conflict. All members who participated in any of the episodes are identified (by pseudonym) in Table 2.1. By September 29, at Faculty Orientation Day a week later, our entry was taken by Sr. Claudia and Sr. Catherine to be a *fait accompli*: I was introduced as a 'consultant', and I gave a brief presentation of my purpose, concepts, and activities. A researcher's 'entry' into a host organization is not a single, unified move nor an accomplishment in itself. 'Entry' must be as differentiated a concept as 'reality', in that it is always relative to persons and issues. The partial, step-wise nature of an entry process was to be demonstrated in the course of the year and specifically in the course of the conflict episodes taken up in Part III. Consider the first episode, an attempt to solve an organizational problem by writing a constitution for the Trinity council.

Table 2.1. Participants in One or More of the Trinity Episodes During the Year 01–02 or the Year 02–03

The Year of Our Observations, 01–02

The Executives

> Sr. Claudia (Dilorenzo) — Co-Director, in charge of academic affairs, personnel, and, as Curriculum Director, in charge of curriculum; also Chair of the English Department
> Sr. Norma (Erskine) — Co-Director, in charge of student affairs, including all student activities and discipline, and including all scheduling of Trinity's large auditorium.
> Sr. Catherine (Norton) — Associate director, in charge of publications, public relations, and the business office.

The Trinity Council

Administrative Representative
> Sr. Norma

Faculty Representatives

Sr. Janet (Acker)	Norine Cohler	Naomi Higgins
Katherina Logue (Mrs.)	Louise Nolan	Sr. Mary Nannette (Noyes)
Sr. Mary Sabrina (Snedden)		Stanley Sullivan

Table 2.1. (continued)
_____

Student Representatives

Dale Devlin, Vice President (junior)   Beth Dolan, Treasurer (junior)
Roslyn Donahue (freshman)   Mary Donnelly (freshman)
Lucy Ellen Garvin, Secretary (junior)   Hester Dulany, President (senior)
Laura Hanrahan, (sophomore)   Sonia Griffin, (senior)
Donna Laughton, (junior)   Kathy Kuhlen, (sophomore)
Fran Novak (freshman)   Joan Noonan, (freshman)
Leonore (Leo) Phelan, (senior)   Nora Quinn, (junior)
Eleanor (Ellie) Sanford, (sophomore)   Pamela Roe, (sophomore)

> *Participants in One or More of the Trinity Episodes During the*
> *Year 01–02 or the Year 02–03*

From The Regional Administrative Board (the seven-member 'Regional Team')

St. Georgette, member in charge of all schools in the region
Sr. Jeanine, Chair (Former Principal of Trinity)
Sr. Mary Iver (Kallahan), member in charge of sisters' health and hospitalization

Staff

Sr. Mary Sonia (Hallahan), Coordinator of Buildings and Grounds
Mrs. Molly Larkin, Sr. Claudia's clerk-typist
Sr. Mary Lucille, member of the Guidance department and chair of the ad hoc
    faculty committee on student-faculty relations.
Mrs. Sybil Shulman, Sr. Norma's secretary
Mrs. Nellie Wagner, Sr. Claudia's receptionist-secretary

Researcher-Consultants

Susan Allan
Frederick Lighthall
Franklin Patrick, intern

The Year After Our Observations, 02–03

The Executives

Sr. Claudia, Director
Sr. Mary Patricia (Johnson), Senior Coordinator
Sr. Mary Ann (Cross), S.I.C, Sophomore Coordinator
Sr. Catherine, Associate Director
Irma Carey, Junior Coordinator
Sr. Jeane (Parnell), Freshman Coordinator

Persons From Earlier Years

Sr. Florence Ellen, Associate Director, business office, 00–01.
Sr. Mary Florentine Rose, Principal of Trinity after Sr. Jeanine
_____

Notes

1. Precise figures might identify the school, so these figures will suffice. Pseudonyms are used, too, to refer to the academic years at Trinity, e.g. 01–02 for the year of our observations, 02–03 for the year following, and 00–01 for the year preceding.
2. I had long since forgotten, if I ever knew, that Sr. Claudia herself had attended our conference at the university. While I thought I was recruiting Trinity as a resource for our training program and myself, Sr. Claudia and Sr. Sabrina had, before our May 13 meeting, begun to recruit an intern from our program for Trinity. Thus, Sr. Claudia and I had complementary solutions to our respective problems.
3. It embarrasses me to see how insensitive I was to Sr. Claudia's problem of stepping on toes and of coming on so strong with her colleagues. In this passage, instead of asking her to say more, I interrupt with my own quickly guessed version of her meaning. The repeated experience of retrospective embarrassment at my insensitivities revealed in the data brings home in this context an important fact noted first by Heider (1958) and explored in the laboratory by later attribution theorists (e.g., Jones and Davis 1978; Jones, 1978; Ross, 1978a, 1978b): As actors and as reviewers of action we are in sharply different situations. Add to this the fact that quite a few years have transpired since I was at Trinity, and the reader may understand that I regard myself then and now as having different sensitivities, skills, concepts, and outlooks.

   In order to solve my problem of wanting in this account to be true to the data, on the one hand, but seeing myself there in the data as often acting inadequately, judged by my current standards and images, I had to achieve a distance between myself now, trying to be as methodical and reliable a reporter as possible, and my earlier self then, as consultant-researcher, too often missing events and implications that, in retrospect, should not have been missed. A useful device to achieve this analytical distance was simple enough: I would think and write in the third person about 'Lighthall': 'That [past] Lighthall was not this [present] Lighthall, so go ahead and be as openly (or coldly) analytical of that Lighthall as you are of any other actor'. I use this device in Parts II, III, and IV, but remain in the first person in these introductory chapters.
4. This comment may well have been the basis for Sr. Norma's conception, expressed to her colleagues later, that the focal purpose of an intern was to criticize.
5. Sr. Florence Ellen, the fourth member of the executives, had recently and unexpectedly been granted leave to sort out confused thoughts and feelings about her position at Trinity and her goals more broadly. She re-appears later, briefly, as a participant in the conflict between Sr. Claudia and Sr. Norma considered in Part III.
6. A definition of 'episode' given in a hand-out to the Trinity council on October 20, 01 reads: 'An episode is, in its simplest form, a social interaction between person or group A and another person or group B. Episodic data are the words and behavior of the individuals involved, including their thoughts and feelings to the extent that they are evident in their comments or behavior'. The concept of episode at that time, thus, had no connection with the concept of problem but was merely another word for 'social interchange' or 'social interaction'.
7. The phrase, 'to capture and review episodes', places episodes in the world out there, as something given, to be captured. Convenience sometimes dictates that such shorthand be used, but 'episode', like 'history', is constructed, and an episode is properly conceived to be an account of events, a history, whose unitizing is done by the observer not by nature. On the other hand, I am willing to argue that the condition I call 'problem', is well nigh universal (e.g. can be found clearly in the fairy tales and myths of widely varying cultures), even though my focusing on it as a unit of data may reflect culture-bound values and outlooks.

8. The question of how impervious organizational processes are to observer influence is a knotty one. Surely it requires differentiation: some processes, like those of choice or decision, for example, may well be sensitive to observer's presence and interventions. But other processes, particularly those dispersed across persons, roles, and levels, like the problem solving captured in this book's episodes, will be relatively impervious, both to the presence and to local interventions of consultants. Unlike the dominant position that experimenters hold in their experiments, and thus the dominant influence they have over subjects' behavior — which is always short-term behavior — the organizational consultant or researcher holds a dependent position and a subordinate agenda in a host organization whose members have strong agendas of their own.

On the question of the influence of those interventions that we did carry out, Appendix II describes each of our organized interventions. They were designed to help participants in some particular way to become more aware of, and increase their collective control over, the organizational processes in which they were participating. In general, while at the time we would have been delighted to have observed noticeable changes in levels of awareness or behavior, we observed only minor, short-term instances of impact. This is not surprising, given their occasional, ad hoc natures and given our increasing commitment to collecting narrative data.

While our specific interventions had little discernible effect, our continued presence, particularly in the executive committee, did have a noticeable effect. That becomes part of the narratives of Parts III and IV. Part III conveys how I, and to a considerably lesser extent Susan Allan, became participants, at first unwitting, in the conflict between Sr. Claudia and Sr. Norma. Our becoming enmeshed in the co-directors' conflict opened some doors for obtaining data and closed other doors.

Part II
The First Constitution Episode:
Abortive Problem Solving

Chapter 3

Constitution: From Originating Problem to Collective Action

The problem solving in this episode failed almost completely — an instance of organizational incompetence, of maladaptation. It failed in the sense that it did not solve its originator's problem and its collective problem-solving momentum died out. It is important not for what it alone did to its participants or to Trinity, but because it depicts the kind of mundane failure that happens so often in schools and other organizations. In this case, for all participants except its problem originator, Sr. Claudia, action guided by the original problem or by any transformations of it simply ceased. The 'constitution' became unimportant for each participant except Sr. Claudia. Sr. Claudia's problem was not solved, but she returned to it later, in a new context and with new resources. We trace the later, more successful re-addressing of her problem in Part IV. Here, we trace the abortive attempt which recruited efforts but came to naught — except a net loss of resources.

Overview

The episode began with the problem, synthesized by Sr. Claudia, of the proper function of the new student-faculty Trinity council. The Trinity council had been created primarily as an advisory body. Besides its primary function of advising, it was to make decisions only where it had resources itself to implement them (e.g., sponsored dances). It was now, however, making decisions and policy that affected the faculty, large segments of the student body, and parents. On one hand, Sr. Claudia wanted and had expected a faculty-student council that would make recommendations for improvements in school life and functioning. It would advise. In contrast, she saw the Trinity council not only make school-wide policy, but also set in motion implementing actions. She regarded both the policy and the implementing attempts as beyond the council's knowledge and legitimate authority. Her focal problem, therefore, involved an intention opposed by perceived conditions.

Sr. Claudia initiated a series of actions to solve her problem. One of them led to a discontinuity in the problem-solving process, a severing of the problem-solving process from its originating problem. The solution, now labeled and therefore communicable as a set of actions in the abstract, was seized upon as a solution for an entirely different problem from the originating problem. How this seizure was accomplished, how it subverted the solving of the originating problem, and how it led to confusion and some bitterness will become clear in the analytic narrative. Readers familiar with the 'garbage can' theory of organizational decision making (Cohen, March, and Olsen, 1972; March and Olsen, 1979) may recognize in this severing of a process from its initiating purposes the ambiguity and seemingly random joining of problems, solution, and opportunities featured in that theory. I will comment on that interpretation in Part V.

Immediate Context

While Sr. Claudia's focal problem was the incompatibility between the expected (advisory) and perceived (decision making) function of the Trinity council, that focal problem formed but a nucleus of a larger problem complex. Part of that complex was Sr. Claudia's expectation, on the one hand, that her co-director, Sr. Norma, would represent administrative concerns and constraints in the council, and her perception, on the other, that Sr. Norma was absent from work and was not carrying out a number of her administrative duties. In fact, Sr. Claudia had synthesized this problem regarding Sr. Norma's absences from her office and from the building before Sr. Claudia had become troubled by the council's functioning. Sr. Claudia's problem with her co-director, which evolved into a full-blown interpersonal conflict and is pursued as its own episode in Part III, constituted an important contextual constraint on her focal problem of the council's functioning. It is important to synopsize briefly a bit of background to that conflict.

The previous year, Sr. Claudia had overstepped the boundaries of her own administrative jurisdiction (curriculum and personnel). She had asked some maintenance men to do a task. Her request conflicted with plans of Sr. Florence Ellen, whose jurisdiction was maintenance. When the matter was brought up in conversations and in a meeting of the four executives, Sr. Claudia was criticized for overstepping her boundaries. Sr. Norma spoke in support of Sr. Florence Ellen's position in this dispute. Sr. Claudia was embarrassed and, as the narrative of Part III will show, took very much to heart her colleagues' sensitivity to proper jurisdictional boundaries: henceforth she would be very cautious in taking any action or suggesting any policy that came under her co-director's bailiwick. With that background we can turn to the immediate context of events.

The actions by the Trinity council which Sr. Claudia found objectionable were taken on October 5 and 20, relatively early in the first year of the council's operation. It was responding to two sets of conditions experienced by council members. One set concerned the parking of automobiles in the school's large parking lots and narrow connecting roads. The other related to freshman girls' dissatisfaction with their uniform and to the onset of cool weather and some drafty and occasionally underheated rooms in the school.[1]

There had been parking difficulties from the beginning of the school year. Many students drove to school; every lay faculty member and some of the sisters commuted by automobile. Parking close to the building was desirable, since walking distance to offices, classrooms, and lockers was considerable, even from the near edge of parking lots. Members of the faculty had adopted the habit of parking along the narrow connecting road, thus causing them to be narrower, and holding up traffic in the rush of the morning by their parking maneuvers. Complaints were lodged about dents and scrapes in parked cars. At its October 5 meeting the council passed a motion, spearheaded by its students but approved by the faculty members, proposing a graduated set of steps to solve 'the parking problem'. They ranged from a request over the school's public address system for no parking in the bottleneck areas to the deployment of the school's policeman to direct traffic, and having cars ticketed and towed at owners' expense.

The Trinity council took a second action on October 20 that Sr. Claudia regarded as beyond its proper authority, an action that added salience to her problem of advisory vs. decision-making functions. The council considered, voted down a motion to table, and referred to a sub-committee a motion to add a regulation school sweater to each class's school uniform. Sr. Claudia saw this as a move not merely to add a sweater to each class's uniform. She saw it as an initial move in an attempt to 'change the whole uniform policy of the school' — i.e., to do away with uniforms.

A word about the narrative form. A narrative of an episode traces the history of its problem-solving events and on-going interpretation by its participants insofar as our data capture them. Parts II, III, and IV of this book each contain a single episode of organizational problem-solving which is narrated and analyzed. The narrative of each episode in each of those parts is punctuated by analytic comments to help the reader sort out patterns. Shifts from narrative to analysis to narrative are explicitly signalled by: *   *   *   *.

Early in a narrative readers require more orientation than later, so each narrative will be analyzed at first in rather brief segments, at first with a high ratio of punctuating analysis to data. As analytical dimensions and recognition of patterns become established, fewer commentaries on our part will be necessary, allowing a reading of increasingly extended portions of uninterrupted narrative data. We begin our first narrative.

The First Episode

On October 20, after the first council discussion of a change in dress code, Sr. Claudia met with Hester Dulany, student chairman[2] of Trinity council, to voice her objections. Sr. Claudia described to Lighthall her interchange with Hester:

> Sr. Claudia: ... I told them [sic: she later verified she had talked to Hester alone] that I thought they were in an untenable position as far as having no administrative input was concerned but that they were moving ahead as if they did have, do you see? And that I felt that they should know that I couldn't move with that and that I would not be able to support a policy that would pass that no administrator had any voice in. ... I gave them [sic: Hester] examples. They passed a thing on .. you know: cars would be towed away. And I said, 'Tell me, which cars have been towed away? You know, you said that cars that were invalidly parked would be towed away [emphasizing her words by firm taps of her hand on the desk in cadence with each word]'. So I said, 'Look out the window. ... Nothing has been done in terms of this. You acted outside, you know, your ability to put into practice and outside of the kind of ..[3] we weren't asked our opinion....'
>
> Lighthall: When was this?
>
> Sr. Claudia: ... After council meeting Wednesday night (10/20/01) when they were moving to change the whole uniform policy of the school. ... I feel it very strongly,' cause I get the phone calls. They don't. (FL: 10/26/01; C1:795–830)[4].

✿   ✿   ✿   ✿

Communication: Aim. If the council is to be persuaded to alter its function, it is the council, not individual members of it, that must re-direct itself as a collective entity. Sr. Claudia's first move outward to solve her problem, however, is not to the council, but to a single member of it, its (student) president. Sr. Claudia's communication aim is either off-target or indirect, attempting to reach the council by an intermediary. Sr. Claudia's communication here is aimed at a level of social complexity (the individual) well below the level implicated by her problem (the group). In other words, Sr. Claudia communicates important realities to some members of a constituent group but excludes the constituent group itself — excludes on two counts: (1) she excludes it from her own realities, specifically *her problem* concerning its functioning, and (2) she excludes herself from its realities, specifically *its problems* of parking and sweaters.

Cognitive Functioning.   Sr. Claudia construes her interchange with Hester, the council's president, as an interchange with the council itself. This kind of mental collapsing of a socially plural, differentiated, and complex entity into one more singular, undifferentiated, and simpler excludes many realities that are important to cumulative effort in organizational problem solving. It excludes, for example, the resources, the extent and complexity of communication and the power of resistance which twenty-five members of a council represent as contrasted with the single person of their presiding officer. It expresses as already accomplished communication that has not been accomplished: telling 'them', the council, that they were 'in an untenable position'.

Communication: Flow/Blockage.   An important part of Sr. Claudia's complaint to Hester is 'we weren't asked our opinion'. That is, administrative positions' opinions opposing the issuing of ticketing and towing instructions are either not expressed or not heard. How come? Sr. Norma was the administrative representative on the council. She met weekly and had other contacts with Sr. Claudia. How come Sr. Norma did not provide the council with the executives' views opposing a policy of ticketing and towing cars? But even more fundamental than such substantive positions was the fact that the council was acting *procedurally* as a policy-making, order-issuing body rather than as an advisory body. What prevented Sr. Norma from conveying that reality to the council? Data are lacking for a solidly grounded answer. We do know, however, that Sr. Norma was deeply distracted by other concerns in this period and was withdrawing her motivational investment from her work at Trinity and, indeed, from her commitment to being a nun. Whatever the cause of her failure to provide administrative input to the council, the data clearly show that she did not do so on this matter.

Reciprocity in Problem Solving.   The council's actions on parking and the uniform dress codes, from Sr. Claudia's viewpoint, promised immediate difficulties but also represented a far more serious and continuing malfunctioning within the school's structure. These difficulties and this malfunction was in the foreground for Sr. Claudia. But those actions on the council's part were also attempts to solve its own problems, to overcome its own difficulties. The physical dents and scrapes and the mental anguish in regard to parking and the students' experiences that pushed for the addition of a sweater to the uniform also constituted realities in their own right. These council difficulties received no mention in Sr. Claudia's interchange with Hester.

   Sr. Claudia's attention to problems can be characterized here as exclusionary rather than inclusive. A more inclusive reality, more open to others' problems as well as one's own immediate and local problems, could have been expressed to Hester in the following manner:

Sr. Claudia: You have taken action on parking and uniforms without administrative input. I want to do what is necessary to help you solve whatever problems you have with parking and uniforms, but I want you to know that the way you are now going about it cannot solve those problems because the administration is left out of the action. See those cars still parked out there? Nothing has been done to ticket or tow them because we are the only ones who can issue such orders, not you. So let's go back to the beginning with your problems, and develop a solution to them that will also not create the problem we now have with the council acting as if it had powers it does not have.

This more inclusive reality, one neither foreign to administrators nor beyond Sr. Claudia's general capacities, would have tended to counter the reciprocal exclusion that had thus far been established regarding each other. This reciprocal exclusion can be expressed as 'I respond only to my own local and immediate problems and can't be bothered with — or am ignorant of — your problems'. This reciprocity was asymmetrical in one sense. While the council was uninformed regarding Sr. Claudia's problem, Sr. Claudia was manifestly informed that the council was responding to difficulties: it was taking action on two fronts. Sr. Claudia was more attentive to the actual and potential effects of these actions than to their causes.

Here two local realities, the council's regarding scraped fenders and a concerted voice calling for sweaters and Sr. Claudia's regarding the proper functioning of an organizational unit important to her, were generating action into which the other party's local realities were not integrated. Since Sr. Claudia and the council were each constituents of the other's problem, each was excluding a constituent reality from their own problem solving.

Motivational Investment. Sr. Claudia's act of calling Hester in, her tapping of emphasis on her desk, and the language of her complaint all reveal a motivated, mobilized person. She would be the one to get the phone calls — an assessment on Sr. Claudia's part that all of our evidence would confirm. At the nub of her problem was being held responsible (by the people who would do the phoning, the faculty in the case of parking and the students' mothers in the case of uniform changes) for actions she had no hand in influencing.

            ✿   ✿   ✿   ✿

Three weeks later (November 16), with both Sr. Claudia and Sr. Norma present but only peripherally participating, the council added a regulation school sweater to all four class uniforms. In those three intervening weeks between October 20 and November 16, however, momentous events took place regarding the relationships of Sr. Norma and Sr. Claudia to each other and to Trinity High School. Those events are traced in their broader context in Part III. It is relevant at this point to note that Sr. Norma's intention not to return the following year to Trinity had been officially received and accepted at the regional level of the Blessed Sisters of Trinity. This fact was known to Sr. Claudia and to us but it was still to be announced publicly only by Sr. Norma. Her announcement was expected sometime before the end of December.

At the regular December 3 executive meeting Sr. Claudia expressed misgivings about Trinity council's decision-making posture to Sr. Norma:

[Sr. Claudia turned attention to up-coming executive meetings, indicating that she wanted to set aside some time for 'talking about the relationship of administration and Trinity council in terms of policy making and decision making'.]

Sr. Claudia: . . . I have a fuzzy idea of how some of those things work. And so, I'd like . . . to hear how you think they work and how they should, not how they are [functioning] now necessarily, but how they should [function]; and how the council sees itself in decision making. And how these committees [council subcommittees] see themselve . . I think they see themselves as feeding information in and that's how I could agree with it, too. But I have questions about Trinity council's *decision making.*

Sr. Norma: Umhmm.

Sr. Claudia: . . . and also how administration . .

Sr. Norma: It was never intended to be a decision-making body.

Sr. Claudia: No. Right.

Sr. Norma: It was to be an advisory body . .

Sr. Claudia: Advisory body — when we okayed it, you know.

Sr. Norma: . . not policy making. And it's, you know, that's the whole thing with regard to students today, you know, and the desire for the power and authority to be able to come to some decisions on their own and I think we have to get down to the nitty-gritty things about wherein their authority lies to make, um, decisions and where it does not.

Sr. Claudia: And spell that out and work with them in terms of what they expect, d'you see, and then how much they're willing, you know: 'If you make this policy, are you willing to enforce it?'

Sr. Norma: And, see, they don't have a constitution. There's nothing, you know, to go on. You know, it's more or less trying to, um . .

Sr. Claudia: Experiment.

Sr. Norma: . . experiment and draw up the constitution towards the end of the year after we've had a year of experiment.

[Sr. Claudia then turned attention to a time schedule for future meetings to help her 'especially in terms of interviewing people' for the following year. Sr. Claudia asked whether Sr. Norma thought discussion at the next executive meeting should be devoted to Trinity council functions or to administrative structures for the following year. Sr. Norma said she thought administrative structures should be discussed first. That became an agreed agenda item for the next meeting.] (E:12/3/01; 2:238–257)

Shortly thereafter, either that very Friday or the following Monday, Sr. Claudia had an occasion to talk with Mr. Sullivan, the only male faculty member of the Trinity council. The subject of the Trinity council came up. We do not have any record of the contents of that discussion except testimony from Mr. Sullivan, given a number of months later, that 'the idea of a constitution came up' in his interchange with Sr. Claudia.

One of the Trinity council's bi-weekly meetings fell on December 7. Without prior preparation and, according to his later testimony, without an initial intention to do so, Mr. Sullivan brought up at that meeting the matter of a constitution for the council.

Hester: . . . we move on to New Business. And . . . Mr. Sullivan, you're the first under New Business?

Mr. Sullivan: Yes. I'd like to present a motion for discussion that a new committee be organized in the Trinity council and that some faculty member and some student who are not presently chairing a committee be appointed as co-chairmen of the committee. I think we need a constitution for this organization. We have as of right now no by-laws. We have absolutely nothing written down with the exception of a series of minutes from every meeting, and I think we need a constitution, a written constitution. And so I would therefore move that a constitution committee be organized and that, um, Hester appoint a faculty member and a student, um, council member who are not presently members of a committee as the co-chairmen of that committee. [Miss Nolan seconds, Hester calls for discussion. Mr. Sullivan omits any mention of his conversation with Sr. Claudia, who is absent.]

Nora Quinn: Mr. Sullivan, I don't get how .. I mean, like, I don't know. . . . Explain to me, like, what they would write.

Mr. Sullivan: A constitution, um, [laughter] is a constitution. Well, I .. you know, there's no other way to explain, what's a constitution. A constitution is a .. a statement of the by-laws of an organization, in other words, all the rulings that we have made, the things that we have passed, the laws that govern our assembly, see?

Nora: Do thos .. do, like, the previous minutes and that, do those go into a constitution?

Mr. Sullivan: Not word for word, but any vital decisions that were made go into the constitution.

Hester: The motions that were passed.

Mr. Sullivan: Right. Any ... any laws regarding the council itself go into, into the constitution .. In other words, it ... a constitution includes ... it ... a constitution is described in Roberts' *Rules of Order*, the book we all have. Now there's a very adequate explanation of what a constitution is, I mean, how it's organized. It includes a description of, for example, the jobs of each officer at the assembly, which I think is important, we should know. It includes any deviations from parliamentary procedure that we use, which we do .. we do have several.

Hester: Sr. Norma, was your hand raised?

Sr. Norma: I .. the thing I was just going to add, you know, that it was in Roberts' *Rules* and that a sample constitution, I think, is probably there and can communicate the necess .. the necessary things that *must* be included in a constitution of an organization.

Hester: Mrs. Allan?

Allan: May I ask a question? Is this a constitution for the Trinity council or for the student body or ...?

Mr. Sullivan: No, for the Trinity council.

Hester: But ...

Allan: Thank you.

Hester: You .. you're asking for a constitution. I think it's a good idea and I hope that .. that your motion passes, but .. what do I ask? Oh. Would it be a constitution just for this year or would it be to carry on the next year and ..

Mr. Sullivan: No, no. You see, a consti ... that's really the primary purpose for having a constitution is so that it *can* carry on 'til the next year because, now it's feasible that everyone that is sitting here right now will not be sitting here next year.... It's not probable, but feasible. So that the people that come in here next year will have something to pick up and read and see, okay, this is what the president does.... For example, our, our assembly deviates from parliamentary procedure in a great number of ways. One of them is that the presiding officer is not impartial, this ... is a deviation of parliamentary procedure. It's not bad, you know, but it's just the way we have it. That should be in the constitution, so that people know that. They .. it's not a difficult task to write a cons .. constitution. All, all that's involved is picking up that book and looking in there and putting it down on paper.

❖   ❖   ❖   ❖

Communication: Aim. To return to analysis, once more Sr. Claudia moved outward with her problem, once again selecting an individual, Sr. Norma, not the council, as her interlocutor. Choosing Sr. Norma was more relevant to her problem than her first choice, Hester, since Sr. Norma was implicated in the council's inappropriately taking on executive functions (deciding and implementing policy). But Sr. Claudia did not broach Sr. Norma's own role in allowing the council to proceed in its 'decision making'. If she had done so, her aim would have been precise and direct. Sr. Claudia merely opened up the subject of the council's 'decision making' and the necessity to 'work with them in terms of what they expect'. If Sr. Claudia were hinting that Sr. Norma should be the one to 'work with' the council, her communication aim would have been direct. But she had no intention of having Sr. Norma work with the council, partly because she knew that Sr. Norma would not be at Trinity the following year, but mostly because the malfunctioning of the council developed in the first place under Sr. Norma's supervision. Bringing the matter up with Sr. Norma, therefore, was an indirect approach to the body (the council) that was focally implicated in her problem.

A third such indirect approach was made. Sr. Claudia spoke to Mr. Sullivan — quite possibly, a fleeting hallway conversation. And it was Mr. Sullivan, not Sr. Claudia or Sr. Norma, who carried the idea of 'a constitution' to the council. Sullivan was more influential informally than either Hester or Sr. Norma in the council, but still constituted an indirect link between Sr. Claudia and the body focally implicated in her problem.

Since the connection between a constitution and the directors' shared problem of the council's malfunctioning was broken in that interchange between Sr. Claudia and Mr. Sullivan, it is a pity we neither observed nor recorded it, nor interviewed either party soon after the conversation. It seems likely — since both participants tended to move decisively toward constructive action as quickly as possible, and given Sr. Claudia's proclivity for pushing ahead in thought, beyond difficulties to imagined solutions — that Sr. Claudia's conversation with Mr. Sullivan focused on the accomplishment of a constitution and de-emphasized or omitted altogether her problem and purpose. Thus de-contextualized, the proposed action was left for Sullivan to interpret on his own, to provide his own problematic context.

Sequential Integration of Realities: Success vs. Failure. An old parlor game provides a useful metaphor for thinking about one important dimension of organizational functioning. Participants sit in a row and the person at one end reads, in a whisper so no one else can hear, a brief story or joke to the person sitting in the next seat. That person whispers what he or she can remember of the story or joke to the third person in the row, and so on. The whispered contents travel down the row to the end. The amusement comes from hearing the last person's version and comparing it with the initial written one.

In organizational life matters are complicated by the fact that the communicated content that moves outward from a problem originator to others is not a story or joke but is problematic content to be acted on in some way. Of course, organizational processes often do not take the simple linear form of the parlor game. They often include check points and corrective mechanisms to prevent the accumulation of errors that a merely linear system of communication tends to produce. The extent to which each problem-solving process in an organization succeeds in mitigating the dangers of linearity is always an important question, however. So the parlor game remains a useful metaphor.

The idea of writing a constitution for the council traveled from Sr. Norma to Sr. Claudia to Mr. Sullivan to the council. Note the linearity here. The course of the migration of that solution from its origins to its implementations may strengthen, weaken, or completely nullify the solution of the originating problem. But if that migration is linear and if that linearity is unmitigated, solutions and plans will tend to be expressed in the absence of the problems from which they arose.

In more general terms, we can hypothesize that a linear structure of sequential communications in organizational problem solving will tend to retain *most recent and immediate transformations of content* and to delete the 'oldest' content. Since the originating problem soon becomes the oldest content in such a linear structure, that soon becomes de-emphasized or lost altogether. In other words, contents that pass through a linear sequential structure tend to become *sequentially and progressively re-contextualized by each successive participant.*

Sr. Norma suggested a constitution as a corrective: a constitution would reverse the fact that the council had 'nothing, you know, to go on'. From his conversation with Sr. Claudia, Mr. Sullivan took up the idea of a constitution for the council. His description of a constitution at the December 7 council meeting, however, showed that in the transfer of problem-solving contents from Sr. Claudia to Mr. Sullivan, its original corrective function and problematic context had been lost. In its stead Mr. Sullivan had construed a problem of his own to give the solution causal and contextual meaning. The writing of a constitution was now to support the council's *continuity and efficiency in its current mode of functioning* — precisely opposite to Sr. Claudia's intent.

Sr. Norma participated in the December 7 discussion of Mr. Sullivan's version of a constitution. She was thus in a unique position to correct the discontinuity that had crept into the problem-solving process. Sr. Norma was the very person who had originally suggested a constitution as a corrective for the council's inappropriate decision-making function. Now here she was four days later, having just heard Mr. Sullivan's entirely different rationale for a constitution, in a position to bring 'constitution' back into connection with the originating problem of advisory vs. decision-making function. It was as if the first person in the whispering parlor game were able, after whispering the initial joke or story, to take up a position further down the line and to hear and to correct the errors that had accumulated in the message. But she expressed no such connection. Sullivan's problem of the council's possible discontinuity of functioning thus replaced Sr. Claudia's problem of the council's possible continuity of functioning, problems of exactly opposed content.

∘ ∘ ∘ ∘

> Hester: Can I ask one thing before we vote? This is just to clear accounts. This is stupid. Um, is there a faculty member and student who will be willing to chair this? Miss Nolan? Okay, good. I was just .. out of curiosity. Is there any more discussion on the motion? [silence] All those in favor of Mr. Sullivan's motion please raise your hand. Okay, the report is that the motion is unanimously carried ... Then at this time I'd like to appoint Miss Nolan and Joan Noonan as co-chairmen of the constitution committee ... (C:12/07/01; I:162–195)

In just under five minutes a motion had been put forward, discussed, passed unanimously, and partially implemented.

Four and a half months later we gave a transcript of the December 7 council discussion of Mr. Sullivan's proposal to Hester and, later, to Lucy Ellen. We explained that we were following up the writing of the constitution. They were asked to read the transcript and to indicate with a pencil mark wherever they remembered a thought or feeling they had at the time of the meeting. Clearly, retrospective testimony of this kind, so remote from the original event and experience, must be scrutinized critically and skeptically for its validity. It is possible, and often the case, that retrospective 'memories' are a mixture of accurate memories and of construings and experiences intervening since the original events, casting the original memories into a mold quite different from the original. But it is also possible for a person to register thoughts and feelings with sufficient specificity for later accurate and detailed retrieval — especially using this kind of stimulated recall.[5]

With these difficulties and possibilities in mind, consider the part of the discussion to which Hester addressed herself and her reconstruction of her reactions at the time:

> Lighthall: Will you read that over, and put a little mark with the pen here in the margin as to where you have a reaction, you know, ah, where you can remember what you thought or felt while it was happening?
> Hester [reads and makes some marks; then addresses herself to the first section marked]: Okay. Oh, when Mr. Sullivan was asked what a constitution was, he goes, 'A constitution is .. well, a

constitution'. I felt intimidated. Because I myself wanted to know what he meant by a constitution and, um, I thought some other people might have felt intimidated, you know . . .

Lighthall: When you say 'intimidated . . 'Say a little bit more, if you can, about why that's intimidating? What does that say?

Hester: He's saying, 'You don't know what a *constitution* is? I mean, a constitution is a constitution. It's common knowledge. I don't even have to explain it. It's self explanatory when I say 'constitution'. Now that would make me feel like, wow! I . . I . . I . . I'm dumb. You know? . . . 'You're not all there, kid. Watch out. You . . you better read up a little more before you ask questions like that'. [proceeds to her next marginal mark]

Oh. Then when Mr. Sullivan is saying, 'It's described in Roberts' *Rules of Order*' — which, to him is very clear because he's read Roberts' *Rules of Orders* [sic] . . um, nobody had really read Roberts' *Rules of Orders* . . . — I think probably nobody spoke up and said, 'Well, we haven't read Roberts' *Rules of Orders* so we don't know exactly what kind of constitution you're talking about'. (FL:4/25/02; cl:228–255)

Hester responded to two other parts of the transcript, expressing thoughts and feelings that were unexpressed at the time but which she said she had thought and felt at the time:

Hester: Oh, and then, um, Mrs. Allan asked if it was for the Trinity council specifically or for the student body. Mr. Sullivan said, 'No. For the Trinity council'. And I started to say, 'But . .' and then, um, I never finished it and, uh [sighs] I remember I was thinking, 'A constitution should be open to the whole student body, to be seen'. But I don't . . . I don't know why I never pursued it . . .

Lighthall: I'm not sure you didn't later. I don't know. But that seems to be the end of it in that segment . . .

Hester: I'm a little surprised now that it's not stated at all there. I must have been confused or frustrated or something. God. [continues scanning the transcript] Oh, then at the end, when I was supposed to appoint a student . . a faculty member and a student? Um, I remember feeling very inadequate. Very, like, [sighs deeply] you know. I'm supposed to be the chairman and I wasn't really elected by this body of twenty-five people to be chairman. I was elected by students. And here I am, I'm supposed to elect . . . like, me, a student, is supposed to appoint a faculty member, as chairman. It just . . I could never feel right . . feel comfortable doing that. You know? It's just . . I felt very out of character . . . I can tell. I would stutter and things like that. . . . I was scared to, almost, ask a faculty member if, you

> know, you know, 'You're supposed to chair a committee' . . . not
> scared, but it's not me who should be doing it. It's .. a faculty
> member should volunteer or, you know, 'You, a faculty member,
> had nothing to do with me being chosen chairman of this group,
> so who am I to say to you, "I'm appointing you"?' You know? . . . it
> had to be carried through, so do it even though you're not
> comfortable doing it. (Ibid., 255–317)

Much later, seven months after the meeting, Lucy Ellen Garvin responded
to the transcript and to a similar request for a reconstruction of her
experience at the time:

> Lucy Ellen: First thing I remember from this meeting .. I
> remember talking about the meeting and I don't know if I
> thought this at the meeting. I think I did. But when ... Nora
> Quinn asks, 'Well, Mr. Sullivan, I don't know what ... exactly it
> would be?' and he says, 'A constitution'. And the way he said it
> was very condescending, you know, like, 'What do you mean?
> How could you ask such a stupid question?'. . . That was the
> whole air of the meeting, as far as I was concerned . . . . Mrs.
> Allan says . . ., 'May I ask a question? . . . is this for the student
> body?' and Mr. Sullivan cut in [snaps her fingers] right away and
> said, 'No. It's for the Trinity council.' . . . Like, he knew what he
> was talking about and couldn't understand why everybody else
> didn't.
> And then, on the second page [of the transcript] when Sr. Norma
> and Mr. Sullivan both say .. they explain that everything's in the
> book and the book'll tell you how to do everything, well that
> seems kind of funny. Why couldn't they just explain it, I mean,
> you know? It seems like if it's in the book everybody should know
> it . . . . . Mr. Sullivan couldn't understand .. you know, people
> who understood it couldn't understand why other people didn't
> understand it. (FL: 7/12/02; cl: 150–185)

These retrospective views offer only straws in the wind, of course. The
evidence about operating realities these two testimonies provide is suggestive only. It is also incomplete: other members of the council were not
interviewed. Still, such evidence as they provide tends to corroborate the
confusion and hesitant doubt about the meaning of 'constitution' evident in
the utterances captured in the transcript of the December 7 meeting.

Summary

So far we have accomplished two things. First, by following in some detail
the unfolding of a single problem and attempts to transform it, we uncover
the strong hold localism has exercised on this particular problem-solving

effort. Sr. Norma was preoccupied with her personal agenda of making a new niche for herself in the world. Sr. Claudia, seeing that administrative outlooks had not been integrated into the Trinity council's actions on parking and uniforms, and realizing she would be the one to receive any faculty or parental complaints, diagnoses the trouble (advisory vs. decision-making powers) and begins action to bring the council back in line with original expectations. Sullivan hears Sr. Claudia's mention of a constitution for the Trinity council, construes his own problem for which the constitution would be a fitting solution, a problem entirely different from Sr. Claudia's. Hester and Lucy Ellen reveal realities regarding Sullivan's proposing a constitution that, again, were strikingly different from Sullivan's. Discontinuity and separateness, not community and cohesion, characterized these problem-solving efforts.

The second accomplishment is a modest beginning at identifying qualitative variables affecting the extent to which local realities become integrated into, or blocked from, problem-solving action. The problem originator, Sr. Claudia, ignores the problems that the council grapples with (ego-centrism vs. reciprocity in problem synthesis); addresses corrective action to individuals rather than to the body centrally implicated in her problem (peripheral vs. central aim of communication); confuses the council with one of its powerful members (cognitive functioning); and sets in motion a process depending importantly on an already weak relationship between Sr. Norma and the Trinity council (communication flow vs. blockage); Sr. Claudia's original problem becomes replaced by another (sequential integration of realities); and the problem originator's motivational investment appears to be much greater than that of other participants (distribution of motivational investment). Each of these variables does the same thing in a different way: it constrains the extent to which the local realities in which participants are invested — their problems, their favored solutions, their necessary routines — become integrated into, or blocked from, the problem-solving action in question. To the extent that those local realities are excluded, the problem-solving action in question will not only compete for their energies but will also be uninformed about organizational commitments antithetical to its efforts.

Notes

1. These two problems, note, were problems to which council members were responding, not problems of Sr. Claudia's. While we might have followed episodes of those problems we did not; here we are following Sr. Claudia's problem which arose partly as a result of council members' pursuit of their 'sweater' and 'parking' problems.
2. Such sexist terms as 'chairman' and 'upperclassmen' are occasionally used here because these were the terms used by all participants at the time.
3. Whenever a person being quoted interrupts his or her own thought, the interruption

will be marked by the double period ('..'). Brief elisions ('...') delete material within the same person's utterance. Such deletions are of material that is repetitious or not germane to the problem at hand. Extended elisions ('....') delete material from two or more persons, again, because it is either repetitious or not germane.

4. References at the end of quotations are to specify where they are taken from in our corpus of data. An interview is designated by the initials of the interviewer (FL or SA); followed by the date; designation of a cassette tape (C) or the absence of a C, indicating a reel tape; followed by Roman numerals I, II, or III if more than one tape was used or, if only a single tape was used, an Arabic numeral, 1 or 2, indicating the side of the tape; and, finally, if the taped interview or meeting was a long one, the last designation consisted of the tape recorder counter numbers where the quoted segment began and ended. Counter numbers are from the Sony TC-55, for cassettes, and the Wollensak, for reel tapes.

Recordings of scheduled or ad hoc meetings of participants are identified by E, C, or RAC indicating, respectively, an Executive meeting, a Trinity council meeting, or a meeting at the Regional Apostolic Center; followed by the date; Roman numerals designating tapes if more than one; followed by the side of the tape; and if needed, the tape recorder's counter numbers where the quoted segment began and ended.

Field notes, all written by Lighthall unless Allan's initials appear, are identified by contact number, date, book, and page.

5. Specificity and accuracy are assisted by the method of stimulated recall that we adapted from Eugene Gaier (1952, 1954). This kind of retrospective data would have been strengthened by interviews with all or a systematic sample of the council members, and by much more prompt interviewing. At the time, we were not sure we would pursue the writing of a constitution and our attention was diffused for want of a clearer conception of 'episode'.

Chapter 4

The Re-Contextualized Solution Plays Itself Out

A constitution committee had now, on December 7, been approved and appointed to write a constitution for the council. The constitution, having now been equated variously with a summary of minutes and a set of by-laws, was to ensure continuity, not change, of functioning. Some confusion had been expressed before the vote. The unanimous vote was followed by attempts to clarify what had ostensibly been decided by the vote:

Hester: Elaine?

Elaine [a homeroom representative to the council]: Is this going to be an open committee or just one for members of the Trinity council?

Hester: Miss Nolan.

Miss Nolan: I hesitate say, now. I would imagine at the present it has to be closed, then, because at present information taken is mainly from what we have done so far. I mean, because the constitution will be what has been done, so far. I'm not going to assume what's going to be done.

Hester: Mr. Sullivan.

Mr. Sullivan: The job is primarily clerical. There's not a whole lot of opinion that goes [laughter from Mr. Sullivan and others] into it. It's primarily a clerical duty, to sit down and transcribe the things that have happened and to investigate, you know, what's going on. And I don't really see any opportunity for any type of dialogue in it or anything. I think they probably need help. I think they need two or three people to serve on the committee, but as far as a larger number of people, I don't think it is necessary.

Hester: If they found out you needed an open committee, we would publicize it, I guess.

❅   ❅   ❅   ❅

Communication: Flow/Blockage. The homeroom representative's question about an 'open committee or just one for members of the Trinity council' is significant because it gets directly at a basic organizational issue: whose organizational realities will be represented in the formation of a guiding document? When the homeroom representative asked about the openness of the constitution committee's membership she was asking, in effect, about the structure by which other organizational realities might be expressed and therefore integrated into the instrument, the constitution, which, in turn, might well control local homeroom action in the future.

The answer she received was, in that regard, exclusionary. Miss Nolan and Mr. Sullivan categorized 'constitution' as a means of preserving the past — keeping procedures and guidelines already established. Further, they assumed that the council's minutes contained in recognizable form just what those established procedures and guidelines were. The realities that Mr. Sullivan and now Miss Nolan intended to be included, in other words, were those realities that had been sufficiently shared by council members in the past that they were publicly acknowledged (in the minutes) as the council's realities regarding its functioning. Both Miss Nolan and Mr. Sullivan were here ruling out consideration of (1) realities regarding the council's functioning from other parts of the organization, viz, homerooms (to say nothing of Sr. Claudia's realities); (2) realities that referred to the future; and (3) realities that had not been voted on and thereby established as the council's collective realities. So restricted was the frame they thus adopted that the procedure for constructing a constitution could be reduced to a clerical task of 'transcription', without 'a whole lot of opinion'. We return now to the narrative.

o   o   o   o

Lucy Ellen Garvin: Are we back .. are we .. did we move on [to the next agenda item] already?

Hester: No. We were just about to and there was a question.

Lucy Ellen: I have a question.

Hester: Lucy Ellen.

Lucy Ellen: How .. the constitution that you write .. you said just now that you're only going to write for now? Like, for what, what we've already done?

Mr. Sullivan: You asking me? Yeah.

Lucy Ellen: Anyone who wants to answer.

Mr. Sullivan: Right. Well, we can't very well write it for what we're going to do, 'cause we don't know what we're going to do.

Lucy Ellen: Yeah, I know, but .. [laughs lightly] doesn't a constitution, you know, like ..?

Hester: Sister Norma?

Sr. Norma: Well, a constitution can be operative for a certain period of time. And it can be then changed by vote of the members or can be amended.

Mr. Sullivan: You see, the thing is, every time . . . this constitution committee would be in charge of making any deletions or changes in that constitution, once it's written.

Lucy Ellen: Ohhh! Okay.

Mr. Sullivan: So, like, if a month from now we were to happen to note that, oh, we need another officer on the Trinity council or we had one too many officers, or something like this, you see, [laughter] then that would have to be changed. It's important to remember, the constitution doesn't include things like we're allowed to wear sweaters at Holy Trinity. It's not that type of thing.

Lucy Ellen: Yeah, I know. Yeah, I know.

Mr. Sullivan: It's just involving an internal type of thing.

Lucy Ellen: Thank you very much.

Hester: Okay, is there any discussion on this now? Then the next one is . . . (C:12/07/01; I:195–235)

❖   ❖   ❖   ❖

Communication: Flow/Blockage. Lucy Ellen Garvin raised a question about the forward-looking and future-guiding functions of a 'constitution . She did so haltingly, but not so haltingly that Mr. Sullivan did not catch her drift. He understood she was referring to the council's future but he ruled out its consideration on the grounds that the future was unknown. Lucy Ellen tried to bring the constitution into a more inclusive frame ('but . . doesn't a constitution . . .') but was cut off by Hester's calling on Sr. Norma.

While Lucy Ellen was halting and then gave up when Sr. Norma and Mr. Sullivan assured her that the constitution could be changed in the future, no one explored what she was after. No one asked, for example, 'What are you driving at?' or 'What's the problem?' or 'What's your point?' Communication that integrates realities penetrates to the realities behind the fumbling attempts to find words. Lucy Ellen's expression was halting, but an exploration of her operating reality that could help her express those realities was absent. The same was true for each of the other questions raised: responses were given to interpretations of the meanings of words. Those who fielded questions about the constitution — Miss Nolan, Mr. Sullivan, and Sr. Norma –- apparently assumed that the words first expressing a question or an idea capture the only meaning to be attended to, ignoring or oblivious to the realities that gave rise to the question or idea in the first place. Such word-centered interchanges must be clearly distinguished from reality-exploring interchanges if we are interested in understanding how local realities, like Sullivan's, become integrated with other local realities, like Lucy Ellen's. Let us return to the narrative.

✿　✿　✿　✿

How did the episode's successive problem-solving actions play themselves out? With respect to the sheer number of meetings, the process was simple. Miss Nolan and Joan Noonan did not recruit others to help. They met together only once for the sole purpose of working on the constitution — at Miss Nolan's house for about two hours during the Christmas vacation. Early in January they met a couple of times during lunch and conversed about the problems they were having in carrying out their task. Then, at the January 18 meeting of the council, the matter of a constitution came up in connection with the evaluation of the council's effectiveness.

The number of meetings, structure of participants, and outcomes present a fairly simple structure. The psychological experience of the participants, their unfolding action, and its relation to the originating problem were more complicated. Consider events in four segments: (1) efforts and experiences up to the January 18 council meeting; (2) problems regarding the function and writing of the constitution and their solutions revealed in the discussion of the January 18 meeting; (3) abandonment of the task, with retrospective reflections; and (4) conditions after the Committee abandoned its task.

The Committee's Efforts Up to January 18

Joan Noonan's later assessment of her experience and activities with Miss Nolan in that Christmas vacation meeting was in these words:

> Some of the minutes were mixed up and some of them really didn't concern what we really thought should be in the constitution. Like, it would say something that we carried ... [i.e., a motion that the council passed] it wasn't really self-explanatory, like we didn't really get what it meant out of [the minutes]. So we wrote down all the information about who should we see and who should we talk to about it. (FL: 4/14/02; cl)

Joan remembered her orientation to the task and to the problem it presumably would alleviate:

> The first thing ..., I really wasn't sure about, like myself, I wasn't sure what the constitution committee was supposed to be doing. Like, I didn't know. I really didn't understand it. She [Miss Nolan] explained it to me.... Mr. Sullivan had suggested that we do need a constitution because ... we'd go around in circles ... I mean like we weren't getting very much done.... A part of the school ...

had a complaint and we'd bring it up at Trinity council and we'd take a vote on it, the issue would be passed. And then maybe, the whole school didn't hear about it and therefore another group of kids would bring up the same issue. And instead of saying, 'Well, you look in our constitution. Look at the written documents about set rules for the school', we'd just bring it up and like forget that we ever had ... passed on it before. (Ibid.)

ο   ο   ο   ο

Continued Linearity and Re-contextualization. The parlor-game effect continued: the solution, a constitution originally proposed to establish an advisory function, progressively disintegrated and was successively infused with local realities as it passed along the line of successive participants. This transformation of solution content continued, furthermore, even though the structure of sequential participation contained loops. That is, even though Miss Nolan and Joan Noonan had both been present earlier when Mr. Sullivan had explained the need for a constitution, Miss Nolan had now substituted her own rationale, her own problem for which the constitution would be a solution. Mr. Sullivan had claimed that the constitution would support continuity of council functioning from one year to the next. Now Miss Nolan was claiming — according to Joan but later corroborated by Miss Nolan — that it would address the problem of repetition, circularity, and non-cumulativity from one *month* to the next.

As Sr. Claudia's problem-related content passed to Mr. Sullivan, her problem became replaced by Mr. Sullivan's problem, and Mr. Sullivan's became replaced by Miss Nolan's. In both cases the structure of participations was to some degree against the parlor-game effect. In the first, Sr. Norma was present not only at the beginning but also when Mr. Sullivan explained the substituted basis for a constitution. She somehow never made the connection, or did not give any importance to the connection, between Sr. Claudia's constitution problem and Mr. Sullivan's constitution problem. (Sullivan made it easier for Sr. Norma not to make any such connection by failing to mention to council members that the idea of a constitution had come from Sr. Claudia.) So Sr. Norma's presence both early and later (creating the loop in the sequential structure) was not sufficient to mitigate the parlor-game effect.

Then when Joan Noonan later expressed confusion about the constitution, the person who did the explaining, Miss Nolan, was again a person who had earlier been present when Mr. Sullivan had given his explanation. But so had Joan herself been present earlier! Their presence both on December 7 and later in their joint meeting created another loop in the sequential structure. Loops in the structure, therefore, were not sufficient to mitigate the parlor-game effect on the functioning within that structure. We shift again now to the narrative.

*   *   *   *

Miss Nolan's recollections also indicated some confusion at that meeting with Joan. She voiced her recollections during a council meeting in May, at which some aspects of the constitution episode were discussed:

> At that meeting [during Christmas vacation with Joan] we both had questions to ask. We were missing a couple of pages of notes [minutes of the council]. We went through every note, or every minute, that we had, to get information that we needed. And it was a hair-raising experience. Because all of a sudden .. you sit there and you think to yourself, 'I know what it is I am looking for, but I don't know if what I'm seeing is what I am looking for. What is it? What do I do with this statement: "that we have an All-School Functions Committee?" (C:/2/02; 1:437–462)

The January 18 Council Meeting

The week of January 25 had been written into the school calendar for an evaluation of the Trinity council. On January 18 the council discussed at length its own evaluation. An evaluation questionnaire had been prepared and circulated to council members. The Elections Committee (a standing sub-committee of the council) was proposed to administer the school-wide distribution and collection of the questionnaires. At the point where Hester Dulany asked for a vote on a motion to approve the questionnaire, Sr. Norma demurred:

> Sr. Norma: I don't think I understood. I think it should be open for discussion for some suggestions that council members feed into the Election Committee. For example, ... how can they evaluate unless they know specifically what the goals and objectives are? .... I would like to raise the question to the committee that's working on the constitution how soon do they see themselves presenting a constitution to the council? And then I think we have to ... put it to the students and faculty, and maybe after that happens, we could see ourselves evaluating the council in light of what our goals and objectives are. (C:1/18/02; c2)

Some students responded favorably to Sr. Norma's suggestion. Miss Nolan disagreed:

> Miss Nolan: I'm going to take the opposite side. I do not think that this problem of giving the goals and objectives of Trinity council should be given to the constitution committee. As one of the chairman of the constitution committee, I could not handle that,

and neither could my co-chairman, because there's nothing in the minutes of any of our meetings that states any of our goals or objectives. Our notes carry the formation of committees but in no way is there any indication that twenty-five members of one body agree to a goal. And I would not take that on, personally. (Ibid.)

* * * *

Linearity: Resistance to Correction. The January 18 council meeting created another loop in the structure of unfolding problem-solving. Sr. Norma, the originator of the proposal that a constitution might solve Sr. Claudia's problem, was again at a meeting in which the members of the constitution committee were present. They were present, moreover, after having struggled with the task that Mr. Sullivan had constructed by providing a substitute meaning for 'constitution'. This time, unlike the December 7 meeting, Sr. Norma did attempt to bring the writing of a constitution closer to her original intent. She saw the constitution as providing the 'goals and objectives' of the council by which it now would be evaluated. To be sure, she did not say, 'The original idea of a constitution was to force examination of the council's basic role in school affairs and to make it more clearly an *advisory* body'. Nonetheless the thrust of her influence attempt was to make evaluation contingent on statements of goals and objectives coming from the constitution committee's constitution. For Miss Nolan and Joan Noonan to present a statement of goals and objectives for council discussion, they might have been forced to raise the issue of the council's advisory vs. decision-making function.

So we see two things in this January 18 meeting. First, we see a *structural* opportunity for re-instituting the original context for problem solving, an opportunity provided by Sr. Norma's presence at this meeting. Her presence provided a 'loop' in the linear structure of participations, that is, a repeat of her earlier presence in the original discussion of Sr. Claudia's problem with the council, where Sr. Norma had originally suggested the need for a constitution. And second, we see a kind of functioning of the individuals within that structure that did in fact bring the solution (constitution) back into a much closer *semantic* connection with its original problem (advice vs. decision making): Sr. Norma was not only present but she also spoke about a constitution as a means of setting goals.

What came of that attempt? It was successfully resisted. Miss Nolan refused to take on the task of presenting a statement of collective goals. She held to Mr. Sullivan's original procedural limits: that the 'constitution' be transcribed from minutes. She resisted what she regarded as a much larger, more complicated task — one she saw requiring the securing of agreements, not merely clerical transcription — on the grounds that it would not be accomplished from the minutes alone. It would be a different task from the one she and her co-chairman had volunteered for and they would not, she said, volunteer for this larger task.

Thus can a substituted context (Sullivan's for Sr. Claudia's) produce a radical transformation of one solution into another under the same label ('constitution'), and thus can this radical transformation take on power of its own to resist corrective re-transformation into the original solution (a task too great for the constitution committee to take on, one for which they had never volunteered). The end-workers, the intended producers of the intended product, can become committed to a radically re-contextualized solution and resist later attempts to restore control over action to its original context, the originating problem. Or, in still other language, once a solution has parted company from its originating problem, *it can take on a life of its own despite attempts to re-connect it to the original problem.*

ο   ο   ο   ο

Continuing our narrative, a debate ensued over whether the council could identify its goals, or had done so already. The debate raises for us and raised for some of them an important and recurrent issue in organizations: to what extent do official statements, or widely 'accepted' statements, of collective goals or purposes capture the actual psychological commitments operating in the collective's members?

Louise Nolan supported the distribution of a questionnaire, not necessarily the present one, she said, but one which included a question such as 'What, in your words, is the goal of the Trinity council?' She said, 'That's the evaluation, to come up with the goals. . . . It is working a little bit backwards, but I think because we are experimental it is the way we are working'. Hester argued that members did have goals for the council and had made them explicit in their speeches about the council at the beginning of the year: 'Those speeches were accepted by the council first, and in those speeches they used words such as "our aim is this", "we want to do this", and the council automatically accepted it . . .'

Louise Nolan responded to Hester's argument, picking up on the idea of people 'automatically accepting' others' statements of goals and intentions. Louise said that it was evident that everyone had forgotten those statements about goals. If a new statement were to be distributed, she said, what would prevent the same thing from happening?

> Miss Nolan: You're saying that we should give a statement to the students. Well, if we do that, and we use terms such as 'an advisory board', 'a sounding board', 'policy making', something like that, those are all fine and good and . . . [all of the] students are going to do exactly what 25 members did: we sat, we listened to the speech, we accepted it, and now none of us can remember what it is. . . . A lot of people are going to look at it and rather

than having to put it in their own words, they're going to accept what's written down, maybe not understanding what the terms mean. (Ibid.)

Sr. Claudia, who had begun to attend council meetings,[1] supported Hester's point, that goals had been made explicit in the platforms that various students had circulated in the previous spring's council elections. A student homeroom representative commented that 'Everyone has their own idea of what Trinity council should be or is', and Sr. Nannette expanded on Hester's and Sr. Claudia's argument that goals had been made explicit. She referred to the very early meetings of the council, in July of 01, where a number of objectives had been talked about: 'I'm sure you could find them someplace in the minutes of those previous meetings'.

  Discussion then took the form of arguments and counter-arguments with respect to whether the council 'had' or 'knew' its objectives. Support for Louise Nolan's point, that it was important for people to say in their own words — i.e., to have internalized — the goals of the council, came from Dale Devlin, who rarely spoke. She said that it is possible that statements of goals could be found 'back there' in the files some place, but that 'we should really get it in our heads'.[2]

  Sonia Griffin brought the council's discussion closer than it had previously been to Sr. Claudia's and Sr. Norma's originating problem, that of its basic function. Sonia suggested the appointment of a committee to consider the 'roles and functions of the new Trinity council' for the following year. Louise Nolan *again resisted*:

> Miss Nolan: Now to just set up . . . just to pass off and say, 'Okay, let's form another committee, and let them . .' . . . What you are doing is saying, 'Somebody else can figure it out, so let's give somebody else the chance'. . . . You can't say, 'All right, ad hoc committee for this'. It has to be a group effort. (Ibid.)

As discussion continued, Hester Dulany gave her own idiosyncratic view of 'the constitution':

> Hester: The council decided that each minute . . . each segment of the minutes would be a running .. run-through of the constitution; that, as we made progress, as we changed, as we .. every meeting would be a section of the constitution. . . . And the minutes have been open to anybody in the school. . . . That's the part of the constitution you see. (Ibid.)

She then turned to Miss Nolan and asked if she wanted to say something about the constitution committee. Miss Nolan commented on the magnitude of the task:

> Miss Nolan: Now this means going back and taking all the minutes of the past meetings and it means a little bit more than the

> minutes, as we found out in going through the minutes. It's
> something that will not be written in the *near* future, I mean . . .
> before the next meeting, perhaps before the meeting after that.
> It cannot be done like that. It is not an easy task to do. (Ibid.)

Eventually it was moved that a 'reaction survey' be undertaken about the
council's functioning. The ensuing discussion included a comment by
Lighthall that he thought council members were unclear about how such
information would help them or how they would use it after they obtained
it. The motion failed.[3] Hester turned attention to the next item, the school's
benefit drive. It was to be advertised and promoted by a council-sponsored
skit. The girls on the council wanted the faculty members to participate, if
only in non-speaking roles. All but one or two of the faculty resisted that
idea, complaining about 'time pressures' and the need to meet a deadline
for submitting grades. Several of the girls expressed frustration and
disappointment at the faculty's reluctance.

Abandonment of the Task

Louise Nolan's later comments about the January 18 meeting suggested
that the animated discussion about the skit, completely pre-empting the
topic of council goals or constitution, turned her away from writing a
constitution. She recalled the conversation she had had with Joan Noonan
immediately after that meeting:

> Miss Nolan: It was kind of: 'Well, Joan, what do you think?'
>   'I don't know.'
>   'Well, I say let's hold on it until we decide exactly what's going
> to happen, where this statement [of goals] is going to come from,
> if it is going to be a part of the constitution, or what direction this
> whole thing is taking.' (FL: 4/7/02; c2)

Joan Noonan's recollection of her abandonment of the task was that it had
become obsolete:

> Joan Noonan: I was supposed to confer with Mr. Sullivan. . . . But
> then, as it happened, at one of the future meetings Hester said
> that we should drop the constitution .. not drop it. She didn't
> say, 'Drop it'. She said we were not going to use it for a while but
> it was still there. . . . In the meantime, while I was getting all
> that information, Hester told me that, and I told Miss Nolan.
> Lighthall: I see. Hester told you that.
> Joan: Well, I said to Hester .. this was the day that we were
> starting out talking about her future Trinity council [2/8/02]. I
> think it was that day. And I went up to her .. 'cause I thought,
> how could we write up a constitution when we were changing

the whole structure of the council and we didn't have our aims down yet and what our duty was, really.... we didn't know what committees were going to be set up next year because that was part of our constitution — like, the School Functions Committee was in there. And, like, we were going to find out. But I talked to Hester .. I told her that ... it would be worthless if we did write a constitution 'cause it would take a lot of time and then we would have to change it anyway. And she agreed with me. (FL:4/14/02; c1)

Council discussions about more encompassing problems of school governance began soon after January 18. They are followed in Part IV. These new problems pre-empted Joan Noonan's further participation in the writing of a constitution. Miss Nolan and Joan did no further work on the substantive content of the constitution after their single meeting during Christmas vacation. Their commitment to the task was undermined by realities emerging at the January 18 council meeting (for Miss Nolan) and at the February 8 council meeting (for Joan).

Miss Nolan's recollections of what stopped her from further work on the constitution were specific and, as usual, colorfully expressed:

Lighthall: Do I understand right that you were stymied because [pause] you needed the evaluation and the evaluation wasn't forthcoming? Or .. What stopped you?

Miss Nolan: ... I think the thing that stumped me ... the first meeting that Joan and I had ... We took the minutes ... and I thought, to myself. 'I thought we had done much more than this.... There's not much meat here ... to begin ... what I consider a constitution'. And I'm as ignorant on that fact as anybody else is, ... except the constitutions I have read and Roberts' *Rules* that I've seen. And I thought, 'Now, there's gotta be more'.

Then we went through these minutes ... We made a list [of motions and amendments passed] ... And I just thought .. the presentation [Mr. Sullivan's, on December 7] ... just, you know, fresh in my mind, and I thought, 'Now this is ... not working. This is not what is going to come out of this because we just don't have .. there doesn't seem to be the formation of a constitution here' .... And it was something that I intended to bring up. And then it was brought up [at the January 18 meeting] ... but in such a way as we've got to have some kind of a statement .... And then all of a sudden this whole idea of a statement from .. had to come from us, and I said, 'No'. How could I make such a statement from what I had, except out of personal opinion?

.... Then all of a sudden it just seemed that everything went

... down. Because everybody was talking about something different. And suddenly it just seemed like constitution wasn't the thing that was on their mind. . . . the meeting just took such a swerve . . . about this benefit drive. And all of a sudden this was the important topic . . . and everything else is knocked out of priority . . . and this was on my mind and then . . . the next thing that was given to me was, 'You mean you don't want to be involved *in the skit*?!'

. . . I think this committee was formed to *shove it off*: 'All right, somebody's going to take care of it. Everybody else,' you know, 'forget about it'. And I've seen it happen before. . . .

Lighthall: Well, what about .. How do you feel about your participation in that? Is it .. that frustration thing? How does that ..

Miss Nolan: It is frustrating because I .. Yes. It is frustrating because I .. Yes, it is frustrating. Because [pause] I feel like I've been duped. Now how am I going to explain this? It seemed clear to me when I volunteered to do that — and again, I repeat, I volunteered because I wasn't doing anything at the time I got it — it is .. Yes. I understand the presentation. It .. it's a necessary thing. But when I sat down with the actual . . . meat in front of me, I thought, 'Now where am I going to get a constitution out of this?' And all of a sudden .. I mean that's very frustrating because in one person's mind, the person who presents it, it's very clear, or at least it *seemed* very clear and I accepted it as that. And that's *my* problem there. That's *my* fault for doing that at the minute.

I think there should have been more discussion . . . Everybody should have had to look at the minutes and .. come to either, 'Yeah, you can get something out of this', or 'We can't', *before.* (FL:4/7/02; c2)

◦　◦　◦　◦

Motivational Investment: Central/Tangential. Consider the motivational investments of each of the major actors in the unfolding problem solving. Miss Nolan's motivation to volunteer for the task of writing a constitution did not come from any conviction on her part that something important to her would be prevented unless she did participate. She volunteered because she 'wasn't doing anything at the time . . .' Most of the other adults had some kind of committee assignment in the committee; she did not. It was a duty: one should share the load, be a good member.

With such tangential motivation, two conditions constituted barriers which might not have stopped her if she had been invested centrally in the substance of constitution writing — e.g., if she had internalized Sr.

Claudia's problem. First, Mr. Sullivan's definition of the field of resources — a small committee, the council's minutes, and a model taken from Roberts' *Rules of Order* — proved insufficient. Miss Nolan's investment was insufficient to overcome this prior definition of resources, insufficient to push beyond minutes to either other sources (e.g., help from other members) or greater clarification of the original intent. Joan Noonan, to be sure, had been delegated to confer with Mr. Sullivan; but that, again, was not important enough for Miss Nolan herself to do.

The second condition was sufficient to undermine whatever investment Miss Nolan might still have had by January 18: the 'sudden' shift of the council discussion that day from matters pertaining to the council's future to the benefit skit. From Miss Nolan's viewpoint, if a skit could take priority over basic goals and functions, then a constitution could not be considered very important. Again, she was responding to others' behavior and others' apparent commitments, not to any commitment of her own.

Joan seems to have taken as her own a problem whose initial description she attributed to Miss Nolan, namely, the council's alleged tendency to go over old decisions as if they had never been discussed or made. Her investment, such as it was — and it was not sufficient to find time to accomplish her delegated conference with Mr. Sullivan between January 18 and February 8 — was undermined by new discussions about the council's future. Any writing would have to be re-done, she thought. In any case, whatever commitment she had would have been sharply restrained as a source of any action by the limited investment of her senior partner, Miss Nolan.

Mr. Sullivan's investment was limited to his December 7 presentation: after that he was not heard of again on the matter of a constitution.

Sr. Norma, as initiator of the initial message ('constitution') in this linear parlor game, i.e., as the one who first suggested a solution in the unfolding attempts to solve Sr. Claudia's problem, was the chief source of the possibility for overcoming the linearity inherent in any such process. Present at both the December 7 and January 18 meetings, she tried to direct attention to the council's goals, a direction that might well have brought the course of problem-solving closer to the originating problem. Other problems, however, were operating locally in Sr. Norma at much higher levels of priority. These problems — of basic life-style, of commitment to the religious order, of career uncertainty — constituted powerful competition for any investment she might make in the improvement of the Trinity council — or, indeed, in her regular work as administrator at Trinity. This competing context of problems will become clear in Part III. Suffice it to say here that Sr. Norma was withdrawing her motivational investments from her role as a co-director beyond the level required to carry out important duties. On January 17, in fact, she had circulated a note to all Trinity faculty announcing her intention not to be at Trinity the following year.

Sr. Claudia, in contrast to all others, was invested. Her repeated attempts to influence the council via council members and the language she used to express herself attest to her investment. But she was alone in this regard.

Post-Solution Conditions

First, recall that an episode's end is fixed not by successful implementation of a solution but by the cessation of participants' attempts to solve or to implement. All participants but one, Sr. Claudia, stopped substantive work on writing a constitution after the Christmas vacation meeting of the two co-chairmen. Sufficient motivation to undertake any further action on the part of anyone but Sr. Claudia was depleted by January 18. That Sr. Claudia's action had not stopped became clear in January, as we shall see in Part IV, but her problem had by then become considerably transformed. Because she, as initiator of the problem of council functioning, remained active, and she alone, it seems appropriate to call this episode an abortive episode, one in which all other participants expended resources for nought.

The judgment, 'for nought', rests on evaluation of the episode's outcome. How effective was the action of this episode in reducing the incompatibilities, and changing the associated conditions, that gave rise to the action in the first place? Answers to any question of effectiveness bring us back to our five criteria, set forth in Chapter 1:

1. Satisfaction-dissatisfaction of the problem originator, in this case Sr. Claudia.
2. Satisfaction-dissatisfaction of all subsequent participants.
3. Changes-continuity in observable conditions associated with the originating problem.
4. Reduction or elimination (vs. continuation or increase) of confusion or cross-purposes previously leading to wasted resources.
5. Resources mobilized in, or recruited to, (vs. wasted in) the organization as a result of the episode's action.

Sr. Claudia's dissatisfaction remained. Miss Nolan ended up feeling 'duped' by Mr. Sullivan's proposal. Joan Noonan saw the project as obsolete. Council difficulties promised, it seemed to her, to be tackled by the council itself in a more comprehensive way. On the whole, participants' subjective reactions add up to a combination of low investment, frustration, and, on Sr. Claudia's part, a continued sense of problem. On the first two criteria, then, the outcomes were negative.

As to observable conditions, some were changed and some were not. The council continued to make at least one line of decisions that went beyond its authority to implement. Proposals heard on November 16, regarding the monitoring of the school's four cafeteria periods each day, were approved by the council on January 4 and implemented under the council's aegis through at least the middle of March. These proposals had to do with monitoring crowd behavior and controlling litter in the school's cafeteria. The council's actions in this domain were not in the least advisory, although Sr. Norma's approval was sought and obtained.[4]

Another condition to which Sr. Claudia had objected was the lack of administrative 'input' into council's decisions. This condition was changed, by the simple expedient of Sr. Claudia attending council meetings. But her doing so was not the result of anything that happened in this episode. No participant asked her to attend council meetings to help cope with its problems, for example. She attended as a result of her own efforts at working out her conflict with Sr. Norma, efforts that resulted in an arbitrated settlement of the conflict between them that actually did change some conditions. So the episode's action failed to meet the third criterion of effectiveness.

If no conditions regarding the originating problem were changed by participants' actions, were conditions changed that related to Mr. Sullivan's or Miss Nolan's problems? Mr. Sullivan synthesized a problem of continuity. Did the action he helped to set in motion ensure greater continuity for the council? Did any of the participants' actions lead to a cumulative integration of this year's actions or structure or procedures with those of the following year? Following this abortive episode, much joint effort was expended in building a better council structure for the following year. But, as we shall see in Part IV, that joint effort resulted not from the action of this abortive episode but from a direct stimulus and request from Sr. Claudia. And that direct stimulus was possible for her only after she had succeeded in changing conditions of conflict with Sr. Norma, efforts we trace in Part III.

If neither the criterion of satisfaction nor of changed observable conditions were met, did the episode's action clear up any prior confusions or cross-purposes in a way that stopped the wastage of resources? There is no evidence that episodic action clarified realities or economized on resources.

What about the fifth criterion, the release or recruitment of new resources into the organization as a result of problem-solving action? It is possible, for example, that efforts like Louise Nolan's and Joan Noonan's can lead to new contacts between them and others in the organization, contacts which bring together joint interests or skills or values which then lead to productive working relations quite beyond the current task or problem. But in this episode no such new pockets of energy or skill became visible. To the contrary, if anything, Louise Nolan, feeling 'duped', was more ready to withhold her volunteering in the future than readily to give it — a small net loss rather than a net gain of resources.

Summary

A single local adaptation — a problem-solving episode — has been laid out in narrative form. That new unit of analysis has a beginning, a middle, and an end. It began with the emergence of an organizational problem in Sr. Claudia: a perception of Trinity council's functioning that was incompatible with her expectations and goals for it. Its middle consisted of the extensions of problem solving outward from Sr. Claudia: to Hester Dulany, which seemed to go no further; to the other members of the executive council, particularly Sr. Norma, which brought from Sr. Norma the fact that a constitution for the council was lacking; to Mr. Sullivan, who connected 'constitution' with a problem of the council's continuity. Extensions by Mr. Sullivan to the council, by it to Miss Nolan and Joan Noonan, and between Joan and Miss Nolan led to their abandoning the task of 'transcribing' a 'constitution'. The episode's problem solving aborted.

Application of the five criteria of effectiveness shows the episode as a whole to have been ineffective on all counts. A search for variables in this segment finds a number also evident in the first segment. In addition, an attempt to reconnect action to the originating problem met resistance, indicating that a problem-solving process de-contextualized from its originating problem may become robust enough to take on a life of its own.

While the data of this episode included verbatim interchanges of importance, the data are also in some respects sketchy, in some respects glaringly absent (e.g., the interchange between Sr. Claudia and Mr. Sullivan), and in some respects barely adequate. Yet through this mixture of strong and weak data comes a pattern of events from a beginning to a cessation of action, a chain of actions that used participants' energies, yet did not solve the originator's problem, did not change the conditions that originally impinged on her, did not clear up prior confusions or cross-purposes, and did not recruit or mobilize additional resources for the organization.

The following chapter pulls together the characteristics noted in the analytical commentaries of this and the previous chapter. It summarizes a first approximation of dimensions of organizational processes that produce abortive problem solving.

Notes

1. Sr. Claudia had begun to attend council meetings as a result of the arbitrated 'settlement' of her conflict with Sr. Norma on November 2, a settlement which privately, known to the co-directors and those who had been party to the 'settlement', extended her authority and therefore allowed her to enter what previously was Sr. Norma's exclusive administrative bailiwick.
2. Implicitly Dale was making a distinction similar to the one made in Chapter 1 between merely observable reality, $o(x)$, and operating reality, $n(x)$, and $c(x)$. She

and Louise Nolan were seeking goals not recorded on paper or tapes, but operating in psyches, as 'owned' ('own words') with some commitment and thus as actually constraining members' behavior and thought.

3. The January 18 council meeting was recorded on two machines. A cassette machine was used first, while the reel-to-reel machine was being located; then the reel tape was used. In switching between the two, some discussion was lost, including the final discussion and vote on the motion to distribute a 'reaction survey'. The assertion that the motion lost and that Lighthall made his cautionary comment are from memory, not actual record. Just how influential Lighthall's comment was, therefore, in defeating the motion, is difficult to determine. Looking back over the whole corpus of data, Lighthall's influence in this particular January 18 vote seems to have been considerable, not only in articulating participants' already felt doubts, but also in raising doubts. The weight of the consultant role, with a direct intervention in this case, seems to have been telling — particularly since this was the meeting in which participants had assumed individual participant roles (e.g., 'barrier identifier', 'solution identifier', 'goal identifier', 'resistor') to guide their participation. Discussion of the role taking at the end of the meeting suggested that while the assumed roles had had some effect in some cases of participation, the overwhelming majority of comments had been in response to the substantive content of the issues. (Not included in this role-taking exercise were Sr. Claudia, Sr. Norma, Miss Nolan, Miss Cohler, or Miss Higgins, since all had been absent from the previous council meeting when Lighthall and Allan had conducted a two-hour workshop on group problem solving and had passed out brief descriptions of the roles to be 'tried on' at the next, i.e., the January 18, council meeting.)

4. The first two drafts of this book in manuscript contained two other complete episodes, one of which dealt with the development of a second absurdity, one with far more serious potential for organizational damage than did the first constitution episode. It involved the gradual shifting of responsibility for monitoring crowd behavior in the school's four daily lunch periods. The shift was from the faculty, by Sr. Claudia's action, to the Trinity council, and by the council, in turn, to a subcommittee, the 'Cafeteria Committee' — all in the solution of a problem (Sr. Claudia's) triggered by faculty resistance to lunchroom duty. The absurdity lay in the fact that the 'Cafeteria Committee' consisted of a single student, without adult assistance, a student chairman of a committee whose stable membership consisted of its chairman alone. The potential damage to the institution were serious accidents, with resulting law suits, stemming from horseplay in lunchrooms unsupervised by adults. Miraculously (it seems now), no serious accidents happened; at least none was reported. While the cafeteria episode provides rich suggestions about processes that produce and maintain organizational absurdities, its publication in the present volume was prevented by space limitations.

Chapter 5

Variables Affecting Problem-Solving Effectiveness: A First Culling

The narrative and analytical commentaries of Chapters 3 and 4 suggest seven variables as affecting problem-solving effectiveness. They are summarized in Table 5.1, ordered more or less as their effects appeared in the narrative. Each bears some comment.

1. Problem Synthesis: Inclusive-Cooperative vs. Exclusive-Defensive

Sr. Claudia's exclusion of the council's problems of dented cars and cold rooms continued an exclusion, begun by the council, of the executives' realities. Each party's exclusion of the other's problem-solving realities relinquished an opportunity to secure, via reciprocity, the other's investment in their own problem.

Similarly, Sullivan's synthesis of his problem was sufficiently obvious and universally acceptable, in his eyes, that it was impervious to hints, to which he might otherwise have been sensitive, that his conception and procedures created problems for others. Both Lucy Ellen's questioning and the homeroom representative's question about openness were excluded as paths to be considered or explored in the December 7 meeting.

2. Aim and Level of Intervention: Constituency Analysis

Each problem's contents indicate more or less clearly which persons and groups must somehow be involved in or affected by any solution to that problem — which persons or groups, that is, constitute that problem's constituent members. Sr. Claudia's problem vis à vis council functioning implicated the council as a collective constituent — not Hester or Sr. Norma or Mr. Sullivan. Sr. Claudia's intervention with each of these individuals, therefore, was aimed if not inappropriately then at least indirectly. Her

Table 5.1. Initial Culling of Seven Variables Affecting Organizational Problem-Solving Effectiveness

No.	Name of Variable	Page References in Narrative
1.	Problem synthesis: Inclusive-cooperative vs. Exclusive-defensive	50, 53
2.	Aim and level of intervention: Centered on constituency vs. Non-constituents	50, 53, 54
3.	Communication-blocking authority structure: Segmented vs. Interpenetrating authority	50
4.	Degree of cognitive slippage or reduction of complexity by the problem originator	50
5.	Sequential integration (vs. non-integration) of participants' problems, solutions, and actions: Linear vs. Looped structure and linkage of content	54, 55, 64, 66, 68, 71, 72
6.	Face-to-face communication: Expression and exploration (vs. denial or obscuring) of relevant organizational realities	54, 59–60, 64–5
7.	Distribution of motivational investment: Broad vs. Narrow	50, 74

* This variable is discernible only by review of all participants' actions over the whole episode.

indirection lengthened the communication line along which problematic content had to pass, making that line more vulnerable to the parlor-game effect.

3. Communication-Blocking Authority Structure: Segmented vs. Interpenetrating Authority

Sr. Claudia and Sr. Norma were constrained by a norm they and previous executive teams had developed regarding authority. The norm can be stated thus: 'Each of us has her own bailiwick of functions to take care of, and each of us should stay out of the other's bailiwick'. Thus, Sr. Norma, in charge of student activities and discipline, was exclusively in charge of student afairs, as Sr. Claudia was exclusively in charge of curriculum.

This norm of strictly segmented areas of authority arose subsequent to, and as a subordinate part of, the more encompassing norm, arising out of more sweeping changes in the authority structure of the Blessed Sisters of Trinity, of egalitarian participation at the executive level. All executives were to be equal in power; there was to be no individual chief executive. The effect of this egalitarian norm, together with the subsequent norm of segmented bailiwicks, was to replace the usual chief executive, the school 'principal', with two chief executives, the co-directors.

This structure of authority was established in order, among other purposes, to enhance communication among executives. An unanticipated effect, however, was to block communication between any executive and any person or group not in their bailiwick of authority. For Sr. Claudia to have communicated directly with the Trinity council, as an instance, would have violated the joint norms of egalitarianism and exclusive bailiwicks. She would have been acting outside her area of authority — a transgression for which she had been criticized by her colleagues the previous year.

Even within the co-equal directorship a communication blockage between Sr. Claudia and the Trinity council was not a logical necessity. Actions in one area, the Trinity council (Sr. Norma's area), for example, had effects that crossed that area's boundaries into another area, dealing with the policeman, and with teachers and parents, regarding damage to automobiles (Sr. Claudia's area). If the two sisters had developed norms of *primary but not exclusive* responsibility, supporting *negotiated* intervention across boundary lines wherever effects promised to spill over, then Sr. Claudia could have been free on October 20 to negotiate a meeting directly with the council rather than work through three of its individual members.[1] The critical and debilitating norm, then, was that of exclusive authority over segmented domains, not the norm of equality between co-directors.

4. Cognitive Slippage or Reduction of Complexity by the Originator

Sr. Claudia's misconstrual of Hester as 'them' reduced the complexity of communication necessary to obtain her desired shift in the council's functioning.

5. Sequential Integration of Problems, Solutions, and Actions

Since the chief means of integrating operating realities regarding emergent events and problems is communication, any blocks to communicating operating realities about events and problems constitute blocks to integration and thus to cumulativity. Two threats peculiar to sequential integration have been identified.

First is structure. A linear structure of participation, the prototype of which is the parlor whispering game, minimizes contact between early participants' realities and late participants' realities. This minimized contact between early and late participants maximizes the accumulation of error through the successive subsitution of merely local, not coordinate problems and solutions. If Peter approaches Paul with a *solution* regarding X and Paul communicates the solution to Mary, Mary's *local problems* are far more likely to guide Mary's actions regarding X than are Peter's (uncommunicated) problems — far more likely to the extent that Peter and Mary remain separated by their first and third participant positions in the problem-solving sequence. If, on the other hand, the sequential structure is not linear but has loops, with multi-positioned participants (participating early *and* late), then the parlor-game effect will be mitigated proportional to (some function of) the number of loops. So the structure of sequential participation (linear vs. looped) is one sub-variable related to the integration of organizational realities into organizational action.

The second threat to cumulativity via integration is cognition and communication within and between loops that fails to make connections among problems and solutions. Thus Sr. Norma was in a *position in the sequential structure of participations* to hear Mr. Sullivan's proposal and explanation of a constitution and to link it up with her own recent conversation with Sr. Claudia. Despite this early and later participation, Sr. Norma did not make the linkage between the originating problem, communicated by Sr. Claudia to her, and the remedy she herself had identified. Nor was Sr. Claudia able later, during the January 18 meeting, to make explicit the link between her advisory vs. decision-making problem, on the one hand, and the dicussion of the council's goals and objectives, on the other. Being in a structural *position* to link early realities with later emerging realities was not enough. The integration of organizational realities regarding a problem depends both on sequential *structure* and on cognitive and communicative *functioning*.

6. Face-To-Face Communication: Expression and Exploration vs. Denial or Obscuring of Organizational Realities

Local realities at any level are accessible often only by their communication by locals to others. In the on-going groping and stumbling that characterizes coping with emergent problems, locals at all levels (from President to sewer cleaner) are rarely able to articulate even the most relevant realities in initial utterances. In Peter's conversation with Paul, if Paul does not allow time for Peter to articulate his realities, if Paul does not explore Peter's uttered words for their meanings, if Paul attends only to his own realities and not those behind the initial, low-fidelity articulations of Peter, then Peter's realities cannot get over to Paul and cannot be integrated into Paul's actions.

Lucy Ellen's quandaries about whether a constitution referred only to past and not to future actions of the council were not explored by Mr. Sullivan or Sr. Norma. The two adults were more intent upon successfully arguing their case for a favorable vote than in exploring Lucy Ellen's awkwardly articulated but culturally and organizationally relevant realities.

7. Distribution of Motivational Investment Among Participants

This first episode raises the issue of the necessary and sufficient distribution of such motivational investment among participants in a given episode. In this episode only Sr. Claudia, the originator, was invested in the problem. Others recruited into the solution process were never recruited into the problem itself. That is, Sr. Claudia's problem was not induced in them; her incompatibilities never became theirs. Motivational investment, therefore, was concentrated in the originator, not distributed among participants. Some, as yet unknown, wider distribution of motivational investment would seem necessary for a problem-solving effort to be successful, as this one was not.

Each of the variables identified in Table 5.1 and in subsequent analyses is hypothesized to explain the same thing: *how constituent organizational realities regarding a problem become integrated into (or blocked from) organizational action, thereby promoting (or undermining) the effectiveness of that local adaptation.*

The diachronic or historical analytical viewpoint I have taken, i.e., my emphasis on sequence, cumulativity, and reversibility, both reveals and obscures. It reveals these seven, but it obscures an eighth that must also be considered. One ancient explanation for the outcomes of any complex process refers to its constituent elements, irrespective of their organization or of impingements upon them. This is Aristotle's material cause: the nature and effects of a thing are due to the elements or contents that make it up. The degree of organizational competence shown by participants in an episode is, in this view, a direct function of the individual competence of its members.

While it can be argued that Sr. Claudia and Sr. Norma were in some sense certifiably competent, having had successful experience in administration, all other participants in this episode are easily seen as amateurs. How can amateurs produce anything but amateurish levels of competence? But this episode reveals much more about individual competence as a variable than is suggested by the general category of amateur. Mr. Sullivan's single-minded construing of a 'constitution' was peculiarly out of touch with conceptions widely available in the surrounding culture. It was a manifestly deviant conception. And Mr. Sullivan played a key role in this episode. Sr. Norma, too, was a crucial actor: it was largely her non-supervision in the first place that allowed a decision-making stance to replace an advisory one. And her non-supervision was largely a function of her own transition from nun to lay person.

Can it not be argued, then, that the abortive nature of this episode's problem solving was due to the participation of two idiosyncratic individuals, and that the chief variables were (1) incomplete acculturation of one member (Sullivan, with a deviant conception of 'constitution') and (2) defection of another member (Sr. Norma)? The more general argument would be, then, that to the extent that individuals in an episode are sufficiently integrated into group culture and membership, the problem-solving process will be either (1) effective (with participants like Mrs Sullivan properly construing things like constitutions) or (2) unnecessary, the problem never having arisen because adequate supervision prevented malfunctioning of the advisory group.

I reject this argument. These two persons did not act in a vacuum, but in an organizational setting. That setting, with members whose acculturation included full commitment and culturally sensitive conceptions of 'constitution' was sufficient to produce some counter-action — e.g., Nora Quinn's and Lucy Ellen's questioning, as well as Sr. Norma's call for goal setting — but *insufficient to reverse the discontinuities observed.*[2] The proper focus for understanding these discontinuities is the functioning of the full range of organizational resources, not the deviant functioning of two individuals. The effects of local deviance can be reversed, after all. Organizational problem solving takes time to engage the persons and groups relevant to the problem. That time — which often seems wasteful to participants themselves — releases important resources for reality integration: time in which people re-think their actions, in which they talk to others about an individual's or a group's action, in which people become more aware of, and organize around, sentiments and purposes they share in common with others. Low levels of individual competence and the presence of individual deviants can, through ongoing interactions of other members that clarify and winnow content, accumulate into a level of competence and saturation of culture collectively higher than the incompetence or deviance of its members. When local deviance and incompetence are not reversed in the context of otherwise acculturated and competent participants, one wants to look to the social and organizational dynamics that allowed deviance and incompetence *to prevail.* We are left, then, with seven variables suggested by this episode as constraining the effectiveness of local adaptation in an organization. Table 5.1 is the first entry in a running box score on those variables that appear, upon diachronic analysis, to contribute to an explanation of levels of effectiveness in problem-solving outcomes.

Summary

The reader can see now at least the outlines of the new unit of organizational analysis I am proposing, a new way of seeing and thinking about organizational events. Organizational behaviors and actions are not merely decisions or communications or uses of power and the like: they are (to be thought of as) all of those things unified by a single function, *adaptation*. Emergent actions, like the one set in motion by Sr. Claudia, are usefully thought of as collective responses to perceived disruptions in organizational functioning, disruptions from particular vantage points, disruptions sufficiently serious to correct, to achieve a better fit to some person's or group's values or ideals for the organization. The new unit, the problem-solving episode, draws our attention to the origins of collective action, problems; to the origins of problems in particular persons' mindings about the organization; and to the extent to which problem-solving action as it unfolds across persons, roles, and levels stays in touch with a unifying problem or becomes fractionated and non-cumulative, using up energies and commitment in self-defeating, self-interrupting efforts.

This first, relatively brief episode concerns much more, therefore, than a Catholic school administrator's frustrated action regarding an experimental council's errant functioning. It concerns the kind of disruption of organizational functioning that frequents every activity, every role, every level, of every organization continuously: locally identified and diagnosed disruption, calling forth locally framed corrective action, which unwittingly denies, rejects, or otherwise fails to integrate into its guidance other local commitments, understandings, and resources on which it depends for the corrective it seeks. It is about otherwise intelligent people combining their efforts in a way that results in organizational absurdity — like trying to *change* the functioning of a group by drawing up a constitution whose stated purpose is to assure *continuity* of its functioning. It is not only in schools where collective absurdity is achieved by individually intelligent members. What we have begun is more, however, than showing how unfolding action can be unitized regarding 'problems' and thought of as adaptation. We have drawn out seven initial 'variables' suggested at certain points in the unfolding episode that might account for the triumph of localism over integrated effort. This kind of variable promises to give us, both as abstract researchers and as pragmatic members of our organizations, more specific understanding over what participants in problem-solving efforts may do to integrate necessary organizational realities into their action and to avoid blocking necessary realities from the action. Those initial variables suggest that how the problem originator frames a problem psychologically can restrict which realities are integrated and which blocked out organizationally; how communication about problems can be truncated by choice of person or group with whom to communicate, which in turn may be restricted by authority structure based on categories of work rather than integrated functioning; how face-to-face communication focused on expressed words rather than probing for problematic meanings may block out needed, corrective realities; how a sequence of participation which takes a linear form, like a whispering parlor game, can maximize the influence of transient local realities, subverting or utterly negating cumulative and integrative efforts to solve a given problem; and how the distribution of motivational investment among participants may be an index of the extent to which their realities have been integrated into the action. This starts a task to which Parts III and IV will add, by accumulating these specific variables and then discovering more encompassing, more stable, and less ad hoc, less episode-specific variables which then would guide inquiry into episodes in other organizations.

We now turn to the second episode, one in which interpersonal conflict about organizational functioning is salient but in which the starting point is, again, an organizational problem synthesized by one person, Sr. Claudia. Some conceptual distinctions are required in Chapter 6 before reading the narratives and analytical commentaries in Chapter 7 and following.

Notes

1. See Townesend's (1970) practically informed commentary on the sharing of administrative authority by two co-equal chief executive officers.
2. An organization's capacity to reverse maladaptive problem-solving action receives focal attention in Parts III, IV, and V.

Part III
The Co-Director Episode:
Conflict and Its Management

Chapter 6

Conflict: Initial Distinctions

In some regards, Part III's episode shifts from an orientation to 'problem', which dominated Parts I and II, to an orientation to 'conflict'. This shifts analysis from the individual, psychological level to the interpersonal, social level of analysis. But that shift is less abrupt or discontinuous than perhaps meets the eye. For it turns out to clarify much if we conceive of problems, as defined in Parts I and II, as the *individual components* of interpersonal conflict, where such conflict is experienced and responded to at the individual level as a problem — one in which the intentions, problems, and solutions of another person are focal. The transition, therefore, from the previous episode to this episode of conflict will turn out to be relatively easy, not discontinuous.

Some conceptual distinctions are necessary at the outset. The conflicts and conflict managing processes that we want to understand are complicated enough without our adding confusion by using terms carelessly or by glossing over important distinctions. Current conceptions of conflict, based overwhelmingly on the very brief and very contrived encounters that happen in experimental settings, are insufficient to cope with the complexities of conflicts that play themselves out in natural settings. To convey some important initial definitions and distinctions I shall anchor discussion in the concrete details of an instance of conflict in a natural setting.

A family of four on vacation in Europe — husband, wife, and two sons aged 18 and 20 — were eventually reunited in Paris after the two sons had returned from a sojourn to Amsterdam — on their own and unexpected by their parents. Earlier, while the parents toured some chateaux in the Loire valley, the two young men had been allowed to go on ahead to Paris without them for a few days. The older son, Peter, was to meet a high school friend in Paris. The sons had enough money for two days' lodging and food in Paris, and a book titled *Europe on Twenty-Five Dollars a Day*.

Parents had arrived in Paris only to find a note at the

American Express advising that sons had gone on to Amsterdam. 'Give them an inch and they take a mile!' is a softened translation of the father's sentiments. Two days' freedom in Paris had been stretched, without prior consultation, to two in Paris and two in Amsterdam. The parents were exasperated because they had had to interrupt what was to have been a whole-family enjoyment of Paris. A Friday of worry due to quite incomplete provision by the sons as to how to re-establish contact with the parents was followed by a Saturday's worried waiting, searching, and telephoning before contact was reestablished.

The eventual telephone conversations between Peter, the 20 year-old, and his father revealed two conflicts between them:

Peter: Dad! We need to get together to make plans.

Father: We need to talk, all right. Your mother and I are anything but delighted, Pete, at your decision to go to Amsterdam [conflict #1]. Do you have any idea how much we've worried about even getting back in touch with you? We've spent the whole morning just finding you.

Peter: Yeah. I'm sorry about that. We had no idea the American Express would be closed. We need to talk 'cause Don [Peter's high school chum] is here. We were just about to go out. He and I plan to go to Italy tomorrow ...

Father: What?! No way, Peter! [conflict #2] This is a family vacation and you are staying here with us. We are at the M. Hotel. I want you and Burt [second son] to get your bodies over there. Here's the address and metro station ...

Peter: Yeah, okay. But Dad, Don has been in Paris for a week and he wants to leave. He thought we were going to go to Italy as soon as I got here.

Father: No way are you going off to Italy before we leave. These last few days we are going to be together. Don can wait that long. Or he can go along and you can catch up with him later. I am [expletive meaning angry] at your going off on your own. I bet that wasn't Burt's idea. We will meet you both at our hotel. The man is signaling that the post office is closing now [noon]. We'll meet you there at two o'clock.

At the appointed hour the boys arrived, Peter having arranged to meet his friend at Nice after his parents and brother had flown home. It turned out that Peter had, indeed, been wary of parental objections and had made his plans with his friend with the stipulation that they might have to be changed. He just didn't say so over the phone. It also turned out that younger brother Burt had been wary, earlier, of parental objections to their trip to Amsterdam and had actually tried to sell his train ticket to Amsterdam upon having second thoughts. As time ran out without buyers, and with doubts about faring well alone in Paris with his high school French, Burt went along to Amsterdam — with ambivalence.

After a serious family review of the sons' decisions and implicit priorities, parents and sons enjoyed in a much lighter vein the son's narratives of their experiences in, and to and from, Amsterdam. All's well that ends well.

The first distinction to be made is between conflict as substance and conflict as process. Two people are *in conflict* when (1) their fates or interests are interdependent, (2) the goals that impel them are incompatible, and (3) they are both aware of the incompatibility of goals between them. The substance of conflict consists of incompatible goals. There were two substantive conflicts in the foregoing narrative. Both conflicts were between parents and son, Peter. The first conflict was over the sons' leaving Paris for Amsterdam. That is, the *substantive issue or content* of conflict was whether to stay or go. I shall reserve the term, 'conflict', for this meaning, the issue, the whether-or-not content unless the context or modifiers make clear otherwise. Conflict, thus, is that over which opposition arises.

There would not have been a conflict if Peter and his parents had been independent of each other. For example, had Peter and parents each been able to attain their respective goals without any impact on the other, there would have been no conflict. But Peter was dependent on his parents in many ways and his parents could not enjoy a whole-family vacation without Peter and Burt. So the first criterion of a conflict, interdependence, was met.

Conflict in this substantive sense, this sense of issue content, must be distinguished from any *processes* by which the substantive issues are managed or resolved. The generic terms I shall reserve for such processes are 'conflict management' or 'conflict resolution'. What Peter and his parents *did in response to* their conflict constituted their conflict management. The distinction between conflict and conflict management is exactly parallel to the distinction between problem and problem solving. Just as 'problem-solving' refers to the process by which the substantive incompatibility *within persons* (problem) is worked on, so 'conflict management' is the process by which the substantive incompatibility *between persons or groups* (conflict) is worked on. Just as problems precede problem solving, so conflict precedes conflict management.

A second distinction required is one between conflict and problem of conflict. 'Conflict' we shall reserve to refer to an incompatibility of goals that *both* parties are aware of (my third criterion, above). It happens often, and did in this case, that one party becomes aware of a potential conflict before the other party. Peter was aware that his parents would take a dim view of his leaving Paris for Amsterdam. His awareness of parental objections was reinforced, furthermore, by Burt's active hesitancy. Between the time

Peter became aware of that potential conflict and the time, some days later, that his parents also became aware of it was a period of asymmetric awareness, a period in which Peter but not his parents was mentally active in dealing with that potential conflict. In this period it is appropriate to speak of Peter's 'problem of conflict' with his parents, an incompatibility so far only in his own minding, not theirs. It is not appropriate to speak of a 'conflict' with his parents at this stage, since 'conflict' is the term to be reserved for the truly dyadic, social entity, incompatible goals of two interdependent parties *who are both aware of the incompatibility.*

We, as observers of Peter and his parents and seeing the asymmetry developing, become aware of an *incipient conflict* between them. The difference between incipient conflict and conflict proper, then, is a difference in awareness. In conflict proper, both parties are vigilant regarding the other's actions and motives, since both are fully aware of the mutually conflicting goals. A situation of incipient conflict is psychologically different from, and potentially more unwittingly dangerous than, a situation of conflict. In incipient conflict the potential is high for unwitting and unrestrained exclusion by the first-aware party of the second-aware party, since in an initial period of asymmetrical awareness the second-aware party is still blissfully unaware of the conflicting goals.

This asymmetry in the timing of awareness of incompatibilities of goals between persons implies a distinction between conflicts where both parties know early of an incompatibility from conflicts where there is a first-aware party and a later-aware party. In the latter case, the period of asymmetrical awareness is a period in which the first-aware party solves his or her problem of conflict. The solving of a problem of conflict is a one-sided attempt to resolve an incipient conflict before it becomes known by the other party. The way in which this problem is solved, both as process and as outcome, constitutes an important *environment* for the second party's awareness, an important *psychological context* in which the second party synthesizes his or her conflict with the first-aware party.

For example, Peter, Burt, and Don decided to go to Amsterdam without waiting to confer with Peter's and Burt's parents. That is, knowing of parental objections and being further reminded by Burt's second thoughts, Peter took preemptive action before his parents could even become aware of a possible conflict. That was Peter's way of solving his problem of conflict. His solution, going to Amsterdam, and his process of solution, deciding to go before his parents could become aware of the possibility and ignoring his brother's doubts, later constituted an important social psychological environment for his parents' first becoming aware of a conflict. They became aware of the incompatible goals, in other words, in an environment of not being able to do anything about them, an environment that rendered them mute, dependent, helpless.

The period of asymmetrical awareness, then, was between Peter's first commitment to leave Paris for Amsterdam, on the one hand, and his parents' reading the note at the American Express. In that period, the young men had not only confronted the problem of staying vs. leaving, they had solved it, by deciding to leave, and had implemented the solution by actually leaving. In the same moment, the parents became aware of the conflict and an irreversible action managing the conflict on the part of the sons, i.e., experienced the exclusion of their realities regarding staying in Paris vs. leaving for Amsterdam at the same moment they became aware that those realities were relevant to any matter of importance.

A second conflict ensued, somewhat different from the first. The second again was between Peter and his parents. The issue was similar: whether Peter would or would not leave Paris for Italy with his friend, Don. The process of Peter's solving his problem of conflict and of his and his father's joint resolution of their conflict were rather different from the first, however.

First, Peter and his friend made plans which took likely parental objections into account. They made two plans. Plan A was to be put forward, Plan B to be held back, to be offered in case Peter encountered intolerable or insurmountable parental opposition. Peter put forward plan A, then substituted plan B in response to his father's angry opposition and arguments. A second difference was that the period of asymmetrical awareness was short and, more particularly, that the period was not exploited one-sidedly by Peter and his friend by taking irreversible action before parents could influence decisions. To the contrary, Peter advised his father that they needed to plan together and told him of his goal to go to Italy. The brief negotiation thus triggered was, to be sure, not an even-handed one, but reciprocal influence attempts did ensue. The parties to the conflict had direct interchange regarding the substance of conflict. Their process of managing their conflict was, therefore, mutual in the sense that each party had the opportunity to exercise influence before action was taken.

One more initial distinction is necessary before narrating and examining the co-directors' conflict. It is the distinction between exclusionary and inclusive *modes* of managing conflict. I think many of the characteristics that Deutsch (1973) calls 'competitive' in contrast to 'cooperative' stand up to naturalistic observation but are usefully regarded as a contrast between inclusion and exclusion: a contrast between the infusion of what I have called constituent realities into, and the exclusion of constituent realities from, collective action.

When Peter, Burt, and Don went to Amsterdam without waiting to negotiate with parents, they effectively excluded from that action any expression of parental realities. Parents were constituents of Peter's problem of conflict because he could not effect a solution without influencing their normal functioning in the family and, in particular, their functioning with respect to his own freedom to act in the future.[1]

The second conflict was managed much more inclusively. That is, the operating realities of the parents regarding travel, meeting, and the like, not altogether unknown to young men of this age, were given considerably more weight even in the planning stage: Plan B was prepared in advance, in response to the knowledge that Plan A's goals would be incompatible with parental goals. The incompatibility in that case was known by Peter; what was unknown was whether the incompatibility could be reduced and overcome. Peter's bringing forward his plan at the first opportunity, on the phone, also was an inclusionary move in that it opened an expressive channel for the inclusion of his father's realities as an influence over action. His father's response tended toward the exclusionary: he would not negotiate. Instead, he issued commands. None of the inclusive or exclusive moves were as extreme as they often can be in conflict management, but exclusionary tendencies are nonetheless identifiable.

Much more can be said about these two substantive conflicts and their management. Enough has been said, however, to illustrate some initial distinctions and to define some basic terms. In summary, the term, 'conflict', will hereafter refer to the substantive issue or incompatible goals over which opposition arises unless the context makes clear otherwise. 'Conflict management' and 'conflict resolution' will refer to the process through which the parties work to resolve their incompatibilities. A period of 'asymmetrical awareness' has also been identified, a period in which one party but not the other is aware of an incipient conflict and therefore can be said to have (i.e., to have synthesized) a 'problem of conflict'. Finally, two modes of conflict management have been distinguished, one whose process tends to include both parties' operating realities as influences on definition of problems and on problem-solving action, the other of which tends to exclude opposing realities from expression or exploration.

Chapter 7 describes some problems salient in the operating realities of Sr. Claudia and Sr. Norma, problems (at the individual level of analysis) which led to conflict (at the interpersonal level). Chapter 8 and beyond will trace their management of that conflict, particularly Sr. Claudia's management of it.

Notes

1. Deutsch (1973) argues that cooperative processes of conflict resolution (i.e., inclusive processes) are 'productive', while competitive (exclusionary) processes are 'destructive'. I used to agree, but now prefer to leave the matter open to empirical exploration — and to make explicit my criteria for productivity or effectiveness. Observation of conflict-managing processes and outcomes in natural settings, and of the kind of process Janis and Mann (1977) label 'groupthink', convince me that we must entertain the hypothesis that what Deutsch calls 'competitive' processes and what I shall call exclusionary processes can, under certain circumstances and for certain periods, lead to effective resolutions of conflict, and that what he calls 'cooperation' and I call inclusive processes can lead to resolutions of conflict in which disappointment, dissatisfaction, and alienation can result.

Chapter 7

The Co-Directors' Problems

The conflict of primary interest in Part III is that between Sr. Claudia and Sr. Norma. The co-directors' conflict was to be emotionally draining for them and affected their interactions for the entire year. On Sr. Claudia's part, her problem of conflict was so severe, and its management was initially so frustrating, as to require the intervention of the Regional Administration, at the next higher level of the religious order. Their conflict resulted first from a problem in Sr. Norma and then, in response to her solution of it, as a problem in Sr. Claudia.

To speak of 'a problem' in this way is, of course, over-simplification. For each co-director an over-arching problem (with respect to their conflict) can be inferred. But each over-arching problem implied a family or cluster of nested problems — as is always the case. For example, Sr. Norma's over-arching problem — the one implicated most directly by our focus on the co-director conflict — was that of wanting personal and professional fulfillment, on the one hand, and finding, on the other, that religious life increasingly frustrated fulfillment.[1]

That over-arching problem was made up of sub-problems of personal relationships, freedom of choice, residence, employment, and the like, each of whose solutions would contribute to the solution of her over-arching problem. So the conflict between the two sisters can be more accurately described as a *problem complex* arising in, and solved by Sr. Norma over a period of time, a problem complex whose emerging solutions gave rise to a very different complex of problems in Sr. Claudia.

The conflict between the two sisters grew out of the incompatibility between aspects of Sr. Norma's solutions and aspects of Sr. Claudia's commitments (expectations, values, and desires). Our focus is the process by which the two co-directors (1) solved their respective problem-complexes and, in so doing, (2) managed their joint conflict, but our data are more complete for Sr. Claudia than for Sr. Norma.

Sr. Claudia's Problem Complex

A problem of conflict first arose in Sr. Claudia's awareness in December of the year before we arrived. At that time and for six to eight months afterward Sr. Norma was apparently unaware of Sr. Claudia's problem of conflict with her. Sr. Claudia's problem of conflict concerned Sr. Norma's administrative performance. The effectiveness of the administrative team depended on each of the three executives' taking care of the functions each had agreed to perform. Sr. Claudia regarded Sr. Norma's absence from Trinity during the entire summer of 01, and especially during the planning week before school opened, as an intolerable failure of performance. She also regarded it as a failure to honor prior agreements. On Sr. Claudia's part, the school simply could not function, and she herself could not, if Sr. Norma continued to absent herself. So since the December before we arrived, Sr. Claudia had been tolerating a growing incompatibility between her expectation of Sr. Norma and Sr. Norma's visible performance.

But there had been difficulties beyond Sr. Norma's lapses in effectiveness. The four-member administrative team the year prior to our observations had had other difficulties. Sr. Claudia had perceived something of a split in the quartet's relations, Sr. Norma and Sr. Florence Ellen, the Business Manager, 'siding with each other' on a number of issues against Sr. Claudia and Sr. Catherine. It was not an immobilizing split, but it was there and worrisome to Sr. Claudia.

In addition, Sr. Claudia had been accused of 'overstepping' her bounds, of acting outside her domain of authority. Her functions were to handle personnel and curriculum (she also held the title of Curriculum Director). Sr. Florence Ellen, as business manager, was in charge of building and grounds — a not inconsiderable domain, given the multi-acre campus and sprawling school-convent building. Sr. Claudia had been called to account by Sr. Florence Ellen and Sr. Norma when she had issued a directive to the maintenance men to take care of some maintenance condition she regarded as deficient. The resulting interchange with her two colleagues made Sr. Claudia wary of taking action that might be regarded as outside her own domain.

Sr. Claudia had gradually synthesized a problem of conflict with Sr. Norma, in the period from December of 00 through the spring of 01 and with increasing acuteness through the summer of 01, a problem regarding Sr. Norma's continued and increasing failure, in Sr. Claudia's eyes, to fulfill Sr. Norma's administrative duties. But that problem of conflict, itself, arose in the context of a wider problem synthesized by Sr. Claudia, the problem of working relations among the quartet of executives, of the split into two factions and of Sr. Claudia's coming on 'so strong'.[2]

An over-arching problem in Sr. Claudia, therefore — the problem for which her attendance at our conference at the University of Chicago on the new school role was a move to solve — was the incompatibility between her commitment to effective school governance, on the one hand, and a set of immediate and urgent perceptions of tension and miscommunication among the executives, on the other hand.

Sr. Norma's Problem Complex

In this same period Sr. Norma was struggling with her own, quite different problems, growing out of a single problem complex that seemed to pre-empt all others. These following facts became plain only *after* the entire episode had played itself out. Indeed, some crucial facts became known only a decade after the conflict had been resolved.[3] The first fact about Sr. Norma's side of the eventual conflict must be introduced by the mundane statement that at the time of our observations, and increasingly since then, members of religious orders in their thirties and forties often gave up the religious life for the more conventional life of making one's own way in the world, a life often including marriage and family. The first retrospective fact about Sr. Norma, then, is that in the period just preceding our observations she took the first steps in the transition from nun to lay woman.

Other facts, drawn retrospectively from the completed episode, and not available to us (nor to more than one or two others) at the time, were the following:

1. During a three-week workshop in New England two summers before our observations at Trinity, Sr. Norma struck up a friendship with a priest whom she would marry three years later. Sr. Claudia was then aware of Sr. Norma's friendship with the priest. It was not until more than a decade later that she told me that it was then she realized that Sr. Norma's 'struggle [with religious life] had begun'.
2. In the week before November 2, Sr. Norma did make known privately (including us) that she would not be returning to Trinity the following year.
3. In May of 02 Sr. Norma applied to the Regional Administration for, and was granted, official leave of one year ('exclaustration') from the Bessed Sisters of Trinity.
4. In the summer of 02, in the early period of her exclaustration, Sr. Norma accepted a post as principal of an elementary school operated by another religious order. She has been the principal of that school continuously for many years.
5. In May of 03, after a year as principal, Sr. Norma ended her period of exclaustration by permanently leaving the religious order.
6. About that same time, Sr. Norma married. Her husband had left the priesthood about the time Sr. Norma had left the Blessed Sisters of Trinity.

These facts, together with her absences from Trinity during the Fall of 01 and some plausible assumptions, point to the conclusion that Sr. Norma had basically solved her problem regarding staying in vs. leaving her religious order at least by the Fall of 01. I assume, in keeping with the data we do have and with experiences of other nuns who left their order, that (1) her acquaintance more than a year earlier with the priest was an important (but probably complex) part of her decision to leave the religious order, (2) her doubts about remaining a nun for the rest of her life had been gradual, not sudden, originating probably before the Spring of 01 and possibly well before then, and (3) these doubts probably antedated her friendship with the priest. Sr. Norma's basic decision to leave the order became clear-cut, but only over time and in anything but a rectilinear process. To renounce one's perpetual vows, vows symbolic of one's marriage to Christ, was to go through a divorce with especially deep emotional and social dimensions. She would be leaving friends of more than 20 years, with whom she had entered the religious order. On top of all that was the financial dimension. Religious life had been for more than two decades her main or sole source of friends, housing, employment, and financial support, but also of deep satisfaction, honor, status, regularity, and abiding values.

In the period of our observations, therefore, Sr. Norma was struggling with a family of problems. The over-arching problem was her long-time devotion to and satisfaction from religious life, on the one hand, and on the other, her dissatisfactions with it and her attractions to a lay life of womanhood. In a word, Sr. Norma in this period was deeply ambivalent. She does seem to have made the basic decision to leave, but to do so opened up, in the vernacular, a whole new can of worms.

One of the immediate, organizational uncertainties that leaving the order would bring was a comfortable exit: Sr. Norma was, as we shall see, committed to publicly finishing the year as co-director of the school, a position that assumed she was a member of the religious community. Another uncertainty evidently was living arrangements: should she continue to live in the convent or should she move out, as many other sisters had done? Moving out would bring her closer to the laywoman's life style, but required a whole new set of decisions and uncertainties not present in convent living. Finally, the timing of her leaving must have posed some quandaries, since she had contracted for the coming year to co-direct Trinity high school. She could most comfortably loosen her ties with the school only toward the end of the current school year or in the following summer.[4]

The stage is now set for the narrative of the conflict. The narrative will again be interspersed with commentaries, the shifts from narrative to commentary and back signalled by four asterisks: * * * *.

* * * *

Notes

1. As has been hinted at various points in Part II and as will become clearer as the narrative of this episode unfolds, many of Sr. Norma's realities were not directly available to Allan and me except infrequently. We infer them from the contents of her interactions with Sr. Claudia and from her overt actions. To put the matter succinctly, Allan and I were regarded by Sr. Norma somewhere on a continuum from nuisance to threat. If she had cooperated fully with our inquiries and probes, her own solution to an encompassing problem could have become unmanageable, could have created for her, in her words, a 'crisis'. So our data regarding Sr. Norma's problem and her conflict with Sr. Claudia are much more limited than our data regarding Sr. Claudia's problem and the conflict with Sr. Norma. The overview of their respective problems and of the conflict we now offer must be read in that light.

2. Sr. Claudia's colleagues remarked, in quite independent contexts, that Sr. Claudia intimidated them by the penetrating and comprehensive thinking that she brought to discussions of problems. One faculty member spoke of her 'multisimultaneous' thought: the capacity to keep a large number of dimensions of a problem in mind at once. The fact that her colleagues could be intimidated by her; that she had been called to account for overstepping her bounds; that she believed it necessary and proper to monitor the functioning of *all* fundamental aspects of education at Trinity, not just segments of it; and that she regarded advice as useful so long as it was relevant and competent — these facts in no way diminished her conscious commitment to restructure the mechanism of school governance to 'build in' (a favorite phrase) more frequent and more heterogeneous participation in decisions and policies.

3. Sr. Claudia and I have stayed in contact over the years since our observations at Trinity. She has read and commented on various drafts of this entire manuscript. Had her post-Trinity testimony not been available, our facts and interpretations would have been seriously deficient at a number of points. I am deeply grateful to Sr. Claudia for her continued thoughtful investment in this project.

   It is nevertheless with some ambivalence that I present the reader at this point some of these 'delayed facts' about Sr. Norma's side of the co-directors' conflict. For the reader to know them before reading the narrative may prevent understanding the immediate causes of confusion, surprise, and anguish that the participants, who could not know many of these facts, went through at the time. Much of Sr. Claudia's action at that time, and the anguish that accompanied it, had to do with her uncertainty about the very issues the factual conditions eventually settled. If we all had known these facts, i.e., had we participants been able to predict outcomes certainly, all of us would have come out looking more rational and intelligent. Knowing them in advance makes it much easier to dismiss the behavior as 'stupid' or 'hostile' or merely 'incomprehensible' and much more difficult to understand the participants' grapplings with the ambiguous and the uncertain.

   Yet to postpone disclosure of these facts, as a novelist might, in order to recreate in the reader some of the experience undergone by the participants, would merely obfuscate unnecessarily. The reader is warned to bear in mind, then, that many of the conditions and forces that this account reveals were unknown or only vaguely and dimly known or, indeed, unknowable by the participants at the time. Their and our operating realities at the time, in other words, have to be distinguished from the narrative picture that now can be presented.

   One cause for this separation of present-knowledge from then-operating realities — beyond the principal fact that we have widely gathered and intensively reviewed data of the kind never available to ongoing participants — was that many of the relevant realities then operating were defined by the participants at the time (and by their wider culture) as personal, intimate, and private. By private and intimate realities I mean those realities consciously and unconsciously kept secret by the participants. Sr. Norma, especially, had much to keep secret from us, but also from her colleagues at Trinity. She had much to keep secret, that is, given her choice of strategies of solving her over-arching problem. On a scale of accessibility of their operating realities to us from 1 to 10, Sr. Norma would be somewhere in the 2–3 range while Sr. Claudia would be 7–8, Sr. Catherine, 8–9.

4. I place Sr. Norma's basic decision to leave the order sometime between March and late August, 01. If she had fully decided to leave before March of 01, she would have had time and opportunity to begin her exit from Trinity in the Spring of 01. A dating of her decision to leave the order later than summer of 01, however, would be incompatible with her professional behavior and her deepening friendship with the priest.

Chapter 8

The Incipient Conflict Extends to Our Presence and Sr. Claudia Takes First Steps

Chapter 2 has already described how Sr. Claudia and Sr. Norma had different views regarding Lighthall's proposal to work out an internship, a 'research-consultation', at Trinity. Their differing views constituted part of their larger conflict. In the early weeks of the 01-02 school year, however, the conflict was incipient since it is doubtful that Sr. Claudia and Sr. Norma exchanged views directly on the matter.

✿   ✿   ✿   ✿

In what way was the introduction of Lighthall and Allan in this new 'internship' role relevant to the incipient conflict between the two co-directors? Substantively, the new role — concerned with organizational analysis and consultation among the executives and in the Trinity council — constituted part of a *solution* for Sr. Claudia but something of a *problem* for Sr. Norma. The very commitments that led Sr. Claudia to immerse herself in the difficulties of improving governance, the very commitments that led her to surge ahead with action and to sometimes crowd out others' participation (or at times overstep her bounds), were the commitments that made this particular kind of internship appealing, a positive aid toward improving executive functioning. But the very commitments that led Sr. Norma away from immersion in administrative tasks and toward protecting temporarily the privacy of a transition from one life to another were the same ones that made the new internship upsetting if not downright dangerous. Open analysis by others of problems such as Sr. Claudia had spoken of, of overstepping boundaries and of miscommunication among executives, implied examination of executive functioning. Such examination could easily open to scrutiny precisely what Sr. Norma wanted to keep private. The introduction of this internship, therefore, was a matter over which Sr. Norma and Sr. Claudia were opposed, though they did not raise this matter for actual discussion between them until later in the school year.

But their opposing commitments impinged on more than the substance of the internship. It impinged as well on the process by which the internship was structured and legitimated. Very simply put, while Sr. Claudia was present at all discussions where expectations were set regarding the new roles and persons in the school — including the desirability of having them at all — Sr. Norma was absent from many of them. Both in the August discussion regarding Lighthall's and Allan's presence in the executive council and in the September discussions regarding their observing and later consultation with the Trinity council, Sr. Norma was absent. She had simply no influence, therefore, over the legitimating or shaping of the new research-consultation project.

The new project, therefore, was assimilated into the structure and process of the co-director's incipient conflict. Willy nilly, it became allied with Sr. Claudia's values and purposes and either irrelevant or antagonistic to Sr. Norma's values and purposes. And that alliance, on the one hand, and irrelevance or antagonism, on the other, set differential restraints on, and biases in the kinds and amounts of data available to us. Sr. Claudia and Sr. Catherine supported data gathering while Sr. Norma resisted it. In on-going organized life, therefore, both the legitimacy and the scope of data gathering can become (must inevitably be?) subject to not only the purposes of, but also the incipient (and presumably the actual) conflicts among, those being studied.[1] Let us return to the narrative.

✺   ✺   ✺   ✺

In late August and again sometime between September 25 and 30, Sr. Claudia went out to the Regional Administrative Center to enlist higher administrative aid in solving her problem with Sr. Norma. Sr. Norma's absences from her office and from the Trinity building had become intolerable to Sr. Claudia. Sr. Claudia could not believe that the absences were due simply to Sr. Norma's illness — not when she could see that Sr. Norma was present each morning to make announcements over the public address system, with no apparent symptoms. Sr. Norma was again absent from the October 1 regular weekly meeting of the executives, which met as scheduled in Sr. Norma's office near the school's front office in the main wing.

Lighthall and Allan, having been at Trinity about two days a week since September 10 and having concentrated their time in the Trinity council and executive council meetings, were still, on October 1, unaware of Sr. Norma's absences. They had heard Sr. Norma's regular daily morning announcements over the public address system, but were unaware that she often disappeared from the building immediately after the announcements.

At the October 1 executive meeting, attended by Sr. Claudia and Sr. Catherine and with Lighthall and Allan sitting in (by now regularly), discussion turned at the end briefly to Sr. Norma's absences. Sr. Claudia said, 'I think it's very difficult for us to have a council meeting like this when only two of us are here,' and went on to explain that there was information that she really needed from Sr. Norma. She began to explain why she got 'hysterical as far as Sr. Norma is concerned,' when Sr. Catherine interrupted:

> Sr. Catherine: I would also like to say I haven't the slightest idea. You [to Sr. Claudia] asked me where she was — really, where she was. And I think you ought to know that. You, too [turning to Lighthall and Allan].
>
> Lighthall: Where ... who? Sr. Norma?
>
> Sr. Catherine: I mean I know she's been sick. But there's been no contact and I don't know when she's going to be .. [Sr. Claudia says something inaudible] Oh, *did* you?
>
> Sr. Claudia: I wanted to see how she was, and so forth, and she says the doctor says she could be up and so on, but not to do her work .. So, ah, I'm uptight about it, frankly... This week Sr. Norma's been out and, ah, it forces me into a position of making decisions in areas of [Sr. Norma's] competence. And I know that this gets people uptight when you do that. And yet I don't think the whole school can just close down. (E:10/1/01; 1:304–346)

The previous year, the co-directors had agreed explicitly that each would stick to her own domain of authority unless the other declared that she would be physically absent or were actually incapacitated. Had Sr. Norma now reached the point where she was incapacitated? How could she have reached that point when she was up and about? But how could she not have reached that point when she was too ill to be regularly in her office? The two sisters had never explicated the criteria by which illness or absence would be judged an 'incapacity'.

Sr. Claudia still had not, by October 1, confronted Sr. Norma with the effects of Sr. Norma's absences. If Sr. Norma had some sense of being a cause of problems for Sr. Claudia, her own over-arching problems prevented her from doing anything to diminish Sr. Claudia's problems. It is entirely possible, too, that her preoccupations with larger questions prevented any awareness of Sr. Claudia's problems. If so, she was presently to be enlightened. In any case, Sr. Norma was entirely unaware of the intensity of Sr. Claudia's problem regarding Sr. Norma's absences. In particular, Sr. Norma would have been surprised to learn that Sr. Claudia had initiated formal discussions out at the regional center about Sr. Norma's absences.

✧   ✧   ✧   ✧

Embedded in this narrative is the beginning of a period of asymmetrical awareness of conflict. Sr. Claudia's problem of conflict with Sr. Norma was crystallizing to the point of action: formal discussions with the chair of the regional administrators. Sr. Claudia was recruiting help in solving her problem. But Sr. Claudia was communicating with the higher administrators before she communicated with Sr. Norma. Her first moves in this period when she alone was more than marginally aware of conflict, therefore, were exclusionary moves.

In her own mind, Sr. Claudia was seeking help to fill an important gap in school functioning, a gap that she was unable to fill by herself. But she was doing so on her own. That is, she had not induced that problem in Sr. Norma as a joint problem. She had not communicated so that Sr. Norma, too, could help influence either the conception of the problem to be solved or the solution of Sr. Claudia's problem. While Sr. Claudia intended to take care of the administrative gaps due to Sr. Norma's absences, her assumption of the task of taking care of it bilaterally with the higher administration created unilaterally an environment for Sr. Norma's eventual coming to awareness of the problem that could only severely constrain Sr. Norma's options. For example, Sr. Norma now would have to contend with the fact that the problem of her absences was not merely a matter between herself and her two co-executives but was a matter that had come to involve the regional administrators. Further, the fact that Sr. Claudia had now recruited the aid of those administrators could easily be felt as, or even consciously construed as, a power play on Sr. Claudia's part, an amassing of forces against Sr. Norma. Sr. Norma's exclusion from Sr. Claudia's problem-solving process, in the period after Sr. Claudia was aware that some action was needed, created a vacuum of information for Sr. Norma that would inevitably be filled in by Sr. Norma from a context of having been excluded from Sr. Claudia's actions.

But for one fact we would conclude that *when Sr. Claudia unilaterally approached Sr. Jeanine, the chief regional administrator, about her problem regarding Sr. Norma, she set in motion an exclusionary process of conflict management.* It is manifestly apparent that to bring Sr. Jeanine into the problem before including Sr. Norma did accomplish an exclusion of Sr. Norma's operating reality and an exclusion of Sr. Norma from Sr, Claudia's process of synthesizing and solving the problem of conflict. What, then is the fact that makes the italicized conclusion above inaccurate?

It is the fact that Sr. Claudia's actions were already in response to an exclusionary process, an exclusion initiated by Sr. Norma in her unilateral and private withdrawal. If we focus on Sr. Claudia, as our more complete data about her incline us to do, then it appears as though she initiates the exclusion. But just a little contextual sensitivity brings Sr. Norma's problem-solving into the picture as a *prior environment* for Sr. Claudia's synthesis of her problem. A reformulated conclusion, therefore, would run something like this: *When Sr. Claudia unilaterally recruited Sr. Jeanine into her problem-solving regarding Sr. Norma, she continued an exclusionary mode of problem-solving initiated by Sr. Norma.*

In the October 1 meeting of Sr. Claudia and Sr. Catherine, Sr. Claudia for the first time voiced to a colleague at Trinity her problem about Sr. Norma. A pointed element in her problem was her fear of overstepping her bounds of authority (her 'area of competence'), which was incompatible with her sharp realization that she had been forced actually to overstep those bounds, to make decisions in Sr. Norma's absence that would ordinarily be Sr. Norma's. To the extent that now Sr. Catherine, too, would have to fill gaps or temporize during Sr. Norma's absence, a structure had emerged that could easily be felt as a power coalition by Sr. Norma, namely, two co-workers who both shared an incipient, and then an actual conflict with Sr. Norma.

Unwittingly, then, a social psychological environment was emerging for Sr. Norma, one in response to the exclusionary environment she had earlier created for Sr. Claudia. This emergent environment excluded Sr. Norma from influencing the course of action on a problem of which she was a key element. It was an environment being created for Sr. Norma, furthermore, by not only Sr. Claudia but also at the regional level, by Sr. Jeanine. In short, the parties in this incipient conflict were not only solving their own respective problems, a matter uppermost in their minds. *They were also unmindfully creating reciprocal socio-emotional environments of exclusion, each excluding the other from her own problem synthesis and problem solving.*

We now return to the narrative.

✿   ✿   ✿   ✿

Notes

1. Because of this bias in kinds and amounts of data from (and about) Sr. Norma as compared to Sr. Claudia, the current episode and its analysis cannot be considered more than a skeletal study of interpersonal conflict as defined in Chapter 6. Rather, it is a study of one side of a conflict, with the other side as an appearing and disappearing backdrop. At the level of the individual, of course, this is an adequate study of *problem solving* where the problem happens to be one of conflict with another person.

    An adequate study of interpersonal conflict in the natural setting would require either (1) that the conflict be managed inclusively, where both parties regarded the investigator as legitimate and in a positive light, thus allowing the investigator to have access to both parties' data, or (2) two investigators working more or less independently at the site of study, each becoming accepted by one of the parties who was excluding the other. The investigators would then later pool their data, each providing data from which the other had been excluded in the conflict.

Chapter 9

Sr. Claudia's Efforts Intensify

On October 5, four days after Sr. Claudia first voiced to others at Trinity her problem about Sr. Norma, Sr. Claudia confronted Sr. Norma. Soon thereafter, Sr. Catherine, too, brought up to Sr. Norma her problem of Sr. Norma's absences. A week after Sr. Claudia first broached her problem with Sr. Norma, i.e., on October 12, Sr. Claudia went out to the regional administration center, now for the fourth time, to convey her desperation and to urge some action.[1] All of this came out in the Friday executive meeting on October 15, a meeting Sr. Norma did not attend. She had decided to move out of the convent and to convalesce temporarily at her family home, some distance from the school. Her decision and her whereabouts had become known to regional administrators and to Sr. Claudia only the previous evening. Toward the end of that October 15 executive meeting, Sr. Catherine spoke of her confrontation with Sr. Norma first:

> Sr. Catherine: And then ... I ... I confronted her once. I said that things were really tough over here... My confrontation with her was: 'Yes, you're sick,' and I *do* think she's sick, 'Please let us appoint someone'. .... and she got very angry with me and said, 'I have been running this office from my bedroom perfectly well'.
> Lighthall: Umhmm.... Yeah.
> Sr. Claudia: My confrontation with her in terms of that was the same. One evening I went to see how she is ... how she was. I said that [inaudible] I felt that I, you know, was doing the very thing that she objected to so strongly last year, that I found myself in the position of having to make decisions. And she said, 'Well I'm covering most things in the office'. And I said, 'You're not covering the things that are coming to my office. You're covering the things a girl walks to Mrs. Shulman [Sr. Norma's secretary] with. But if a girl walks in and sees that you're not there, she does not go to a secretary to talk over the serious problem.'

So I said I was finding this difficult and I said I would appreciate knowing how long it would be before she felt she could assume her full position and I was suggesting that in the meantime we take some steps to .. either to hire some .. my suggestion was [to hire] someone that we had talked about earlier in the year, in terms of some stu .. some faculty assistance in the area of discipline, and, ah, giving them part-time teaching positions. [Lighthall: Umhmm. Umhmm.] And, ah, I said I'd like to recommend that we move to that now and I'd hire, you know, additional academic help and she said .. um, she got very upset and she said, you know, that here she was sick and it seemed as if we were trying to push her out of a job or something. I said that it wasn't it at all and that I was trying to cover. So then she said, 'Well let me think about it'. (E:10/15/01; c2:125–142)

Neither of them pursued the matter on their own initiative. Events were to bring them face to face again, but under very different circumstances.

❋   ❋   ❋   ❋

In this short bit of narrative two things should be noted. First, we can assume that after these two interchanges between Sr. Norma and her colleagues, Sr. Norma was on her way to knowing that she had come into conflict with them and, specifically, that the focal issue was her administrative performance, her 'covering' in absentia. By October 5 or shortly thereafter, therefore, at least some definite parts of the incipient conflict had become known by both parties: the period of asymmetric awareness of conflict had started to come to an end.

Second, we cannot know fully what actually was said in those two interchanges between Sr. Norma and her two colleagues. How much Sr. Claudia and Sr. Catherine left out of their accounts of those interchanges we cannot know, nor how much distortion of emphasis nor how many additions. On the other hand, it seems unwise to dismiss their testimony out of hand. We can use it as an indication, at least, of how inclusive or exclusionary they were being with Sr. Norma at this point in the conflict.

Let us focus on Sr. Claudia. Sr. Claudia started her description by saying she went to 'see how she was'. Sr. Claudia was not neutrally gathering objective data about Sr. Norma's health out of disinterested curiosity. She was, rather, trying to solve her problem vis à vis Sr. Norma's absences and the effects of them which came to rest at her door.

Sr. Claudia's attempt to *narrate the effects of Sr. Norma's absences on her own behavior* was precisely in line with what a perspective of multiple realities would imply as effective: 'Narrate to the other, in the first person singular, specific, detailed, factual information of the sequence of events caused by the other so that he or she can accumulate substantially the experience which has brought you to synthesize the problem you are trying to solve. In this way, induce in the other your own problem'. Evidently Sr. Claudia's narrative was confined to her reference to doing 'the very thing she objected to so strongly last year' rather than specific details of the who, what, when, where, and how of a number of absences and their effects on her. The kind of first-person, problem-inducing narrative suggested by a perspective of multiple realities, furthermore, would have included in Sr. Claudia's narrative as specific effects caused by Sr. Norma's absences *both the number and the contents of her prior conferences with Sr. Jeanine*. Sr. Norma's defensive retort about 'covering most things in the office' led Sr. Claudia to draw a general conclusion about the kinds of events Sr. Norma was not covering; Sr. Norma's retort did not, apparently, lead Sr. Claudia to re-create for Sr. Norma any details of a specific student who had found Sr. Norma absent, had come to Sr. Claudia, and had said such-and-such.

After these few and brief references to effects, omitting mention of her having conferred with Sr. Jeanine, Sr. Claudia abandoned any attempt to convey her problem and shifted instead to corrective action. By proposing the corrective action, Sr. Claudia tacitly assumed one of three possibilities, all false from the standpoint of a multiple-reality perspective. She may have assumed, first, that it was possible to induce Sr. Norma to adopt a *solution* to a problem that she, Sr. Claudia, had synthesized without first inducing that *problem* in Sr. Norma. Or, second, she may have assumed that she had induced in Sr. Norma her problem as she proceeded to detail a solution (hiring someone to be part-time academic and part-time administrative) and to recommend a timing for implementing the solution (i.e., immediately). Or, finally, Sr. Claudia may have assumed that Sr. Norma already had synthesized her problem and was therefore ready to consider suggestions for a solution.

Of course, Sr. Claudia did not think in terms of multiple realities or of problem-solving theory. The foregoing rhetoric is just my way of pointing up what in effect she may have been assuming: in effect, that direct communication of one's own favored solution is an effective way to secure acceptance of it by the person whose actions one is trying to change.

Sr. Claudia's success in inducing cooperation from Sr. Norma was mixed. While Sr. Norma's first response was to become upset, derogating the intent of the action ('. . . trying to push her [Sr. Norma] out of a job'), a second reaction was to ask for time to think about Sr. Claudia's proposal — a partial opening of the door to Sr. Claudia for further communication and negotiation ('let me think about it'). While perhaps leaving the door open, Sr. Norma's asking for time was also a simple negation of Sr. Claudia's request to take action 'now'. Having failed to induce her desired solution, however, Sr. Claudia apparently did not see Sr. Norma's partial opening for later communication. Or more accurately, Sr. Claudia saw and, indeed, remembered and reported Sr. Norma's request for more time, but did not construe it as an opening she wanted to pursue. In sum, even if taken in the most positive light, there was little inclusiveness by Sr. Claudia in this interchange, and only an ambiguous opening by Sr. Norma.

Sr. Claudia's October 5 approach to Sr. Norma was to be the single opportunity for their joint exploration of their respective different realities before Sr. Claudia's problem was successfully induced, finally, in Sr. Jeanine and matters were taken out of Sr. Claudia's hands. That interchange may have been as crucial for the co-director episode as Sr. Claudia's interchange with Mr. Sullivan was in the first constitution episode — a point at which communication of the focal *problem* was absent or swamped by a solution, creating a void that put its stamp on the rest of the problem-solving process. Let us return to the narrative.

o o o o

Sr. Claudia and Sr. Catherine conducted the October 15 executive meeting in the usual manner: each reported to the other her administrative actions, plans, and questions from the previous week. Sr. Claudia turned to a problem of noise in the halls, a problem ordinarily in Sr. Norma's bailiwick. She said she had phoned Sr. Norma at her family home that morning, telling Sr. Norma of the increasingly intolerable noise levels in the halls. Sr. Norma said that Sr. Claudia should meet with Sr. Sabrina and 'ask her to get going on it with the discipline board [a subcommittee of the Trinity council]'. This prompted Sr. Catherine to laugh aloud:

> Sr. Catherine: I just think Sr. Sabrina will be wild; that she'll say it's Sr. Norma's job. And Sr. Norma's saying it's hers . . . . it just seems to me more and more . . ah, Trinity council is getting these responsibilitities to handle, jobs that by rights belong to Sr. Norma . . . (E:10/15/01; cl: 313–377)
>
> Sr. Claudia [expressing a pronounced sigh]: 'I don't know when Sr. Norma will be back'.
>
> Sr. Catherine: Did she give any indication when she called you? [A seven-second silence ensued, during which Sr. Claudia seems to have said 'no' non-verbally.]
>
> Sr. Claudia: So, I don't know. I know, you know, that the Apostolic Center [the regional administration] is waiting for a . . . report, I guess, from the doctor, as far as Sr. Norma is concerned.
>
> Sr. Catherine: Oh. [turning to Allan and Lighthall] As you may or may not have guessed, we're in a heck of a mess with her absence and not knowing . . [her voice trailed off]
>
> Sr. Claudia: I haven't heard from her . . . since last week until this morning. (E:10/15/01; cl: 742–780)

Sr. Claudia went on to explain that Sr. Norma, in phoning Mrs.

Shulman that morning, had left a message that she was not to be called back because such calls would disturb her.

Sr. Catherine: . . . I'm really uptight about it. I *wish* she would *say*, 'I'm coming back in X days', or 'I'm *not* coming back', so we could *do* something.

Sr. Claudia: Well, I've asked her that, you see, and she will not say this, you know. Obviously I'm uptight . . . [Lighthall: Yeah, right.] I'm on the hot seat, so there's no way that I'm not *angry* [raising her voice volume and laughing].[2] (Ibid, 870–85)

◦   ◦   ◦   ◦

Sr. Claudia felt '*on the hot seat*'. By that she meant that she would be held responsible for Sr. Norma's failures. This was not merely her own aberrant egoism or delusion of grandeur. Informally, Sr. Claudia was widely regarded as the principal administrator of the school. Formally, Sr. Claudia's official responsibilities — personnel hiring and evaluation, budget, and curriculum, not to mention her chairmanship of the English department — made her authority much greater than Sr. Norma's.

Yet in legitimate power Sr. Claudia was officially only equal to Sr. Norma, without authority to 'step in' to perform functions of Sr. Norma's for whose failure she could easily be blamed. Being 'on the hot seat' but unable to act was explicitly acknowledged by Sr. Claudia as the cause of anger.

◦   ◦   ◦   ◦

Continuing about that October 15 executive meeting, Sr. Claudia repeated a complaint and then elaborated on her assessment of Sr. Norma's condition. She said, 'Sister really will not let us know [when she will return] . . . . And I think it's a whole psychological problem, it's a whole physical prob . . It's a lot of things, you know. It concerns religious life. It concerns a lot of things.' This was the closest Sr. Claudia came, until a decade later, to disclosing Sr. Norma's friendship with the priest.

In that same meeting on October 15 Sr. Claudia indicated that she had met three days earlier with not only Sr. Jeanine, the chair of the regional administration, but also with Sr. Sonia Hallahan, who was in charge of convent life. Each had initiated 'investigations' about Sr. Norma's health 'and so forth'. Lighthall asked whether the two executives had ever brought up as an executive meeting agenda item, for joint discussion with Sr. Norma, their problem with her absence and refusal to legitimate their assuming her duties. Sr. Claudia replied that, yes, there was one time when they might have, but did not do so. She described her wished-for scenario:

Sr. Claudia: . . . I think that then I should have had . . . as one of

> my points [on her agenda sheet]: 'How can we deal with the fact, you know, that it's very upsetting when you're not fulfilling your own role in terms of August, you know, in terms of the first two weeks of September,' and this sort of thing. Now, in retrospect, what I mean is I wish I had faced it then [Lighthall: Sure.] because it would have saved this thing. (E:10/15/01; c2:55–85)

Sr. Claudia said that Sr. Norma had not been in her office, now, for three weeks except for three or four days when she came in to make brief announcements over the public address system in the morning. After her talk out at the regional center with Sr, Jeanine, she said, she had started to think of 'alternatives'. Just the previous night 'in *bed*' she had lain awake at night listing and organizing the specific functions that made up Sr. Norma's domain: 'there were three aspects of this job that would have to be taken care of — the disciplinarian function; the activity aspect of it; and the detail aspect of it'. She had thought Mrs. Shulman, who now was already taking care of so many of the details, could step in and continue that aspect.

So Sr. Claudia at this time was thinking very specifically about how Sr. Norma's functions could be systematically allocated to other persons. She ended discussion of Sr. Norma by asserting that an important juncture had been arrived at: 'I think it's only honest of me to say that I've been thinking about alternatives. And I feel that very soon we're going to have to be discussing them, because I can't see that this will continue.'

Five days later the Trinity council met, again without Sr. Norma. On October 22, just a week later when the usual Friday executive meeting was to have taken place, Lighthall wrote the following field note:

> 10/22/01 — Contact #40: Call to Sr. Catherine about why the meeting today was called off. They were expecting a call any moment during the AM from the regional center re: Sr. N. If possible, I asked, could we be notified of the meeting or, if not, if it could be recorded. Sr. C. said she'd check ...

The following Monday, another field note:

> Contact #41, 10/25/01 — Call from Sr. Catherine. She asked [us] to come to a mtg at the regional center tomorrow at 10, and at school with Sr. Claudia earlier if I wanted to be filled in on the mtg that took place on Sunday (yesterday) ... I will go to the meeting tomorrow. (Bk. IV, p. 105)

∗   ∗   ∗   ∗

We see how clearly Sr. Claudia's October 12 conference with Sr. Jeanine at the regional center had made its mark: she had induced in Sr. Jeanine, and via her, in other members of the regional administration, problems that were yet to be clearly defined but that had, in any event, produced their own actions. While Sr. Claudia remained active, thinking more boldly of 'alternatives', she had now created a new center of activity, one with an energetic life of its own.

Summary

The present chapter's narrative reveals an attempt to bridge the gap between two starkly different operating realities regarding work responsibilities. While Sr. Claudia regards herself on the 'hot seat', being held responsible for matters which also include effects of Sr. Norma's absences, Sr. Norma regards Sr. Claudia's attempt to fill those absences as intolerant to the point of pushing her out of her job. Each is responding to a threatening disruption each regards the other as perpetrating. Sr. Norma's more general adaptational agenda is to create a better life as a whole, one that integrates more of her deeper aspirations. She is responding less to an external disruption, generally, than to impulses to expand and improve her whole life. Sr. Claudia's adaptational agenda is less expansive, more defensive and corrective, as she lies awake in bed at night thinking how various functions of Sr. Norma's might be handled.

Sr. Claudia then approaches Sr. Norma to bridge the gap as she sees it. Her communication, focusing more on a solution to her own problem than on the details of the disruptions she has experienced, fits no reality Sr. Norma can see, feel, or value and is antagonistic to realities Sr. Norma does see, feel and value. Sr. Claudia's focus, here, was not on her local problematic realities. It was on her own transformation of those realities into a solution. She communicated not something Sr. Norma might understand, but something Sr. Norma should do. In this regard the chapter's narrative captures a kind of problem-solving communication frequently met in organizations: one that privileges action over understanding and that construes self and other in either-or terms, emphasizing localism, rather than both-and terms, emphasizing trans-local integration. This kind of mutual exclusion of the other's realities and defense of localism is not merely a *cognitive* blindness. The mutual failure lies in being prevented from crediting the other's otherness as legitimate or weighty in the solving of one's own problem.

Notes

1. The regular Friday executive meeting on October 8, attended by all three executives, together with Mr. Stagg, the regional administration's accountant, had been devoted entirely to another set of problems, centered in Trinity's business office. Nothing was said in that meeting about the incipient conflict between Sr.

Claudia and Sr. Catherine, on the one hand, and Sr. Norma on the other, regarding Sr. Norma's absences.

2. Lighthall commented at this point on Sr. Claudia's admission of anger. Her reply revealed how she wanted the adults, herself and Sr. Norma in particular, to present themselves to the students and a kind of implicit theory of why that was necessary:

> Lighthall: Yeah, right, but you sit on your anger so well.
>
> Sr. Claudia: Yeah, right. [Lighthall laughs] Yeah, well, I've got to tell you .... I think if ... the girls knew how angry I was and ... the faculty members knew how angry I was, it would do no good.
>
> Lighthall: I agree with that. [Only partly, at the time, and only in a restricted sense now. FFL]
>
> Sr. Claudia [continuing]: So that .. In other words, so that the thing moves and so that there's a minimum of turmoil for them, see. Because no way .. I feel so strongly about the fact that one thing students need to see is the possibility of adults getting along together [laughs lightly] somehow, and working things out. And ah, you know, I just .. we don't, you know, and so forth, but th .. I .. I just have the feeling that the less they knew about that the better ... [the tape ran out at this point, missing the rest of Sr. Claudia's comment.] (Ibid., 885–900)

The 'thing' that was to 'move' was the school — as well as any enterprise Sr. Claudia might be involved in. The ideal school, then, was one that 'moved', perhaps with turmoil among the movers, but with a minimum of turmoil showing to the students. It is important, in other words, for students to learn that the adults can get along together even when the adults are not getting along together. Students learn from the appearances, not the underlying realities. It is important, therefore, to control the appearances, just as one might select a curriculum.

Chapter 10

The Co-Directors Reach Their Limits;
The Regional Administrators Get Moving

In her meeting with Sr. Jeanine at the regional center on October 12, Sr. Claudia said, she later reported, that she could no longer 'handle the situation' with Sr. Norma's absences and that she was at the point of 'a nervous *break*'. In response to Sr. Claudia's discussions out at the regional center, a call was put through to Sr. Norma's physician by Sr. Mary Iver Kallahan, the regional administrator in charge of health services. This set off a series of eight interchanges that revealed how Sr. Norma's withdrawal had become a pointed exclusion of Sr. Claudia, and how the regional administrators had internalized Sr. Claudia's sense of crisis. The sequence of interchanges is not completely clear but they probably occurred in the following order.

1. Sr. Norma's physician conferred with Sr. Mary Iver in his home. They talked about the community's role in regard to Sr. Norma's sickness and about its nature and severity. The physician said Sr. Norma was not incapacitated, but did evidently have a virus.[1]
2. Sr. Norma's physician conferred also with Sr. Norma, reporting his conversation with Sr. Mary Iver. Sr. Norma's response to his having informed others of her physical health is not known, but it may have fueled an angry and abortive interchange she had with Sr. Claudia on the telephone at about that time.
3. The abortive interchange by phone happened quite by chance. Sr. Sonia Hallahan had to reach Sr. Norma about a business matter. When Sr. Norma returned Sr. Sonia's call, Sr. Sonia was not able to come to the phone and asked Sr. Claudia to take the message.

> Sr. Claudia: ... she [Sr. Sonia] asked me to take the message and Sister [Norma] refused to speak to me. She told the switchboard girl she wouldn't.... I was kind of thrown by this in terms of the fact that we were covering, you see, so I knew that she was still very

upset. And I didn't know what about, at that point. So
that was the only contact I had [for about 5 weeks] ..
was her refusal .. you know, I could hear her on the
other end of the phone refusing .. (FFL/Sr.
Cl.:10/26/01; cl: 610–625)

4. The seven regional administrators met to discuss options thus far
   evident regarding Trinity's administrative conflict. They authorized Sr. Georgette to abolish the co-directorate at Trinity if she felt
   that was necessary, and to create a single executive in its stead,
   with Sr. Claudia as the acting executive director as an interim
   measure.
5. Meetings between regional administrators and Sr. Norma were
   arranged and then cancelled by Sr. Norma. Sr. Norma reported to
   them she was well enough to go back to work and that she
   intended to do so. Sr. Mary Iver told Sr. Norma that the issues had
   gone beyond health or illness and that Sr. Norma should not return
   to work but should confer with Sr. Georgette (responsible for all
   regional schools).
6. Sr. Georgette asked Sr. Norma to confer with her out at the
   regional center on Sunday, October 24. Sr. Jeanine also attended
   that meeting.
7. Immediately after that meeting, Sr. Claudia and Sr. Catherine met
   with Sr. Jeanine, Sr. Georgette, Sr. Mary Iver, and Sr. Sonia, to
   clarify matters as Sr. Claudia saw them.
8. All parties met immediately after Sr. Claudia's views had been
   canvassed. The last three of these interchanges (#'s 6, 7, and 8),
   from the regional administrators' point of view, were three stages
   in a single meeting: a stage to hear Sr. Norma, a second stage to
   hear Sr. Claudia, and a stage to reach a temporary closure with the
   two co-directors.

About Sr. Norma's part of the meeting we know very little. Sr.
Claudia's description of her own part of that Sunday meeting informs us
that she reported to the regional administrators' she had found herself
'constantly overstepping my area of responsibility' by making decisions in
Sr. Norma's domain — e.g., student suspensions. She knew, she said, that
every time she did this Sr. Norma would be upset. She elaborated on her
relationship to Sr. Norma in that second-stage meeting on Sunday:

Sr. Claudia [to Lighthall, on 10/26/01]: I had to say that I could not
continue as we presently were, that I felt that at this time it was
impossible for us to *share* decision making.... I knew that my
trust in her was gone and, you know, that I couldn't do it when
someone won't talk to me. (FL/Sr. Cl.:10/26/01; cl:781–87)

Sr. Georgette announced her decision, when they all convened, that Sr. Claudia was to assume the position of 'Acting Principal' of Trinity, effective immediately, until a permanent solution was found. The change was not, however, to be made public for the time being. Sr. Norma said she thought it was a good idea for Trinity to be under a single head, but that the shift should not take place until the following school year. Sr. Norma's reply to Sr. Claudia's query, probing whether Sr. Norma could work under Sr. Claudia, was later unclear in Sr. Claudia's mind — except that Sr. Norma would not allow poor health to be used as an excuse for Sr. Norma's returning to Trinity in a different capacity. Sr. Norma said she was well, that she wanted to return to work immediately. Sr. Jeanine demurred, not ready for a decision. Another joint meeting was set for two days hence, again at the regional center.

There was a brief, poignant exchange between the co-directors at the end of that Sunday's extraordinary meeting:

> Sr. Claudia: Before we left, Sr. Georgette and Jeanine had to go out for their coats or something and so I said, you know, 'I'm sorry that this is the way the whole thing has been .. you know, worked out,' hurtful to her and she said she was, too, and she said, 'I think I should tell you that I can't possibly at this moment see myself returning in any capacity'. (FFL/Sr. Cl.:10/26/01; c1)

These extraordinary actions by the regional administrators had already transpired when, on Monday, October 25, Sr. Catherine conveyed to Lighthall Sr. Claudia's invitation to meet with her the following day and be brought up to date, just before going out to the regional center. (Lighthall's offer to be helpful in any way he could in that regional center meeting — an offer motivated more by a desire to observe an obviously important set of organizational decisions than by any clear image or hope of being effectively helpful — had been forwarded to the regional administrators and had been accepted.)

◦   ◦   ◦   ◦

Four things are notable here. First, a structural change: Sr. Claudia was named Acting Principal. From a dual executive, with all of the difficulties apparent so far, Trinity was to move to a single executive, a reversion to the previous and traditional hierarchy, away from the concept of shared decision making at the top. But this structural change was to be kept private, known only to the regional administrators, the Trinity executives, and Lighthall and Allan. The 'structure' that was changed, then, was definitely hybrid: social structures take their structured quality from the *public* knowledge and acceptance of their form, structure deriving from commonality among members' categories of thought, accepted norms, mores. This change extended only to an inner circle, a limited structural change. Sr. Georgette and the regional administration were moving toward a change in Trinity's structure.

The second matter to be noted is that Sr. Jeanine and Sr. Georgette had created an organized force that was on the march, marshalling the raw realities from which it would fashion a solution to their own problems, solutions which might differ in important regards from Sr. Claudia's.

Third, to say that the regional administrators were on the march is also to imply that their tread in some respects was not delicate. To obtain information from a physician about a community member's health was certainly not unheard of; but in the context of a struggle between two sisters over the possibility that one might replace the other temporarily due to that sister's illness, such information gathering was anything but neutral. Given the regional administrators' failure to inform Sr. Norma of their approach to her physician, it was simply a form of espionage.[2]

Finally, the intervention by the regional administrators accomplished something of a reversal. They broke the blockage of communication between the two co-directors by interposing themselves in between as listeners to both sides. To be sure, in some respects they were still exclusionary in their interposition. They gathered information about Sr. Norma surreptitiously and they heard the two co-directors separately, not together. Nevertheless, they had begun to integrate organizational realities heretofore completely blocked from integration. That process of reality integration would continue — up to a point.

✻   ✻   ✻   ✻

For about an hour (on Tuesday, October 26) Sr. Claudia brought Lighthall up to date about the events just described. In the course of her account, she revealed a mild but significant confrontation with Mrs. Shulman, Sr. Norma's secretary, reflecting Mrs. Shulman's close relationship with Sr. Norma which extended the communication blockage between the two co-directors:

> Sr. Claudia: I'd get typed notices saying such-and-such a thing has happened and signed by Sr. Norma, but typed by Mrs. Shulman .... I asked her [Mrs. Shulman] once to meet with me and she said she didn't think it would be necessary, Sr. Norma was coming back. And on a couple of occasions she said, 'Sister, I can't talk to you about it. Sister has asked me not to'. So then, just removed myself ... There is a real loyalty there which I think in the future may be a problem. (FL/Sr. Cl.: 10/26/01; c1: 741–58)

Sr. Claudia also became aware of another aspect of the conflict between herself and Sr. Norma. In the preceding week, apparently, Sr. Claudia had had occasion to confront Sr. Norma about comments she had heard attributed to Sr. Norma about our consultation-research. Her account gave more evidence of communicative blockage between the co-directors:

> Sr. Claudia: She [Sr. Norma] had told a number of people that she thought that it [the consultation-research] was a sensitivity thing [as in 'sensitivity training'] and that we should be careful about it and so I asked her if she'd want to reflect on that because I had heard this and I had found it difficult to understand because she hadn't brought it out directly. And she seemed to feel that she never really got to make a decision on whether you were a part of the thing and I .. and I take exception to that, do you see, because I feel very strongly that she did and that she accepted it, do you see. And she didn't want to discuss that very much. She really wanted to say, 'Well, the people on the Trinity council should have the say and the people on the academic senate should have the say', and I said, 'Well, they have'. (FL/Sr. Cl.:10/26/01; c2:02–10)

Sr. Claudia also told Lighthall he should know that Sr. Norma had said she was considering leaving the religious order. Sr. Claudia told of another sister, a nun for many years and close to Sr. Norma, who left the religious community. Her leaving had deeply affected all of them and, Sr. Claudia guessed, Sr. Norma especially.

Sr. Claudia's lengthy summary had left Lighthall feeling overloaded with new and detailed information. He observed that Sr. Claudia had omitted reference to her own feelings, but guessed that she was 'dubious' about continuing with Sr. Norma. She responded:

> Sr. Claudia: I'm filled with anxiety about that . . . I have to admit, you know, I find it very difficult sleeping for the past two weeks. I can't keep my food down, you know. So I *know* there's a tremendous amount going on. (FL/Sr. Cl.:10/26/84; c2:82–85)

Sr. Claudia said, with uncharacteristic emotional intensity, that it would be 'an awful hassle' for her if Sr. Norma's decision later that day would be to continue as co-director. Lighthall mused about the future, doubting that the upcoming meeting would change very much if Sr. Norma did not resign. His use of the first person plural indicates that he had identified with Sr. Claudia in her current plight:

> Lighthall: If she does not do work or if she does not fulfill expectations as a subordinate in the way that she has not been fulfiling expectations as an equal, ah, we're back in the same ..
> Sr. Claudia: Except I would feel absolutely free to confront her with this. I really feel .. and I said that to her the other day. And I really think I would.

> Lighthall: Yeah. The *position*, now [Acting Principal], has changed
> inas .. that would be your *role* and expectations of *you* to
> confront her. I see.
> Sr. Claudia: Because I .. I find I'm able to confront Sr. Catherine.
> She's an associate director.
> Lighthall: Well, Sr. Catherine's a very different person to confront.
> Let's face that. (FL/Sr. Cl.:10/26/01; c2:141–150)

✧   ✧   ✧   ✧

We learn two things in the preceding segment. First, Sr. Claudia felt, though she did not often express, intense anxiety regarding continuing to work with Sr. Norma as co-director. Her anxiety was sufficiently intense to lead to loss of sleep and severe indigestion. Second, we see that Sr. Claudia believed that with a clear change in authority, where she was the single chief executive, she would be able to confront Sr. Norma about any further failure of performance. Her attribution of ease or difficulty of confronting Sr. Norma to their respective authority positions (Sr. Norma as equal vs. as subordinate) was doubted by Lighthall, who attributed a good part of the ease or difficulty of confronting to qualities of the person being confronted. It was Lighthall's observation at the time that Sr. Catherine received influence attempts rather easily in this period, while Sr. Norma presented a peremptory, brisk, even brittle attitude, one that suggested the Revolutionary War battle flag, 'Don't tread on me' — a phrase that seems to capture well the message Sr. Norma was trying, by her actions in this period, to send to Sr. Claudia.

We next shift to the meeting out at the regional Apostolic Center, where the two co-directors and Sr. Catherine were to meet with Sr. Jeanine and Sr. Georgette.

Summary and Comment

Sr. Claudia tried, once, and failed to open up communication with Sr. Norma. The narrative of this chapter brings an outright refusal of Sr. Norma even to communicate through Sr. Claudia. Mutual avoidance has become intense. The mutual antagonism has recruited Mrs. Shulman, Sr. Norma's secretary, as a loyal lieutenant to Sr. Norma. But Sr. Claudia's efforts to mobilize help from the regional administration have succeeded: we get a glimpse that a process of information gathering has begun in which testimony from the two sisters was gathered separately and then tentative assessments reported to them jointly. Thus, superordinates introduced new reality-integrating possibilities just when the two sisters themselves were reaching the point where their capacity to reach common ground had been exhausted.

But our pragmatic constructivist outlook, emphasizing each person's commitment to her own adaptational agenda, prompts us to ask whether and to what extent the information gathering process helped the two co-directors to integrate their problematic realities themselves, thus enlarging their respective realities, or promoted, instead, merely the enlargement of the regional administrators' realities. If A and B are in conflict, to enlarge C's understandings of it does little to resolve that conflict unless C's enlarged understandings are turned back upon A and B in a way that induces in them some common or complementary problems. From that same vantage point, we are warned to watch for the extent to which the regional administrators have *substituted their own problem* for Sr. Claudia's problem — a disturbance in Trinity's administration to be simply settled. To what extent could their busy lives as regional administrators accommodate the conflict between the two sisters as a problem with the magnitude experienced by either Sr. Claudia or Sr. Norma or, responding to more local demands at the regional level, accommodate that conflict as a disturbance to be handled rather routinely, and one to be judged as settled so long as no more complaints were heard from Trinity? Finally, we must also wonder whether Sr. Claudia has been successful in inducing in the regional administrators her own problem to the extent that they form merely a coalition with her against Sr. Norma, thus being pulled into the mutual antagonism on one side rather than adding new, relatively dispassionate, reality integrating possibilities.

Notes

1. The source of information about these meetings was Sr. Claudia in her meeting with Lighthall on 10/26/01. Sr. Claudia had been informed in conversations with regional administrators. The events and their basic themes of discussion were all corroborated in later discussions among the principals.
2. Deutsch (1973, p. 353, 367) lists espionage as one of a number of (exclusionary) modes of getting and giving information which characterize what he calls 'competitive' processes of communication.

Chapter 11

Conflict Management From Higher Up: A Closer Look, A Researcher-Consultant's Dilemma

Sr. Claudia went to the regional center hoping to emerge from the meeting free to act in Sr. Norma's significantly absented domain. Sharing decision making with Sr. Norma was no longer possible for her. She had already been appointed Acting Director, and hoped that Sr. Norma would carry out her earlier sentiment of not returning to Trinity 'in any capacity'. Sr. Claudia was to be disappointed.

Both Sr. Norma and Sr. Jeanine, the chair of the order's regional administration, had made new assessments of their respective situations. Lighthall, on the other hand, was to be anything but disappointed: he would be allowed to see, and to record, the inner workings of an organizational conflict and its management from a higher level. Those 'inner workings' would reveal an organization's capacity to mitigate and in certain respects reverse exclusionary conflict management processes between the two co-directors: a new and freer flow of information from, about, and to the two co-directors became set in motion. Lighthall would also be drawn much further into active participation than had been the case, before or afterward, at Trinity itself.

The Meeting

All this became apparent as the meeting unfolded — in five fairly clearly discernible phases:
1. Assessments, complaints, and counter-complaints of the immediate parties, the three Trinity executives;
2. Sr. Jeanine's assessments of problems and the responses of those present to her assessments;
3. the production of 'options', of various solutions to the various problems — a phase interrupted by an exploration of Sr. Norma's realities;
4. resistance to closure and a decision to think more; and

5. a review of the results of the meeting by Lighthall, Sr. Norma, and Sr. Claudia, and some conjectures about the future.

Phase 1.   Assessments, Complaints, Counter-Complaints

Rather than provide a narrative of each phase, it will serve present purposes better to summarize for each successive phase the major themes relevant to problem solving and conflict management. The first theme to be sounded, by Sr. Catherine, is perhaps best labeled *'the accumulation of unfinished business'*:

> Sr. Catherine: ... I would expect, as an executive in charge of student affairs, that you [Sr. Norma] would be at dances and so on. And ah, apparently you didn't. Well, I would revise that [expectation], but every time you weren't there it wasn't my expectation. And *I never confronted you with this.* And I think this is the sort of thing where I would say [inwardly], 'You were absent'. And you would say [inwardly] 'I was not. I delegated this thing.'
> Sr. Norma: Are you talking about this year?
> Sr. Catherine: *No, no.* I just . . *Last year.* This year you were sick.
> (RC:10/26/01; I, 1:0–6. Emphases added.)

Sr. Norma's absences and delegations the previous school year (i.e., the 00–01 year, before our appearance) still rankled. No doubt one factor in their continued capacity to fuel Sr. Catherine's conflict with Sr. Norma was Sr. Catherine's failure to communicate to Sr. Norma or, in her words, to 'confront' Sr. Norma. For such business to become 'finished', communication about it is frequently necessary.

Sr. Norma herself, a short while later, responding to a comment by Lighthall, saw a communication failure between herself and Sr. Claudia:

> Sr. Norma: ... I haven't responded to her in the way that she expected me. And *we haven't really been able to sit down — and I think this is one of the problems —* [emphasis added] to sit down and actually point out to *me* where I have failed to account for myself to her, beforehand. (Ibid. 37–40)

Sr. Claudia, too, in lodging a complaint of her own, mentioned unfinished business that had accumulated, adding tension:

> Lighthall: As I understand it, when, uh, Claudia or Catherine, when you have felt it necessary to do something that was in Norma's area and you have done it, that you had the experience of Norma coming back and getting angry at your doing it. Is that correct?

Sr. Claudia: Not so much in specific cases, and it has not happened this year. *But last year* my experience was, you know, in terms of what both you [glancing at Sr. Norma] and Sr. Florence Ellen said, that I was .. that it was my tendency to take over their areas of responsibility ... Part of the anxiety that I have been under, and I told this to you, ah, a couple of times this fall, that I hated to make a decision *because* of what we went through last year [emphasis added] and I came in when you were sick on two occasions with a list .. and when you called me ... a week ago Friday I believe it was, I had a list of things so that I would keep you in .. aware of the kinds of decisions outside my area of responsibility.

And I found myself really under tension attempting to do that, you see. So that .. that's one of the things I mean when I say that this tension is *not* of five weeks duration. *This tension goes all the way back to the spring* ... I told you that at the time: I find it very difficult to handle an emotional reaction to my doing this. (RAC: 10/26/01; I,1:51–65, emphases added)

A few comments are in order at this point. First, the concept of 'unfinished business': in the context of interpersonal relations, this refers to any issues of any conflict whose non-resolution continues to provide for one or both parties the basis for distrust, anger, fear, anxiety, or other negative affects toward the other. Such affects are always accompanied by interpretive and attributive dispositions that cast the other as capable of acting incompetently, inappropriately, insensitively, or malevolently and therefore as the necessary and proper object of one's vigilant, suspicious scrutiny.

Evident in these excerpts and in the executives' unfolding behavior are three facts bearing on the executives' interpersonal relationships. First, each acknowledged that their communication with each other had not been sufficient to control or regulate some important part of their work environment — monitoring of adolescent behavior at a dance, making a decision in the absence of the other, or clarifying violated expectations. Somehow, the executives had not been able to find the time or personal resources to communicate about how they were working together or ought to work together better. *Failures to each other were kept out of their talk with each other.*

Second, feelings and thoughts about these failings did not go away. They remained alive. They tinted, colored, and finally etched deeply each one's image of the other as co-worker. Going on with business as usual, ignoring these past failures, was insufficient to dilute the poisoning acid of their effects.

A third fact of importance regarding the accumulation of unfinished business was that, while Sr. Claudia and Sr. Norma constituted the focal parties in conflict, Sr. Catherine was by no means immune to its force. She was caught up because her own work depended on a communicative relationship between the co-directors. No one in Sr. Catherine's dependent situation without exceptional skill in mediating conflicts could avoid choosing sides.

Thus, a failure in communicative *process* led to accumulations of unfinished interpersonal business; such accumulations led gradually, in turn, to a poisoned *relationship* between the co-directors, a relationship that, in turn, further weakened communicative tendencies. Further, that poisoned relationship then recruited Sr. Catherine into its structure, as a coalition of two against one. Thus, a superficial and 'confrontation'-avoiding communicative *process* produced a deeply riven *structure*.

A second theme in this phase of complaints and counter-complaints was *an asymmetry of acknowledged culpability* regarding the conflict. Sr. Claudia acknowledged several of her own failings, but Sr. Norma, while able to point up Sr. Claudia's mistakes, acknowledged virtually no contribution of her own to the conflict. Sr. Claudia felt 'resentment' at bearing 'the whole onus of the thing', where 'the thing' was being the cause of Sr. Norma's 'psychological destruction'. She, too, had suffered 'psychological damage', she felt — in apprehension about Sr. Norma's emotional reactions, in loss of sleep, and in not being able to keep food down. While Sr. Norma's embarrassment or loss of face was being acknowledged by the regional administrators, her own earlier psychological damage was not, she felt.

A third theme evident in this phase — evident upon analysis, not to the participants at that moment — was their heavy reliance upon *a priori categories* of work and abstract *agreements* in the delineation of responsibility, and upon an implicit theory that once you clarify categories or procedures of work sufficiently through discussion and agreements, you remove all significant problems of overstepping proper boundaries of authority. The categories and procedures allowed one to sit back, as it were, and coast along, as one rides in a dependable vehicle. In this theory, prior clarifications and agreements about such categories, not on-going communication and negotiation, are the guarantors of administrative peace and tranquility.

Following Sr. Norma's comment, quoted above, about the co-directors' not being 'able to sit down' together, Sr. Claudia responded, revealing her reliance on agreements rather than on up-dated assessments of reality for maintenance of a working relationship:

> Sr. Claudia: Could I respond? What *we had agreed to early last year* was that if any of us was unable to be where she .. you know, to take care of her responsibility that she notify some member of the team and that that person would agree to cover for us. *We had that agreement built in* so that we wouldn't be running against a misunderstanding.

And *we also agreed at that time* that if a decision was made in the absence of the other, the person making the decision would attempt to do it in the way ... they [the absent person] ordinarily handle that situation. But that, if they [the one who was 'covering' for the absent person] handled it in a different way in the absence of the other, that they still had the right to .. you know, they did the best they could and the other one would understand. (Ibid., 40–51, emphases added)

A few minutes later, Sr. Norma narrated a brief account of Sr. Claudia's episode of 'overstepping her bounds' the prior year. Her account shows the executives' shared reliance on a categorical division of labor:

Sr. Norma: We [the four executives, the previous year] had agreed upon the movement of the guidance office at one of our [executive] meetings. But then apparently some of the people in the guidance department had asked to have these rooms painted and shelves made [as part of the transfer into new offices]... And that went actually through Sr. Claudia. And one day apparently when [Sr. Florence Ellen] wanted men [inaudible] to do something, she didn't know what was going on and she was expecting the men to... be doing something else. In reality they were doing this [preparing the rooms for transfer to the guidance department] and she didn't know anything about it. And she felt this *came under maintenance* and ..

Lighthall: And that was her bailiwick. [Sr. Norma: Yeah]. How did you enter into it? ... You didn't enter into it.

Sr. Norma: Well ... I was in the *middle* [laughs]. I really thought it did fall under maintenance and that this is one of the areas that probably should have been talked out... I felt it should have been *channeled*... (Ibid., 80–96, emphasis added)

Such categories of work entail two difficulties. First, any given work is always interpretable as belonging in different categories. And second, while such categories tend to be mutually exclusive, or at least viewed as mutually exclusive, work itself is part of a system of interdependencies. It is almost never the case in organizations that work at one site and in one category is without effects in another site and another category, effects that have to be dealt with at the other site and in the other category.

Consider, for example, the matter of interpretation in the episode narrated by Sr. Norma. The maintenance men were painting rooms and putting in shelves. In the context of the prior executive decision to move the guidance department into these rooms, this painting is easily categorized as part of that decision. Office moves rarely take place without some painting and renovation, since it is easier to do that when people are out of the office than when they are in it. Such work, while done by maintenance men, becomes categorized as work in relation to the requests for faculty support and work conditions and therefore as being in Sr. Claudia's domain. But since it is done by maintenance men, it is also easily interpretable as falling under maintenance, Sr. Florence Ellen's domain. The guarantor against 'overstepping boundaries' in such cases, therefore, cannot be categories. Rather, it is frequent, mundane transactions about how work will be interpreted in this particular case.

The fourth and final theme evident in this first phase of the meeting was the impact of emotionality and in particular, Sr. Claudia's 'hating' of the emotional confrontations with Sr. Norma: 'I hate the emotional part of it, you know, the accusations and weeping that came with these. I did find those difficult . . .' (Ibid., 105–109) Later in the meeting she explained how what she perceived as Sr. Norma's anger directed at her caused her to 'remove' herself from further pointed communication with Sr. Norma.

The first phase of the meeting (complaints and counter-complaints) ended with an interchange between Sr. Catherine and Sr. Norma. Sr. Catherine told Sr. Norma, 'Everyone has felt this way about you'. Lighthall asked her to clarify, which she did: 'That she's, ah, derelict in her duties. That's getting hard, but . . [leaves sentence unfinished]'.

Sr. Norma explained how a 'flu' virus had alternately attacked and subsided that Fall, concluding: 'I asked my doctor, "Is it in my head?" He said, "No, Sister. It isn't in your head because that's how viruses react. One day you feel you can really go in there and do it and the next day your strength is absolutely drained" '. (Ibid., 280)

The first half hour of this meeting, then, produced complaints and counter-complaints centering on the co-directors' relationship. Seven dimensions of that relationship can be identified. The following causal chain of these dimensions is at least plausible:

(1) Reliance upon prior static agreements and categories of work and a norm against 'overstepping' separate bailiwicks — assuming no change in the *basis* of those agreements — rather than upon jointly recognized interdependence,

together with

(2) a clear asymmetry between the co-directors in their orientations to emotionality — Sr. Norma expressing emotionality freely, intensely, and defensively while Sr. Claudia suppressed her own emotionality and withdrew sharply from Sr. Norma's weeping and angry accusations which struck Sr. Claudia as degrading self-pity,

produced

(3) a communication process that barred communication about the working relation thus excluding their exploration of important interpersonal problems,

which led to

(4)   the accumulation of unfinished interpersonal business,
which, in turn
(5)   acidified their relationship in mutual mistrust and vigilance for threat,
a relationship rendered more acid by
(6)   asymmetry in the parties' readiness to acknowledge complicity and culpability in their actions,
all of which
(7)   forced a choice on Sr. Catherine of taking sides, ending in an executive triad of two against one.

When various conditions lead to unfinished interpersonal business between two people whose organizational roles dictate that they must work together, that unfinished business will not only debilitate their organizational performance but will also lead other parties to 'take sides', thus creating structures of alliance and antagonism quite beyond the dyadic relation — to triads and clusters. Conditions and processes that promote the finishing of unfinished business, therefore — supporting a 'working through' by the parties of their suspicions and mutual antagonisms before they harden — are conditions and processes that promote the integration of organizational realities quite beyond the immediate antagonisms.

Phase 2.   Sr. Jeanine's Assessments

Sr. Jeanine's special position as head of the regional administrators gives her assessments special importance to us just as it did then to the executives.

> Sr. Jeanine: It seems to me that there are two very different points of view here . . . a basic lack of understanding as I see it, in the areas of expectations and perceptions in three . . . very significant areas: accountability, responsibility, and presence to each other.
>   Sr. Claudia . . . feels very much put upon and has had to, in her judgment, assume responsibilities which were not legitimately hers and then is trying to cope with doing the thing and handle the attending question and being on tenterhooks as to when allegations will be flung at her again for, quote, overstepping.

By accountability, Sr. Jeanine meant the frequency and completeness with which each kept the other informed of any deviation in action from expectations previously set. By responsibility, she meant both the content and the manner of executing duties, especially whether a duty would be carried out personally or by delegation to someone else.

> Sr. Jeanine [continuing]: And I hear Norma differently. I hear

Norma saying, 'I'm in perfect health. The doctor concurs, the doctor attested to this and I was only absent four days recently in the last two weeks for this. But then .. the virus occurred last August and this accounted for my, um, erratic physical presence in the job'. But I'm hearing: 'But I handled my job because, you know, everything that was my responsibility I somehow engineered through others'.

I didn't hear all of that today, but this is the kind of thing ..

Sr. Norma: I think I attempted [inaudible] due to the absences, I tried to do as much as possible.

Sr. Jeanine: See, if I were Sr. Claudia or Sr. Catherine I would be so mad at you for telling me you were only absent four days. If I have to pick up for you all year and then I hear, you know .. oh, yes, later in the discussion you say it was more than that, because you can't tell, you know, from one day to another . . . the virus is incipient within you . . . I think Claudia was left on tenterhooks . . .

If she knew that you were sick on a particular day — you could phone her: 'I can't make it'. [Sr. Jeanine here is assessing Sr. Norma's 'accountability'] — I think Claudia would be free to .. to act . . . You haven't done that. I think what she can't cope with now is [taking Sr. Claudia's perspective]: 'You weren't accountable in August .. or at least you weren't responsible in my terms, and I don't know where you are. And how can I go into a team situation lacking this?'

Okay, now you've been saying, 'I will be. I will be. I will be'. And I think Claudia, at this point, if I'm understanding you correctly, you can't hear Norma say any of these things. (Ibid., 280–310)

Sr. Jeanine's assessment may have attempted objectivity and even-handedness, but her own conclusions about Sr. Norma's and Sr. Claudia's relative contributions to the conflict are fairly clear. Her disbelief in the effectiveness of Sr. Norma's delegation of duties to others ('responsibility') is evident in her phrasing of Sr. Norma's defense of her 'erratic physical presence on the job', namely, 'I handled my job because . . . everything that was my responsibility I *somehow engineered* through others' [last emphasis added].

Her assessment of Sr. Norma's minimizing of her absences to her colleagues ('presence to each other') followed directly Sr. Norma's defense, 'I tried to do as much as possible'. Sr. Jeanine became sharply explicit: '*I would be so mad at you* for telling me you were only absent four days. If I have to pick up for you all year . . .'

As for accountability, she used concrete detail: '. . . you could phone her: 'I can't make it.' I think Sr. Claudia would be free to act . . . You haven't done that.'

Sr. Claudia's earlier efforts were clearly effective in inducing her problem in Sr. Jeanine. As we shall see, Sr. Jeanine had synthesized other problems regarding the conflict as well.

We have already seen that Sr. Norma's response to Sr. Jeanine's assessment was mildly defensive. Sr. Claudia's response acknowledged some weakness, but also analyzed why she would 'remove' herself from confrontations with Sr. Norma regarding her absences:

> Sr. Claudia: No. I can hear her say, 'I'm sorry for all of this . .'
> Sr. Jeanine: No but . .
> Sr. Claudia [continuing]: . . . and I can hear her say, 'I will do it'. But now I can't believe it. And I can't believe that I can respond as I should. I should add that. I hear her saying this. My experience now, in terms of times when Sr. Norma feels guilt for not being present when she thinks I expect her to be, is anger. And I think it's not with herself, but it comes out in anger with me. And so I know that I just [voice becomes unsteady] remove myself from it.... (Ibid., 310–340)

As to Sr. Norma's reality regarding her shifting commitments, Sr. Jeanine was still in the dark. Sr. Norma had mentioned nothing about her doubts about religious life in the meeting; nor would she. Evidently, she felt she had to protect that reality from examination by others. By doing so, however, she unwittingly assisted Sr. Claudia in exporting Sr. Claudia's problem to Sr. Jeanine. Thus Sr. Jeanine and then Sr. Georgette joined Sr. Catherine in a coalition informed by Sr. Claudia's reality, not Sr. Norma's. To protect one's reality from examination is, in such situations, to allow the extension and validation of others' realities — at least in the short run.

Phase 3.   *Identifying and Exploring Options*

Five options for dealing with the conflict were suggested and responded to. Two commentaries also briefly interrupted this search for the right solution.

Option 1 (suggested by Lighthall). 'To suspend action', 'to continue this kind of discussion' was the first suggestion, and Lighthall offered a procedure for 'each party in a dispute to clear the air'. Sr. Claudia's response was that 'we went over this same ground Sunday'. For her, more discussion directly with Sr. Norma would be redundant. Sr. Jeanine repeated remarks earlier, saying that the discussion so far had given her new insight into three things: 'accountability, presence to each other, and responsibility'. Queried whether she was impatient, Sr. Claudia replied, 'I'm impatient for some kind of . . After these months, yes, I am'. Sr. Norma said that she was, too. Warned by Lighthall that a choice might require later backtracking, Sr. Claudia understood, but also warned that 'to put it off, put it off, and put it off is a danger'. Upon further probing by Lighthall, Sr. Claudia explained her resistance to further discussion of the kind he had suggested. It was the emotionality:

> Sr. Claudia: I don't think I can say we don't need any more discussion. I think [sighs deeply] I'm saying [pause] to talk this out again .. I guess I go back to what I said earlier, the confrontations. The number of confrontations on these same issues have multiplied to the point of my exhaustion. (Ibid., 540–546)

Option 2 (suggested by Sr. Norma). 'Why can't we pick up from here?' asked Sr. Norma. She argued that she could, indeed, live up to Sr. Jeanine's three categories of performance (responsibility, accountability, and presence). Sr. Norma said that she knew that eventually Trinity would have to have a single head, but indicated she couldn't see that being done immediately.

Sr. Catherine asserted again her loss of trust in the capacity of the co-directors to work together. Sr. Claudia spoke of the emotional drain of that working relationship and urged that it was important to use that energy in the running of the school, not in continually working out their relationship. She gave a recent example of once again having to fill in for Sr. Norma's absence — a confrontation with parents about the school's uniform purchases, a matter in Sr. Norma's bailiwick. Sr. Claudia concluded: 'It is my conviction that whether she is there or isn't there, I probably wouldn't be able to work as a co-director' (Ibid., 693).

Sr. Georgette's response to Sr. Norma's suggestion of carrying on business as usual was to focus, instead, on Sr. Norma's agreement that eventually there should be one person at the head of Trinity. She started to ask Sr. Norma a question with the premise about Sr. Norma's being willing to accept a single head and Sr. Norma interrupted, adding that another premise was what she, Sr. Norma, felt she could live with back at Trinity.

> Sr. Georgette: Yet you do see the better way is with a single director. If so, why can't you change your mind [and agree to a single director immediately, rather than at the end of the year]?

Sr. Norma replied that she could simply not bring herself to return to Trinity in a subordinate position. Clearly, a public demotion back at Trinity was unacceptable to her.

Sr. Georgette's response to Sr. Norma's plea for business as usual was to ask her directly to change her mind, to institute now what she agreed was best later. Sr. Georgette wanted clear, overt change then and there, and saw Sr. Norma as the resistance.

Lighthall, too, tried changing Sr. Norma's mind. He gave an example from earlier that year of a teacher who had had to accept an embarrassing withdrawal of a position when the executives overturned a widely held expectation of this teacher's appointment. Yes, it had been embarrassing, but the executives had not given that teacher's personal feelings precedence over organizational effectiveness then. Why, was the implication, should they now? But even if Sr. Norma did return as co-director, Lighthall mused out loud, perhaps little would change between the co-directors.

Sr. Catherine suggested not an option, *per se*, but a criterion for judging options: 'I'm not sure I want to be committed unless [the solution] is long term and has stability' (RC:10/26/01; II, 1:0–43). The current arrangement — and Sr. Norma's suggestion of business as usual — was unstable in Sr. Catherine's eyes.

A weakly audible response by Sr. Norma, probed by Lighthall, briefly side-tracked discussion of options. Sr. Norma revealed that the purpose of the Sunday's meeting had become clear only when she had arrived at the meeting itself. The revealing discussion began with Sr. Norma's weakly audible and vague reference to the past Sunday's meeting: '. . in the light of Sunday, you know, that comes into it a bit'.

> Lighthall[to Sr. Norma]: What does Sunday mean for you?
> Sr. Norma: Well, I have a lot of mixed-up feelings about how this thing got going, and everything. I thought, Sunday, I was going to just meet with Sr. Georgette. I must .. I realized that eventually I was meeting with Sr. Jeanine and Sr. Claudia, but for some reason in our communication that didn't come through to me, that this was going to be what was taking place on Sunday. So what I thought I was doing on Sunday was ... filling Sr. Georgette in on our high school situation from my point of view, because she hasn't been involved in the high schools. Where in reality, that isn't what really was taking place. And I wasn't conscious ..
> Sr. Georgette: What was taking place?
> Sr. Norma: .. then I learned that Sr. Claudia and Sr. Jeanine were present and that there .. [responding to Sr. Georgette's question] Well, I got the whole picture of, you know, just a lot of rumors, like I had walked out on Trinity, or you know, something like that. And this is not the case at all.
> Lighthall: It's certainly not your perception of the case.
> Sr. Norma: No.
> Lighthall: But other people may have been affected that way.
> Sr. Norma: Right. (RC:10/26/01; II, 1:44–62)

Here Sr. Norma denies any complicity in Sr. Claudia's problem and diminishes to mere rumors her absences at Trinity. Responding perhaps to Sr. Catherine's parameter for an acceptable solution, stability, Lighthall set out a parameter of his own: dependence not on categories but on communicative process:

> Lighthall: One of the things we have to deal with somewhere along the line is this dependence upon categories for role definition. They will never work. They're a good starting point. [Opens the Trinity handbook-calendar.] You look in the thing here [points to the 'specific areas of responsibility' in the handbook-calendar], there they are, nice and neatly laid out. And if everybody is rational and knows what everything here means, then they will go [i.e., will communicate problems] up these lines. But the trouble with categories like that is that they deal with humans and humans are interdependent and therefore the categories are interdependent.
>
>   So when somebody brings to you something to do with teacher recruitment [Sr. Claudia's bailiwick], it may immediately have student implications [Sr. Norma's bailiwick] because this guy is a radical type or whatever the heck . . . or community implications [Sr. Catherine's bailiwick].
>
>   So you had a good start but it seems to me that where it broke down was [pauses] in the assumption that it would work [loud laughter led by Sr. Claudia and Sr. Jeanine] .. alone, alone. It will work, but with something else.... Categories are not enough. And that means communication. (Ibid., 69–83)

After giving some examples of oblique communication and suggesting that outside consultants might assist the co-directors in establishing better communication about their roles, Lighthall identified a third option, related to Sr. Norma's public embarrassment of what would amount to a demotion in administrative position.

Option 3 (suggested by Lighthall).   Following the regional administrators' previous private appointment of Sr. Claudia as Acting Director, Lighthall suggested that the titles not be changed publicly, but that it be agreed privately among the present members that Sr. Claudia would have final authority whenever there were differences of opinion, that each might be able to return.

> Lighthall: If that kind of thing could be done, then you [Sr. Claudia] might be freed up [to act without being blocked by resistance or absences of Sr. Norma] and you [Sr. Norma] might not have to deal with the public aspects of a shift in role. Now that's just off the top of my head. I don't know if that makes any sense at all. [pause] I don't get very much favorable reaction.
> Sr. Claudia: I'm thinking about it (Ibid., 133–139).

Sr. Catherine's response to that option was definite and immediate. She saw duplicity in it: 'Either she is [full director] or she isn't. And I think our faculty has a right to know that . . . [turning to Sr. Georgette] I'm sure that even you would find this objectionable, would you not?' Sr. Georgette said she was not sure, that probably most faculty members would not care one way or the other.

Option 4 (suggested by Sr. Georgette). In view of everyone's agreement that there should be a single head 'at the top' of Trinity, Sr. Georgette said, 'I don't see why they don't start moving toward that immediately ... So I can see the rest of this year moving into that' (Ibid., 240). Earlier Sr. Georgette had asked Sr. Norma directly to change her mind. Now she was urging the immediate beginning of a transition to a single head.

Lighthall said he foresaw not much change in one respect no matter which option was taken: the two co-directors would still have to communicate in order to coordinate action, and that communication would still be difficult and emotional for Sr. Claudia. Without fairly close communication, he said, 'You're still going to get in each other's way' — so long as they both returned to Trinity. Sr. Claudia, too, saw no way out of what for her was a depressing prospect of having to communicate with Sr. Norma. Lighthall said he thought their communication could be 'vastly improved,' 'but not without energy expended, emotion lost [sic: spent], hostilities felt'. Lighthall said he, himself, could not spend much more time at Trinity than he had been, thus obliquely ruling himself out as an 'outside consultant'.

Sr. Claudia tried clarifying the implications of Lighthall's scenario:

> Sr. Claudia: So you're saying that our energies go into trying to get along, instead of into the ... [running of the school] .. For the rest of the year, now, we attempt to ... continue to drain off our psychic energies, and so forth, attempting to begin to make decisions together.
>
> Lighthall: No.... Whatever decisions are made, ... you still are going to have violated expectations and you're still going to have to deal with those. Now, if you deal with them by burying them, you're still going to have emotional drain. And if you deal with them by talking about them, you're still going to have emotional drain. But one has an end to it and the other doesn't. (Ibid., 290–306)

Option 5 (suggested by Sr. Claudia). Sr. Jeanine said that she was due at another meeting 'momentarily'. After indicating that she had given up hope for a decision at the present meeting, Sr. Claudia offered the fifth and last option:

> Sr. Claudia: The other alternative we haven't suggested is my resignation.... And I don't feel I would lose face in resigning. I really don't. I really don't have so much of a problem with that. I feel I could resign from Trinity and I think you could place me

someplace. And I'm perfectly willing to accept this. (Ibid., 319–323)

Sr. Jeanine's response was immediate: she disagreed. Once Sr. Claudia had made a commitment for a year, as she had, she told Sr. Claudia, 'You could not live with not being faithful to your word' (330). Sr. Claudia said she thought an explanation that she was resigning for the good of Trinity would be accepted and that she could live with that 'without the kind of psychic hurt' that Sr. Norma would feel. 'See, I think psychically I could take it.'

Sr. Claudia's offer to resign, taken by Sr. Georgette as a threat to resign (as she indicated later), precipitated a decision and phase four.

Phase 4.   Decision to Deliberate More

Sr. Georgette's response to Sr. Claudia's argument (or challenge) was quick: 'I'm not ready to make that decision right now, and I don't think Sr. Jeanine is. And the decision we came to last week, which still stands, is, like, for this interim time' (368). But Sr. Jeanine demurred, arguing that the decision to make Sr. Claudia Acting Director was under the assumption that Sr. Norma was not present in the school. If she were to be present while Sr. Claudia was acting director that was, for her, a quite different situation and a very different decision. As Sr. Georgette pressed her case, she disclosed a contrast between an ideal and her actual assessment:

> Sr. Georgette: I would love to see these two come to some consensus, along with Sr. Catherine, about what would be the best thing. That, you know, is the way you would really like things to happen: [have the co-directors] make the recommendation to us, then we weigh it. But when you're in opposition and one is exclusive of the other, you know, that's pretty difficult for them to have to make the decision. (Ibid., 410)

Sr. Jeanine countered Sr. Catherine's argument that it would be disruptive to have Sr. Norma remain as co-director while knowing she would be leaving the following year — a lame duck situation. Sr. Jeanine then summed up: 'More time is needed . . . We are not ready for a dramatically different decision today'. She and Sr. Georgette then departed.

Phase 5.   Some Residual Worries

Lighthall was worried that he might have had a dysfunctional effect on the process. In exploring his worry, he opened the door for Sr. Norma to express some unfinished business of her own, a door which Sr. Catherine opened further:

Lighthall [to Sr. Norma]: What do you feel about my presence here?

Sr. Norma: I welcomed it. I wanted it. And, you know, I want to get back to work. I was due back last Monday. I don't want to go into all the details of why I was held up.

Sr. Catherine: I'd like to know, or is it none of our business?

Sr. Norma: Why I didn't? [Sr. Catherine: Umhmm.] It's simply because the last time when I was ready .. actually going even to come to the Fall dance, the Regional Center was involved in it. And the doctor didn't seem to know why even the Regional Center was involved. And so I was forced into a meeting with Sister [Mary Iver Kallahan] and I've been through this thing ... a million times. And it was Sr. Mary Iver who said to me, 'Don't go back to Trinity' .... I've been ready to go back.

Lighthall: Well, I .. How do you [to Sr. Catherine] feel about my being here?

Sr. Catherine: I liked it.

Lighthall: Okay? Well see, I always have the fear that I am new, and if something goes the wrong way, I may in fact have pushed it that way.

Sr. Claudia: I don't think that anything went the wrong way or anything like that.

Sr. Norma: No. No.

Sr. Claudia: Like, I don't foresee a decision, now, for ages, frankly [laughs lightly]. And it has nothing to do with you. (536)

Lighthall: My view isn't that the thing will be pushed off to ages ..

Sr. Claudia: I think 'til next June, you know. Then we'll do it [reorganize the executive] again, you know, and go through this. So, like, I kind of am pessimistic ... I've been through it three times, in terms of redefining the same team.

Sr. Norma: I've been through it twice ... And there's a lot of back history through all of it, too.

Sr. Claudia: So .. But .. I think if it has to be, it has to be.

[Lighthall predicts that in January Sr. Claudia will see more stable structure and will feel some 'relief'. Sr. Norma says, 'Relief for me, too'.] (Ibid., 560).

Lighthall realized he had been more active in intervening and was worried whether Sr. Norma saw him as taking sides against her. He was confident of Sr. Claudia's support, but worried about Sr. Norma, because he felt she was opposed to his and Sue Allan's being at Trinity, from her earlier comments. Further, Sr. Norma's absences and self protectiveness rendered him simply more of a stranger to her, where his ignorance was easily filled with his own defensive constructions about her, constructions not a little tinged with Sr.

Claudia's views of Sr. Norma. Being dimly aware of that one-sidedness, Lighthall was now worried about further alienation. He was surprised at Sr. Norma's answer, a surprise that can be taken as further evidence, if any is needed, of his ignorance of her reality.

Sr. Norma revealed in her explanation of why she was 'held up' an attitude of having been actively prevented from doing her job by the regional administration — as if the absences in question had been those in the previous week or two.

Sr. Claudia saw continued conflict with Sr. Norma over their working relation, conflict that would continue to drain energies away from what she regarded as her own, and their joint, legitimate mission: effective school governance.

All of this demonstrated clearly that Sr. Claudia had dropped all thoughts of resigning from Trinity. And she never mentioned the idea again. The next months might be bleak, but 'if it has to be, it has to be'. Her earlier offer to resign, in this light, must be seen less as a real option than an expression (a) to Sr. Jeanine and Sr. Georgette against their taking her for granted as a stalwart at Trinity, (b) to Sr. Norma against her falling back on personal psychological comfort as justification — an indirect challenge that she, Sr. Claudia, could 'take it', while Sr. Norma was acting like she could not, (c) to all present against the prevailing assumption that Sr. Norma's psyche was being put in jeopardy or damaged while Sr. Claudia's was not, and (d) especially to Sr. Jeanine, rejecting the loss of 'face' by one person as the legitimate grounds for a decision affecting something as important as Trinity's executive-level functioning.

Back at Trinity: Lighthall's Dilemma

The Trinity executives and Lighthall departed separately from the regional center. That afternoon Lighthall put identical copies of the following note in Sr. Claudia's and Sr. Norma's school mailboxes:

> To two difficult and struggling sisters:
> I have an inner urgency to express deep withness to both of you. Each of you may resent my sympathy for the other, but my most prominent impression is that both of you feel very alone now. You are alone, each one, and I wish I could do more to mitigate that loneliness. A few words on paper is all I can do at the moment. May peace come out of your turmoil.

Returning to Trinity three days later for the regular executive meeting, Lighthall met Sr. Norma. She thanked him for the note, adding, 'It was just the right thing'. She also said the executive meeting had been cancelled since it was a day of testing for the students. Sr. Catherine confirmed that it had been cancelled but gave different reasons; not much business that needed taking care of but mostly the emotional tensions between Sr. Claudia and Sr. Norma.

Lighthall found in his Trinity mailbox a reply from Sr. Claudia, written the day after the Tuesday meeting at the regional center:

> Dear Mr. Lighthall,
>
> Thank you very much for taking time to offer sympathy. Please know that my gratitude for your help and concern outweighs my confusion as a result of Tuesday's session. As I reflect on yesterday, I must admit now to seeing aspects of religious community that I hadn't experienced before and must learn to cope with somehow.
>
> I so long for peace — but not at any price!

Lighthall took the opportunity of the cancelled meeting to talk with Sr. Claudia, as usual with tape recorder running, about her conflict, about the Tuesday meeting, and about her.[1] He asked Sr. Claudia if the postponement of a decision on Tuesday was 'hanging things up' for her. Not only was it hanging things up, she said, but it had caused her to re-interpret what was going on. She said she really wanted a decision, one way or the other:

> Sr. Claudia: Somehow, you know, you do this or you do *this* in terms of the decision. But I .. but dang, I'm .. you put your finger right on it the other afternoon when you said to me, 'You are dissatisfied and impatient'. [Sr. Claudia emphasized the words, 'you', 'dissatisfied', and 'impatient' by three forceful taps of her hand on her desk.] I am impatient, you see.
> Lighthall: Now. I didn't get as clear a statement there at the Regional Apostolic Center, that you are, as you said just now. Maybe you've done some thinking ...
> Sr. Claudia: I *have* done thinking on that. (FL: 10/29/01; C2: 62–96)

Her 'thinking' and 'interpreting' of events had focused on what for her was surprising vacillation. A path to a decision seemed to have been reached, in her appointment as Acting Director, and then retreated from. She had feelings about that kind of 'business' (her word).

> Lighthall: What would be a better word for it than 'business'?
> Sr. Claudia: Human relations ... or the real use of authority ....
> It's no use of authority, the way I think authority should be used ... In three years I probably have only referred about three problems to the regional level and I thought they were serious problems or I wouldn't have gone diddling out here ... I know that my impatience the other day was that: I expected it [a decision] that day and it wasn't forthcoming .... I had pretend .. I had said, as if, well, maybe I'm not that impatient. But when I got a good perspective on it ... I think I was thrown by, you know,

> what happened in terms of what my expectations were and in
> terms of what I had thought Sr. Georgette and Sr. Jeanine . . . had
> decided. (Ibid., 105–129)

Lighthall, too, had been doing some pondering — about his dual role as
researcher and consultant:[2]

> Lighthall: . . . I've said to myself, 'Now listen, you're not in there to
> impose your, ah, preferences or even perceptions on the situa-
> tion. You're there to facilitate the people there, facilitate their
> progress toward their goals'. And then I say, 'Well, wait a
> minute, now. Who can progress toward any goals in a very
> unsettled situation?' . . . There's a difference between the
> professional and the scientific aspect. I'm trying to do both [Sr.
> Claudia finished Lighthall's sentence simultaneously with him,
> . . . 'both'.], see? And now, which one? (Ibid., 186–210)

Specifically, he asked, 'Should I call them [the regional administrators] up
and say, "Would it be useful for me to come and talk to you?" and facilitate
their movement so that you can move a little faster?' Clearly, Lighthall had
been caught up in Sr. Claudia's impatience, giving her desires for closure
greater weight than the regional administrators' possible need for time to
think and talk together. Thinking aloud further, he moved closer to closure
for himself:

> Lighthall: Then on the other side I turn and say, 'If you do that,
> then what you are studying is your own behavior.' [Sr. Claudia: I
> see. (laughs)] And so, what is that? . . . I'm here to study your
> behavior, not to go around and do things and say, 'Oh, yeah,
> that's what I did'. So what? You know? . . . . That's the dilemma I
> have and I think my answer to myself is that I prefer to study the
> processes in here [at Trinity]. And it seems to me that . . . the
> processes in here are being disrupted by a non-decision out
> there. And I think I could . . not only might facilitate something
> out there but might also learn more [by offering to help the
> regional administrators think things through]. So it's not just
> either-or [between facilitating and studying].
>
> [Turns to Sr. Claudia] What would you . . what would your
> preference be, given that dilemma?
>
> St. Claudia: . . . If you could facilitate a decision's being made, see,
> then I would like to say, 'Do it'. . . . That's the thing that's
> necessary. Not which decision so much as, you know, a deci-
> sion. . . . What I find I cannot deal with is no decision . . .
>
> Like, I want right now to dig right in and get some things
> accomplished. It's the end of a quarter . . . I'd like to just free
> myself of these other kinds of pressures that I think are

secondary in one way, but have become primary .... I would appreciate it if you took an active role. (Ibid., 270–320)

Lighthall left a phone message for Sr. Jeanine that he was available for consultation to them if they might find that useful. A field note records that 'Sr. Jeanine called back almost immediately and asked me to come to sit with them while they considered their decision'.

        °   °   °   °

As we shall see, Lighthall represented to the regional administrators a consultative resource not only out at the regional center but back at Trinity, a resource whose even-handed availability to the co-directors at Trinity he would have denied if he had been asked directly at the time. His offering of his services to sit with the regional administrators no doubt helped to reinforce their image of his active and available consultancy to both co-directors at Trinity.

Summary

The narrative of this chapter provides a glimpse of several parts of yet another impediment to communication and reality integration, unfinished interpersonal business. Participants' capacity to handle emotionality, or their fearful avoidance of emotional expression, becomes relevant to their capacities to express, probe, and integrate their different organizational realities. Just when differences regarding organizational conditions, opportunities, or functioning come into conflict is when emotion is prompted around those very matters. Avoidance of emotionality can lead, as this chapter's narrative reveals, to regular avoidance and retreat from precisely those persons whose behavior one wants to change and precisely those realities which must be understood and coped with. The rigid use of work categories again appears in the narrative as an impediment to cross-role communication. The categories or bailiwicks of work and the norm against overstepping boundaries were paralleled by a tacit norm against including as meeting agenda disturbances in working relationships themselves. Each of these sources of avoidance or blockage between the co-directors seems to have combined to create and sustain an exclusionary process that pulled others into its initially two-person structure to create small camps. Thus Mrs. Shulman was pulled into the exclusionary conflict management between the co-directors on Sr. Norma's side, and Sr. Catherine was pulled into it on Sr. Claudia's side. Lighthall, too, was pulled into their exclusionary management on Sr. Claudia's side, raising research vs. consultation dilemmas of the kind depicted in the narrative. Unfinished interpersonal conflict, in sum, can perpetuate and augment its capacity to impede communication across realities and thus to block the integration of participants' realities into their collective action.

Notes

1. At the end of an earlier draft of this chapter, read by Sr. Claudia about a decade after the events themselves, she wrote in the margin these words: 'Why didn't Lighthall check out Norma's reality at this time?' Certainly an astute question. Lighthall's relationship with Sr. Norma was tenuous and fleeting and not a little defensive. He had never resolved his sense of her opposition to his and Allan's consultation-research at Trinity, never allowed her the opportunity, really, to express directly to him her opposition. Why? Quite simply, he feared (unrealistically only in retrospect) that she would not only express opposition in words but would press her feelings in action. On several occasions Lighthall had observed Sr. Norma take peremptory action to stop something she did not like. If she had insisted to Sr. Claudia that our project be stopped, Sr. Claudia would have had to honor her co-equal position — or so Lighthall believed.

    The difference between his relationship to Sr. Claudia and his relationship to Sr. Norma is reflected in their responses to his note. Reading Lighthall's note these years later, it seems a mixture of authentic, even-handed concern and rather saccharine sentimentality. As it happened, both Sisters seemed to respond to the positive, not the negative. But while Sr. Norma's response was ad hoc, triggered by a fleeting encounter, and was accompanied by an explanation of the cancelled meeting that ignored emotional tensions between herself and Sr. Claudia, Sr. Claudia's response was immediate, written, and authentic about her feelings.

    So the answer to Sr. Claudia's question, written in the margin of the manuscript, is twofold. First, Lighthall's relationship with Sr. Norma was distant and defensive and was more or less reciprocated. And second, Lighthall did not have the resources, either within him or in linking networks of friends who could help bridge the gap to Sr. Norma, to overcome the constraints of that relationship. That differential relationship of Lighthall to the two co-directors puts its stamp on these data. It dictates that this could not be more than an incomplete inquiry into a conflict, since one side of the conflict was not reached.

2. Lawler and others (1985) have considered thoughtfully some costs, benefits, and complications of participant-observer research; the essays by Hackman (1985) and Goodman (1985) come closest to considering the issues facing Lighthall at this point in his research-consultation.

Chapter 12

The Regional Administrators: Local Problem Solving, Conflict Management and Misleading Assumptions

---

The present chapter underscores the localism of organizational adaptations. Just because one is a superordinate does not mean one has superordinate grasp of organizational realities. Superordinacy can be, and often is, as local as subordinacy. Superordinate relationships, power advantage, commitments, obligations, and access to information, put their particular stamp on superordinate members' problems, diagnoses, and solutions. The following narrative identifies a number of assumptions Sr. Jeanine and Sr. Georgette made which constituted important parts of the reality that was only locally theirs but which they regarded as encompassing Trinity.

o   o   o   o

Lighthall travelled out to the regional center to meet with Sr. Jeanine and Sr. Georgette. At the outset, Sr. Jeanine asked Lighthall for his assessment of the previous meeting. Lighthall's only comment was that 'there was a discontinuity between the information being given and the affect behind it', that it had been 'all very businesslike, but we weren't talking about "business"'. The implied suggestion that attention might be given directly to matters that most affected the co-directors *personally and emotionally* was pursued neither by Lighthall nor by the two regional administrators, Sr. Jeanine and Sr. Georgette. The two administrators spent the hour and a half exploring and then negotiating their respective preferences regarding a solution to their respective problems regarding Trinity's administration. Lighthall listened for almost the entire discussion, asking some questions toward the end.

Conflicting Views

Sr. Jeanine and Sr. Georgette had conflicting views, initially, about what needed to be done: they had synthesized different problems. Sr.

Georgette's problem was, on the one hand, wanting an unfettered, functioning administrator at Trinity and, on the other, being sharply aware that the co-directors had bogged down in a debilitating conflict. She had narrowed the issues to an either-or decision: either Sr. Norma or Sr. Claudia would take the reins at Trinity. Sr. Claudia was her clear choice.

Sr. Jeanine, however, saw two reasons for keeping Sr. Claudia and Sr. Norma in their present positions at Trinity. First, Sr. Jeanine felt Sr. Norma's interpersonal style was 'a lot gentler' than Sr. Claudia's, that Norma offered the Trinity faculty 'a buffer' from Sr. Claudia: 'People coming to her [Sr. Norma] sometimes find her more empathetic, initially, than Sr. Claudia'. Her second reason was more crucial, in her eyes. On no account, she felt, could their decision be such as to make it seem as if Sr. Claudia were replacing or 'displacing' Sr. Norma. To understand Sr. Jeanine's rooted commitment to keeping Sr. Norma visibly in place at Trinity, we need to present Sr. Jeanine's view of recent history at Trinity.

Two years before our arrival at Trinity, according to Sr. Jeanine, Sr. Claudia and another sister, who then held the position of Principal at Trinity, had come into conflict. The other sister had left Trinity after a good deal of tension and unfavorable sentiment toward Sr. Claudia. Sr. Jeanine's perception (whose validity Sr. Claudia expressly and forcefully doubted some years later) was that a substantial number of the school's staff, both lay and religious, had attributed that sister's leaving to Sr. Claudia's forceful will. There remained, Sr. Jeanine felt, a good deal of sympathy for the departed sister and some unfavourable sentiment toward Sr. Claudia. Later in the meeting Sr. Jeanine would express herself on this point:

> Sr. Jeanine: I submit that if we do one thing that publicly displaces Norma, Claudia is dead. Not just for this year but for good. And we might just as well face it. I don't think she could sustain the kinds of rejection she would get. (RAC:10/29/01; 1:360–364)

Sr. Jeanine shared that part of Sr. Georgette's problem that called for a freeing of Sr. Claudia to act, but doing so in the straightforward way Sr. Georgette wanted would 'displace' Sr. Norma and result in disastrous rejection of Sr. Claudia.

Sr. Georgette proposed a solution to her own problem. She was 'pushing', she said, for Sr. Claudia to be director knowing that 'they're still going to have all of their problems'. As director, Sr. Claudia would have sufficient 'psychological relief' to 'continue to operate'. Sr. Georgette was torn. Yes, she had to consider the persons. But she had to consider the organization, too, an organization with 'an awful lot of persons'. Her conclusion: 'So I'm not going to, like, save Norma's psyche or save Claudia's psyche and destroy Trinity'. Her 'working premise' was that 'the only person at this time, right now, that can keep Trinity going' was Sr. Claudia.

Sr. Jeanine worried about a statement she recalled Sr. Claudia had made: 'No matter what we [the co-directors] do for the rest of the year, . . .

I'm sure our communication will be written [not carried out face-to-face]'. Sr. Jeanine believed, she said, that Sr. Norma 'would really make an effort to be present for meetings physically'. She felt certain conditions must be fulfilled at Trinity: If they can't be person-to-person, once a week at a meeting where they're looking at the projection for the next week, I think it's impossible. (Ibid., 265–7) She was hopeful that the two sisters could work together, but only if Sr. Norma were not displaced by Sr. Claudia. She noted that Sr. Georgette had suggested earlier that 'we appoint her as director for the next year and a half but this not to be by way of announcement', that is, elevating Sr. Claudia from Acting Director to Director but continuing to keep that decision for a period of time private. Sr. Jeanine repeated that she could not 'possibly at this time say that the best action on our part is to say she is *the* executive director'.

Misleading Assumptions

Sr. Jeanine then stated her own position, reading from notes. As the notes are quoted, it will be useful to insert commentary on the assumptions being made.

> Sr. Jeanine: One: That . . . we affirm the role description to which they made commitments last Spring.

✻   ✻   ✻   ✻

> *Assumption 1:*   That re-affirming a role description that had already led to conflict would help clarify misunderstandings and mitigate conflict.[1]

In fact, the words of the descriptions themselves, using general labels for different areas of work and for procedures, had never been in dispute by the co-directors.

> *Assumption 2:*   That conflict could be avoided by dividing up areas of responsibility and conferring on the co-directors autonomy of control over their respective autonomous 'roles' or 'areas of responsibility'.

But this had already been a major assumption of the Trinity administration, one that denied functional interdependence among the 'areas' of the two co-directors.

✻   ✻   ✻   ✻

> Sr. Jeanine (continuing): Second: In the event of a default of either of them, it's our understanding that the other will act, assuming whatever responsibility and accountability is called for, with real

authority. And I think that gives Claudia all the authority she needs.

◦   ◦   ◦   ◦

Assumption 3: That the conflict that had occurred was due to the absence of, or confusion over, this stated principle of take-over rather than over a mechanism for invoking the principle. Sr. Jeanine was assuming either that the sisters had agreed to a mechanism for determining when default had occurred or that such a determination was a simple, straightforward matter.

In fact, both sisters understood this take-over principle in the abstract and agreed to it. It was not the words that were in dispute. What had been in dispute was whether, at any time, Sr. Norma had defaulted, i.e., whether the principle applied. In Sr. Norma's eyes, she had not defaulted sufficiently to invoke the principle. She had been ill, then had been prevented from assuming her duties. With two co-equal directors, there existed no super-ordinate mechanism — except repair to the regional level of authority — for determining when default had occurred. Sr. Jeanine's second point remained silent on such a mechanism.

◦   ◦   ◦   ◦

Sr. Jeanine (continuing): Then, thirdly: That in planning for 02–03 [the following year], which should already be in progress, it's understood that Sr. Norma is resigning. Therefore, the dominant role is Sr. Mary Claudia's and that Sr. Claudia is shortly, you know, after Norma's resignation . . . has come in, Sr. Claudia actively involves herself in a role description for the kind of associate she sees. And that we ask her to do this yesterday: 'You are director, 02–03 . . . What are the supporting roles that seem most reasonable, most effective to you?' . . . So that she has status in moving ahead for the next year and that her right to act is definitely affirmed at this level and that they continue to meet, you know, once a week [turning to Lighthall], with your outside help . . with your inside help and reflecting on the process . . . to keep the ship afloat and to keep their psyches somewhat intact for the year. I submit that if we do one thing that publicly displaces Norma, Claudia is dead . . .

◦   ◦   ◦   ◦

Assumption 4: That it would be possible for Sr. Claudia to move ahead quickly, after Sr. Norma's resignation 'has come in'. For her to move quickly would require a quick public announcement from Sr.

Norma. Until Sr. Norma made her intention to resign known, Sr. Claudia could not take any action toward personnel or policy planning as director for the following year. If she did, she would, in Sr. Jeanine's eyes, appear to be seeking a replacement for Sr. Norma before the latter had ruled herself out — an act to 'displace' Sr. Norma. Thus, it was assumed that Sr. Norma, herself, would initiate an early announcement, 'yesterday', to clear the way for Sr. Claudia's action.

To put the matter another way, Sr. Jeanine was making assumptions that we can see, with distance and focal thought unhurried by decision deadlines, were contradictory: (1) that Sr. Claudia should act immediately ('yesterday') and (2) that she wait for Sr. Norma to announce her resignation.

Assumption 5: That perhaps because a failure of the co-directors to meet weekly would render the Trinity situation 'impossible' and because a decision from the regional level would weigh heavily with the co-directors, they would actually meet weekly. Behind this was the assumption that new conditions, like new resolve and the constraint of superiors' decisions, could cause new behaviors in the absence of a change in old conditions — an implicit theory of change from the outside in, that is, a materialistic view, implicitly denying idealistic and constructivist views.

Assumption 6: That Lighthall's relationships with the two co-directors were, or could become in the context of a decision from the regional level, sufficiently positive to assist the co-directors in their working relationship at Trinity. In this assumption, Lighthall concurred at that point, having been encouraged by Sr. Norma's comments at the end of the previous regional center meeting. Let us continue the narrative.

         ☼   ☼   ☼   ☼

Sr. Georgette: Can I go back to ... where you say, 'We affirm the role description ... as you have them and our understanding .. defaults ...', then 'the other person assumes the responsibility' — which is their role. This is nothing new. [Sr. Jeanine: Umhmm.] ... What I'm saying is, like, that didn't help Claudia before. How come that's going to help her now?

Sr. Jeanine: Because I think that Norma's understanding of her role was that if .. well, she, first of all, admits that she wasn't present as much as she could have been. Now that admission didn't come out all the way, here, the other day.... But she also has made the statement of apology.... I think it was very hard for her to walk into the room and apologize to Claudia. And she did it and Claudia accepted it ...

＊ ＊ ＊ ＊

Assumption 7:　That Sr. Norma's admission (in private company) of past deficiencies and her offering to Sr. Claudia an apology which was then accepted constituted evidence of realities sufficiently changed to promise a change in interpersonal behavior and role performance.

But mere recognition of past behavior and expression of guilt or remorse, by themselves, have little or nothing to do with causes. In particular, they would not change the force of Sr. Norma's starkly (though not suddenly) shifted reality vis à vis the religious life vs. life as a laywoman, a force that operated outside the regional administrators' realities — and outside of ours. (Sr. Claudia had once mentioned casually to Lighthall that Sr. Norma, over the years, had expressed doubts about being suited to the religious life. There was no indication that such doubts had earlier interfered in Sr. Norma's performance of her duties.)

＊ ＊ ＊ ＊

Sr. Jeanine (continuing): Now I think that she [Sr. Norma] clearly understands that nobody around this table thinks you take care of things from a ... telephone to a secretary who's not empowered to act, that this is not adequate.

＊ ＊ ＊ ＊

Assumption 8:　That what those 'around this table', i.e., Lighthall and the two regional administrators, thought had some effect on Sr. Norma's role behavior at Trinity.

Sr. Norma was in important and focal ways unresponsive to what her closest co-worker thought. In some organizations someone in her position might be expected, nonetheless, to be influenced by what superordinates like Sr. Jeanine and Sr. Georgette thought. But the administration at the regional level had had a long history of purposefully granting wide autonomy to the school administrations under its jurisdiction. They did little more than approve budgets, appoint administrators, and intervene in crises, like this one. So in the press of daily activities Trinity executives rarely thought about how regional administrators might react to this or that decision or internal policy. (Sr. Claudia would continue to expect that degree of autonomy, supported by the regional administration's preoccupation elsewhere. Sr. Norma, moving away from the religious life, would be even less inclined to worry about what Sr. Jeanine or Sr. Georgette thought was appropriate role performance at Trinity.)

Assumption 9: That Mrs. Shulman, Sr. Norma's secretary, was not empowered, through Sr. Norma's delegations, to 'take care of things'.

Mrs. Shulman had become, through Sr. Norma's delegations, much more like an administrative assistant than a secretary.

> Sr. Jeanine (still continuing): So I see her [Sr. Norma] with a clearer understanding of her responsibilities and her saying she will do that. Now this has never happened before. They had never talked about what their mutual expectations were. (RAC:10/29/01; 1:334–425)

✽   ✽   ✽   ✽

Assumption 10: That the two sisters had, in fact, now talked through 'what their mutual expectations were'.

To the contrary, mutual avoidance characterized the co-directors' relationship; certainly the interchange of the previous meeting at the regional center in no way constituted a mutual setting of expectations.

✽   ✽   ✽   ✽

The extent to which Sr. Jeanine believed that Sr. Norma had reoriented herself to responsibility, accountability, and presence is revealed in an interchange with Sr. Georgette, where she demonstrated clear understanding of the impact of Sr. Norma's previous pattern of behavior on Sr. Claudia's reality:

> Sr. Jeanine [speaking as she believed Sr. Norma would, in response to Sr. Claudia's dissatisfactions with Sr. Norma]: ... 'I'm filling [my role] because I've covered this dance. So-and-so's there'. And then so-and-so .. [Sr. Norma] isn't even sure if she's [i.e., 'so-and-so' is] going to be there. She's [Sr. Norma has] sent her a note telling her to come. And so-and-so said, 'I'm nobody's fool. I'm not going. Call so-and-so'. So she [Sr. Norma] doesn't even know that Claudia has had to get into the act, which must have been infuriating — to appoint somebody to be there.
> And then Claudia would further punish her by not only appointing somebody to be there but Claudia would be there physically. So word would get out that besides running the school all day long, Claudia's been up at night at a dance. (RAC: 10/29/01; 1:425–432)

Sr. Georgette: But ... see, this is what I mean. Do you think that Norma is going to change her whole idea of, well, take that example.

Sr. Jeanine: Yeah, I do. I think that she heard Claudia say, 'Physical presence'.... But I think I would want to say it again: 'This means that you are going to be physically present to each other and physically in your place of business [i.e., office] every day'....

o   o   o   o

Assumption 11: That reinforcing admonitions from the higher administration would combine with apparent cognitive reorientations to induce changed behavior on Sr. Norma's part.

Assumption 12: That if the problem of mutual physical presence of the two sisters could be solved, their working relationship would be sufficiently restored. The implicit assumption behind this was that the failure of mutual physical presence was cause rather than effect. Sr. Norma's absences were, of course, cause. But they were also effect, caused by factors — e.g., Sr. Norma's alienation from the religious order and from executive meetings — which Sr. Jeanine was assuming were absent. She also seemed to be assuming that emotions — the mistrust and antagonism that had grown up between Sr. Norma and Sr. Claudia — were much less important than the co-directors' thoughts about role and responsibility.

o   o   o   o

Sr. Georgette (pursuing her objection): But what about student activities? ... Norma doesn't see any reason for her[self] to be physically present at every single student activity ... if she sees to it that a responsible person is there. Claudia's expectation is 'You are there', you know. And I don't know that Norma either can change that or should change it.

Sr. Jeanine: I don't either. But I think there are a couple of gray areas where Claudia's position could have been modified ...

o   o   o   o

Assumption 13: That for Sr. Norma to arrange for a responsible person to supervise a given student activity was a simple matter.

Such arrangements were not simple on three counts. First, what constituted 'responsible' supervision was not easy to determine in precisely those kinds of activities, like dances and pyjama parties, where hundreds of adolescents might be most difficult to supervise both wisely and effectively. Failures in adequate supervision could easily happen when the number of participants was large. And such failures almost always led to aroused parents on the telephone — as likely to be calling Sr. Claudia as Sr. Norma. The first stumbling block, then, were differences between the two co-directors in what constituted 'responsible' supervisors. Sr. Claudia believed that there were certain faculty members who would say yes to Sr. Norma's request to supervise but who would not supervise either wisely or effectively.

In the second place, finding persons willing to supervise extra curricular activities was not easy. One often had to take persons who were merely willing or compliant, not those whom one preferred. Sr. Norma had little real power in this matter. For example, Sr. Claudia, not Sr. Norma, evaluated the faculty and negotiated contracts with them. While a general clause in contracts bound faculty to participate in extra curricular activities, the clause was general. In any particular instance of an activity, faculty members could, and often did, refuse. As Sr. Jeanine had said, they were 'nobody's fool'.

Finally, Sr. Norma's 'requests' often took the form, as Sr. Jeanine earlier indicated, of commanding or assuming their cooperation, rather than asking, seeking help, or gentle persuasion.

While evidence of these three factors was clearly available to Sr. Jeanine (from her own experience as Principal at Trinity), they were not integrated into her thinking in the matter of whether the co-directors had 'talked about what their mutual expectations were'.

This lack of integration within Jeanine's own reality regarding the co-directors' mutual understanding was reflected in her reply to Sr. Georgette's further pushing. Sr. Georgette wondered why, if they could not come to a mutual understanding last spring, and if their relation would end in June, the co-directors should go through all the pain of further negotiation? Sr. Jeanine countered that from now until June was 'not a vacuum', and they had to work their way beyond 'their own closed understandings of what their role calls for'. But if they still had 'closed understandings', how mutual could their talking about their expectations have been? It was a question not asked by any of the three in that meeting.

○ ○ ○ ○

Sr. Georgette directed Sr. Jeanine's attention to the precise issues 'where we really differ':

> Sr. Georgette: Maybe what I'm saying basically is: 'They're never going to work it out. Never' . . . . They're going through the memo writing stage right now. . . . And so therefore . . . [six second silence] don't spend a lot of time . . . coming to a better

> understanding of their roles. I think time would be better spent projecting toward next year ... And in order to do that, I would like to have Claudia be able to take the direction of that. (RAC:Ibid, 438–485)

Sr. Jeanine had no difficulty with that, she said. But how could the two of them work together, she asked, if 'they don't understand what they are doing now'? Sr. Georgette saw their working relationship improving out of the initiatives that Sr. Claudia would be taking as sole director. She envisioned a scenario:

> Sr. Georgette: Sr. Claudia is Director. She sits down with Catherine and Norma, and Mr. Lighthall perhaps, and says, 'All right now, we have an area that we have not covered ... the business office ... We have to look at that area. We also have to look at Catherine's area again.... And Norma, we also have to look at your area. What things are we going to change?' ....
>
> In that kind of conversation, with a futuristic look, Norma's going to get insights into what's bugging her, Claudia is going to get insights into, maybe, where Norma's been overloaded or gotten all the ... unpleasant things [student discipline], which I would, maybe, resent too, and they're going to have to rearrange that. And so maybe Claudia will come to a better understanding and Norma will come to a better understanding, but it's not just looking at me. It's like looking at what would I plan for another person. (Ibid, 485–510)

In her last two sentences, Sr. Georgette was trying to imagine how the two sisters would re-negotiate roles without focusing directly on themselves — a negotiation, as it were, not in the first person, but in the third person.

Sr. Georgette tried to summarize Sr. Jeanine's position in a way that focused on the area of their agreements. The co-directors' 'role descriptions' would be the same as they had been, and 'if one defaults, the other has not only the right but the responsibility, the obligation, to step in and assume that responsibility. Okay'. They also agreed, she said, that in view of Sr. Claudia's appointment as director next year, Sr. Claudia would assume the directorship 'in plans and projections for next year'. Sr. Jeanine agreed, giving as a specific example Sr. Claudia's right to make 'final decisions on the kids who are coming January 8 to apply for next year ...'

At this point they had reached the major points of agreement they would put in writing four days later. Sr. Jeanine had secured the privacy of the shift, protecting Sr. Claudia while simultaneously acquiescing in Sr. Norma's position, stated at the previous meeting, that no shift in titles or authority be publicly visible back at Trinity. Sr. Georgette, in turn, had secured the authority she sought for Sr. Claudia to act. They had, thus, solved their respective problems regarding the Trinity co-directors. And in doing so, they had managed their initial conflict cooperatively — by inducing in each other a common reality from the initially conflicting ones.

Sr. Jeanine returned to her colleague's conclusion that the two co-directors would never be able to 'work it out'.

> Sr. Jeanine: I do think that without a lot of emo .. [laughs] without a lot of emotion, they have to hear each other say, 'These are ... my expectations ... of my role, and I commit myself to this. [And, referring to the other co-director's response:] These are the expectations of my role, that's going to be my nitty-gritty, day-to-day stuff, and I commit myself to that'. And then [mutual] challenge [she used gestures to indicate give and take over such statements]. (Ibid, 560–570)

✦   ✦   ✦   ✦

Assumption 14: That the two sisters could, and should, work out the 'nitty-gritty' of their commitments without a lot of emotion.

Sr. Jeanine's laughter in the midst of her assertion I take as evidence of her own doubts about the possibility of the sisters' avoiding emotionality in talking out their own role expectations. Was she assuming that the agreement that Sr. Claudia would assume the directorship regarding all matters related to the following year, that this official but private subordination of Sr. Norma to Sr. Claudia, would make face-to-face communication between the co-directors easier than it had been as co-equals?

✦   ✦   ✦   ✦

Sr. Georgette clarified with Sr. Jeanine that the date on which Sr. Norma would be expected to announce her decision not to continue at Trinity would be January 21, 02, the date when all new position openings in the region would be announced. None of the three noted the implications of this clarification for Sr. Jeanine's assumption that Sr. Claudia would begin authoritative planning 'yesterday', that almost two full months could pass before Sr. Claudia could consider 'yesterday' to have arrived.

Lighthall summarized his understanding: the wording of Sr. Jeanine's proposals called for the roles at Trinity to be transformed toward a single directorship. Sr. Jeanine demurred. She wanted, she said, to steer clear of any public implication that the role they were thinking of for Sr. Claudia for the rest of the year was that of single and sole director. Rather, they would emphasize only that they would be moving toward that kind of role for the following year. She explained the basis of her fear.

She had previously given Sr. Claudia a clear indication, she said, just before the Sunday, October 24 meeting, that she would be moved into the position of single, executive director at Trinity:

> Sr. Jeanine: ... we felt that Norma's health was such that she could not re-enter.... I said to Sr. Claudia, 'It is eminently clear to me that you cannot run a school with fifty per cent of total responsibility absent and that your evolution as *the* director is just as plain as anything you could possibly see. So I would suggest that you begin to look at ways that you can compensate for Norma's lack'.
>
> So I think she came [to the Tuesday, October 26 regional meeting] with the expectation of putting this on the table, you know. And it never got on the table. It's never been referred to again. So she may wonder, you know, did we have a hidden agenda in that meeting. Did we intend this to be a confrontation with her?
>
> I have no idea what she's dealing with in terms of us, you know. I gave her that as a strong [suggestion] ... [in response to Sr. Claudia's report, made to Sr. Jeanine as a friend who knew her, 'I've had it'.] So I said to her, 'I think that [finding ways to compensate for Sr. Norma's 'lacks'] would be positive, not just fault yourself because [taking the voice of Sr. Claudia's inner self] 'Have I been such a tyrant she can't work with me?' She said, 'I'm not saying that'. And I said, 'Not all the time, but you do say it once in a while'. And she does, you know, because she .. she really is very tender. (Ibid., 655–670)

o   o   o   o

The distance between the co-directors' realities and those of the two regional administrators is evident in the foregoing interchanges and assumptions. That distance was reflected in Sr. Jeanine's last comments. She knew she had pulled the rug out from under her friend, Sr. Claudia, reversing herself. She was able to empathize with the confusion that reversal must have caused in Sr. Claudia. She knew Sr. Claudia must be making interpretations of the reversal and of the fact that the matter had never 'got on the table'. Yet Sr. Jeanine had not been in touch with Sr. Claudia in that time to explain the basis of the reversal, or to promise explanations later, and thus bring Sr. Claudia's mystified wondering and interpretation to an end — or at least to a slow walk.

o   o   o   o

Reflections

Sr. Georgette turned to next steps in communicating with the co-directors. They talked of meeting with Sr. Claudia and Sr. Norma separately first, then together. Lighthall asked: Why separately?

Sr. Georgette (after a seven second silence): I guess I think that if .. I don't know. My first response would be .. I don't think Norma's going to have any problems with this at all. I don't know if Claudia will. And, like, if we have Claudia by herself [laughs], maybe we can cajole her into it, you know. That's my first reaction.

Lighthall: I see. Okay. Well, that tells me what you're driving toward.

Sr. Jeanine: See, if Claudia makes a public statement, it's awfully hard for her to get off it .. [Sr. Georgette: Right. Yeah.] .. and if she says, 'I won't do it', you know, 'That's okay. Go on, Norma, you can be principal', you know, then it's going to be awfully hard for her to accept ..

Lighthall: Okay, I see what you're driving at. The costs, of course, are that if they both accept what you say and interpret ..

Sr. Jeanine (interrupting): And interpret different things.

Lighthall: .. and each doesn't know what the other was told, then the stability [of common understanding] is lost. (Ibid, 780–811)

      ❍   ❍   ❍   ❍

Sr. Georgette's candid disclosure, that separate meetings with the two co-directors was to prevent Sr. Claudia from rejecting the solution that the two regional administrators had now forged, indicates not only her commitment to that solution but also her exclusionary stance regarding the legitimacy of Sr. Claudia's objections and, in general, Sr. Claudia's reality. It was all well and good to work cooperatively with one's immediate colleague, Sr. Jeanine, but Sr. Georgette preferred to substitute one-to-one cajoling of Sr. Claudia for the kind of negotiation she had just completed with Sr. Jeanine.

Sr. Jeanine supported the separate meetings with the two co-directors, but on different grounds. She feared Sr. Claudia making an impulsive public statement and then feeling so committed to it that it would be 'awfully hard for her to accept' the regional administrators' agreement. Both Sr. Georgette and Sr. Jeanine, then, were committed foremost to Sr. Claudia's acceptance of their agreement. Each wanted to avoid further difficult conflict management and so wanted to short-cut open discussion by arranging for the two of them to meet with one co-director at a time — a more forceful, 'cajoling' arrangement. In short, it was time, not for reality exploration and integration, but for compliance, for Sr. Claudia to agree overtly to constraints already worked out, not for her to continue to influence what those constraints might be.

      ❍   ❍   ❍   ❍

Sr. Jeanine had to rush off to a noon meeting. The two sisters hurriedly compared their crowded schedules and set meetings with Sr. Claudia the following Monday morning and with Sr. Norma Monday afternoon. (Sr. Jeanine indicated she did not even want to risk the two co-directors meeting in passing!) A meeting was scheduled with Lighthall and with all three Trinity executives on Tuesday. Sr. Jeanine rushed off.

Sr. Georgette and Lighthall then talked about two matters. First, what would be the details of a workable criterion by which either Sr. Claudia or Sr. Norma would determine when the other had been 'in default' and could assume the other's duties legitimately? The second question Lighthall raised was what Sr. Georgette and Jeanine had meant by comments earlier that Sr. Claudia had 'limitations' in 'participative management'.

Discussion of the workable criterion led to specifications that will be evident in a document to be presented in the next chapter, describing the full set of agreements that the regional administrators hoped would manage the co-directors' conflict for the rest of the school year.

Sr. Georgette's assessment of Sr. Claudia's limitations in participative management, however, sums up a tendency toward closure and action in Sr. Claudia that Allan and Lighthall had also observed, and that is evident in our narrative at various points. We close this chapter's narrative with Sr. Georgette's description, in response to Lighthall's question:

> Lighthall: I wanted to bring up your notions of Sr. Claudia's being limited in ... participative management. It's my observation that both Sr. Claudia and Sr. Norma have limitations and strengths in this area. And I wonder why you picked Sr. Claudia particularly.
>
> Sr. Georgette: Yeah. I don't know about Sr. Norma ... I've worked with Claudia .. we've worked together a lot ... for about the last four years [on matters relating to the religious community] ... and I'm not ... saying that Claudia is more limited than Norma.... Why I say this about Claudia is because, ah, she gets impatient. She can't wait. She sees a solution, say, ... she *sees* a thing, you know, and [speaking from Sr. Claudia's vantage point:] 'Why aren't we all?' you know .... We've talked about it, you know, to one another, because I thought I was bad on that until I saw her, you know. And then I realized ... you just can't go that fast ... (RAC: Ibid, 2:217–225)

Summary and Comment

The narrative and commentary of this chapter reveals how far super-ordinates' realities may make assumptions that do not correspond with observable realities, and thus be guided in diagnoses and corrective actions by their merely local, not validated realities despite energetic, focused gathering of data and despite deliberation.[2] While *routines* of the subordinate's situations come to be well known by superordinates, the capacity to penetrate realities relevant to emergent disturbances appears limited. Thus, superordinates' sense of the 'big picture' of their organization tends to be a routinized, smoothed out picture of normal, even ideal, functioning — where, for example, responsible executives, like Sr. Norma, do not delegate decisions to 'secretaries' like Mrs. Shulman. Under these conditions, this chapter's narrative illustrates, their intervention into emergent disturbances is easily vulnerable to misleading, even seriously misleading or observably false assumptions, undermining the effectiveness of their intervention.

Superordinates can reverse or exacerbate the effects of missing or distorting their subordinates' organizational realities, however, depending on their type of intervention. Briefly, if they intervene in such a way that they support reality exploration and integration by their subordinates, and where they resist any temptation to 'settle matters' by issuing orders or guidelines or solutions fitting their own realities, then the untoward effects of their localism can be mitigated or reversed. Interventions that would exacerbate the effects of intervening with merely local, routinized understanding are those which constitute forming a coalition with one of the conflicting subordinates or taking on the role of binding arbitrator without the monitoring and policing resources that such arbitration requires.

Notes

1. These assumptions became clear only later, reviewing transcripts of the meetings.
2. To be sure, the superordinates in this case had granted their subordinates (at all schools, not just at Trinity) great autonomy, thus becoming somewhat out of touch with the schools under their authority. Two connections put the more powerful of the two regional administrators in closer touch with Trinity than with other schools: the fact that the sisters on Trinity's faculty and Sr. Jeanine lived in the same convent and that Sr. Norma and Sr. Claudia had both been assistant principals under Sr. Jeanine at Trinity three years earlier.

Chapter 13

A Memorandum of Agreement and Autonomy Versus Interdependence

Back at Trinity, the co-directors were politely businesslike, but their actions showed tension. A field note, written after lunch on the day of the meeting with Sr. Georgette and Sr. Jeanine, gives a glimpse of that tension:

> Contact #50 — 10/29/01 — back at lunch in Trinity. Norma comes in and we sit, me eating and she drinking 7-Up ...
>
> I noticed Sr. Norma [across the table from me] stiffen and tense up at one point and felt vaguely aware that someone had come into the dining room behind me (but in view of Norma). In a few seconds, I glanced around, with the hunch that Sr. Claudia would be there. Sure enough, she was; writing something on the end table with her back to us. I had the impulse then to go over and tell her about the meeting [just finished, out at the Regional Center], but I did not. I continued the conversation with Norma and two male religious teachers ... and a moment later looked over to see if Sr. Claudia was still there. She had gone without a word to any of us. (Book IV, p. 112)

The separate meetings between the regional administrators and the co-directors took place on Monday, November 1 as scheduled.[1]

A Written Agreement

The Tuesday (November 2) meeting at the regional center, lasting an hour and a half, focused on a six-point memorandum of agreement. It had been written jointly by Srs. Jeanine and Georgette, setting forth products of their separate conversations with the co-directors. It is reproduced in facsimile as Figure 13.1. At the top right hand corner of Lighthall's copy of the memo appears the note: 'Confidential until January 30, 02, but "operationally this is effective now"', the last clause quoted directly from Sr. Jeanine.

The only information not on the memorandum itself which is worthy

Figure 13.1. The memorandum of agreement discussed and affirmed at the November 2, 01 meeting with the Trinity executives at the Regional Apostolic Center.

Confidential

Blessed Sisters of Trinity

Regional Apostolic Center

To	Sister Mary Claudia, Sr. Norma and Sister Catherine
From	Sister Mary Jeanine and Sr. Georgette
Regarding	Future Directions for Trinity High School Date

It has been affirmed by all concerned that Trinity High School's interests would best be served by a single administrative head. In view of Sister Norma's intentions for next year and our decision to appoint Sister Mary Claudia as Director for the next two years, we postulate the following:

1. We affirm the evolutionary roles of Sister Claudia and Sister Norma toward the effecting of this new role. We consider regular administrative meetings an imperative for this purpose.
2. We anticipate a modification of these roles throughout this present year. Such modification will be effected by a mutual working through of these roles with the assistance of Mr. Lighthall. Sister Mary Georgette will also try to be present to these meetings.
3. We expect that Sister Mary Claudia will function as Director in all those matters that pertain to the organization and planning for the school year, 02–03.
4. We expect that in the event of default of responsibility and/or accountability** on the part of either one, that the other director will assume full responsibility and accountability.
5. At this time, it seems to us, the retention of the present administrative titles is most beneficial to all concerned.
6. Sr. Norma's intentions for the 02–03 school year will be communicated at the appropriate time according to the personnel placement process. Trinity staff will be advised at this time, and negotiations for placement for 02–03 school year will take place as roles are evolved.

*   *

a. if one or the other fails to provide a 'working presence' to the other for more than 24 hours without a previous mutual agreement.
b. there will be no recriminations if this is effected.
c. this principle will apply until new explicit roles and expectations are developed mutually that pre-empt this condition.

of note, from Sr. Georgette's reading and commentary which opened the meeting, was her clarification of the sixth item — Sr. Norma's public communication of her intentions for the following year. Whereas the earlier date mentioned had been January 20 or 21, Sr. Norma was now expected, Sr. Georgette said, to announce her decision not to renew her present position in 'late December or early January'. Not only would this earlier announcement bring the 'yesterday' of Sr. Claudia's planning three weeks earlier, but also it would allow Sr. Claudia 'first crack' at recruiting the best administrative talent available for Trinity's administration.[2]

Even before Sr. Georgette had finished her opening, Sr. Claudia voiced a concern directly to Sr. Norma, about the Trinity council's autonomous functioning and her feeling an absence of executive influence over it. Sr. Norma said she could forestall votes by making sure matters had Sr. Claudia's input, but Sr. Claudia countered that she already was attending the meetings. What worried her was the actual vote. She did not want to end up vetoing, since that would undermine council members' commitment to the council. Lighthall extended the issue of influence and control:

> Lighthall: ... it seems to me that there's another issue here and that is how much power does either of you have to affect the council? .... That's got to be kept separate from the idea of getting the input in there ... Once you have a voting body, there it is. You have to deal with that. So, you may not have the kind of control you want anyway, but not because Norma has it.
> Sr. Claudia: No, no. No. I think .. that's one of the things that has to come up in terms of, you know, that group to change uniform policy for the whole school ... which is what they're asking to vote on ... at the last meeting ... Where do they make policy and where don't they make policy? If they are a policy-making .. I didn't realize, see, they were a policy-making group until [Sr. Norma: Well, I really ..] they started doing it.
> Sr. Norma: That wasn't the intent. The intent was that they would feed in to the administration ... (RAC:11/02/01; 1:177–188)

❁   ❁   ❁   ❁

Sr. Claudia was not only looking ahead to the council's future the next year; she was making yet another attempt to solve her problem of autonomous council functioning, the problem whose abortive solution, followed in Part Two, was still playing itself out back at Trinity.

❁   ❁   ❁   ❁

As the discussion about the council reached a lull, Sr. Norma addressed Lighthall in a way that was at once characteristic of her and wholly unexpected by Lighthall, catching him flat-footed:

> Sr. Norma: ... the whole question of the Trinity council, ... it's an experiment and there's lot of things we have to, you know, straighten out and I expect your [to Lighthall] assistance on that.
> Lighthall: Yes. Ri .. Well, that wh .. you know, that's where we started. I mean, I'm not here [at Trinity] because I had any

idea I'd ever be *here* [at the Regional Center]! (RAC, Ibid, 294–297)

    ✿   ✿   ✿   ✿

Sr. Norma often requested assistance from others by telling them simply that she expected it. What she had in mind is difficult to say, since she never referred to the matter again and continued to play only a peripheral role in the Trinity council.

    ✿   ✿   ✿   ✿

Sr. Claudia expressed her feelings about the second sentence of item one, regular administrative meetings:

> Sr. Claudia: . . . we could cop out and take care of things by means of, um, memorandum, you know . . [Sr. Norma: Sure.] . . . and so putting this in here, that we do have the meetings, you know, I see why you put that in there [laughs] . . . We could take that way and, you know, the temptation is strong. I'll be very honest. . . . So I think that's something that we should say, right out: 'This is here so that we don't cop out on it. And we're willing not to cop out on it'. (RAC: Ibid, 330–335)

    ✿   ✿   ✿   ✿

Sr. Claudia was almost certainly not merely summarizing an agreement in saying these words; she was adressing Sr. Norma obliquely, hoping to avoid a problem she feared. She held deep doubts about whether Sr. Norma would attend executive meetings regularly. By summarizing an agreement in these words, she was trying to urge Sr. Norma (and perhaps herself!) not to give in to the temptation to avoid face-to-face communication, not to 'cop out' by communicating via memoranda. Sr. Norma, it will be noted, was non-committal in reply.[3]

    ✿   ✿   ✿   ✿

Autonomy vs. Interdependence

Sr. Georgette explained that her work load would prevent her from attending executive meetings in the next few weeks. (Sr. Georgette would attend only one of the executive meetings the rest of the year, much to Sr. Claudia's well controlled disappointment and anger.)

Sr. Jeanine expanded on the necessity of communication between the two co-directors. In doing so, she revealed a way of construing the dual directorship and division of administrative labor at Trinity that sounded the theme of interdependence of functions, a theme heard before and to be heard again:

> Sr. Jeanine: I think that it's important for the two people who are at the top of *two different columns within the school* [emphasis added] to communicate on the process ... *Forget* their own roles. But Norma is going to be aware of some tensions within the school which will have serious ramifications for the faculty. Claudia is going to have some other considerations, things that she intends to do, like, next week, or things that she's had to modify and I think that besides projecting [toward the future], they have to keep informing each other about what's going on. Not what's going on in their lives or their roles, but what's going on in their areas. (RAC:Ibid, 339–345)

✿ ✿ ✿ ✿

Sr. Jeanine was focusing on the issue of ease and openness vs. avoidance of communication between the two sisters. She was using the weight of her voice to break down the barriers that had grown up between them. But the very terms of her urging unwittingly reinforced a major source of communication blockage between the sisters. She referred to 'two different columns within the school', by which she meant the two sets of functions and responsibilities that the co-directors had defined as their bailiwicks: for Sr. Norma, all matters pertaining to students — activities, discipline, dress code, attendance, and the like; for Sr. Claudia, curriculum, admissions, and all matters pertaining to the faculty — hiring, evaluation, termination.

Sr. Jeanine was aware that these two 'columns' of school life had 'serious ramifications' for each other, and gave one example of Sr. Norma being aware of something amiss in Sr. Claudia's domain, an instance where cross-domain communication was called for. But so long as the terms, 'column', and 'their areas' were used without addressing the powerful norm that had developed *against 'overstepping' one's domain*, the use of those terms would reinforce an outlook of separate domains. 'Overstepping' had come to mean not only taking action outside of one's domain, but also *concerning oneself* with the other's domain: one must avoid both.

To put the matter another way, no norm had developed among the Trinity executives supporting discussion by *all* of the executives of the school's functioning *as a whole*. To the contrary, the counter-norm had developed of not overstepping boundaries, boundaries delineated by the 'columns' or 'areas'. This counter-norm, easily seen now from a reading of all of the transcripts, was seen at the time only as an isolated fact, a norm that the participants would all agree had developed — if their attention had been drawn to it. But its implications for, and connections with, the communication blockage between the co-directors were not understood then by any of the participants.

Lighthall had earlier (see page 136) sounded the same theme Jeanine was here voicing, the *interdependence* of the 'areas' of functioning. But even in that earlier voicing of the need for communication, he did not see that it was the norm against overstepping boundaries that stood crucially in the way of effective cooperation between the co-directors.

❂   ❂   ❂   ❂

Continuing the narrative, Sr. Claudia responded with a clarification of her own, about what should and should not be the focus of their communications. She verified that Sr. Jeanine was advising that she and Norma 'not go back and reflect on the past', but rather 'to go ahead and do the present and the future ... We've had the other things out now and that's finished ...'

❂   ❂   ❂   ❂

If by this last sentence Sr. Claudia meant that the emotional antagonism of their relationship had been worked through to the point of resolution, she was, as we shall see, simply inaccurate in her assessment. Their interchanges had been sparse and fleeting for some time and as emotional as they sometimes did get, they never penetrated the core of Sr. Norma's shift in emotional commitments or their implications for, or connections with, her absences at Trinity.

❂   ❂   ❂   ❂

To a question from Lighthall about how the co-directors felt about moving away from 'the idea of a collective administration', Sr. Claudia replied that just because 'ultimate responsibility' lay with one person that did not mean that 'a decision is made by one person'. She said, 'I still believe that the more people are involved in a decision, the better chance you have of a wise decision'. Lighthall asked if she could think of a case where a single, final authority had been needed during the last year or two at Trinity. After denying that there had been a single case, Sr. Claudia described one where she was 'least sure' of a solid agreement with Sr. Norma:

> Sr. Claudia: ... I felt least sure of our agreement [about] curriculum changes that involved discipline ... [turning to Sr. Norma:] Last Spring, when you said, 'If you do this, then I can't be involved in it'. Do you see? You know, the study hall thing, for instance.
> Sr. Norma: Right.
> Sr. Claudia [speaking from Sr. Norma's vantagepoint at that time:]

'If they're not all assigned to study halls, then I'm not going to be involved in it'. Well, ... I didn't put them all in study halls. . . .

Sr. Norma: ... It isn't that I basically disagree in the theory of unscheduled time ... but in the ability of, you know, one person as the disciplinarian to handle the problems that arise due to it, is what our prob .. my problem was . . . .

Sr. Claudia: The whole thing last spring of whose fault, you know ... the problems of when students are free and they're misusing their time ... vandalizing and so forth, you know, well then it comes back and it's the fault of curriculum [the Curriculum Director, i.e., Sr. Claudia] ... or is it the fault of this one? ... If one person says, you know, 'That was a decision that I'm responsible for ..'

Lighthall [finishing her sentence:] .. then you can live with your bad effects ..

Sr. Claudia [with emphasis]: *You can live with your bad effects!* Do you see, then?

Lighthall: .. but if it's something that *he* did, [playing that role]: 'I ain't going to live with that!'

Sr. Claudia: Right. Right. [laughs] When it would be easy for me to say, 'Okay, you [Sr. Norma] didn't take care of it, you know, you weren't around'. Or for her to say, 'I can't help it. You made that kind of decision, and you freed all these people. How can I possibly be around [i.e., everywhere] in a school? ...' So either way .. But if one person does it and takes the responsibility for it then the chips fall there ... And I didn't really think that three years ago. (RAC:11/2/01; I:425–460)

o   o   o   o

Sr. Claudia was specifying effects of decisions made in one domain upon events in the other domain. But further, she was saying that decisions made in the other's domain held little commitment for oneself: while the effects were not restricted to a domain, the commitment to its legitimacy was so restricted. Even further, she was asserting a tendency to blame all untoward effects of a decision in X domain on the person whose domain that was, to wash one's hands of the matter — as an outsider might.

The correction for this condition, Sr. Claudia now saw, was a single person in 'ultimate' authority in the school.

o   o   o   o

A number of years later Lighthall read Sr. Claudia the foregoing transcripts of discussion of the 'study hall episode' and asked her about it. A segment of that later interview gives a glimpse of what Sr. Norma's reality probably was at the time:

> Lighthall: Let's see now, do I understand you correctly that . . . you did have unscheduled time and she did oppose it?
>
> Sr. Claudia: . . . her stand as I remember it was, you know. 'I can't continue to deal with it. It's just beyond me. And no one will help me'. [Uhhuh]
>
> I think what she was caught in was the fact that, like homeroom people wouldn't help her, teachers wouldn't help her and I think that she felt, probably, I didn't [help her]. Because I held to the thing of .. that part of the educational thing is the choice making [i.e., giving students free time to force choices, even if the choices are sometimes destructive]. We've got to find ways. (FFL:2/24/–; 1:75–83)

✿   ✿   ✿   ✿

Under the system of separate bailiwicks, one co-director could 'hold to' a policy that she knew was having disastrous effects on the other co-director's functioning and even in face of the other's lack of resources to cope with those spill-over effects. The events of the school were interdependent and ramified across all bailiwick boundaries. But the authority for, and commitment to decisions were specific to bailiwicks. Sr. Norma did not have the legitimate authority to veto Sr. Claudia's policy of allowing juniors and seniors free time out of class and study halls even though that policy was having overwhelming effects in Sr. Norma's bailiwick. The very definition of legitimate authority, via the norm against 'overstepping', denied the interpenetration and interdependence of causes and effects across these categories of authority, these 'columns' of responsibility.

The narrative to this point reveals that the regional administrators had tacitly made an important choice regarding the co-directors' conflict, a choice among three alternatives. They might have elected, first, to address Sr. Claudia's problem primarily, forming in effect a coalition with her against Sr. Norma. Sr. Georgette initially leaned in that direction. Second, they might have taken the role of mediator, addressing the conflict by, first, insisting that the two sisters confront their conflictful working relationship and, second, assisting their efforts in working through to a mutually acceptable resolution. In this approach, the regional directors would resist becoming the agents of reality integration themselves, leaving that agency with the co-directors. Finally, they might take an arbitrational role, assuming the task themselves of reality integration and from the realities integrated, fashion a settlement whose substantive terms would then be imposed and then policed.

By assuming the arbitrator's role, Sr. Jeanine and Sr. Georgette implicitly decided that they, not the co-directors would integrate whatever realities were to be integrated. Their various meetings with Sr. Claudia and Sr. Norma were to inform themselves of their relevant realities and then to test them out with the two co-directors and with each other. The arbitrator's imposition of a solution from such a process can work, however, only when the parties in conflict are so pained by their own failures in resolving their conflict, that they secure an arbitrator they both can trust and hand over to the arbitrator total control for settlement. When the arbitrator also has resources and legitimate authority to monitor the parties' degree of conformity and to sanction violations, then arbitrated settlements can force integration of realities from the top down because desperation has readied the parties from bottom up. Were these conditions met in the present instance? Sr. Claudia said she wanted just some decision. She seems to have suspected at some unconscious level, however, that there would be pressures to 'cop out', to avoid regular meetings. Her suspicion had at least one solid basis: Sr. Norma had never legitimated the regional directors' role as arbitrator. She believed she had been called to the meeting with Sr. Georgette in order to inform Sr. Georgette about conditions in high schools, but found that it had something to do with 'rumors' that she had 'walked out on Trinity', which she flatly denied. Would the weight of the regional administrators' efforts prevail nonetheless, and bring about new dispositions and outlooks sufficient to replace the co-directors' mutual exclusion with an effective, working relation? Thus far, Sr. Claudia and Sr. Norma had served Sr. Georgette's and Sr. Jeanine's attempts to integrate the constitutent realities. Sr. Georgette and Sr. Jeanine had not promoted reality integrations by Sr. Claudia and Sr. Norma. Could the memorandum of agreement of November 2 bring that about?

Summary

The narrative reveals an arbitrational approach by the regional administrators to solving their problem regarding the debilitating conflict at Trinity. Commentary on that implicit choice from among alternatives, on the conditions and resources required for arbitration to achieve reality integrations, and on the question who should work out reality integration all lead to the question whether the memorandum of agreement can lead to sufficient 'meeting of minds' for the co-directors to re-establish a working relation at Trinity.

The narrative and analysis also disclosed once again how the participants organized their realities regarding the co-directors' roles around relatively autonomous categories of work and how these categories might undermine cross-role communication about work when they were accompanied by a strong norm against 'overstepping' one's domain. The narrative also revealed how the co-directorship's separate domains had led Sr.

Claudia and Sr. Norma to reject responsibility for 'bad effects' in one's own domain that resulted from decisions made by the other co-director in her domain — another triumph of localism in organizational realities over integration of organizational realities.

Notes

1. The only data I have regarding these separate meetings are comments from the meeting of all parties on Tuesday, whose taped excerpts appear in this chapter.
2. A contradiction lay undetected in Sr. Georgette's statement that Sr. Norma's announcement would come in late December or early January, on the one hand, and Sr. Jeanine's statement, noted on Lighthall's copy of the letter of agreement, that its contents would remain confidential until January 30. If this agreement was to be kept confidential until January 30, then so could Sr. Norma's announcement.
3. While the letter's first 'postulate' made explicit provision for regular meetings among the executives at Trinity, no provision was made for the parties to review either the agreement or the co-directors' working relationship. The letter and its accompanying discussion meeting settled matters for the regional administrators.

Chapter 14

The Relationship Between the Co-Directors Improves, Then Deteriorates

---

Relief

The November 5 regular Friday executive meeting was the occasion for genuine collaboration between the co-directors. Not the slightest uneasiness or antipathy between Sr. Claudia and Sr. Norma was evident. The three executives expressed themselves actively and were open to each other's quite conflicting realities on a matter of admissions policy. Right after the meeting all who were there went to lunch together. Sr. Claudia and Sr. Norma sat side by side. Lighthall thought the seating and the tone of the conversation remarkable, and wrote a field note depicting the seating with the comment: 'An easy-going lunch with Norma and Claudia exchanging with remarkable ease and fluidity'. Later he talked with Sr. Claudia about 'the freedom that you seem to be having in interchanges with Norma today at lunch and the other day [out at the regional center]'. He asked, 'What happened?'

Sr. Claudia said that she and Sr. Norma had not 'discussed the thing' (i.e., their previous conflict) outside of the meetings at the regional center. She said she felt a great sense of relief. Responding to Lighthall's query regarding the source of her relief, she answered, 'a decision . . . I think that's what I was asking for all along: "Could we please have a decision?"'. She repeated, 'I feel, you know, a great deal of relief . . . . And I honestly interpret that Norma does, too'.

> Sr. Claudia: When we were coming home [from the regional center, three days earlier], the three of us, . . . I did say, 'Norma, now, does this make you feel . . you know, do you feel that you can move in this direction . . . that we can move on, plan for the future and, you know, we won't be looking back thinking recriminations?' And she said she felt very strongly that there would be no reason why we couldn't . . . .
> The way things have gone this week, . . . that's the way we

were almost three years ago, you know, in terms of her being able to pick up the phone and say .. without any tension, you know, ask me a question and how I feel about it and I can do the same ... a great relief.

Sr. Claudia said she was surprised at how smoothly their interactions had been going, even doing complicated and previously difficult joint tasks like the morning's discussion of the admissions policy for the next year. In reply to Lighthall's question about how she saw that morning's (November 5) meeting, she said, 'It was one of the best executive meetings we've had in terms of ... that policy on admissions'.

Why had the morning's interaction been so fluid and easy? Perhaps each was on her best behavior, and wanted to make the settlement work. Perhaps the recent clearing of the air between them, while by no means complete, had neutralized enough of their mutual antagonism to promote feelings of good will. Perhaps Sr. Claudia's unusual move of bringing a genuine problem to the meeting, rather than a pre-formed solution, stimulated genuine participation. Most likely all of these contributed to the noticeably increased ease of that morning's interaction.

The executive meeting the following week also revealed cooperation and good will between Sr. Norma and Sr. Claudia. If we take as our unit of analysis Sr. Claudia's problem-solving and conflict-managing episode with Sr. Norma from September through November 12, therefore, we have in hand an instance of successful problem-solving on her part, and successful conflict management by both co-directors. The processes which led to the November 2 letter of agreement, therefore, most notably Sr. Claudia's recruitment of the help of the regional administrators and their arbitration of the co-directors' differences, would constitute effective problem-solving and conflict-managing processes.

But this problem solving and conflict managing went on in the context of a larger cultural unit of time, namely the school year. Did the processes lead to an outcome that endured through that school year? No. Relief from conflict was short lived.

Underlying Conflict Emerges Again

An early sign of Sr. Norma's renewed disengagement came to Sr. Sonia Hallahan. Sr. Claudia's mother had cancer and Sr. Claudia had gone out of town to be with her because she had learned her mother was dying. Characteristically, Sr. Claudia telephoned Sr. Sonia from her mother's home to conduct some unfinished work. She asked Sr. Sonia to inform Sr. Catherine and Sr. Norma that she would be unable to return in time for the Friday (November 19) executive meeting. Sr. Sonia delivered the message about Sr. Claudia's delayed return and about her mother's condition. Sr. Norma's response to the news struck a discord in Sr. Sonia. As Sr. Claudia later related it from Sr. Sonia's account, Sr. Norma's first response to the news was, 'Oh, good. We won't have the meeting tomorrow'. It was only after that response that Sr. Norma expressed sorrow at Sr. Claudia's mother's condition. Part of the discord for Sr. Sonia was that she was aware that Sr. Norma had known Sr. Claudia's mother for twenty-five years. This event was just a little over two weeks after the November 2 letter of agreement, and just a week after an executive meeting in which communication and collaboration between the co-directors was easy and fluid.

Sr. Claudia later inferred that Sr. Norma's aversion to the executive meetings stemmed from Sr. Claudia's (overt and businesslike) planning of administrative roles for the next year. Sr. Claudia felt that her discussion of administrative roles in the previous executive meeting might have reminded Sr. Norma of Sr. Norma's (now firm) decision to leave Trinity. At least as important, I believe, was the evidence plainly visible to Sr. Norma from that previous discussion that the Trinity administration would continue matter-of-factly without her. To be made conscious of one's easy replaceability as one leaves an organization is likely to accelerate, not decelerate, one's withdrawal.

As it happened, Sr. Norma did attend the November 19 executive meeting, making her own brief report of actions taken and pending[1]. Four days later, Sr. Norma was absent from a regularly scheduled meeting of the Trinity council. Sr. Claudia had asked Sr. Norma to come to the regular executive meeting on December 3 prepared to describe her various responsibilities as co-director. This Sr. Norma did. She elaborated in a way that throws light on her disaffection from her own role:

> Sr. Norma: I don't know what the solution to this thing is, because it's been a hassle that I've been going through myself, you know. Um, to give somebody just discipline [without other contacts with students] is a pretty hard task ... you have to have something else, I think ... you know, the image you create. If that's the image that the students have [of one's role as disciplinarian], and that's the only image that they have, then I don't think you have the power, when you're dealing with an individual discipline case, to have them realize that there's another side of you.[2] (E:12/03/01; 2:40–50)

On December 7 the first of two bulletins (the second on Dec. 16) to homeroom teachers from Sr. Norma showed signs of her deep frustration at the faculty's response to 'the uniform problem'. The bulletins were couched in a demanding, peremptory tone and placed responsibility for detailed monitoring of the girls' attire and for enforcing even small deviations from the dress code squarely with the homeroom teachers.[3]

The tone and content of Sr. Norma's demands are captured in the following sentences:

> If there is no parental note, a personal detention must be issued to the girl and the homeroom teacher is responsible for the girl serving it for her (or him).
>
> In the event a class teacher finds a student out-of-uniform during the day, the girl is to be sent to Sr. Norma's office for an out-of-uniform slip and a detention. The detention slip will be sent to the homeroom teacher to take care of.[4]
>
> The uniform problem is out of control, and unless EACH homeroom teacher cooperates, it becomes more difficult to handle.

Excerpts from Sr. Norma's December 16 bulletin reflect increased intensity of insistence:

> The 'uniform problem' is out of control and the students and teachers are not cooperating with the directions stated in my bulletin of December 7.[5]
>
> If a girl is sent to the office after homeroom period by a subject teacher, we will follow the above procedure and notify the homeroom teacher in writing of his/her oversight.

◦　◦　◦　◦

These bulletins do little to present the realities to which Sr. Norma and Mrs. Shulman were forced daily to respond. Instead, they present detailed solutions, solutions to problems in *their* local realities, not the realities of the homeroom teachers. In effect, Sr. Norma is directing the teachers to respond with her solution to her (unstated) problem, thus by-passing or ignoring the teachers' own realities. Sr. Norma was thus assuming either that the teachers' realities were substantially the same as hers in this matter of uniform violations or simply that homeroom teachers do what Directors of Student Affairs tell them they must do — both assumptions normally false.

But her reality exclusion in these bulletins goes a good deal further. It is manifestly clear that Sr. Norma (and Mrs. Shulman, who probably composed them from dictated notes) had not beforehand sought out a sampling of homeroom teachers' realities in face-to-face conversations — opportunities for which presented themselves daily at lunchtime. The homeroom teachers did not have the opportunity, as Lighthall had on November 19 (see note 1), to present a portion of their own reality to Sr. Norma and thus set off an exchange of realities, each enlarging the other's, so that a shared reality emerged to which both could respond in common. Sr. Norma, thus, not only excluded her own realities from these bulletins, but also excluded the homeroom teachers' realities regarding the uniform problem.

Finally, the realities which do find their way into the bulletins are contradictory. While the manifest *content* of the bulletins reveals that Sr. Norma is observably dependent on the homeroom teachers — and therefore, that they have the power to control outcomes important to her, the dominant *tone* of the bulletins denies dependence and asserts, instead, directiveness and power. The dominant tone, thus, denies a reality otherwise evident, and provides a challenge to the homeroom teachers, thus further diluting any cooperative effort the bulletins might elicit.

The procedure which Sr. Norma had (unilaterally) established made homeroom teachers vulnerable to class teachers' later actions. For example, if Mary O'Neill came to school wearing a sweater (not considered part of the uniform) which went undetected by a homeroom teacher but was later detected and reported by a class teacher, the homeroom teacher would now be reminded by Sr. Norma's office of her 'oversight'. Sr. Norma was implying that she would now supervise the homeroom teacher's behavior!

These bulletins, together with Sr. Claudia's merely referring the complaining teachers to Sr. Norma, bespeak a lone administrator increasingly frustrated by widespread non-cooperation — just one more reason for Sr. Norma to accelerate her withdrawal from Trinity.

o   o   o   o

Sometime between December 7 and December 14 a number of homeroom teachers complained to Sr. Claudia about Sr. Norma's new demands. Sr. Claudia referred them to Sr. Norma, but our data do not include any subsequent interchanges. No more bulletins on this problem were forthcoming.[6]

On December 9 Sr. Florence Ellen, returning to Trinity to repair her relationships with Sr. Claudia and Sr. Norma, having left precipitously the previous summer, added new signs of Sr. Norma's alienation. As Sr. Claudia related it the following day, Sr. Florence Ellen had put her arms around Sr. Claudia and apologized, weeping with remorse. After she had 'got that out', as Sr. Claudia put it, she explained that she had felt impelled to come to Sr. Claudia to straighten out their relationship. After seeing Sr. Claudia, she had planned also to see Sr. Norma, but explained that that was not going to be possible. She said Sr. Norma was too upset to see her, reporting to Sr. Claudia, 'Sister, you just have to know that she's leaving'. The next day, when Sr. Claudia related the interchange to Lighthall, he asked and Sr. Claudia confirmed that she meant leaving the religious community. Lighthall then asked whether that made 'a hassle' for Sr. Claudia.

> Sr. Claudia: It doesn't make a hassle for me. But it sure makes a hassle for her. I don't think somebody who's been under vows for [more than twenty] years gives it up ... in terms of somebody who's waited this long to do it, it must mean a tremendous

amount. And so I was thinking of that kind of tension working with the school tension as probably, you know, [leaves sentence unfinished].... If this is true, then I understand the fact that she find .. you know, evidently finds it more and more difficult to remain [at work in the school]. She's out in the evenings and she finds it hard to deal with. And she finds it very hard to remain in her office ... She's leaving her office by thr .. before three o'clock or something. (FL:12/10/01; I, 999–1061)

Sr. Norma called Sr. Claudia early in the morning of December 10 from her office to explain that she would be unable to attend that day's regular executive meeting. She felt too ill, she said. On his way out of Sr. Catherine's office, where he had heard about the cancellation, Lighthall met Sr. Norma. His field note records that 'Norma seemed to have a slight cold but otherwise seemed brisk and in good spirits. She laughed heartily [about how wrong certain girls had been in predicting a low turn-out for a traditional vacation trip over the up-coming holiday]'.

In the course of discussion with Sr. Claudia immediately thereafter, Lighthall voiced worries about an apparent increase in Sr. Norma's emotional tensions — evidence for which Lighthall took to be the December 7 and 16 bulletins to the homeroom teachers together with an abortive attempt by Sr. Norma in the December 7 Trinity council meeting, successfully resisted by the council, to halt after-school student activities promptly at 4:30. Sr. Claudia's first response was to worry that she had again caused pressure for Sr. Norma by moving on with plans for the following year. Then she enlarged on her relationship with Sr. Norma:

> Sr. Claudia: We're back at a point where Sr. Norma can hardly communicate with me outside of the business situation again, you know. And the same is true [of Sr. Norma's communication] with Sr. Catherine.
>
> [After an extended discussion of the meaning of Sr. Norma's December 7 bulletin to the homeroom teachers] ... and now she's withdrawing more and more from the Community and more and more from me in any kind of a social relation — not that we have had .. we have not had any kind of unpleasant discussion at all. But we haven't had any discussion that hasn't been a business thing ... So I feel we've regressed in terms of what was occurring after our understanding [on November 2].

If December was a period of increasing frustration and alienation for Sr. Norma, it was also a period of increasing frustration for Sr. Claudia, but frustration born of *increased* commitment and involvement in the governance of Trinity. All the evidence suggests that what Sr. Claudia wanted to say to Sr. Norma at this point, was the following:

Norma, in order to get on with hiring the very best people possible for these new administrative positions, the faculty needs to know, from you, that you are not returning next year. Until you make that announcement publicly, I cannot talk with anyone. Time is running on, and I am increasingly anxious about people who might be available for these positions making other plans for next year. So, in order for me to let them know about these new positions and for me to talk to them, will you please make your resignation known to the personnel office by the end of December and then make your public announcement to the school community by the first week in January?

Sr. Claudia could not bring herself, however, to speak plainly to Sr. Norma and to make that request explicit. What she did say to Sr. Norma was indirect, a kind of hinting around, hoping that Sr. Norma would catch her drift:

> Sr. Claudia [to Sr. Norma]: I think, like, I don't want to put us under pressure of time, but, you know, we'll have the month of January to get sister personnel. You know. And so I'd like to think in terms of the fact of, um, if we're going to pull a department chairman out, for instance, of someplace, to put her in [into the new role of class disciplinarian][7] then I think in fair . . . you know, I really would like to be able to try to contact a sister or . . if you're going to get somebody with the credentials to take care of the . . or whoever you pull out from any place, if possible, like, for economic reasons if for no other. And, um, so it's . . it's im . . that's why I picked . . I'm pressuring, I think, a little bit. I'm feeling a time pressure.
>
> Lighthall: It's not premature at all.
>
> Sr. Norma: Right.
>
> Sr. Claudia: Especially . . and then if we say, you know, the whole training time I think is going to be so important for the people coming in, to give them a chance to work through all the things that happen in the Spring . . .

This attempt by Sr. Claudia to influence Sr. Norma's time schedule went right by Sr. Norma. In a conversation with Lighthall four days later, when Sr. Norma was absent, Sr. Claudia could be quite explicit and straightforward: 'In the kind of time schedule I am thinking of, by the end of December Sr. Norma will make her resignation known to the personnel office . . . and in early January I'd like her to make her position . . you know, her resignation known to the school community itself'. She complained that her current attempts to feel people out regarding their possible willingness to take one of her administrative posts were 'so sub-rosa'.

By January 7 Sr. Norma still had made no move to make her resignation known, and Sr. Claudia's slightly increased directness was still embedded in vagueness:

> Sr. Claudia: Sr. Carrie [in charge of personnel at the regional center] will be communicating with the sisters by the end of next week [Sr. Norma: Umhmm.] about administrative openings. And I was wondering if .. how we wanted to handle this, you know, in terms of notifying the whole faculty or do you want to keep it just with the sisters and have the faculty, you know, hear about it through them?

Sr. Norma replied that she was to meet with Sr. Carrie 'early next week' and that she would follow Sr. Carrie's announcement, due on January 14, with one of her own. By January 14 Sr. Claudia had decided to go ahead even in the absence of an announcement from Sr. Norma 'because there are certain people I want'. She had reached the point, she said, 'of absolute frustration [uttered in high-pitched tones] as far as how to push along through this year without, um, running into barriers'. But the following Monday, January 17, Sr. Norma did circulate a letter to the entire faculty announcing that she would 'not be returning to Trinity for the 02–03 school year' and asking for their 'continued support during the second semester'.

✿   ✿   ✿   ✿

Sr. Norma's pursuit of her path toward autonomy was untouched by the November 2 letter of agreement. She continued to withdraw time and energy from her Trinity commitments to other commitments. Sr. Norma's private and unilateral decision to leave the parent organization brought into her relation with Sr. Claudia an *asymmetrical dependence*, and therefore asymmetrical power.[8] One way to think of Sr. Norma's withdrawal is to see her as seeking her own independence. That is partly accurate: she was seeking independence from the Blessed Sisters of Trinity. But she was also seeking a new dependence, a dependence upon people and conditions outside the religious order. She was, in short, shifting her own base of dependence, from the relatively protected and protecting religious order to other persons, institutions, and conditions in the wider society and culture. She was doing so, however, independent of the Blessed Sisters of Trinity and of her co-workers, and without telling them of her withdrawal of time and energy from her own administrative functioning. In our terms, she was solving her problem regarding lay vs. religious life in an exclusionary mode, preventing some of those most severely affected by her solution (and her implementation of it) from any part in integrating their realities into either solution or implementation. In Sr. Jeanine's terms, Sr. Norma was again failing in 'accountability, responsibility, and presence'.

Sr. Claudia's increased responsibility for Trinity's administration (or, as she thought of it, governance) the following year made her *more, not less* dependent on Sr. Norma. In regard to a number of dimensions of administrative life (all those involving Sr. Norma's bailiwick), Sr. Norma's power over Sr. Claudia had increased in precise proportion as Sr. Claudia's dependence on Sr. Norma had increased (Emerson, 1962). Sr. Claudia's 'absolute frustration', was a frustration of being *responsible* for setting up a new administrative structure while being *powerless* to do so, a powerlessness due precisely to her dependence on Sr. Norma's choice of timing.

The foregoing focuses on the co-directors' relationship. If we look closely, however, at Sr. Claudia's own attempts to communicate to Sr. Norma her salient realities of time pressure and dependence on Sr. Norma's timing, it becomes clear that Sr. Claudia's own indirect, vague, 'pussy-footing' mode of communication to Sr. Norma played an important role in creating Sr. Claudia's own 'absolute frustration'. We cannot know how Sr. Norma would have responded to a forthright representation of Sr. Claudia's reality regarding timing of the public announcement, but it is clear that Sr. Claudia's own communications prevented Sr. Norma from even receiving a clear representation of Sr. Claudia's reality regarding Sr. Norma's delayed announcement.

Summary

Sr. Norma's reality, dominated by her social, emotional, and economic shift from religious to lay life, again exerted its dominant influence in her work and relation with Sr. Claudia. That dominant reality of a wrenching shift was still kept private, protected from integration with Sr. Claudia's realities. Having escaped integration by the now completed efforts of the regional administrators, it was, so to speak, home free. It was a reality of independence seeking, of denying dependence, with all that that implied for sharing realities. Sr. Norma would protect her emotional alienation and re-alignment while still maintaining organizational membership and position.

Notes

1. She stayed only long enough to hear Sr. Catherine's brief report, leaving before a lengthy discussion among Lighthall, Allan, Patrick (a student intern) and Sr. Catherine of a problem in Sr. Catherine's bailiwick. At this point it is important to include an interchange between Lighthall and Sr. Norma that bears on their relationship.

    In the half hour before that November 19 executive meeting, Sr. Norma tersely asked Lighthall into her office to voice an objection to her 'being involved in this' — her reference was at first vague. Lighthall thought at first that 'this' referred to her entire participation in the research-consultation project. He began to become inwardly indignant that she should so peremptorily, so unilaterally, and apparently so whimsically be able to bring the entire project to a halt. He asked her if she shared the espoused values of the Blessed Sisters of Trinity in self improvement through self examination, values that could be served by examining the kinds of data that he and Allan were gathering. She had not been prepared to deal with this larger issue, having had in mind, as it turned out, a much more limited one, and suggested that they talk further, after she took care of an emergency. When she returned, she closed the door and pulled up a chair obliquely to Lighthall's, choosing not to sit behind her large desk, and clarified herself further.

She objected to a question he had asked her earlier, a question she had readily answered at the time, about the most important part of the text, *The Ways, Virtues, and Directions*, universally used in the training of novitiates of the Blessed Sisters of Trinity during the period of Sr. Norma's and Sr. Claudia's novitiate. She felt that matters of religious life were private. In the subsequent clarification, she said she had been holding back a great deal so that what she did say could be published.

When Lighthall asked about her part in the executive council and the Trinity council, she indicated that her being involved in those observations was all right, but that more personal or private matters she did not want to get involved in. A field note goes on to report that 'she said she was going to leave at the end of the year and she did not want to make any investment in any change'. She could 'go along with' others' desires to have him and Allan involved in the Trinity and executive councils, but that private life was different. Lighthall agreed, explaining that he had been interested in some general impacts of religious training on the sisters, not on Norma in particular. She seemed relieved to know, he noted in his field notes, that he had asked Sr. Sabrina the identical question. They went on, indeed, and explored a wholly different episode between Sr. Norma and a student (not reported here), with Sr. Norma quite forthcoming in relating details.

A nascent conflict between them, then, was talked through, with the outcome first, that Lighthall avoided further inquiry with Sr. Norma on anything pertaining to religious life and second, that the way was clear to proceed with the research-consultation with Sr. Norma as (an increasingly withdrawing) participant.

2. Sr. Norma and Sr. Claudia had defined Sr. Norma's role in the context of an earlier Trinity administration in which they both were assistant principals. As defined, the role included not only student discipline but also all extra-curricular activities with a good deal of direct contact with students possible. Evidently Sr. Norma was no longer able to make that side of her role a source of satisfaction or a way to present 'another side of you' to the students.

3. Homerooms were classrooms where girls of a given class (freshmen, sophomores, etc.) gathered at the beginning and end of each day for fifteen minutes to hear announcements about school and class events and to participate in brief prayer. The homeroom teacher's ties with homeroom students was the weakest of all teacher-student ties, since it was the briefest and entailed no curriculum or instruction. The rewards of homeroom duty came, if they came at all, from teachers' informal, friendly interactions with students. If the homeroom teachers accepted Sr. Norma's demands that they take seriously the policing and enforcing of the dress-code, it would have two effects. It would insert an evaluative and punitive quality into the otherwise informal relationship between homeroom teacher and student and it would add yet another non-teaching duty, a duty that required scrutiny of the dress of upwards of thirty students each morning — to say nothing of the unpleasantness of confronting students even partly out of uniform with an after-school detention. If that weren't bad enough, in the homeroom teacher's reality, she (or he) would in all likelihood have to stay after school personally, with the student, to enforce the detention, a local reality Sr. Norma gave little weight to in her attempt to influence the homeroom teachers.

4. The use of the phrase 'sent to Sr. Norma's office', using the third person rather than the first, probably indicates that Mrs. Shulman composed the bulletins, along lines indicated by Sr. Norma.

5. In a hallway count, Lighthall tested his hypothesis that no serious deviation from the uniform code existed. Out of 55 persons passing he counted 2 girls with minor variations in uniform — 96.4 per cent conformity. Lighthall's conclusion that there was no uniform problem, let alone one that was 'out of control', and that Sr. Norma was therefore over-reacting was, however, erroneous. In the context of hallways and homerooms, 96.4 per cent conformity could be no problem. But in a school of more than a thousand girls, dealing with 3.6 per cent of the population *each day* as deviants would be an overwhelming task for a single office. All the more so when one contemplates the emotional responses of the girls *and their mothers* to assertions that they were not in proper attire. Lighthall's error was to assume that his local reality in the hallway was Sr. Norma's local reality in her office; his attribution of the cause of Sr. Norma's confronting a problem where he saw none existing to Sr. Norma being psychologically 'overloaded', was a simple case of what Ross (1978a) calls the 'fundamental attribution error'. In fact, Sr. Norma may well have been *both* psychologically overloaded, with her own shifting commitments, *and* confronted with an objective overload of uniform violations.

6. Sr. Claudia's referring the homeroom teachers to Sr. Norma might be seen as reflecting once again the separation of bailiwicks. But teachers' duties were also a part of their contracts, which were in Sr. Claudia's domain. This matter, as with so many others, crossed bailiwicks. Sr. Claudia selected Sr. Norma's involvement as dictating a referral of the teachers to Sr. Norma; she could as well have selected homeroom teachers' contractual obligations, thus synthesizing it as her own problem. That would have brought her into a three-way interchange with the homeroom teachers and Sr. Norma, however, an unpleasant prospect for her — one that could easily have tipped the scale in favor of her coding their complaint as being in Sr. Norma's domain.

7. The new role was to receive a number of titles before settling on the final one, 'class coordinator', among them 'administrator-counselor' and 'class-administrator'.

8. While Emerson's (1962) analysis assumes an ever-present struggle for those in dependent positions to equalize power with those in power positions, a clearly untenable assumption, its intimate connection between power and dependence and its focus on the inter-party *relationship* rather than on one party's *perceptions*, as does French and Raven's (1959) formulation, offers advantages to social and organizational psychological theory and analysis over French and Raven's more limited individual psychological orientation.

Chapter 15

A Wider Rift, A Revulsion, A Raw Deal, A Regret

Four days after Sr. Norma distributed her letter announcing her June departure, she told Sr. Catherine, in the words of a field note by Allan,[1] that she was 'sorry' but she 'just couldn't face' the Friday executive meeting. 'She couldn't sit there while people talked about her role and the reorganization of her role'. Sr. Norma told Sr. Catherine, in addition, that she 'couldn't deal with' Lighthall and Allan, particularly Lighthall, towards whom, she told Catherine, she was developing an increasing aversion.

Allan had received confusing information about whether an executive meeting would be held that Friday (January 21). It was a marking day (when teachers recorded students' grades); no students and few lay teachers were in the building. She stopped in to see Sr. Claudia, who was alone. They talked briefly about Sr. Claudia's plans to meet with the Trinity council some evening, to talk about its advisory vs. decision-making functions (see Part IV).

When Sr. Catherine arrived she explained that Sr. Norma had thought there would be no meeting that morning since it was marking day. Sr. Catherine said she had disagreed, telling Sr. Norma that it had been specifically said at the last meeting that there would be a meeting, and that she had relayed to Sr. Norma that there would indeed be a meeting this morning. It was at that point that Sr. Norma had indicated she couldn't 'face it'. When Sr. Norma added her comment about her aversion to Lighthall, Sr. Catherine explained that he would not be at that day's meeting. Sr. Norma again said, Sr. Catherine reported, that she could not talk about planning for her role for the following year, and would not come to today's meeting.

Sr. Claudia asked Allan if she was aware of the strength of Sr. Norma's reaction to our presence. She gave as an example of a particularly strong reaction, Sr. Norma's putting her head down in her arms in response to Lighthall's comments at the January 18 Trinity council meeting,[2] comments that raised a question about the clarity of council members' purpose in conducting a school-wide questionnaire survey. Sr. Norma had favored the survey and right after Lighthall's comment the survey was voted down.[3]

Discussion among Sr. Claudia, Sr. Catherine, and Allan that morning of January 21 turned to another ramification of the growing (or returning) remoteness between Sr. Claudia and Sr. Norma. She had objected to Sr. Norma's setting a date in August for the delivery of the students' uniforms for the following year. That was too late in the summer to make corrections in time for the beginning of school, she said. But Sr. Norma had delegated the matter of uniforms to Mrs. Shulman, who had been making some fairly substantial decisions. So, for Sr. Claudia to pursue the matter, she had to communicate with Mrs. Shulman — *by written memoranda*, Allan reported. Sr. Claudia took to writing because, as Sue Allan reported the thrust of Sr. Claudia's meaning, 'Mrs. Shulman has evidently put her loyalties with Sr. Norma and has been very defensive any time she talks to either Sr. Claudia or Catherine'. Sr. Claudia used written means to communicate with Mrs. Shulman apparently to avoid the tension of face-to-face conflict.

It would be Sr. Claudia, not Sr. Norma, who would have to live with current decisions about uniforms, but these decisions were being made in Sr. Norma's office by Mrs. Shulman. Mrs. Shulman had become assimilated into Sr. Norma's orbit and had become actively resistant to Sr. Claudia's exercise of authority in what Mrs. Shulman regarded as Sr. Norma's bailiwick.

Sr. Claudia related to Allan earlier interactions with Sr. Norma which she now regarded as obstructing her planning and as reflecting an attitude that could be obstructionistic.

> Allan: A lot of the comments that she's made [Sr. Norma has made] to both Claudia and Catherine have continually been of this sort of thing: [simulating Sr. Norma's viewpoint] 'Well, that one [that person] can't handle that; that one can't handle that' — i.e., 'there's nobody else who can handle my role' — even when you're talking about the role being broken down into parts. So Claudia is starting to be of the feeling that maybe it would be better not to have Norma in some of the discussion about her role.

Sr. Claudia sought some way, other than face-to-face communication with Sr. Norma, to solve her problem of disliking decisions Sr. Norma was still making, or that Mrs. Shulman was making, but being blocked by their not being available or open to consider alternatives. Allan said that Sr. Claudia 'really looked like she was looking for a reprieve' from having to talk directly with Sr. Norma about her decision making and avoidance of executive meetings. They eventually agreed that the best way for Sr. Claudia to cope was to set up a time for her and Sr. Norma to talk about progress and difficulties since November 2 regarding the November 2 agreements.

As it turned out, Sr. Claudia's approach to set up such a meeting became the meeting itself, the only meeting in which post-November 2 difficulties were discussed between them. Sr. Claudia's foreboding of emotionality on Sr. Norma's part was borne out. She described the interchange about a month after it occurred:

> Sr. Claudia: When I went to her at that time I said . . . 'Is there any way that we can make this any easier for you?' I said, you know, that there was no way we wanted to punish her or anything . . . but that we had mutually agreed that this was what we were going to do this year and is there any way I could make it easier for her. Well at that time, no. That was a crying scene and all, but it wasn't anger.
>
> She said that she found these meetings impossible when we were talking about the future; that she couldn't sit here and be a part of it. And I said, well then, I wouldn't find that it would be necessary for her to sit there and be a part of it, but that we did need the feed-in of her decisions. Because it's very hard to get her decisions from a parent on the phone, you know, who differs with that decision. And I explained that to her and she understood that.
>
> And then she cried and she said, 'You don't know, you'll never know what it's like to be all on your own completely and having to find a job'. So I said, 'Norma, now, I know I don't know that'. And then I talked to her in terms of what I saw her expertise to be and . . . I gave her a list . . . of at least five places that I would suggest for her to apply, in terms of the things she indicated she'd like to do.[4] (E:2/18/02; 330–358)

The two co-directors reached agreement on two other matters related to planning for the following year. The executive meetings would be separated into two parts. The reporting of decisions made or up-coming Sr. Norma would participate in; she would absent herself as soon as that part was finished so she would miss planning for the following year. With respect to Sr. Norma's description of how she had administered student activities (e.g., dances, clubs, fund drives), Sr. Norma thought Allan's idea of a handbook was a good one, and she agreed to provide Sr. Claudia with written descriptions of rules and procedures. With each of these agreements the two sisters had diminished the number, the duration, and the regularity of their face-to-face contacts.

Just before a Trinity council meeting on February 8 Sr. Claudia complained in passing about Sr. Norma's 'physical and psychological absence from executive meetings'. Four days earlier Sr. Norma left in the middle of an executive meeting, prompting Sr. Claudia to say to Sr. Catherine, 'We end up talking to one another at this meeting all the time'. Lighthall suggested that it might be necessary to find a way to proceed with Trinity's administration without counting on Sr. Norma's participation.

As it happened, Sr. Norma's subsequent participation as an executive was neither wholly outside the Friday meetings nor wholly within them. She was absent from the February 11 and 18 meetings (and frequently from the Trinity council meetings), but participated in the usual reporting format of the February 25 meeting. From the first of February onward, Sr. Norma was devoting increasing portions of work days away from Trinity, finding a position for herself for the following year. Her participation in the administration of Trinity from the beginning of March to the end of the year can be accurately represented, as far as our observations, interviews, and recorded meetings reveal, as the irreducible minimum to keep student affairs and discipline operating.

This noticeable diminution of her investment, and Sr. Claudia's reaction to it, were reflected in an interchange Mrs. Shulman initiated with Sr. Claudia.

> Sr. Claudia: She [Mrs. Shulman] came over to the south wing to see me last Friday afternoon [February 11] . . . She said she 'should bring out the fact' that it seemed to her that Sr. Norma was 'preparing to leave'. You know, early, before June. And she wanted to be sure that we were giving Sr. Norma a gift when she left [Sr. Claudia released a short half-laugh].
>
> The thing hit me with such force. She came to tell me this bombshell, you know [laughs]. And she starting: Give her a gift! And I said, 'Well, you know, we were having our regular faculty dinner and we would, you know, certainly be giving her a farewell gift'. And she said, 'Well, what will happen if Sr. Norma leaves before that?'
>
> That's how I found out, you know. And I said, 'Well, what makes you think she will leave beforehand? She's agreed to stay until June'. She said, 'Well, Sister, I just sense she's not going to. This has been a very hard year for her'. And I said, 'Yeah'. [Sr. Claudia pronounced her 'yeah', as Yeaaaah. She emitted three short, loud bursts of laughter, saying:] 'Riiight! Riiight!' And I said, 'Well, I think, you know, it certainly has been a hard year for all of us but that I ..' I said, 'Frankly, you know, I'm shocked'. (E:2/18/02; 1:350–368)

Sr. Claudia telephoned Sr. Carrie, the regional administrator in charge of personnel. She found out that Sr. Carrie could throw no light on whether Sr. Norma would leave early because she, herself, had been unable to reach Sr. Norma by phone. She had taken to writing letters to Sr. Norma. As it happened, Sr. Norma did not leave, as Mrs. Shulman had feared, before the end of the school year.

Lighthall probed to find out more about what it was that prevented Sr. Claudia from communicating about this and other problems directly with Sr. Norma:

Lighthall: You know, I can't help thinking that in a business organization the reaction to that information [that a co-administrator was about to leave without prior notice] would be for a manager to go down to another [sic: the other] manager and say, 'Hey! Guess what I heard today? You're leaving. Right or wrong? Ah, 'cause if it's right, we've got some things to do that you won't be doing, and if it's wrong, I mean, I'd like to kind of know that'. But it's difficult to do.

Sr. Claudia: It's impossible for me to do right now. It would be an impossible drain at this point for me to go in and discuss anything.

Lighthall: Well, I didn't .. really? Discuss? I just .. You know, a quick answer: 'Yes or No?'

Sr. Claudia: I could not do it at this point. I could not. I don't wish to. I have no desire to. If she walks out, I'll take that rather than go through this thing again [pronounced AI-gaen] .... I don't wish to work out her personal life with her.

Lighthall: ... Look Claudia, I'm not suggesting that you should. I just don't have a glimmer of an idea of what happens in those encounters. It must be just terrible. What is it? A temper tantrum?

Sr. Claudia: No! It's emotion. Cry. We cry: 'I can't do another thing, Claudia. Don't come to me with this sort of thing. I'm doing the best I can. What do you expect of me?' You know, I don't expect anything of her ... I expect zilch! [releases a short laugh] (Ibid., 495–590).

Sr. Claudia described her reaction to the emotion of those interchanges in unusually acrid terms: 'It's revolting to me at this time. I find it extremely revolting on every level'.

                    ○   ○   ○   ○

I think we get closer here than any other time to the center of the co-directors' work relationship in this period. Sr. Norma is simply overloaded. She literally cannot take any more of Trinity than she is already handling. Why? Because she has taken on a whole new world. And she apparently has taken it on without much support from colleagues within the religious order.

So when Sr. Claudia approaches Sr. Norma with mundane matters from Trinity, she is bringing to Sr. Norma just exactly what Sr. Norma can no longer take. Sr. Norma's response, in turn, gives Sr. Claudia just exactly what she can't take: intense emotionality, particularly the emotionality of self-pity and despair. It revolts her.

We also see that Sr. Caludia has reached the point of reversing, or beginning to reverse, her dependence on Sr. Norma: she is learning to expect 'zilch'. From about this point on Sr. Claudia increasingly views herself as, and acts as, Trinity's principal. Any significant bounds which she might be accused of overstepping gradually and increasingly recede as her bailiwick virtually absorbs Sr. Norma's except for individual disciplinary cases.

❁   ❁   ❁   ❁

> Lighthall [continuing]: In other words, you really couldn't get . . . a yes or no answer.
> Sr. Claudia: I could *not* get an answer. I'd get another scene. And I'm just up to here with it. . . .
>
> Georgette called and said, 'Claudia, what do you want me to *do*' . . . And I said, 'I have no idea. . . . But I want you to know what the effects of our meetings [at the Regional Center] were and [what the effect of] our agreement was. [The regional administrators had had little contact with the Trinity conflict or 'settlement' since November 2.] It's the kind of thing that I think that I suggested would happen . . . this year's role would not be changed . . . that was our agreement.
>
> 'But in actuality, now that she finds we are going ahead and planning and that things are moving on, she feels out of it and she feels personally hurt and any inch of security she had is gone. Therefore she wants out. I think I predicted this, that she wouldn't want to stay through all this change'.[5] Do you see? Nobody would.
> Lighthall: . . . .Well, I think Norma feels she's gotten a raw deal. She used the term, 'raw deal' to me. . . .
> Sr. Claudia: Did she say what that deal was?
> Lighthall: No. (E:2/18/02; 1:590–615)

The context of Sr. Norma's remark was Lighthall's November 19 discussion with her of a series of interactions she had had with students in a disciplinary action. The 'raw deal' remark was made in global reference to the depersonalizing, opposition-absorbing nature of the disciplinarian's role as it had developed. She may have referred *specifically* to the chronic lack of help from teachers and colleagues in her role as disciplinarian, a lack well described earlier by Sr. Claudia (see page 168).

In April, Sr. Norma applied for and was granted the religious order's special status for sisters who want to reconsider their ties to the Community, a year's leave of absence officially called 'exclaustration'. From September, 02 through the following June, Sr. Norma was the principal of a school run by another religious order. At the end of that year, Sr. Norma was released from her vows and left the Blessed Sisters of Trinity.

Sr. Claudia characterized her year at Trinity from the perspective of April:

Sr. Claudia: The whole year has been a bad scene in terms of my personal security in my role. There is just no way that I've handled well the whole Norma thing. And I know it. Personally, in my reactions to it I just didn't like the way I allowed myself to be consistently hurt, hurt, hurt, you know. And resentful.

And in terms of the people I deal with [faculty members whose contracts she did not renew], I probably am weighing what they're saying in terms of the fact of what has been said about me: 'Pushing Norma out and so forth . . .'

Catherine came to me and said, 'Claudia, I hope you haven't heard what I've been hearing in terms of the fact that I'm leaving because I can't take it working with you any more'. And I said, 'Well, I haven't even heard that, Catherine'. She said, well, you know, two of the sisters had come to her to say that, you know, Norma was being very talkative. And so, Catherine said, 'No way. I enjoy working with you'. You know. That was it.

But I know it's lodged in the back of my mind and I'm saying: 'Are people feeling that I am just not handling this well and pushing people around?' And I think I felt it strongly . . . when I wasn't renewing someone's contract: pushing somebody else out. You know? (FL:4/7/02; II, 1:119–145)

Summary

The narrative reveals how an interpersonal alienation, having recruited others into its orbit, as Mrs. Shulman became allied with Sr. Norma, reduces communication to memo writing and minimal reporting of decisions — media suitable for well formed routines but ill suited to handle emergent disturbances and therefore ill-suited for adaptations. Once again avoidance of emotionality is revealed as a factor in perpetuating the alienation. We see a final attempt by Sr. Claudia to stabilize a working relation, resulting in Sr. Norma's expressing, and Sr. Claudia integrating, a new reality: Sr. Norma's inability 'to be a part of' planning for the future. The resulting accommodation transforms Sr. Claudia's realities to fit Sr. Norma's, settling and legitimating Sr. Norma's retaining a position at Trinity while reducing performance and communication to an irreducible minimum: a presence constituting an increasing absence — in Sr. Claudia's reality. On Sr. Norma's part, she was merely doing what everyone else does: protecting, maintaining, and enhancing her own adaptational niche, seeking her own, coherent adaptation — where 'own' signals localism and where 'coherence' means 'locally rational'.

Finally, the narrative once again reveals the non-neutrality of the position of investigator in matters of human behavior. Sr. Norma's increasing aversion to Lighthall in the context of decreasing contact between them

parallels her increasing aversion to contact with executive planning generally and Lighthall's increasing contact with Sr. Claudia and the Trinity
council.

Notes

1. Lighthall was absent from this meeting. It was also not recorded. Three days after
    the meeting Allan dictated a field note from notes taken at the time of the meeting.
2. See p. 68 ff. and note 3 on page 79.
3. As note 3 on page 79 explains, this was a clear instance of a direct intervention and a
    telling effect by Lighthall. Such interventions and effects were occasional in the
    Trinity council and, besides exceptional instances which I describe in some detail
    (e.g., Lighthall's participation at the Regional Center), rare in the executive council.
    These occasional interventions beyond those described, interventions like
    Lighthall's on the survey questionnaire, tended to be brief and confined to actions
    remote from problems and problem-solving reported in this book.

    There is no escaping the Heisenberg principle in social science, however: data
    collected are always affected by the process of data collection, and that process is
    always stamped with the closeness of the data collector to the acting 'subjects' being
    observed or the remoteness of the data collector from them. No distance from the
    data source is neutral or objective. This implies that data pertaining to the scientist's
    substantive interests always should be accompanied by data about the relation
    between scientist and 'subjects', data of the kind I have taken some pains to include
    at various points in the narratives and analyses of this book.
4. A colleague raised several questions regarding this and earlier passages in this
    chapter. The first was, 'I am amazed that you pass over this woman's torment so
    lightly. Doesn't it constitute a relevant "sub-episode"?' Sr. Norma's period of
    torment does constitute a sub-episode in her own problem-solving. Our relationship
    and my personal and interpersonal resources to deal with it were such, however,
    that I was unable to pursue her problem-solving except from the distance which
    both she and I kept. At the time, however, Sr. Norma's 'torment' was (1) visible
    directly only to Sr. Claudia and others with whom she felt comfortable showing it
    and (2) accompanied, no doubt, by positive feelings of having made a decision, of
    anticipating a new future, and the like.

    My colleague raised a second question: 'Was Sr. Norma's disdain for you simply
    a matter of your taking part in the division of her organizational possessions? Or is
    something more involved — something having to do with your being the outsider
    she will eventually become herself (recall the matter of her religious training on
    which you "intruded")?' I think the primary source of Sr. Norma's antipathy toward
    me was her conclusion that our project was 'a sensitivity thing', that I intended to
    induce people to reveal themselves at vulnerable levels of exposure. Given the brief
    contact with my explanations of the research consultation occasioned by her
    absences, and by my failures to secure her understanding, and given our intro-
    ductory statements in the Trinity council that by examining episodes together the
    participants could learn how to be more effective members, it is not outlandish of
    her to have concluded that some sort of collective self examination would take place.

    Sr. Norma could reasonably have feared, therefore — at least before our
    conversation about keeping her religious life private — that her private shift away
    from the religious order might have become the subject of discussion in a similar
    episodic review with the executives. My questions about early religious training
    unwittingly hit that very tender spot.

Sr. Norma's later complaint to Sr. Catherine that she did not want to attend executive meetings because Allan and I would be there was tested by Sr. Catherine herself, who told Sr. Norma I would not be present. Sr. Norma's refusal to attend showed that Allan and I were rather secondary aversions, that Sr. Norma was chiefly burdened by the discussions of how her administrative functions would be handled the following year. I believe it was Sr. Claudia's matter-of-fact, instrumental way of discussing the dividing of those 'organizational possessions' that did more than anything else to remind Sr. Norma that her niche at Trinity was shortly to be no longer hers, and to remind her of all that that signified: that she had now burned her bridges and was on her own, that those at Trinity would no longer be dependent on her, that she was to be an 'outsider', and so on.

5. Sr. Claudia may have 'predicted' this outcome to herself; we have no evidence that she did so explicitly to anyone else. Sr. Claudia did express the fear, in the November 2 meeting at the apostolic center, that it would be easy for both of them — but she meant especially Sr. Norma — to 'cop out' by continuing to avoid meeting regularly.

Chapter 16

How Effective Were the Co-Directors' Problem Solving and Conflict Management?

We have now finished the narrative of our second episode of problem-solving. It is an episode, also, of that kind of problem-solving in which two parties come into conflict and come to some kind of management of that conflict. As problem-solving or as conflict management, we can turn the episode into a far more useful unit of data by taking one more step: carrying out an explicit evaluation of its problem-solving and conflict management. We can use the same five criteria used in the first episode: 1) problem originator's degree of satisfaction, 2) degree of satisfaction of the other participants, particularly problem constituents, 3) observable changes in the conditions implicated in the original or transformed problem, 4) reduction or elimination of sources of resource-draining confusion and of cross purposes, and 5) release or recruitment of new kinds or levels of resource into the organization — each as a direct result of the problem-solving. The effects of the problem-solving and conflict management varied across three levels of social complexity: the individual level, the inter-personal level, and the organizational level.

Individual Level

Sr. Norma's Problem

While our data about Sr. Norma's problem are much more sketchy than those about Sr. Claudia's problem, we nonetheless have enough to reach some sketchy evaluations and conclusions. Sr. Norma's problem of leaving vs. staying was largely solved by early Fall. A more immediate sub-problem being solved in the period of our observations was her problem of outward continuity opposed by inner change. Sr. Norma wanted to remain publicly in place, with as few noticeable changes in her position at Trinity or her membership in the religious order as possible, while on the other hand, to engage herself in the energy consuming process of altering dramatically her career, her personal life, and her immediate interpersonal life.

Since both her role as Director of Student Affairs and her personal metamorphosis demanded each day a full day's normal energies, the public continuity vs. private change created a sub-problem of overload in the demand on her resources. A necessary part of her solution to that problem of overload was a minimization of investments of energy in the world she was leaving in order to maximize investments in the world she was joining. How well did she fare in keeping her Trinity world intact and in creating a niche for herself in her new world?

As to her success in creating a satisfying niche in her new world, from Sr. Claudia's repeated testimony in the years after the period narrated (not included in the narrative), Sr. Norma's solution to leave was personally effective: she has remained as principal of the school which first employed her in that position and has continued to appear content with her personal life. Her more immediate and short-term effectiveness in solving her problem of overload and of protecting her change from becoming public was markedly less successful.

With Lighthall's questions about her religious commitments she was very effective: he halted that inquiry immediately after their November 19 interchange (see page 179–80). But her withdrawal of her energies and of her presence from Trinity jarred both Sr. Catherine and Sr. Claudia. Sr. Claudia succeeded, by intervening at the regional level, in bringing Sr. Norma's impaired functioning into the open and to force a private and then a public acknowledgement of her leaving Trinity. The process of regional inquiry and joint meetings with Sr. Claudia and Sr. Catherine at the regional center and the November 2 'settlement' surprised her. She then had to defend herself against claims that she 'had walked out on Trinity', and to face Sr. Jeanine's reaction of being 'so mad' at Sr. Norma's estimate of the extent of her absences. Then later, Sr. Norma had to cope with a confrontation by Sr. Claudia about continued 'feed-in' to the Trinity planning process. Her reduced investment, then, became noticed and, except for the two weeks after November 2, remained out in the open, beyond her attempts to minimize or deny.

Sr. Norma did prevail, however, over fairly strong efforts by Sr. Georgette to publicly demote her at Trinity. Sr. Norma's success was fed by realities operating in Sr. Jeanine, about preventing Sr. Claudia from being seen as 'displacing' Sr. Norma, realities Sr. Norma probably knew nothing about. Sr. Norma also managed, after her renewed withdrawal toward the middle of December, to negotiate acceptance by Sr. Claudia of her lessened participation in all joint administrative efforts, thus securing her reduced investment at Trinity from further challenge.

Thus, Sr. Norma's efforts to maintain an appearance of business as usual vis à vis Trinity and the religious order failed in their immediate aim of preventing confrontation by her colleagues and community. But they succeeded in attaining a more basic goal, the protecting of *at least sufficient* time and energy to continue progress toward establishing a new life. In short, she was forced to 'go public' before she had wanted to do so, but that did not prevent her from effectuating an exit from Trinity, an entry to another school in a more advanced position (thus nullifying her 'raw deal'), an exit from the religious order, and an entry into married life. An immediate *organizational* problem regarding 'business as usual' was solved relatively ineffectively; but a far more consequential and long-term *personal* problem about living one kind of life and wanting to live another kind, was solved successfully.

Sr. Claudia's Problem

Sr. Claudia's problem with Sr. Norma consisted of the following two incompatible sets of elements in her operating reality. On the one hand was her intense commitment to community life and to work: community life that meant a shift from the old, authoritarian order to one of interdependent participation based on negotiated agreements not dicta from above, and work that meant full investment and professional responsibility. Incompatible with this sense of self and set of commitments, on the other hand, was her repeated experience of lack of commitment, non-dependability, and non-professional attitude which she saw reflected in Sr. Norma's repeated absences over the summer of 01 and from the opening of school in late August onward.

In short, she was committed to an effective, shared administration but saw Sr. Norma's undependability as preventing both an effective administration and a shared administration. To fulfill her own commitments she had to rely on Sr. Norma's fulfilling her part of the administration of Trinity but found Sr. Norma repeatedly unreliable in that task.

An immediate sub-problem, part of the problem complex being solved by Sr. Claudia, was that while Sr. Claudia had strong impulses to fill many of the voids created by Sr. Norma's absences, she also had strong inhibitions against doing so, have been previously admonished by former peers against 'overstepping' her domain of authority. But not all of those voids could be filled by Sr. Claudia, even if she had wanted to do so, if she was to fulfill her own side of administration. If Trinity's administration was to be shared, she needed a fully invested co-director.

How successful were Sr. Claudia's efforts to re-establish a dependable, fully invested and shared administration, backed up by legitimate freedom to take action when and if gross administrative failure occurred? First, her single effort on October 5 to arrange directly with Sr. Norma a temporary substitute failed. Part of the failure may be attributed to Sr. Claudia's emphasizing a solution, suggesting what Sr. Norma might do, while communicating to Sr. Norma almost no account of the realities created by

Sr. Norma's absences. Part can be attributed, too, to Sr. Claudia's failure to pursue Sr. Norma's plea to 'Let me think about it'. Instead of keeping the door open for further direct negotiation, Sr. Claudia appealed to the hierarchy, which then produced a solution remotely. How successful was that solution?

The first criterion of effectiveness, satisfaction of the problem originator, was met in part: Sr. Claudia was glad to have some decision and, further, to be freed to plan for the following year. If we were to measure her satisfaction in the week or two after November 2, we would conclude that her satisfaction was complete. But between the third week in November and February 18, when Sr. Claudia had come to expect 'zilch' of Sr. Norma, Sr. Claudia's satisfaction with the solution she had accepted from the regional directors was at best mixed. Afterward her satisfaction with the solution must have increased as she became increasingly involved in planning the following year's governance of Trinity (see Part IV).

How about the satisfaction of the other key participants with the November 2 solution? Sr. Norma, one must infer, rejected the whole process and its product. The whole intervention held no legitimacy for her. To the contrary, Sr. Claudia's problem solving had created a problem for Sr. Norma. For Sr. Norma, therefore, the November 2 solution and the process that produced it was a net loss and made no impact on her main agenda.

Sr. Georgette and Sr. Jeanine worked through a conflict in their preferred solutions, allowing them to get on with their other crowded agenda. From their perspective, their resolution of the co-directors' conflict had finessed the mutually incompatible initial conditions of the co-directors and had gained their joint acceptance, had resolved the regional administrators' own differences, had freed the more capable Trinity executive to take needed authority while still avoiding public displacement of the other co-director, had figured the consultant explicitly into the implementation of a solution, and had done it all through a process of repeated deliberations that included extended input from all the parties — quite enough to be satisfied about.

On the first two criteria, then, the November 2 solution produced satisfaction for the regional administrators, increasing satisfaction for Sr. Norma as she successfully negotiated her withdrawal, and peaks of dissatisfaction on the part of Sr. Claudia followed by increasing satisfaction as she expected less and less from Sr. Norma and was able to shape events for the following year.

To meet the third criterion, observable change in the observable realities implicated in the problem, would require changes (a) in Sr. Claudia's legitimated freedom to act in the case of gross administrative failure by Sr. Norma, (b) in the dependability of Sr. Norma's role performance, largely a function of her motivational investment, or (c) in the co-directors' degree of sharing of Trinity's administration. The first two we shall consider here, postponing (c) until evaluating effects at the interpersonal level.

As to (a), legitimate freedom to act, Sr. Claudia had gained not only a wide new latitude in any domain that pertained to planning for the following year, but also the right and obligation to act in Sr. Norma's domain if she should be absent for more than 24 hours.

While the sheer *predictability* of Sr. Norma's functioning (b) did increase, from about three weeks after November 2 onward, her *dependability and investment* steadily decreased after that point. And by February 18, when Sr. Claudia could voice her expectation of Sr. Norma as 'zilch', Sr. Claudia's subjective realization had caught up with observable facts and from that time onward their relationship can be counted as having stabilized.[1] Could this stabilization, Sr. Claudia's acceptance of Sr. Norma's withdrawal, be attributed, however, to the solution of November 2? Certainly not by intention. That settlement called for Sr. Norma to reestablish responsibility, accountability, and personal presence. She did, by open negotiation, attain a measure of accountability. But essentially she continued her withdrawal. The stabilization came from within Sr. Claudia herself, from her re-arrangement internally of her own expectations to be more in line with the consistently observable reality that Sr. Norma was presenting.

Yet the November 2 settlement, by not including regularized monitoring by the regional administrators of degrees of compliance at Trinity, became unintentionally a mechanism whereby the regional administrators turned their attention away from Trinity, withdrawing both monitoring and authoritative support for the settlement. This allowed Sr. Norma to continue her withdrawal unimpeded by any intervention of the regional administrators. Sr. Claudia was thus forced simply to adapt to that which she had tried to prevent: Sr. Norma's autonomous functioning on her own terms. It seems perverse to conclude that such a settlement can be counted as an effective solution because, unintentionally, it eventuated in a stable and in some respects an effective solution. Yet the intended solution is often, as in this case it was, poorly informed, based on false assumptions, leaving plenty of room for the unintended to be in fact more adaptive than the intended solution. In any case, we are considering here only the single dimension of Sr. Norma's dependability and motivational investment in her role performance: they steadily declined.

In sum, the conditions regarding Sr. Claudia's freedom to take administrative action were definitely changed by the November 2 settlement, but conditions regarding a fully invested co-director changed not at all. As to Sr. Norma's dependability, Sr. Claudia finally realized she could not depend on Sr. Norma ('zilch'). So, while Sr. Claudia obtained greater legitimate freedom to take administrative action related to the following year, she also was forced to compensate for an increasing void in Sr. Norma's current functioning.

The fourth criterion of problem-solving effectiveness is the reduction or elimination of wasteful confusion or cross purposes. One notable advance in this regard was achieved: the November 2 specification of the 24-hour mechanism for invoking the 'default' clause allowed the executives to correct for one member's absences. It might be argued that this advance was moot, however, since it was never in fact invoked and the condition to which it applied, the co-directorship, was dissolved at the end of the year. But without that specific clause, Sr. Claudia's power to act would continue to be in doubt, continuously under the cloud of 'overstepping'. It promoted subjective confidence on her part and legitimate warrant for her action under circumstances experienced previously by her as debilitating. So an important confusion was cleared up by the November 2 settlement.

Finally, the fifth criterion of effectiveness was that episodic participants release or recruit new resources into the organization as a result of either their attempts to solve, or their solution of, the problem in question. As Sr. Norma withdrew and Sr. Claudia increasingly filled the void thus created, a net increase in the intensity of investment in planning was achieved. Sr. Claudia's full-time commitment sparked the release of energies by members of the Trinity council which, joined with Sr. Claudia's own, dramatically increased the amount of energy released into organizational functioning — changes observable in the period and in the events narrated in Part IV. The narrative of the co-director episode only notes that Sr. Claudia planned to meet with the Trinity council the evening of February 2 — evidence of her having taken Sr. Norma's place in providing leadership for that group, an act she was now free to do as a result of the November 2 solution. (Prior to November 2 it would have been overstepping her bounds.) On this fifth dimension of evaluation, then, we can judge the solution to have been effective.

To summarize, Sr. Norma's solution to her short-term problem of carrying on business as usual while withdrawing was mostly a failure: she was called to account and her withdrawal forced partly into the open. Sr. Norma's solution of her long-term problem of effecting a dramatic transition in her life, however, was successful. As to Sr. Claudia's problem solving, the solution resulting from her efforts yielded (1) some degree of satisfaction, grounds for new hope if you like, for Sr. Claudia and the regional administrators, but not (in the short run) for Sr. Norma; (2) an observably expanded domain of authority for Sr. Claudia, coupled, to be sure, with a certain amount of added work from Sr. Norma's lapses, (3) reduction in confusion on an important point of authority (the 24-hour rule), and (4) release and recruitment of new levels of energy into organizational functioning. At the individual level of the co-directors' respective problem solving their efforts must be judged, on the whole, a success.

Interpersonal Level

The nub of the co-directors' conflict was the extent of personal presence and motivational investment that Sr. Norma brought to her role as executive and director of student affairs. Sr. Norma's 'physical and psychological' absence meant that executive functions, premised upon co-equal authority and a clear division of labor, would be seriously curtailed. In the face of this absence and this meaning, for Sr. Norma to refuse to honor their prior agreement — an agreement that, as Sr. Claudia interpreted it, when one sister was absent the other was free, without recriminations, to assume that sister's functions, was to personally and unilaterally bring the very basis of a co-directorate to a halt. Sr. Norma wanted a co-directorate to continue (functioning on her own terms), since it provided her with not only needed esteem but also with an autonomy she needed to apportion her resources in a new way. But Sr. Claudia wanted the co-directorate to be officially dissolved, since the very autonomy Sr. Norma enjoyed had nullified cooperation and had stymied corrective measures.

Having evaluated problem solving at the individual level of complexity, the criteria that remain distinctively appropriate at the interpersonal level are the satisfaction of the key participants *in the management of the conflict* and the change in conditions implicated *in the nub of the conflict*.

While Sr. Claudia coped, in the end, with Sr. Norma's withdrawal from Trinity, she was dissatisfied with how the conflict was managed and with the resulting relationship. Her learning to expect 'zilch' was making the best of a bad bargain. We have no evidence regarding Sr. Norma's degree of satisfaction, but it is clear from the entire episode that she obtained more of what she wanted from Sr. Claudia than Sr. Claudia obtained from her. If there was a winner regarding the nub of the conflict, it was Sr. Norma.

We can entertain two formulations of the dimension of evaluation having to do with changes in conditions implicated in the nub of the conflict. One formulation is that at the nub of the conflict was the degree of Sr. Norma's personal presence at Trinity and of her motivational investment in her work. That condition remained simply untouched by the conflict management.

A different formulation is that at the nub of the conflict was that particular degree of Sr. Norma's personal presence at Trinity and of her motivational investment in her work *which was legitimate for Sr. Claudia and Sr. Catherine to expect*. With the formulation, emphasizing legitimate expectations rather than overt behaviors, observable changes were made. The arbitrated settlement of November 2 changed the basis of legitimate expectations by 1) affirming that Sr. Norma would be leaving at the end of the school year; 2) appointing Sr. Claudia as director for the following year and the year thereafter, thus clearly indicating their support and her assumption of full responsibility; and 3) specifically calling for changes in the co-directors' roles which led to the single position of principal.

While this second formulation is arguable, it is flawed. A clear and repeated theme of the discussions at the regional center was the necessity for the two co-directors, no matter the future or their movement toward a single principalship, to meet regularly to accomplish effective communication about the current year's work. Sr. Claudia repeated the theme in her prophetic warning:

> ... we could cop out and take care of things by means of ... memorandum ... the temptation is strong ... that's something that we should say, right out: 'This [first item of agreement] is here so we don't cop out on it. And we're willing not to cop out on it'.

The scenarios imagined (though, significantly, never communicated to the co-directors) by Sr. Georgette or Sr. Jeanine vividly portrayed lively, authentic, working interchanges. The management of the conflict did not move the two sisters toward a working relationship. No conditions affecting their working relation were changed except those they negotiated between themselves, regarding Sr. Norma's restricted participation in the regular meetings, a change which added further distance between them.

To summarize, the conflict management process yielded less dissatisfaction on Sr. Norma's part than on Sr. Claudia's and had no impact on the nub of their conflict or on their working relationship: it continued, increasingly, to become mutually exclusionary — the very denial of a working relationship or of a 'presence to each other'.

Organizational Level

An important change at the organizational level of complexity brought about by the November 2 solution was the shift in Trinity's executive from a co-directorate to a single principalship for at least the following two years.[2] This single move effectively eliminated 1) autonomous bailiwicks, 2) the need for agreements or norms about 'overstepping', and 3) immobilizing conflict between co-directors. The principal would be charged to deal directly with any gross administrative failure of a subordinate. Any gross failure on the part of the principal herself the regional team would deal with. In short, the kind of conflict experienced by Sr. Norma and Sr. Claudia could no longer occur as a result of that single shift from co-directorate to principalship.

A lesson here, clearly, is that one of the chief benefits and functions of a single head of any organization is avoidance of immobilizing conflict at the head of the organization or, put positively, the assurance of an unfettered capacity to take action on behalf of the organization as a whole. The November 2 solution returned that benefit and function to Trinity.

As Part IV will show, Sr. Claudia continued the spirit of shared decision making in her structuring of the new Trinity governance and, in particular, in her organization of the executive council. There would now be six members in that executive group. That increase in numbers further diluted the impact any future interpersonal conflict could have within Trinity's executive. But that structuring resulted from Sr. Claudia's solving of yet a different problem complex, one that is the focus of Part IV. It is sufficient to note here that the November 2 solution's shift from co-directorate to principalship eliminated *structurally, at the organizational level* struggles which manifested themselves at the interpersonal level, as conflicts, and at the individual level, as incompatibilities in operating realities, that is, as problems.

Dimensions of Evaluation

Confronting this second, more complex episode of problem-solving forces awareness of two dimensions of evaluation present but not salient in the first episode. First is the dimension, levels of social complexity. And second is the dimension of time, of short-term and long-term effects. Further and even more interesting is the fact that even for a given episode of problem-solving or conflict management radically different levels of effectiveness can obtain at different levels of social complexity and in different time spans.[3]

At the level of individual problem-solving, for example, the co-directors fared very well in the long run, i.e., if we take the year observed with the year or two afterward as our time span. In the short run, within the school year, Sr. Norma seems to have had less success in solving her problem of withdrawal vs. business as usual than she had in solving her long-term problem of transition, just as Sr. Claudia achieved more long term than short term success in gaining freedom to act. In further illustration of the multi-dimensionality of effectiveness of outcome is the relatively high degree of effectiveness at the individual level by both Sr. Claudia and Sr. Norma and the very low degree of success in the forging of a working relationship. Not all the resources brought to bear by Sr. Claudia and Sr. Norma and the regional administrators and the (relatively but not totally passive) consultant-researchers could put that Humpty Dumpty back together again. If we move beyond, to the level of the organization, the same processes which aided fairly effective individual problem solving but were ineffective at the level of the working relation were, again, effective in creating a structure of executive authority which would prevent the very kind of conflict at the interpersonal level that it was ineffective in directly resolving.

The necessity of distinguishing among different levels of social complexity in order to clarify different degrees of effectiveness of a given solution brings with it much larger questions about evaluation. Which is to be preferred, for example; a conflict management that leads to positive outcomes at the level of participants' problem-solving, negative outcomes at the level of the working relation, and positive outcomes for the organization, on the one hand, or one that leads to positive outcomes for the individual and the working relation but negative outcomes at the organizational level? Answering these and the fuller set of such questions takes us deep into our basic values and conceptions of the individual and of organized life.

As to the co-director episode, can we extract any general statement of evaluation? No, not a simple unidimensional one. We can conclude, however, that the processes of that episode produced substantial positive changes at the individual and organizational levels and released and recruited substantially increased energy and thought into the organization by one of the conflicting parties, even while failing to resolve the focal conflict itself and to re-establish a working relationship.

We move to the final chapter to analyze the episode's process by drawing out further variables that seemed to affect outcomes, particularly the integration of local realities into organizational action.

Notes

1. Reviewing the manuscript of the book recently, Sr. Claudia reacted to her 'zilch' comment: while it might be true that her expectations of Sr. Norma's performance had lessened at the time, she still kept experiencing occasional frustration with her that last semester, indicating that 'zilch' never reached absolute zero.
2. The administration of Trinity High School has retained its single principalship for more than a decade, and there is no sentiment for shifting back to a co-directorate.
3. In addition, of course, is the dimension of problematic content: a given person can be successful in solving problems of one complex, say an interpersonal problem A, and completely unsuccessful, in the span of that conflict episode A, in solving problems from another complex B, say a problem of cutting costs to meet a budget. Evaluations of effectiveness, therefore, must be problem- and conflict-specific.

Chapter 17

A Second Culling Yields Twenty-One Variables: Some New, Some Old

We shall retain distinctions among levels of social complexity as we identify variables suggested by this episode of conflict. Since our basic unit of analysis is the episode, that is our highest level of complexity, followed in decreasing complexity by the levels of sub-organizational units, inter-personal interactions and relations, and the individual. Variables associated with each level will be taken up, in ascending order of complexity, after briefly describing the level of social complexity itself. Any variables relevant to a given level culled from the first constitution episode (in Table 5.1) will be reviewed first, then any to be culled from the co-director episode will be described. I leave to Part IV the task of identifying the few major, underlying variables from among the twenty-two culled from all three episodes.

Individual Level

Our central focus is the problem-solving episode, which captures the emergent process of a given adaptation. Because an episode's adaptational action ordinarily begins psychologically, that is, with a problem in a single individual's minding, the individual level of analysis is critically important. As is true for each of the levels of social complexity, this level includes both *stable* parts; personality traits, values, basic attitudes, and *emergent* parts; cognitions, perceptions, problems, solutions, plans and actions. Emergent, mobile, and sequential aspects of each level transpire within the constraints of the more stable, structured, already accumulated aspects of that level and of all higher levels. The de-stabilized relation between Sr. Norma and Sr. Claudia became the emergent condition handled by the superordinate and more stable structure, the regional apostolic team.

1. *Problem Synthesis: Mutuality vs. Ego-Centricity*

Important in the first episode and again in this co-director conflict was the degree of ego-centricity or mutuality of problems synthesized. In the first constitution episode, when Sr. Claudia synthesized her problem regarding the Trinity council's decision-making stance she excluded the problems behind the council's two instances of decision making, problems of uniforms and parking. In this second episode, both sisters synthesized their problems of conflict in ways that excluded the other's insistent problems.

In her original meeting with Lighthall in the spring of 01, Sr. Claudia not only took the role of spokesperson for the administration but also spoke of her conflicts with others on the team in terms of 'coming on so strong'. While her role and functions had been compartmentalized on paper and in others' minds, in Sr. Claudia's mind the school was a whole and she was the person most responsible for it: she felt she was 'on the hot seat'. She worried about the effects that malfunctioning elsewhere visited upon her own functioning, but also upon the school for which she felt chief responsibility. Her worries tended not, however, to focus on the local realities others might be responding to. Fulfilling the functions she saw as necessary, particularly solving problems in her own bailiwick, was a distinctly stronger tendency in this period than helping others solve their own problems.

Implied here is one of two alternative ways of committing oneself to the effective functioning of the whole organization. These two commitments involve the basic distinction between substantive contents and directions of functioning, on the one hand, and causative process, on the other. When one is committed to substantive contents and directions, as Sr. Claudia tended to be, one accepts substantive responsibility in one's own mind for effective functioning. One feels 'on the hot seat', sometimes to the point of attempting to alter specific contents and directions by trying to take on others' functions when they malfunction. The controlling image here is 'being on the hot seat' — feeling responsibility for the functioning, and blame for the malfunctioning, of the organization's units.

The other classical way of committing oneself to the effective functioning of the whole organization is, first, by acknowledging that organizational functioning depends not on one's own mental images, but on multiple persons and realities in addition to one's own. It is a realization that the whole requires others, in their otherness and in their own organizational locales. Following from this realization, second, one undertakes substantive correction of unit functioning by means of assisting others to perform up to their local capacities in their local roles by helping them cope effectively with their local realities and most especially their local problems. Third and finally, this second classical way of achieving effective organizational functioning includes recruiting others to help solve one's own problems, which implies, to adumbrate a later conclusion, that one induces in others the problems (or complementary ones) that one needs help to solve. These two modes of commitment and thinking are similar, but not identical to the two dimensions Blake and Mouton (1964, 1966) employ in their 'managerial grid', concern for people and concern for production.[1] These two modes boil down, essentially, to an orientation to reality: one's own reality as *the* organizational reality vs. others' realities as necessary, unknown, and to-be-discovered parts of organizational reality. This difference in orientation is reflected in the ego-centricity vs. inclusiveness (or 'decenteredness', in a Piagetian sense) of the originator's synthesis of her or his problem. The orientation selected (often unwittingly) most likely predisposes one, too, to an inclusionary or an exclusionary mode of conflict management at the dyadic and episodic levels of complexity.

In the present episode, Sr. Claudia again synthesized a problem regarding Sr. Norma's absences that included their effects but excluded causes, an integration of what we might call her own, immediate, 'protagonist' realities but not the 'antagonist' realities of Sr. Norma. Thus, once again, Sr. Claudia's problem-solving efforts were directed entirely toward solving that restricted problem of Sr. Norma's absences, a problem Sr. Norma did not share, a problem that left no room for Sr. Norma's problems. Sr. Norma, of course, preceded Sr. Claudia with an exclusionary problem of her own — presenting herself for business as usual at Trinity while withdrawing herself for a dramatic inner shift, irrespective of any difficulties doing so might create for her co-director. Each was ego-centric in problem synthesis. Mutual exclusion in early problem synthesis contributed to mutual exclusion in later process and outcome.

The first constitution episode suggested that a second variable, also at the individual level, might be cognitive 'slippage' in the problem originator — e.g., the confusion of cognitive assimilation of different constituent realities with one another (variable #4 in Table 5.1). Since no further signs of that were noted, and only one instance in that episode, it seems best to discount that variable at this point.

2. *Orientation to Emotionality and the Expression of Conflict*

Sr. Claudia indicated that she 'hated' 'confrontations' and that she would 'remove' herself from them, and of course avoid them. Since expressing emotions happens precisely when matters of commitment are at hand, especially in the context of problems, avoiding emotionality impinges directly on problem-solving processes where they implicate the strongest commitments and are therefore most consequential. To avoid emotionality is to avoid precisely those situations where realities most require exploring and integrating. A second variable at the individual level of analysis, then, culled from this second episode, is participants' orientation to emotionality, particularly relating to protagonist-antagonist conflict, an orientation that is expressive, exploratory, and inclusive or, in contrast, suppressive, defensive, and exclusionary.

Interpersonal Level

Because organizational problems often can become shared only through communication, as between Sr. Claudia and Sr. Jeanine or, earlier, between Sr. Claudia and Mr. Sullivan, interpersonal transactions are also centrally implicated in any problem-solving process.[2] Relatively stable at this level are the *relations* between two persons, as between Sr. Claudia and Sr. Norma or between Lighthall and Sr. Norma. At this level we keep in focus not only the relations between pairs of participant members, but also between those members and the observer. Emergent at the dyadic level are interactions — conferences, conversations, fleeting or extended interchanges — and the participants' choice of persons, groups, and levels with whom or which to communicate. These take place within the constraints of the more stable, structured aspects of dyadic life, interpersonal relations.

3. Aim and Level of Intervention

In the first constitution episode Sr. Claudia avoided direct contact with the body most directly implicated in her problem, the Trinity council. She chose to communicate, instead, with Hester, Sr. Norma, and Mr. Sullivan, i.e., at levels of social complexity below the one implicated in her problem. In the co-director episode, the co-director relation itself became de-stabilized by Sr. Norma's unilateral, unannounced withdrawal. Interchanges that went on across its instability were greatly affected by that instability. A higher level structure was called upon, the superordinate organization, to bring the relation back into stability. In the episode of conflict with Sr. Norma, Sr. Claudia aimed her communications more directly than she had in the first constitution episode — to Sr. Norma herself and to one level above their co-director relationship. Where she was more (though still incompletely) direct, her problem was conveyed with more influence.

4. Relations: Trust/Closeness vs. Mistrust/Distance

The co-director episode brings into sharp relief the importance of interpersonal relationships for communication. Given Sr. Norma's exclusionary withdrawal, her non-accountability, and Sr. Claudia's resultant antagonism toward Sr. Norma, the amount and kind of communication that might go on between them were severely limited. Given Sr. Norma's emerging alienation from her religious order, the degree of trusting communication between herself and the regional administrators was limited. But given the kind of close, working relationship Sr. Claudia had enjoyed in earlier years with Sr. Jeanine, the frequency, intimacy, and potency of communication that Sr. Claudia could engage in with Sr. Jeanine were, again, testament to the power of relationships to constrain communication and problem solving. The physical locations of the co-directors' respective offices reflected, and strengthened, their mutual avoidance: Sr. Norma's was near Sr. Catherine's, up in the front office of the north wing, where students, faculty, and the public flowed in and out, while Sr. Claudia's was away from any other center of movement in the south wing, buffered by an outer office with two secretaries.

Dyads form only small units in most episodes, but since an individual interchange can be important to a whole episode's outcomes, (e.g., between Sr. Claudia and Mr. Sullivan in the first constitution episode) the relationship between the communicating parties must also be examined. Sr. Claudia's single communication with Sr. Norma, on October 5, did not have the support of a strong bond between them. Indeed, had there developed a strong relationship with some intrinsic attraction, Sr. Norma might well have been much more accountable to Sr. Claudia and much more sympathetic to Sr. Claudia's sense of having been left high and dry. Also, Sr. Claudia might have been much more sympathetic toward Sr. Norma's plight and accompanying emotionality. Their distant relation, as it had grown to be, impinged on the kind of communication that could transpire on October 5, and undermined any readiness on Sr. Claudia's part to pursue further communication with her.

5. Mode of Conflict Management: Inclusionary vs. Exclusionary

Much has been written about 'cooperative' and 'competitive' modes of conflict management (e.g., Deutsch, 1973) characterizing processes of conflict 'resolution' in terms of uses of power, styles of communication, attitudes of the parties, and the like. To that body of theory based chiefly on experimental studies the current conflict episode adds, first, a detailed history of a conflict management by one party, from beginning to end, and second, three new perspectives. First, the dimension, inclusion-exclusion of realities has been brought into focus, replacing the less precise terms 'cooperation' and 'competition'. Two parties can compete in a wide range of domains under many cooperative rules, and cooperation can proceed in varying degrees of mutual and asymmetric reality exclusion. By grounding modes of conflict management in a theory of organizational reality, and relating two principal modes to inclusion and exclusion of parties' realities, conflict theory is brought into *an organizational* context. Second, since parties in the natural setting (but not in experiments) become aware of conflict asymmetrically, a new variable can be identified, a variable of the social psychological *origins* of conflict management: the first-aware party's *transformative response*. That variable is treated at the level of the episode, since it often goes beyond the merely dyadic. Third, since conflict cannot occur where parties are independent, one mode of conflict management, and I would argue a frequent mode in the natural world, is neither 'cooperation' nor 'competition', but independence-seeking. Independence seeking can go on either by inclusive or exclusionary communication. Sr. Norma sought independence in an exclusionary mode. Fourth and finally, since many new and varied possibilities for reality inclusion and exclusion arise from the conflicting parties' giving control over to third parties, a fourth mode of conflict management is identified: conflict management under the direction of one or more third parties.

Basic to a theory of multiple organizational realities, however, is the dimension inclusion-exclusion, and the dyadic choice of a mode of conflict management as inclusionary or exclusionary with respect to the parties' (and observable) realities. The strategic, though non-deliberate or even unwitting, choice of inclusionary vs. exclusionary modes constitutes a commitment, as Deutsch (1973, pp. 365–369) so well points out, to certain attitudes towards the other party, to open or deceptive communication, to uses of power that include or that exclude the other party, and the like. An important variable, then, at the dyadic level, is the parties' commitment to an inclusionary or an exclusionary mode of conflict management.

Sub-Organizational Units

Stabilized at this level are councils, departments, aggregate but un-organized role sets (e.g., homeroom teachers), and ad hoc committees, for example, along with the ways such units are structured. Emergent aspects include problem-relevant transactions within such units, like qualities of member participation in individual meetings and the decision processes of those meetings.

6. Communication: Expression and Exploration of Relevant Organizational Realities

The co-directorate revealed a number of instances of withholding of important organizational realities. Sr. Norma communicated neither the fact that she was losing her commitment to being a nun nor what that implied for her work at Trinity. And she was simply absent from several executive meetings where matters relevant to her functions, and therefore to Sr. Claudia's worries about 'covering' Sr. Norma's area, were discussed.

On Sr. Claudia's part, the problems that she was facing as a result of Sr. Norma's absences and what she was doing about them with the regional administrators were not disclosed to Sr. Norma. While the two sisters' mode of handling conflict was exclusionary, this became more than a dyadic process as it came to characterize the executive council: Sr. Catherine, too, was drawn in.

7. *Mode of Dividing Labor*

The executives had their 'areas of responsibility' and came to executive meetings prepared to up-date the others on events and decisions in their areas. The categories of work each was responsible for had nearly impenetrable boundaries. Sr. Claudia's transgression of one of those boundaries the year before had been explicitly criticized: areas were conceived to be, and addressed as virtually autonomous, independent bailiwicks. The autonomy of each co-director was evident not only in the manner of reporting at each executive meeting, where almost no shared problem-solving went on (the problem-solving alluded to in Chapter 14 being a single notable exception), and not only in Sr. Jeanine's comments about 'two columns' of responsibility. The executive council's compartmentalized structure was also reflected in the fact that the only way for a teacher or counselor to get executive consideration and action on a matter was to approach one of the three executives. The caption under descriptions of each executive's functions, for example, indicates that 'as need arises, faculty and students consult the administrator appropriate to the given area of authority and responsibility'. A matter could not come before the executives as a body, since no mechanism for that had been set up.[3] The executives' roles need not have been so compartmentalized, even with co-equal directors, but at Trinity they were.[4]

The co-directors' use of hard boundaries and prior agreements to the exclusion of consultation about cross-area problems or cross-over effects left them vulnerable to any shift in conditions — or commitments — that rendered the categories or agreements obsolete. While their areas of action generated organization-wide effects, their areas of agenda setting, of communication, and of planning were kept within boundaries. Thus, Sr. Norma could legitimately hold control over functions in her area even when Sr. Claudia complained and asked for relief on October 5. Each co-director's autonomy held heavy implications for communication: one communicates only when one is dependent on another for something. With minimal dependence comes minimal communication. The co-directors' mode of dividing labor, therefore, closed down a channel of communication. One variable of importance, therefore, for stable working relations, i.e., communicative relations, wherever members' roles are systemically interdependent (irrespective of their local conceptions of, or strivings for, autonomy), is reliance on static categories, boundaries, and agreements vs. regular, normal review of the effects each party's plans and actions are likely to have, or have had, outside of the party's own area.

8. Scope of Unit's Agenda Regarding Its Own Performance

Indispensable for the accumulation of 'unfinished business' within the executive council (see page 126 ff.) was its regular exclusion from the agenda of its own meetings any problems of the executives' own functioning — except at year's end, where a general review was often undertaken. Reflecting back on the co-directors' conflict at the regional center, Sr. Catherine told Sr. Norma that she had been forced repeatedly to revise her expectations about Sr. Norma and that she 'never confronted' Sr. Norma with it. Sr. Norma, a few minutes later complained that 'we haven't really been able to sit down ... this is one of the problems'. When one of the executive meetings was cancelled, Sr. Catherine had told Lighthall that it was just as well. They had nothing to meet about, she said, because the two co-directors were so absorbed with their conflict! The idea that the conflict itself, or safely broached parts of it, might become an agenda item for them actually to discuss together was foreign. To the executives as a group, 'work' and 'meeting agenda' were defined exclusively according to the categories of their separate bailiwicks, categories that excluded their work processes and relations.

An important variable impinging on problem-solving effectiveness, then, is a group's readiness to address, or regular avoidance of, *its members' own problems of functioning in their unit*. This would include as legitimate agenda items, for example, substantial problems of setting or meeting expectations, of work processes on particular tasks, or of working relations of its members. A unit that excludes such matters runs the risk, as the executives did, of accumulating 'unfinished interpersonal business' which then poisons relationships and thus creates more *stable, structured blocks against expressing and exploring organizational realities.*

Inter-Unit and Inter-Level Complexity: The Episode

Relatively stabilized at this level of complexity are relations between councils, e.g., between the executives and the Trinity council, between religious and lay teachers and between different levels, e.g., the Trinity executives and the regional administration. Emergent events would be between-group meetings or between-level meetings, e.g., as between the regional administrators and the Trinity executives. The most important emergent unit of functioning at this level of complexity, from the standpoint of adaptations, is the problem-solving or conflict-managing *episode*. This mobile, adaptive mechanism, by which people accumulate their intelligence and action into changed conditions, recruits into itself members and groups from a number of levels of social complexity. Because of its complexity, its duration, and especially its previously unstudied nature, our consideration of it will be extended.

9.   *Communication: Degree of Transformation of Realities*

A frequent tendency in this episode was to communicate highly transformed realities rather than, or far more prominently than, the initial realities of problems themselves. When Sr. Claudia went to see Sr. Norma on October 5, for example, she quickly moved to suggest to Sr. Norma a solution. She communicated very little of her problem — little of the actual work she did as a result, little or nothing of how that affected her, and apparently nothing of her conferences out at the regional center with Sr. Jeanine, visits that would have conveyed the intensity of Sr. Claudia's problem. Sr. Claudia's corrective solution crowded out her problem in that interchange. Similarly, when Sr. Norma sought a change in attitude and behavior from homeroom teachers, she was heavy on solutions and plans and virtually silent on the realities of her problem. Each sister, having progressed in her own problem solving, made public only the most recent mental transformations of her problem, namely solutions, not the initiating, guiding, and energizing realities to which they were initially responding, namely, the *problems*, which alone gave the solutions legitimacy and meaning. Thus, not only in the first episode, but also in this conflict episode, a variable affecting problem-solving effectiveness was the communication of highly transformed or strategically distorted realities vs. authentic communication of early confusion or problems.

10.   *Distribution of Motivational Investment*

In contrast to the motivation of participants in the first constitution episode, investment of parties involved in solving Sr. Claudia's problem was widely distributed — with one key exception, Sr. Norma, who was heavily invested in solving her own problems. In respect to our chief focus, Sr. Claudia's problem of conflict with Sr. Norma, it is clear that Sr. Claudia was able to induce motivated investment of Sr. Catherine, Sr. Jeanine, and Sr. Georgette, and that these, in turn, induced the participation of others. Sr. Norma's non-investment remained telling, however, indicating that the mere per cent of motivated participants in an episode cannot be taken as a sufficient index of reality-including participation.

11. *Relationships/Linkages Among Constituents: Between Groups and Levels*

Relations between the executive council and two other bodies, one at a level below it and one at a level above it, suggest a variable effecting problem-solving effectiveness: linkage — infrequent and weak vs. regular and strong. The Trinity council's attempt to solve parking problems came a cropper because realities at the executive level were not integrated into the council's action — and vice versa. Linkage between the executives and the Trinity council, via Sr. Norma's participation, was infrequent and weak. Similarly, the regional administrators' solution of their problem regarding the restoration of Sr. Norma's responsibility, accountability, and personal presence came a cropper because their linkage was virtually non-existent. They had to make assumptions in the place of valid information because they had no regular linkage with Trinity by which relevant realities there could be conveyed to them.

Affecting problem-solving effectiveness at this level of complexity, then, is the strength of linkage between constituent groups. Indices of strength would be the number of overlapping members, regularity of overlapping members' contacts, and fidelity and completeness of communication by and to these linking members.[5]

Two Classes of Problem Constituents: Protagonists and Antagonists. These episodes and study of other organizations suggest that in virtually all organizational problems the conditions found objectionable and unwanted by the problem originator are associated with some other persons' or group's actions. Part of the originator's problem, in other words, is what other people or groups are doing or have done or are failing or refusing to do. This implies two clusters of conflicting interests. On one hand is the person (for example, Sr. Claudia) for whom condition X (e.g., Sr. Norma's pattern of absences) is unwanted and is taken as the source of a problem. On the other hand are those (like Sr. Norma) whose current functioning supports or has caused or depends on condition X, and who would have to change their way of thinking or functioning if condition X were to be changed. Let us call persons for whom condition X has become unwanted the *protagonists* and those whose functioning supports, has caused, or depends on condition X, the *antagonists*.[6]

It is often the case, as it was with Sr. Claudia, that the unwanted conditions can be changed only with the active assistance or the passive acquiescence of those for whom the unwanted conditions are functional, the antagonists. That is, *the protagonist is often directly dependent on the antagonist for the solution of the protagonist's problem.*

Order of Contact By Protagonist With Other Realities. In such problems, the order in which a problem originator makes contact with other persons, and thus with other organizational realities, is important. In the early phases of one's problem solving, one is still centered on one's confusions and problems and on the upsetting situations that have caused the confusions and problems. When Sr. Claudia first went out to the regional center in late August to see Sr. Jeanine, for example, she was probably not yet committed to a particular solution, like getting a replacement for Sr. Norma. Here, the data present a hiatus, a gap filled only by speculation: she more than likely wanted to vent her frustrations, to get some clarity on her problem, and to seek Sr. Jeanine's advice. It undoubtedly was necessary to describe in some detail the history of Sr. Norma's absences, their effects, and their guessed-at causes.

With one's first attempts to get help from others in solving one's problem, one usually turns to trusted, friendly colleagues to explore how to think and feel about the problem's elements, i.e., what one has seen and how one has interpreted it, what one wants and values, and the like. One seeks confirmation that it is a legitimate problem and also ideas about solutions. With time, however, solutions begin to come center stage and to crowd out discussion of the problem. The originating problem and feelings surrounding it, once conveyed and legitimated by trusted others, move into the background, crowded out by subordinate problems of solution refinement and implementation.

But note: the realities one is encountering early are friendly ones, often similar to those of the problem originator. In any case, the realities that are most unknown, even baffling to the problem originator, the realities associated with the unwanted conditions, are those which operate in the antagonists, those causing, supporting, or depending on the unwanted conditions. (A reminder: antagonists are not ordinarily nasty, obstructionistic people, but merely those organization members on whom solution of the protagonist's problem depends and who happen to also be attached to conditions the protagonist's solution wants to change.) Antagonists are turned to, often, only *after* the problem originator has both crystallized her problem and at least narrowed down the field of acceptable solutions. Considerable cognitive and emotional work has often been completed, often with others, then, by the time the protagonist or someone on her behalf makes contact with an antagonist.

Seven Progressions

Implicit in the foregoing characterizations of the problem-solving process as it typically or often proceeds are seven progressions of action or action tendency that now should be made explicit. Let me list them first and then explain each. I shall be driving toward describing a threat to organizational effectiveness in problem solving, a threat to reality integration, that lies in

213

the cumulative and interactive impact of these progressions. First, the progressions:

1. Progression of Problem Transformations.
2. Progression of Participants' Sense of Corrective Mastery.
3. Progression of Participants' Commitment to Action.
4. Progression of Contacts: Protagonist to Antagonist.
5. Progression of Capacity for Reality Exploration and Integration: Maximum to Minimum.
6. Progression of Incompatibility of Realities to be Integrated.
7. Progression of Delegation of Successive Subordinate Tasks.

1. Progression of Problem Transformations.   The problem originator and protagonists, no matter the content of their problem, their location in the organization, or their personalities, seem to move their problem across a continuum of transformations beginning with the experience of confusion or disorientation, a condition of the originator's psyche, and ending in routinized policies or procedures for action, a condition of the organization.

I assume, with Dewey (1938), that just prior to any incompatibility in operating reality (problem) is a more diffuse state of mind, a confusion or disorientation, a disruption at some level of awareness, a sense that something is wrong, that things are not as they should be, as they were expected or assumed to be.[7] I also assume that more than a few seconds of confusion or disorientation is one of the most noxious states humans can experience, often more noxious than pain. The onset of confusion, therefore, receives immediate allocations of attention and of other resources: mobilization of energy and vigilance, a scanning of environment and of the contents of operating reality. This mobilization and scanning attempt to reduce the confusion to more focal, manageable content, to distill out of that confused content the essence of the trouble, and to bring in into focus.

That distilled content seems always to synthesize two components or two sets of components in (subjectively judged) opposition — a goal and a barrier, a feeling and a proscription against the feeling, a goal and a contradictory value, an expectation and a contradictory perception, and so on. That synthesized incompatibility usually represents an enormous simplification of the prior confusion, from the diffused, gray, many to the focused, black and white, two. With the simplified duality also comes a focal task: reduce the incompatibility to tolerable levels.

I have begun to describe a progression or continuum of problem-solving transformations. Imagine a horizontal line from left to right, representing a left-to-right progression of actions, action tendencies, and capacities, each building — or capable of building — on the action before it, to the left. At the extreme left is mental confusion in some person. At the extreme right is routine social action responsive to, and corrective of, that confusion. Just inside the left extreme of confusion emerges a new state of mind, an incompatibility, the state I call 'problem'.

Problems are transformations of confusion into focal incompatibilities. By synthesizing a problem from confusion, focused energy becomes directed toward reduction of its incompatibility to tolerable levels, tolerable as judged subjectively by the person who has synthesized the problem (whom I have labelled the 'problem originator'). Such energy is expended in one or more of a number of problem-solving moves, familiar to us all, extending to the right in our progression, toward routine social action: imagining actions, some new and some already well tested, that will reduce the incompatibility (solutions); assessing costs and consequences of this and that action (preliminary evaluation) and selecting the most cost-effective action (solution selection, or decision); and specifying component parts of the action, persons who might undertake each part, resources needed, and a time schedule (planning).

Up to this point in the progression of component actions the process may be entirely cognitive, inside the head of the problem originator. But organizational problems, by definition, involve interdependencies: the problem originator *cannot solve her organizational problem alone*. So somewhere in this progression, and no later than the planning stage, others must be recruited into the problem-solving process. Any such recruitment adds entirely new dimensions. It adds new and separate operating realities, realities which capture different parts of the organization from the parts captured in the originator's reality, and different goals, values, and fears regarding the organization and different connectedness to resources.

Just to the right of planning, then, another component is added: recruitment of others into the problem-solving process. These others may be protagonists or antagonists and may participate, in principle, in any component after the initial confusion. The next component after the recruitment of others into the process would ordinarily be thought to be setting plans in motion (solution implementation). But just before that it is useful to accommodate another special kind of recruited participant, the so-called third party in resolving disputes. Because virtually any organizational problem implicitly involves a conflict of interests between the problem originator and those who support or depend on the originator's unwanted condition, conflict-managing processes are implicitly involved. Since these occasionally recruit third parties, we make room for that component just prior to solution implementation.

Each of these moves describes another progression in the transformation of confusion and problem into an action, an action whose final form is so routine that it takes little energy to maintain. That routinized action, at the far right of our continuum of transformation, is immediately preceded by two penultimate moves: an evaluation of the solution implementation (solution evaluation) and a correction or fine tuning of it for repeated, habitual use if the originally problematic conditions may arise repeatedly (feedback). Figure 17.1 summarizes the components of the continuum of transformations from individual confusion to organizational routine.

These components must not be understood as empirical 'steps' in a problem-solving process. Except for a few, they are more in the nature of possibilities or resources. Once confusion arises, the only actions in this continuum of transformations that regularly take place in effective adaptations are problem synthesis, solution selection, recruitment of other participants, and solution implementation. Consider these the minimum necessary components of any transformation. The other ('minor') components (#'s 3, 4, 6, 8, and 10 in Fig. 17.1) are often used to strengthen solution effectiveness. Ready routines of action, even organized action with many participants, are often thrown into the breech of a problem without solution evaluation or planning, and often with effective results. When planning is engaged in, it often leads backward, leftward, to solution generation and selection which, in turn, may well make participants realize that the problem they had first synthesized was a faulty synthesis, a realization that then leads to a new confusion. The 'minor' actions in the continuum constitute *logical* progressions from an episode's beginning to its end (from left to right in Fig. 17.1) but not a linear progression of empirical psychological or social processes. The minimum necessary components (#'s 2, 5, 7, and 9 in Fig. 17.1) seem to be both logically required and empirically engaged in once confusion or disorientation arises.

2. Progression of Participants' Sense of Corrective Mastery. As the problem originator and others recruited into the process move toward a solution, and as they solve the problem's sub-problems, they move from a sense of frustrating difficulty to a sense of mastery and hope. Their efforts are rewarded and validated by an augmented sense of what White (1959) called 'effectance' and 'competence'. Each part of a solution becomes a rewarding accomplishment, a sign they are on the right track. They become more invested in the problem-solving process.

3. Progression of Participants' Commitment to Action. As participants who become recruited early in an episode witness the survival of a solution they have accepted, and as the solution survives and becomes translated into plans of who, what, when, and where, their commitment to actually doing something increases. A movement from disorientation to problem already brings a thrust toward closure, and solutions and plans make closure more tangible and more possible. It is in the nature of the continuum of transformations (progression #1), once entered at the left, to exit at the right with that most tangible and definitive closure, action. It is possible, especially under crisis, for participants to drive toward action in the absence of, and as a quick substitute for, the sense of mastery that comes from working from problem to solutions to plans. In any case, the

1. Confusion, Disorientation

2.* Problem Synthesis*

3. Generation of solution(s)

4. Preliminary evaluation of solutions

5.* Selection of solution(s): decision*

6. Planning: Identifying who, what, when, and where. →...

...→

7.* Recruitment of others to participate in solution or implementation.*

8. Third Party Recruitment: Disinterested help.

9.* Implementation of solution*

10. Evaluation of implementation

11. Routinization of solution

...→

Figure 17.1. Progression of eleven transformations from psychological confusion to organizational routine. Those marked (*) — #'s 2, 5, 7, and 9 — appear to make up the minimum set of effective moves with organizational problems once confusion takes place. All others are optional, often omitted, and any given episode may have moves leftward as well as to the right, e.g.. from planning back to problem, from implementation back to solution, etc.

progression toward action may temporarily bring backward movements, e.g., from plans back to new solutions, but those backward movements come to rest in elements which nonetheless have their own forward thrust toward action. In general, as commitment to action increases, commitment to further transforming earlier (leftward) elements decreases. Thus protagonists' (including supporters') *resistance to re-syntheses of a problem steadily increases* as movement progresses from left to right. The possibility of re-synthesis is always there, but the likelihood lessens with increasing movement toward plans and action.

This progressive commitment toward action casts *early* participants in the role of playwright and director and *later* participants in the role of actor and stagehand. That is, there is an *order effect* in problem-solving episodes. That order effect has a dimension that is distinctly hierarchical and political. The order effect relates, that is, to who governs and who is governed within the limits of episodic action. To control whose problem and which problem will be solved, therefore, is already largely to control whose reality will be responded to. To control the solution as well as the problem is to control just about all that matters — at least within a given problem-solving episode.

4. Progression of Contacts: Protagonist to Antagonist. As I've already indicated, problem originators tend to seek the help of others close to them with whom they have an easy, trusting, working relation. Early assistance in problem clarification and in generating and evaluating solutions, therefore, is from those most likely to operate from realities similar or complementary to the problem originator's with respect to the problem. These co-protagonists are not as likely as others in the organization to support or depend on the conditions which the originator now finds troublesome. The left-to-right action tendency (progression #3) moves *whoever* participates in the process toward plans and solution implementation. Since early participants in problem-solving processes are usually those whose realities vis à vis the problem are similar, initial problem-solving action tends often to be most compatible with the original protagonist's realities and, for reasons already stated, least compatible with antagonist realities. Thus early transformation tends to exclude antagonist realities in favor of protagonist realities.

5. Progression of Capacity for Reality Exploration and Integration: Maximum to Minimum. As already indicated in discussing progression #'s 2 and 3, as commitment to action increases, left to right, so commitment decreases to 'leftward' or 'backward' revisions of earlier transformations. Movement of any kind in problem-solving tends to be movement away from problem. It is in problem synthesizing, however, that the originator is most open to new realities, most ready to forge a new integration. New realities can also be explored and integrated during solution generation and evaluation, but by the time action plans have been made and agreed to by others, exploration and integration of new realities meets resistance from those who have now agreed to the solutions or plans. Thus, the collective capacity for exploring and integrating realities *diminishes* as participants move into plans and toward solution implementation and will be sharply diminished during solution implementation.[8]

6. *Progression of Incompatibility of Realities to Be Integrated.*   As the process of transformation proceeds — problems into solutions, solutions into plans, plans into actions — more participants are recruited. More antagonists are contacted and the realities presented for integration become more and more divergent from the protagonists' initiating realities. These newly recruited realities, after all, are those most supportive of, and most dependent upon, the conditions that protagonists have initially found objectionable. So, at the same time that participants' capacity for integrating new realities diminishes (progression #5), the ongoing process uncovers and recruits realities progressively *more incompatible* with realities integrated earlier.

7. *Progression of Delegation of Successive Subordinate Tasks.*   Once a solution to the initial problem has been chosen by a person or group, its implementation is often turned over to others. These others, in turn, synthesize various problems of implementation, settle on solutions, and delegate these to still others. A considerable distance often grows up in organizations, then, between the initiating problem and the front-line actions — as it happened with the regional administrators' November 2 solution, and as it happened between Sr. Claudia and Mr. Sullivan regarding a 'constitution'. This is the 'whispering parlor game' effect, discussed in Part II, where early participants participate in the episode only early, middle participants only in the middle, and late participants only late — a linear sequential structure without 'loops' in the series of participations.
  Such linear, non-looped structures promote discontinuities in the transformation processes, allowing the successively recruited local realities successively to pre-empt earlier realities as the focus of action, undermining or destroying cumulative problem-solving.

Protagonists' Protective Tendencies   The problem originator and fellow protagonists tend to seek a comfortable protection for the adaptations that, sometimes with considerable and lengthy difficulty, they strive to bring about. Movement from confusion to problem to solution in organizations often requires hard cognitive and emotional work on the part of a number of participants, as it did with Sr. Claudia, Sr. Jeanine, and Sr. Georgette. With a certain degree of movement along the progressions of transformation, sense of mastery, and commitment to action, protagonists feel more comfortable making contact with antagonists to induce their cooperation or compliance in solving 'the' problem. The tendency is strong at that point for protagonists to hold on to their developed solutions, to present them center stage. To do otherwise is often considered weakness, a regression, a denial of their hard-won solution, a denial of its validity, sometimes even a deceptive retreat from their commitments to those who have helped produce the favored solution, and so on. Often, that is, protagonists develop a tendency prior to approaching an antagonist to protect the integrity of the solution they have developed. This protective tendency seems to manifest itself in at least three forms, each more severely solution-centered, and protagonist-centered, than the one before.

The first form this protection of a protagonist solution takes in approaching an antagonist is to briefly describe one or two elements of the problem and then elaborate the solution in some detail. This may open the door for further exploration and exchange of realities, or it may focus attention on the actions to be taken. Sr. Claudia's October 5 approach to Sr. Norma, and Sr. Norma's response, seem to fit this type.

The second form of protection is to focus only on the solution, to 'sell' it as timely and fitting, extolling its virtues by portraying the good things it will bring. Problems are left entirely in the background, as are differences of opinion regarding the solution. This 'positive' presentation may prompt objections or quick acquiescence. The latter inhibits reality exploration, often necessary to integrate the realities of antagonists.

The third and most severe form by-passes any possibility of problem exposure, depending instead on manipulating antagonists into accepting proposals or actions. Antagonists are told falsehoods that point to the necessity or desirability of the preferred solution. Or they are merely ignored long enough for protagonists to make important parts of their preferred solution a *fait accompli*, thus committing antagonists either to accept the full solution in compliance or to raise an unseemly and costly row. This third manner of solution protection — no effective protection at all, of course, from the chronic organizational realities of antagonists — I have already described in the first chapter of Part III as the exclusionary mode of conflict management, available to the first-aware party in the period of asymmetric conflict.

For the problem originator and other protagonists to give in to any of these protective temptations is to risk pre-empting communication about the problems of both protagonists and antagonists. The risk of excluding problems is the risk of foregoing cooperation, since the social psychological basis for any cooperation is similar or complementary problems. Cooperation, here, must be sharply distinguished from compliance. Protagonists who give in to these tendencies toward action often interpret compliance, the outward face of cooperation, as being cooperation itself. Cooperation by antagonists implies, as compliance does not, the continued release of the antagonist's resources into a line of action even when there is no protagonist surveillance.[9] These protective temptations constitute a risk on three counts. The risk increases markedly, from the first to the third of the foregoing protective moves, but risk is present even in the first, most benign move.

The first protective move, to guide antagonists' attention to one's solution and only briefly to the realities behind it, risks failing to induce in the other the very problem one is trying to solve. Solution-mindedness, as Norman Maier (1958, 1970) pointed out long ago, crowds out problem-mindedness. It is the problem which contains the realities to which one is responding and to which one wants the other to respond. Furthermore, solutions are not effective vehicles for conveying two other important parts of any protagonist's reality: intensity of problem and history of efforts thus far to solve the problem. These elements are often necessary to break through the routinized outlooks of antagonists, to let them know that there really are other worlds out here, not just their own, and that the intensity of some problem has caused actions which they would want to know about.

Second, a focus on solutions, even if one is clever enough to present two from which a choice may be made, diverts the attention of both protagonist and antagonist away from the antagonist's realities regarding the conditions unwanted by the protagonist. Since those ignored or avoided realities are the ones which are behind the antagonist's support for and dependence on the unwanted conditions, those are precisely the realities that must be taken into account if the antagonist's needed cooperation is to be secured in changing those conditions. To drive those antagonist realities into the background is to serve only the protagonist's short term *sense* of mastery, not actual joint mastery of the relevant realities. And what are the relevant realities? They are the operating realities of both protagonist and antagonist regarding the condition that the protagonist no longer favors.

The realities that Sr. Claudia, facing Sr. Norma's absences, had to integrate if Sr. Norma's cooperation were to be secured were those behind the absences, namely, the causes of Sr. Norma's depleted investment in her work at Trinity. When Sr. Claudia moved quickly to her solution, in that October 5 conference with Sr. Norma, she precluded the very kind of information she needed in order to understand her co-director's operating reality, that to which Sr. Norma was, in fact, responding in absenting herself.

Sr. Norma's defensive response on October 5 to Sr. Claudia's solution brings us to a third reason why a protagonist's yielding to the temptation to focus an antagonist's attention on solutions rather than on problems is self-defeating. The greater the antagonist's support for or dependency on, the unwanted condition — as Sr. Norma was invested in and depended on being absent from Trinity, the greater the likelihood that the antagonist's operating reality (in this example, Sr. Norma's) will be different from the protagonist's reality and the less the likelihood that the protagonist's favored solution will fit the antagonist's reality. The greater the antagonist's support for or dependency on the unwanted condition, indeed, the more likely it will be that the antagonist will regard the protagonist's solution as *antithetical* to the antagonist's reality and will defend against the solution.

In short, the more a solution fits one's own protected, protagonist realities the less it is likely to fit the realities of those whose actions most support or most depend on the conditions one finds objectionable.

The theory of multiple and diffused organizational realities I am proposing asserts the primacy of the individual's current, local, operating reality in controlling the individual's behavior. When Sr. Claudia brings her own solution to Sr. Norma, who supports or depends on the absences Sr. Claudia finds objectionable, Sr. Claudia is in effect asking Sr. Norma to by-pass or ignore her own reality and to act, instead, on a solution that is responsive to Sr. Claudia's reality, remote from Sr. Norma's. For the protagonist to continue to focus on her own *solution* based on her own problem, is not only to silence the strongest voices of her own immediate reality but also to deny the force of antagonist realities *and to deny the extent to which protagonists depend upon antagonists to solve protagonist problems.*

A protagonist can often force outward compliance with a solution that by-passes the antagonist's local realities, but only because the force itself often becomes a dominant part of the antagonist's reality. Most organizational problems involve members (antagonists) whose actions not only promote and sustain the conditions protagonists find objectionable, but who also have powers of evasion, delay, obstruction, and sabotage in a wide range of alternative actions. Solutions that would gain these members' support for implementation must integrate these members' local realities: they, too, have only so much energy, only so many resources, to expend; they, too, spend their resources on their own local, high priorities.

But even if the antagonist is not defensive, that is no guarantee that antagonist realities are compatible with altering the condition found objectionable by the protagonist. None of us is immediately and completely in touch with the realities to which we respond over the course of a problem's solving. What is important, from the standpoint of multiple and diffused realities, is not that antagonists be immediately willing or satisfied with a solution proposed by a protagonist, but that locally operating constituent realities — their values, commitments to norms, to work routines, their sustained perceptions of local conditions, and the like — actually be integrated into solutions.

The conception of the problem-solving episode as a social enterprise with a forward movement toward action, initiated at the individual level by a movement from confusion to incompatibilities to reduction of those incompatibilities, brings into the spotlight variables related to sequence — chronological sequence and sequence in the progression of problem-solving transformation. This conception and the two problem-solving narratives suggest additional variables at the episodic level to account for degrees of problem-solving effectiveness.

12. *Sequential Structure and Functioning of Participations*

This variable became clear in the first episode, which was so clearly linear in structure: it matters *when* members, particularly antagonists, are brought into the problem-solving process. Some antagonists may be brought into the process early. If a crucial segment of those required to implement a solution participates only early or only in the middle or only at the end, however, its realities may be integrated weakly or not at all. It is the process as a whole that has force, not just some climactic point. The origins are especially important but, as is evident from the first constitution episode, they can be entirely reversed by later participations *if the episode's structure of sequential participations is predominantly linear.* If transformation is always going on in this episodic unit, then realities have to be constantly reintegrated. Integration at the beginning of an episode is not the same as integration at the middle or the end.

In the co-director episode Sr. Claudia and Sr. Jeanine participated heavily in the early and middle segments, but Sr. Jeanine and Sr. Georgette both dropped out entirely from the implementation phase. Sr. Norma participated only in the middle phase, and then only under the constraint of authority. Had Sr. Norma been brought into the process earlier and more regularly with Sr. Jeanine, and had Sr. Georgette followed through with contacts back at Trinity, it seems likely that the November solution would have been considerably modified in response to the central reality initially excluded, namely Sr. Norma's diminished commitment and her continued resistance to executive meetings.

Of course, mere contact accomplishes nothing except to provide opportunity for reality exploration. Opportunity is a necessary not a sufficient condition for reality integration.[10] Each structural opportunity for integrating early realities into late ones must be actually exploited if integration is to take place. In the first episode, Sr. Norma was present in the December 7 meeting where Sullivan proposed the constitution, but was silent about the function she herself had earlier proposed to Sr. Claudia it might serve: the structural loop (her presence on both occasions) did not function as a loop.

13. *Protagonist Action in the Period of Asymmetric Awareness of Conflict*

Those possessed of an organizational problem first possess also the first opportunity for inclusionary or exclusionary action. One index of the amount of unilateral action on the part of the protagonist in the period of asymmetric awareness is the duration of that period. A better index is the number of problem-solving contacts among protagonists before an antagonist is contacted; and a third, even better, is the distance toward solution, plans, and action actually traveled before an antagonist first participates in the problem-solving action. Sr. Claudia and Sr. Jeanine had traveled some considerable distance over more than a month's time before Sr. Norma was approached by Sr. Claudia on October 5.

14. *Communicativeness of Protagonist-Antagonist Contacts*

Are protagonists' contacts with antagonists fleeting, solution-centered, and confined to a few, only one, or no meetings or are they extended, reality exploring, and numerous? Sr. Claudia's October 5 meeting with Sr. Norma was, from her own testimony at least, apparently relatively brief, only briefly centered on Sr. Claudia's reality vis à vis absences and then pointedly action centered — and was not followed up by either sister. Subsequent meetings were held, so the opportunity for probing realities was created. From the data available from the joint meeting at the regional center, it is clear that the reality testing was not sufficient to bring Sr. Norma's overriding preoccupations to light in the deliberations at the center.

15. *Extent of Mutual Induction of Problems by Both Protagonists and Antagonists*

Here we extend to the episodic level the earlier variable at the individual level, inclusive vs. exclusionary problem synthesis on the part of the problem originator. The data regarding Sr. Norma's understanding of Sr. Claudia's problems are skeletal. The data available suggest that any problem Sr. Claudia might have about Sr. Norma's absences was, in Sr. Norma's reality, small potatoes compared to Sr. Norma's problems. So overwhelming to Sr. Norma were her problems of leaving the order and starting a new life that there was no room for mutuality with Sr. Claudia. Sr. Claudia was in a similar situation. It is clear that she had internalized the fact that Sr. Norma might leave the religious order. But that did not necessarily imply that Sr. Norma would not follow through on her current year's work obligations at Trinity. Still Sr. Claudia's problems, including not only a revamping of the school's administration on top of ongoing administrative work and not only the extra load of tasks Sr. Norma was doing, from Sr. Claudia's perspective, half heartedly or not at all, but also the terminal illness of Sr. Claudia's mother — all these left little room in Sr. Claudia's reality for problems Sr. Norma might be experiencing.

16. Strength of Resources and of Mobilization to Reverse Exclusions

Given the high probability of reality exclusion in any problem-solving effort, the capacity to mitigate or reverse such reality exclusions may be the most important capacity of an organization. Let any sub-unit stumble, so long as it has the capacity to recover balance — up to a point. I refer to an organization's capacity to interrupt the kind of mutual exclusion the co-directors had established, for example, by (a) either the protagonist's or antagonist's seeking help, help that actually results in mitigation or reversal of reality exclusions or (b) opposition by constituents who succeed in breaking through the exclusion of their (or others') realities. Examples of unsuccessful opposition, from Part II, were Nora Quinn's and Lucy Ellen Garvin's questioning of Mr. Sullivan in his December 7 proposal of a constitution. There, the adolescents' opposition was too weak to break through the adults' insular, exclusionary minding. The girls evidently were pursuing important realities vis à vis a constitution but had insufficient positional power and were not organized. In the present conflict episode, the two co-directors had no mutually trusted friends in the school itself who were ready to help them individually or together to break through their mutual exclusion. Lighthall's relatively weak attempt at suggesting to Sr. Claudia that she take a matter-of-fact approach to Sr. Norma, regarding rumors that Sr. Norma was leaving, revealed the depths of Sr. Claudia's aversion to Sr. Norma's crying and despair.

The regional administrators, on the other hand, were more successful in mitigating the co-directors' mutual exclusion. They opened up a number of channels of communication, heard testimony from both Sr. Claudia and Sr. Norma, and considered it from a stance much more inclusive, less ego-centric than either of the co-directors. That their own distance from Trinity and false assumptions prevented a more reality integrating solution should not blind us to the fact that, with respect to the co-directors' separate realities and relationship, their intervention did release for relatively dispassionate consideration realities from both sides of this mutually exclusionary conflict.

We turn now to episodic events related to the recruitment and functioning of third parties, whether from outside the organization or from within, third parties like Sr. Jeanine and Sr. Georgette.

An Episode's Third Parties

17. Extent of Third-Party Participation

Implicit in any process of organizational problem solving or conflict management is the participants' choice between maintaining control over the problem-solving process itself or giving some or all control to a third party, someone not particularly affected by or connected to the problematic condition, neither protagonist nor antagonist. Once one turns to a third party for assistance, with all of the cognitive work that implies for a third party, one incurs some obligation to be influenced by the third party. They have given up some of their own normal priorities, after all, to address the protagonist's (and perhaps also the antagonist's) problems. Part of the control over the process, then, is delivered out of the hands of the parties seeking help to the hands of those giving it.

Third parties allow new mixtures of people, new contexts and resources for exploring realities, and bring new operating realities into a problem-solving process. However, while recruitment of third parties itself enhances reality exploration, such recruitment tends to happen only when the parties are unable to manage their conflict. In the large, then, the mere recruitment of a third party would count as a sign of ineffectiveness. Given an exclusionary mode of conflict management, however, the choice to recruit a third party would seem to favor expression and exploration of new realities. So, the first third-party variable is the extent of third-party participation. Indices are the number of third parties and the frequency of contact with the principals.

As we shall see, the regional administrators can be considered to have taken the role of third party only from within the organization, not as independent outsiders. Nevertheless, analysis of their participation as an 'insider' third party brings into focus a number of implicit choices and important possibilities.

18.   *Third-Party Recruitment/Legitimation*

Once that basic choice of recruiting a third party is made, three other choices follow necessarily. The first is the choice between seeking third-party help unilaterally by the protagonist or the antagonist alone, or jointly with both parties cooperating in the choice. A unilateral choice of third-party assistance is a form of exclusion and amounts to forming a power coalition against the excluded party. Assistance from unilaterally chosen third parties may well not be regarded as help by the excluded party, and any solutions or plans produced by the third party are likely to exclude the realities of the excluded party and to be rejected. They may show short-term compliance but probably not cooperation. So the second third-party variable is whether the third party is recruited unilaterally with partial legitimation or jointly, legitimate in the eyes of both protagonists and antagonists.

19. *Third-Party Response to Received Legitimation:*
Passive Vs. Active

Once the basic choice has been made to involve a third party, whether the choice is unilateral or joint, the third party has two further choices. These are choices by the third party alone, independent of choices by the two principal parties. The third party's first choice is between assuming, or establishing, its legitimacy to both of the principal parties. It is not necessary for a third party to be bound by a unilateral recruitment and thereby be confined to the role of ally with the party who unilaterally recruited the third party. It is possible for third parties to reverse the exclusion of a unilateral approach to them by approaching the other party and bringing her (or them) into the decision to use third-party assistance.

Another third-party variable, then, is the extent to which the third party passively accepts the legitimacy received from the recruitment or actively tests for and establishes its own bilateral legitimacy. The regional administrators implicitly chose the passive rather than active mode. Of course, on general principles of authority and hierarchy, they were legitimate: they were the co-directors' superordinates. But in terms of their specific legitimacy *as third parties* in helping to solve a problem, they were, in Sr. Norma's eyes, not neutral at all but assistants of one party, solving Sr. Claudia's problem, not a problem of Sr. Norma's. Indeed, their involvement exacerbated Sr. Norma's problems.

20. *Third-Party Role: Mediation Vs. Arbitration*

The second choice by any third party is between the role of mediator and the role of arbitrator. To mediate is to accept control over the problem-solving or conflict-management process but not over the substantive content of agreements. The process has to do with the timing and conduct of meetings between the principals, the selection of agenda items, support for full exploration of constituent realities, and the like. The substantive content of agreements is left for the principals to hammer out, with the mediator making sure that the hammering continues by both sides. To arbitrate is to take control over both process and substantive content of outcomes. With arbitration, the two principals give up all control over their problem-solving or conflict managing process and in doing so allow realities that are foreign to both of them, viz., the third parties' own realities, to shape the settlement that will be imposed upon them.

Arbitration affects the principals' realities regarding the final settlement in another way different from mediation. In mediation, the parties not only participate directly in the give and take, they also jointly *see each other giving as well as taking*. In arbitration that process is markedly less visible, if visible at all, since the arbitrator is more active and does much private balancing. The resulting relationship between the principals, therefore, will be more grounded in the actual realities of each other from a process of mediation than from one of arbitration.

The regional administrators clearly assumed an arbitrating, not a mediating, role — even to the point of arranging meetings with the two principals so that they would not encounter one another as they came and went from the meeting with the regional administrators. As chapter 13 shows, the regional administrators' realities were distant in a number of respects from those at Trinity, though by and large theirs were more similar to Sr. Claudia's than to Sr. Norma's. Their actions were fast and 'efficient', in the context of their busy schedules. A fourth third-party variable, then, is the type of role chosen: mediation vs. arbitration.

21. Extent of Support for an Arbitrator Role

Necessary for the success of arbitration are at least two conditions besides the third party's legitimacy: (1) the sense of crisis experienced jointly by the principal parties, sufficient to lead them to surrender to others' efforts and to lend strong, shared legitimacy to a settlement and (2) the police powers associated with arbitration, powers of surveillance and forced compliance over both parties, powers lasting the full duration of the agreement. Given the choice of an arbitrator role, what is the extent of support for arbitration beyond legitimation? The regional administrators' arbitration lacked all three of the necessary conditions: shared crisis on the part of the conflicting parties, and powers of surveillance and forcing compliance.

The major contribution of the regional administrators was not as third parties, however, but as superordinate authorities: they and they alone had the legitimate power to give Sr. Claudia Trinity's directorship the following year and to legitimate Sr. Claudia's current authority in all matters pertaining to the following year. It was that line-authority and their use of it, not their third-party role, which solved Sr. Claudia's immediate problem of being held responsible for actions but at the same time being inhibited by the norm of 'overstepping'.[11]

The regional administrators' role as 'insider' third party brought quite another set of views and resources to the co-directors' conflict, brought the two sisters face to face again with the administrators present, and constituted more than merely an ally of Sr. Claudia's. Nevertheless, their role as third party had serious limitations. First, they assumed specific, bilateral legitimacy where only vague and unilateral legitimacy existed. Second, they assumed an arbitrational role before testing mediational possibilities. Finally, they assumed an arbitrational role without the resources necessary for implementing arbitration and monitoring its results.

228

Table 17.1   Expanded Culling of Twenty-One Variables, At Four Levels of Organizational Complexity, Hypothesized to Account for the Effectiveness Of Organizational Problem-Solving

No.   Name of Variable (followed by page references in the narrative)

Individual

1. Problem synthesis by the problem originator: inclusive-cooperative vs. exclusionary-defensive (II:50, 53; III: 109–10, 166–67).
2. Participants' orientations to emotionality and expression of conflict: expressive-confrontive-inclusive vs. suppressive-defensive-denying-exclusionary (III: 127, 130, 133, 155, 187–88).

Interpersonal

3. Aim and level of intervention: centered; addressed to relevant persons and relevant positions (i.e., constituents) vs. off-center; addressed to peripheral, non-constituent persons or positions (II: 50, 53, 54; III: 109, 127).
4. Inclusionary vs. exclusionary *relationships*: trust vs. mistrust; congeniality vs. antagonism. (III: 104–5, 112, 118, 133, 147, 161, 171–72, 176, 183, 187).
5. Mode of conflict management: Inclusionary vs. exclusionary. (II: 50; III: chapter 11 and specific parts of the narrative on pages 118–19, 138, 153–54, 156–57, 183).

Sub-Organizational Units

6. Communication: expression and exploration (vs. denial, withholding, obscuring) of relevant organizational realities. (II: 54, 59–60, 64–5; III: chapters 11 and 12, and pages 109–10, 126–27, 149–50, 153–55, 177).
7. Mode of dividing labor: reliance on static categories and agreements vs. regular communication to review cross-over effects. (II: 50; III: 129, 165, 167).
8. Scope of unit's formal or informal agenda: inclusion and communication (vs. exclusion and non-communication) of work related intragroup, intergroup, and interpersonal problems (III: 98, 113–14, 126–27, 140–41).

Inter-Unit, Inter-Level Complexity: The Episode

9. Communication: expression and exploration (vs. denial or obscuring) of problem-relevant *and relatively untransformed* (vs. transformed) organizational realities (II: 54–5, 59–60, 64–5; III: 109–10, 135, 146, 164, 174).
10. Distribution among episodic participants of motivational investment in the focal problem: broadly distributed vs. narrowly limited (II: 50, 74 ff.; III: chapter 11 and pages 121, 127, 133–35, 137–38, 164, 176, 186, 189).
11. Between-group and between-level relationships/linkages among constituents: number, regularity, communicativeness (vs. exclusionary defensiveness) of contacts (II: 50; III: chapter 11 and pages 112, 121, 156, 185, 187).
12. Structure and functioning of sequential participations: linear vs. looped (II: Part II and pages 54–5, 64, 66, 68, 71–2; III: chapter 11 and pages 118–19, 126, 130).

Table 17.1 (continued)

No.	Name of Variable (followed by page references in the narrative)

13. Protagonists' action in the period of asymmetrical awareness: amount of protagonists' transformation of the problem toward action *before* antagonists first enter the problem-solving process — time, number of pre-antagonist contacts, amount of transformation accomplished toward implementation (III: 104–5, 114).

14. Protagonist-antagonist contact: fleeting, solution-centered, and single vs. extended, reality-expressing, reality-probing, and multiple (II: 50, 54; III: 110, 118ff, 185).

15. Extent of mutual induction of problems and constituent realities by both protagonists (i.e., problem originator and initial supporters) and antagonists (i.e., members dependent on, or in favor of conditions protagonists find problematic): from nil to complete (II: 50; III: 110, 118ff, 168).

16. Strength of resources and mobilization to mitigate or reverse exclusion of constituent realities: (a) to what extent were exclusions of constituent realities expressly opposed or otherwise interrupted and (b) how successful was the opposition (or interruption) in securing integration of previously excluded constituent realities? (II: 63–5, 68; III: chapter 11 and pages 118ff, 126–9, 133, 164, 166–0, 171–72, 183).

Variables Related to Action (If Any) By Third Party

17. Extent of third-party participation. (III: chapters 11, 12, and 13; and specific parts of the narrative on pages 104, 131–34, 137–38, 162).

18. Third-party recruitment and legitimation: unilateral/partial vs. bilateral/full. (III: 104–5, 135, 139).

19. Third party's response to received legitimation: passive, acquiescing vs. actively testing and establishing legitimation (III: chapter 12 and page 145).

20. Third party role: mediation vs. arbitration. (III: 161–62).

21. Extent of support and resources for arbitrator role: participants' sense of shared crisis and arbitrator's powers of surveillance and enforcement (III: chapters 14 and 15, and page 168–69).

** The first page references, following the first variable, II: 50, 53 refer to pages 50 and 53 in Part II of the book. Variables associated with entire chapters appear cumulatively across numerous acts and communications in the narrative, and are only partially captured in small segments of it indicated by page references. Variables found in one episode that also appeared to be of extremely limited generality or durability (e.g., the appearance of a particular reality distortion in a problem originator, as Sr. Claudia's construing of Hester as 'them' in Part II) were not included in this table. Where appropriate, variables first noticed in the conflict episode (III) are retrospectively identified in passages where they appear in the first constitution episode (II).

Summary

In this chapter and the last I have been doing two things. First, I have been gathering variables. I cull them from my interspersed analyses of the narrative and from post-narrative analyses, analyses at the episodic level itself. The second thing I have been doing is to pull together my views of the unit of data I have called the episode and to characterize its components and its diachronic thrust from beginning to end. This characterization suggested variables not identifiable in short segments of narrative but, rather, descriptive of an episode as a whole. Table 17.1. summarizes the twenty-one variables I have culled from both the first constitution episode and the co-director episode, at four levels of organizational complexity. The narrative and analyses of Part IV will provide a few more variables and reformulations of some of these.

Notes

1. BLAKE, R. R. and MOUTON, J.S. *The Managerial Grid*. Houston, Texas: Gulf, 1964; and Blake and Mouton, 'Some effects of managerial grid seminar training on union and management attitudes toward supervision.' *Journal of Applied Behavioral Science*, 1966, 2, 387–400.

   Blake and Mouton's managerial style of maximizing both persons' interests and production is congruent with the working hypothesis of the present work that effectiveness is a function of the integration of organizational realities into action. What this work does not do is to observe on-site action. Their 9.1 management style, based on the premise that 'efficiency in operation results from arranging conditions of work in such a way that human elements interfere to a minimum degree', comes closest to describing Sr. Claudia's working premise in this period. Their 1.1 style, based on the premise that 'exertion of minimum effort to get required work done is appropriate to sustain organization membership', comes closest to describing Sr. Norma's participation in this period.

2. Omitted here because of space limitations is analysis of triadic relations. Analyses of 'balance' (Heider, 1958; Cartwright and Harary, 1956; Davis, 1963, 1968) among linked triadic relations (e.g., among Sr. Claudia, Sr. Jeanine, and Sr. Norma and among Sr. Claudia, Sr. Norma, and Lighthall) reveal important structural constraints on processes at the dyadic level. Triadic relations are discussed briefly in the section on Method in the last chapter.

3. Sue Allan discovered this, and after it was discussed in an early executive meeting, a small notice was put on the bulletin board of the faculty dining room indicating the time and place of the Friday executive meetings and soliciting agenda items. We can identify only one instance, in response to that notice (and none prior to it), of a faculty concern (vacation days) being brought to the executive council as a group.

4. Robert Townsend (1970) is at least one experienced executive who has seen shared power at the top work:

   'I've long held the opinion that a two-man [sic] chief executive is the answer ... But it isn't easy. The two men have to complement each other, and above all trust each other implicitly. They both have to have a sense of humor and they have to enjoy working together. Each must respect the other's fundamental instincts ...

If you're about to do something that your partner might be nervous about, you ask if he has a conviction against it'. (p. 166)

Townsend assumed more than a relationship of trust and enjoyment. He assumed that the legitimate domain of information, thought and action of both co-executives was the organization as a whole. Boundaries of authority varied not with two roles associated with two domains but with *tasks or problems.*

5. Linkage is of course not a new variable. Rensis Likert, for example, made it the central focus of his *New Patterns of Management* in 1961. It finds confirmation twice in this very limited sampling of administrative problem solving and therefore warrants notice. Sr. Claudia's problem solving of Part Four concentrated heavily on linkage, though quite without reference to Likert or other management theorists.

6. The problem of conflict between the protagonist and antagonists, like any problem, may be mild or severe, of short or long duration. I use 'protagonist' and 'antagonist' only in the sense of 'temporarily brought into conflict by the meaning and function of condition X in their respective realities', not in the sense of a repeated experience of conflict between two parties such that they have come to view each other as permanently untrustworthy and as predictable combatants on any issue.

    Chronologically, the first protagonist in any problem-solving episode is the problem originator. The protagonist is always aware of condition X as unwanted before the antagonists; indeed, the antagonists may never become aware either that condition X is unwanted or that the problem originator is against condition X.

    It should be clear that to the extent that organizational problems always implicate members who want some condition changed and other members who depend more or less intensely on those very conditions remaining the same, a theory of problems and of problem-solving becomes necessarily also a theory of conflict and conflict management. The concepts and distinctions regarding conflict laid out in Chapter 1 of Part III become immediately applicable to organizational problem solving.

7. Dewey's (1938, p. 104 ff.) favorite description of his 'problematic situation' was 'indeterminacy', which applies also to the state of mind preceding and accompanying what I am calling 'problem', but 'confusion' and 'disorientation' capture more of the state of mind that precedes problem synthesis. Dewey's problematic 'situation' and my 'operating reality' are clearly different. While his situation refers to a 'contextual whole', or -'field') of perception, it refers to a contextual whole 'out there', in existing conditions. He clearly distinguishes between 'existing conditions' and 'merely "mental" processes' (p. 106): '*We* are doubtful because the situation is inherently doubtful' (original italics; p. 105–106).

8. Cornelius Ryan's (1974) *A Bridge Too Far* (see esp. pp. 131–33, 159–60) narrates military problem solving in which realities close to the planners progressed in transformation and commitment beyond the point where observable realities made known by those remote from the planners could be entertained. These late arriving realities were simply rejected as false, resulting in a military debacle.

9. I have in mind a distinction similar to the one Kelman (1961: *Public Opinion Quarterly.* vol. 25, pp. 57–78) makes between compliance and identification, on the one hand, and internalization, on the other. The kind of aberrant action that can result from an eagerness to comply without internalizing the problem's realities was seen in Part II, where Mr. Sullivan implemented Sr. Claudia's solution of a constitution without integrating her problem.

10. It is also true that those increased contacts have opportunity cost of their own, in diminished resources for other problem-solving processes. Simon's (1976, 1979) concepts of bounded rationality and satisficing are relevant here.

11. Lighthall and Allan might also be seen as potential third parties, and with similar weaknesses in a third-party role. First, they were recruited unilaterally by Sr.

Claudia. Second, they initially assumed that their legitimacy in their role as consultant-researchers was equally strong for the two co-directors and, when evidence arose to the contrary, Lighthall did nothing to attempt to broaden that legitimacy. He and Allan became, willy nilly, associates of Sr. Claudia's, with the same incapacity for exploring the excluded party's realities as was true of the regional administrators.

That Lighthall and Allan never qualified as third parties at Trinity becomes plain when we consider the question of their choice as mediator or arbitrator. They took neither role. The only consulting role they did take at the level of the executives was consultant to Sr. Claudia and that was confined to her thinking, her plans, her perceptions, and her (relatively minor) problems, with no consultation attempted with the co-directors jointly. To put it another way, they consulted at the level of Sr. Claudia's problems, including her problem of conflict with Sr. Norma (mostly by questions and listening), but not at the level of conflict *per se.*

Part IV
The Second Constitution Episode:
An Effective But Vulnerable Solution

Chapter 18

A Look Forward: Results of the Second Constitution Episode

The first constitution episode, whose abortive actions were traced and analyzed in Part II, left Sr. Claudia as the sole participant still pursuing a problem regarding the Trinity council for which a constitution might be the solution. This second constitution episode begins with Sr. Claudia's return to her problem with the Trinity council. In the first constitution episode her problem was that the council had assumed a role of decision and policy making in domains (parking and school dress code) that exceeded its authority and powers to implement, and that it had failed to assume an advisory role in those domains. She had no quarrel with the council's sponsoring a benefit or a campaign for quiet in the halls, for example, but it had begun to assume a role that only the executives should properly carry out. A good part of the council's failure to act within its proper limits of authority, in Sr. Claudia's eyes, was Sr. Norma's failure to carry out proper supervisory functions, failing to represent the executives' views of proper council functioning.

As Sr. Claudia progressed in her management of her conflict with Sr. Norma (Part III) and began attending council meetings, she became aware that not only were the council's role and its leadership dysfunctional, but also that the council was not functioning well in a number of regards. For example, and not in order of importance to her or in the order of her voicing of them, she came to see that: a number of the council's faculty members were physically but not 'psychologically present'; issues discussed were poorly 'winnowed' and prepared; a number of students seemed to her to have been voted as representatives on the basis of 'popularity' rather than any capacity to represent; the council's connectedness to the wider student body and faculty seemed lacking; the issues discussed seemed to her too often trivial, without school-wide relevance; and Hester's chairing of the meetings and Lucy Ellen's writing of the minutes appeared to her wanting in the level of competence such a council deserved. Sr. Claudia's problem with the council, therefore, had expanded to focus on its general functioning: she wanted an effectively functioning council but she saw that the

Trinity council was ineffectively functioning in a number of ways that were important to her.[1] It was that enlarged problem complex that guided her action from early January through May of 02.

The *writing* of a constitution, pursued as a solution to Sr. Claudia's earlier, more limited problem with the council, now was less important. While it now might be part of a solution, what she felt was needed was a new constitution of 'governance' that was not necessarily written but was, in a phrase she used often, 'built in'. By this she meant, in our more sociological jargon, structured in roles, procedures, and norms constraining governance generally and the governing councils in particular. Central themes in her thinking about governance, as we shall see, were *competence, thorough preparation, accountability,* and *responsibility* — all to be 'built in'. Sr. Claudia returned to direct, organized action on that expanded problem at the Friday executive meeting on January 14, 02. By the following May, 02 all components of a solution to that expanded problem were in place, ready for implementation the following school year.

This third and last problem-solving history begins by looking forward in time to its end results. We examine, by before-after contrasts, what the episode's problem-solving and implementing action achieved and only then turn to narrate and analyze the process by which its results were achieved. Problem *solving* took place between January 14, 02, when Sr. Claudia turned actively to her problem of governance for the following school year, and May 3, 02, when the solution had been collectively worked out. Implementation took place the following year.[2] It is the results of that implementation that will be examined first.

Problem in Context

Sr. Claudia's expanded problem of Trinity council's functioning had, by January 14, been assimilated into a still larger problem complex. With Sr. Norma's decision not to return to Trinity, Sr. Claudia was faced with reconstituting Trinity's administration. She rejected the simple expedient of finding a replacement for Sr. Norma. That would leave the whole administrative process once again vulnerable to conflict between its two chief incumbents. From her many comments in meetings, and from interviews, it was clear that, in Sr. Claudia's mind, the executive function must diffuse its functioning among several administrators while at the same time maintaining ultimate authority in a single head.

But the executive group, in her mind, was but part of the whole problem of school governance. Governance went beyond mere administration. Governance included, for her, the mode of discipline used with the students, it included students' taking responsibility for larger segments of their own in-school lives, it included faculty participation beyond teaching duties, and it included, perhaps above all else, development in each person of an internalized sense of 'accountability', of being able to give an account for one's actions. Sr. Claudia's view of governance was dominated by a principle that might be difficult to implement consistently and in which her actions might falter, but where nonetheless she valued, both as end and as means, shared responsibility and shared participation among persons who held each other and themselves accountable. The school was not just a place for teachers to teach, students to be taught, and administrators to administer.

Trinity, after all, was a Catholic school. It was a school of the Blessed Sisters of Trinity. And that should mean, she felt, that it constituted a community — a Christian community, an educational community, but a community. She had been an active leader in her religious order at the national level to institute changes toward local responsibility, local participation, and individual acccountability, modifying the hierarchy of authority and norms of passive dependence and obedience that had obtained before Vatican II. She felt that Trinity, too, should participate in and extend that kind of enlightenment. A reorganized executive and a reorganized Trinity council ought to reflect these community values of shared responsibility and participation in ways more workable and more tangible than previous arrangements had achieved.[3]

Her problem with the Trinity council, then, was part of a larger problem of constituting a governance giving prominence to shared responsibility and that secured its members' invested participation (she emphasized the importance of members being 'psychologically present', not just physically present) in a community effort. She did not have in mind on January 14 the structure of governance that finally emerged. But she was philosophically and emotionally committed to these values. Having such values, her perception of Trinity council's functioning in 01-02, of faculty as seeking too often 'childish' and merely self-serving ends (like more vacation), and of her own administration as caught up in personal issues that pre-empted the very community service she felt religious were there to perform — these perceptions grated against her values and contradicted her conception of the school as an effective community.

The problem whose transformation we shall trace, then, the focal problem of this episode, is Sr. Claudia's enlarged problem of *ineffective council functioning* within her even more encompassing problem of school governance. The larger problem of school governance included her acute problem with the structure and functioning of the executive group itself. The co-director structure had been eliminated for the following year, but that did not eliminate the possiblity of again experiencing debilitating conflict with any replacement she might find for Sr. Norma. It had become apparent to Sr. Claudia, too, that more than one person's efforts were needed in handling student discipline if it were to be handled effectively. For her, as she explained, effective discipline depended on much more of a 'counseling approach' than a 'punishment' approach.[4] An executive structure was needed that would diffuse any conflict and that would somehow increase contact between those responsible for discipline, on the one hand, and students, on the other.

Executive structure and functions Sr. Claudia could alter by herself, simply by deciding what she wanted and hiring the persons. Directors of high schools run by the Blessed Sisters of Trinity enjoyed that kind of autonomy. But her problem of ineffective council functioning, connected to her attempt to broaden participation and share power in governing the school, depended for its solution on the actions, tolerance, and participation of others. Simply to declare by edict that the Trinity council will henceforth do thus and so and will be made up of these many students and those many faculty would deny the very kind of committed participation she wanted to develop. Further, to attempt to institute change by edict would also perpetuate the very kind of hierarchical, top-down governance that she and her fellow Sisters had struggled so hard and so successfully to eliminate in the religious order itself. In the matter of changing governance she knew she had to depend in many important ways on the slow process of persuasion or, as she called it, 'promulgation'.

Sr. Claudia's problem of Trinity council functioning is important because it typifies so many organizational problems faced by managers: it stems from interdependent functions that have come into conflict and can be resolved only with the cooperation of those same interdependent parties. The originator of the organizational problem cannot 'go it alone'. Organizational problems and problem solving are not merely cognitive. Solving them depends on the coordinated action of interdependent members, members whose local operating realities have their own local hierarchies of problems.

It will become clear that the solutions to these two problems, the focal problem of Trinity council functioning and the contextual problem of school governance in general, mutually informed and instructed each other as they emerged. Just as in the first constitution episode Sr. Claudia's conflict with Sr. Norma impinged on Sr. Claudia's solving of her (more circumscribed) problem with the Trinity council, so in this second constitution episode the solving of Sr. Claudia's problems of executive structure and functioning and of discipline in the school will be seen to have effects on the solving of her problem of Trinity council functioning. Let us begin, then, with the ending: the changes that the processes between January 14, 02 and May 3, 02 brought about, as observed from the vantage point of May of the following year, 02–03, the year in which the solution of May 3, 02 was implemented.

The Resulting Changes

The changes in governance in which the Trinity council problem was implicated can be described as before-after contrasts. The focus of these contrasts will be two councils central to an emerging plan of governance, each of which is associated with a school year: Trinity council, associated with the year of our observations, 01–02, the year *before* the changes we are tracing; and the Trinity Thirteen, or simply 'the 13', associated with the following year, 02–03, the year *after* implementation of the changes we are tracing. The reader should clearly distinguish 'Trinity council' (before) from 'Trinity 13' (after), therefore. The before-after contrasts have eleven dimensions. It is useful to list them, then take them up in turn.

1. Function — decision-making vs. advisory.
2. Attributed purpose — student activity vs. governance.
3. Structure — size and differentiation by level and by constituency.
4. Linkage with various parts of the school community.
5. Leadership.
6. Degree and kinds of faculty participation.
7. Agenda — kinds of content, processes of setting, degree of preparation.
8. Technical resources — skills, procedures, and staff roles.
9. Relative power of students and faculty.
10. Decision-making norms: voting vs. consensus.
11. Functioning — degree of effectiveness of problem solving.

1. Function

The council that replaced the Trinity council, called the Trinity 13, was officially advisory and its members accepted that function. Its composition and position within a hierarchy of councils, however, made its 'advice' far more binding on the executives than any decision of the previous year's Trinity council. The Trinity 13 was made up of representatives from eight councils, six of which were new: four class councils (freshman students, sophomore students, etc.), a parents' council, and a faculty council. The two already existing councils were the executive council, whose representative to the Trinity 13 was Sr. Claudia herself, and the Academic Senate, which also sent one representative to the 13. Any matter agreed to by this diverse a group, while regarded by all as officially advisory, was not likely to be rejected by the executive council.

2. Attributed Purpose

The Trinity council of 16 students, 8 faculty, and one administrator was seen as arising out of a long history of *student* councils. These student councils organized benefit drives and dances and other matters almost exclusively in the domain of student activities and student 'spirit'. One of the chief manifest functions of the student councils, in the eyes of both students and faculty, was to give students an opportunity to develop and to reveal leadership qualities. A latent function connected with this leadership opportunity was to provide (elected) students tangible evidence of qualities that college admissions officers look for on college applications. Being able to list oneself as a member or an officer of the student council was a tangible asset for a senior applying to college, as 95 per cent of Trinity girls did.

Both the manifest and latent functions of the student councils were attributed to the Trinity council, giving a continued student-centered orientation to it. Indeed, both faculty and administration were occasionally heard to make slips of the tongue, calling Trinity council 'student council', and then correcting their mistake. The effect of these attributed purposes was to lessen faculty council members' commitment to the Trinity council's processes and problems, and to dissociate the council from anything bearing seriously on conditions or aims of life at Trinity. Sr. Claudia, too, seemed ambivalent in her own attitude toward the Trinity council, viewing it as an important part of the governance that she wanted to develop at Trinity and yet as presently too heavily laden with merely student concerns and activities rather than school-wide concerns.

The Trinity 13 was distinctly different. Its manifest function was to deal with the problems that came to it from various sources, including the administration. One latent function continued to be to provide eight girls with evidence of their leadership to put on their college applications, but that was outweighed in the Trinity 13's functioning by the governance attitude that Sr. Claudia brought to it. About the 13 she was not ambivalent: it fitted her community-building and governing values explicitly and well in her eyes.

3. *Structural*

Clearly, the Trinity 13 was a different bird from the Trinity council the year before — in a number of important respects. One of those respects was its sheer size. While the Trinity council had 25 members, the Trinity 13 was half that size, allowing for much more give and take among members. While the Trinity council was made up of two thirds students, one third faculty, the Trinity 13 was about two thirds students and one third adults from various parts of the school community. Figure 18.1 gives the composition of the 13, showing clearly the differentiated levels of age, position, and section of the school or community represented in the 13.

4. *Linkage*

Figure 18.1 also shows how the successor to the Trinity council was linked to specific sections of the school community. While the students in the

Figure 18.1.   Composition of the Trinity 13: 02–03.

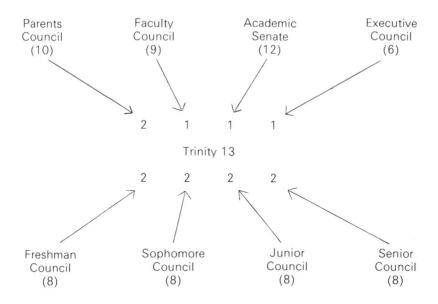

Trinity council of 01–02 were also members of their respective home-rooms, the homerooms had no role in governance — did not meet on issues, did not send agenda items, etc. The students in the Trinity 13 were the voted representatives from each of their class councils. The class councils themselves met every two weeks to discuss their local class agendas, from which arose proposals sent to the Trinity 13.

Just as new and contrasting with the year of our observation was the faculty representatives' linkage to specific other groups. While the faculty members of the Trinity council had been elected by the faculty, they never met as representatives, not with either the faculty at large nor with any group that might speak for the faculty, such as the Academic Senate (chairs of all the academic departments). That fact perhaps more than anything else reflected the 01–02 faculty's general attitude about the Trinity council: the faculty were members of the Trinity council to help the students in a student activity. To assist students in a student activity certainly presented nothing for the faculty to meet about.

In contrast, in 02–03 the two faculty members of the Trinity 13 represented two specific groups of faculty which represented faculty interests: the Faculty council and the Academic Senate. So the linkage between the Trinity council's successor, the Trinity 13, and the faculty changed from nil to explicit, legitimated linkage with two faculty groups.

A second kind of linkage, not so visible in Fig. 18.1, was also extended. That was the linkage between the executive council and the other parts of the school community. Instead of a weak link between Sr. Norma and the

Trinity council, a strong link was produced: Sr. Claudia herself became an *ex officio* member of the 13. The link between the executives and the students was strengthened in another way. Sr. Claudia created, as part of her reorganization of the administration, four new administrative roles, called 'Class Coordinators'. These four would accomplish several important things in Sr. Claudia's problem-solving agenda: (1) increase the disciplinary contact between the administration and the students, allowing a 'counseling approach' (Sr. Claudia's term) to discipline — a change which Sr. Claudia viewed as mitigating what she had regarded as Sr. Norma's punitive, reactive approach to discipline; (2) a diffusion of the responsibilities of administration, disciplinary and other, among a number of executives instead of concentrating them in one person — to avoid concentrated, incapacitating conflict as well as to enable a third change; namely, (3) Sr. Norma's replacements, the class coordinators, would also teach part time, as Sr. Claudia had continued to do, to 'preserve sanity'.

Not only were the executives linked with each student class as a whole, each class coordinator having been recruited specifically for her interest in working with freshmen or sophomores, etc., but also each class coordinator became an *ex officio* member of each class council, meeting with its eight elected girls and guiding their discussion and problem solving. The two elected student representatives from each of the class councils to the Trinity 13, therefore, heard administrative voices in 'downward' communication both at the level of the class council, from their class coordinator, but also at the level of the 13, from Sr. Claudia herself. The reverse linkage, of course, in 'upward communication' from students to administration, was also strengthened.

5. *Leadership*

Leadership in the Trinity council's successor, the Trinity 13, was strengthened in four ways. First, the faculty were elected indirectly from the faculty council, and thus actually represented a constituency and a faculty agenda. They were not merely helping out in some student activity. Second, students, too, were indirectly elected: two came from each of their respective class councils. Selection from each group of eight tended to produce student members of the Trinity 13 who were both forceful and articulate. Third, the chair of the Trinity 13 was not a member of the 13 itself, but a non-voting technical expert whose task was only to chair. Mr. Sullivan, an expert in parliamentary procedure, served in that role. This arrangement contrasted with Trinity council's chair, Hester Dulany, with only student status and who not only was a member but also was inexpert and had easily become drawn into discussion and debate. Finally, Sr. Claudia replaced Sr. Norma as the administrative voice, bringing to the 13 a greatly increased commitment, a higher level of energy, and a far more crystallized vision of community and governance than Sr. Norma had brought to the previous year's Trinity council.

6. Participation

While the Trinity council's student and faculty participation was characterized by activity on the part of six of the eight faculty and perhaps half of the students, the direction of discussion was often uncertain, unstable and confused. With very few exceptions, neither students nor faculty — nor especially the administrator, Sr. Norma — came to Trinity council meetings with more than superficial preparation for discussion. Often many questions were raised and discussed at length about a matter that had just been approved unanimously. Participation by members of the 13 was more distributed, better prepared, more cumulative.

7. Agenda

The agenda setting process of the Trinity council had been an ad hoc affair, Hester Dulany setting it after consultation with student members and sometimes with Mr. Sullivan (whose office was adjacent to the council room). Its agenda content had been almost completely restricted to concerns of students, the parking issue being the notable exception. In contrast, the 13 employed a rotating agenda committee, a student and a faculty member, named and with known deadlines beforehand. The 13's agenda content included a number of school-wide problems and problems from particular constituencies that were sending items previously discussed to the 13 for further discussion at that higher level.

8. Technical Resources

Besides the 13's non-member chair, the 13 had at its disposal another technical resource available in some large companies but rarely available in schools. One of the Trinity council's faculty members, a member also of the religious order, Sr. Janet, enrolled in our training program for Social Psychological Specialists for Schools at the University of Chicago. She received financial support from her religious order. In the 02–03 year, while taking courses part-time, she began actively to integrate a role of internal organizational consultant into her teaching at Trinity. Sr. Janet's senior course in Sociology included a team project that required students to gather data related to some actual organizational problem. Sr. Janet and her sociology students became, thus, a data-gathering and problem-analyzing resource for the Trinity 13. They were recruited, among other purposes, to help the 13 solve that recurrent problem of the parking lot, dented fenders.

Another technical resource, provided for the Trinity council by a student member of the council and often in a relatively weak and delayed form, were minutes of meetings. Sr. Sonia Hallahan acted as staff secretary to the Trinity 13, providing relatively complete and very prompt minutes, strengthening both continuity of discussion and effectiveness of communication to other sectors of the school.

9. *Relative Power of Students and Faculty*

The Trinity council was made up of two thirds students and one third faculty, besides Sr. Norma. The Trinity 13 was composed of eight students and five adults, again roughly a two-thirds, one-third breakdown. The one third of adults, however, contained only two members who identified themselves as 'faculty', and only one of them represented the 'rank and file'. Thus, while the linkage was strengthened between faculty members on the representative body and the faculty at large, their relative numbers in the 13 as compared with the year before were diminished from one third rank and file to one eighth. On a purely voting basis, then, the relative power of students over faculty was greatly strengthened, a fact that did not escape the faculty representatives' notice and that figured strongly in the long-term outcome of this episode's problem-solving process.

10. *Decision-Making Norms*

While Trinity council made its decisions by majority vote, the Trinity 13 adopted, with Sr. Claudia's urging, a norm of decision by consensus, thus nullifying to some extent the effects of unequal numbers from each sector of the school community.

11. *Functioning*

Among the problems addressed by the Trinity 13, a number were more pervasive, varied, and difficult than those addressed by the Trinity council. While the Trinity council focused on only a few school-wide problems — e.g., the parking problem and noise in the halls, and solved them ineffectively, the vast majority of the problems taken up by the Trinity 13 were school-wide.[5] In general, furthermore, the 13 gave its problems more sustained and resourceful consideration, and drew them to more successful conclusions than did the Trinity council.

In sum, the reorganized successor to the Trinity council was dramatically different from its predecessor. In the following section this conclusion is buttressed by examining in some detail its solving of the parking problem, whose process and outcome were, again, very different from the Trinity council's approach to virtually the same problem the year before. Having both characterized and then illustrated the effectiveness of the solution to Sr. Claudia's problem of council functioning, the succeeding chapters trace the process by which this effective solution emerged. In doing so, I will be examining the variables extracted so far, and will be on the lookout for new variables that constitute promising candidates for explaining the difference between effective and ineffective problem-solving processes in organizations.

One Example: The Parking Problem

Consider briefly one episode whose process and outcomes regarding 'the parking problem' illustrate the effectiveness and weaknesses of the Trinity 13's functioning. The Trinity 13's two-hour discussion on October 31, 02 was devoted virtually in its entirety to this problem, a problem whose immediate originator in 02 is unknown but whose conveyer to the 13 was Sr. Claudia. The problem consisted of two parts: (1) commitments to protect one's own automobile from damage versus continued dents and scrapes being complained of and (2) widely shared desires for parking spaces close to the building, to avoid long (and cold) walks to the building. The two parts were connected: the long search in one's car for a parking spot in a crowded parking lot led to loss of time, loss of time led to rush, rush led to hurriedly parked cars and poorly positioned cars, both of which led to scrapes and dents.

Prior to this October 31 meeting, both the 13 and the faculty council had discussed the problem. At the previous 13 meeting, a solution had been reached but had been held in abeyance because the faculty council had not been in touch with the faculty at large. It wanted to obtain faculty sentiment before committing to any solution. (Sr. Claudia was miffed that Trinity 13's problem-solving had to wait for the faculty when the class councils, the students, had all completed their deliberations.) The faculty council circulated a questionnaire to their colleagues, receiving about 50 per cent response, and Sr. Wilma Tisch, their representative, had come to the October 31 meeting with the faculty's proposal.

A Negotiated Settlement

Sr. Claudia opened the meeting with an extended introduction in which she pointed out that each local council would have its own view of problems, but only the Trinity 13 would have a comprehensive view, and that 'frequently the individual councils are going to have to give'. Sr. Wilma asked whether a solution 'will ever be accepted if it implies preferential treatment for one group'. She asked, further, if all solutions would be settled by 'the least common denominator'. 'If there are only so many [parking] spaces that are preferred', she asked finally, 'is it possible that they be allocated to the faculty and not to the students?'

Sr. Claudia replied, easily assuming the role of spokesperson for the Trinity 13: preferences could be granted to one group when they did not preclude the legitimate preferences of another. Each group, she said to Sr. Wilma, had to 'face the music' if it entered the decision-making process unprepared — unprepared, that is (though she did not say so), according to the time schedule of others, and particularly of the Trinity 13.

Sr. Wilma laid out the faculty council's proposal. They requested 40 reserved parking spaces in addition to the 30 faculty already were allocated, a total of 70 of the 77 faculty who now possessed parking stickers. A detailed, focused, cumulative discussion ensued of preferences, inconvenient spots, and uneven incidence of dents and scrapes in various lots.

A student commented that it seemed like a stalemate, that each side, students and faculty, would hold to the same position it had taken, namely, that the students thought first come, first served was fair (early arrivals each morning getting the best parking spots deservedly), and the faculty felt they should be given reserved spaces.

Sr. Claudia expressed the fear that the matter might be settled merely by a vote. She feared a student-faculty split, in which the faculty would simply be outvoted in the Trinity 13. 'There would be one administrative vote here, against twelve, if you looked at it that way,' she said. She pleaded for a solution best for the whole school, one based on consensus.

Sr. Emily tried to focus the group's attention on the part of the problem having to do with damage to automobiles, commenting that reserved spaces still might not prevent car damage. Her comment was lost, swamped by the issue of protected and allocated spots vs. open competition each morning. Discussion revealed that some faculty actually preferred to park in the more remote south lot, complicating the proposal to have reserved spaces for faculty in the north lot only. A student commented somewhat morosely that 'we're going to have to give them half of the spots they ask for', taking a standard negotiating stance. Ellie Sanford, who also had been an active member of the Trinity council the year before, saw an inequity in the faculty's being allocated even 20 new reserved spots (half of the 40 requested) if the faculty were still to be allowed to park anywhere else. Sr. Emily again wondered if they were ignoring the problem of irresponsible driving in the lot, the cause of damage to the cars. It became clear to members that whatever the solution, if there were no monitoring and no penalties it would be only a paper solution. Did they really want to issue tickets? Details and conflicting views were explored.

A compromise solution was proposed, modified, summarized and re-summarized. Certain spaces would be allocated to the faculty for a month, to see what the solution produced. The school's policeman would take notes on which reserved spaces were used and which were not, which area had violations, and the like. A vote was taken, unanimously favoring the temporary solution.

Implementation

Three weeks after the school-wide announcement of the temporary solution, complete parking data were gathered for five days by the policeman and by the Trinity 13's 'Parking Policy Investigation Committee'. The committee was made up entirely of students, since no faculty member agreed to serve on it. Most cars had parking stickers, whose appearance differed noticeably for students and faculty. Tabulations were made of the faculty and student cars parked in the faculty and student areas of both north and south lots, as well as empty spaces in both student and faculty areas, on November 22, 27, 28, 29, and 30. On each day there were no fewer than 10 unused faculty spaces, even though no fewer than 11 student cars were also parked in the faculty area. Vacancies in the student area numbered between one and four. The committee concluded that there was no longer a space problem. It did not gather data, and apparently had no complaints, about automobile damage.

The last three paragraphs of the committee's report were devoted more to the students' frustrations at the lack of faculty response than to an evaluation of the solution itself, but it did end with a terse evaluation:

> Faculty concern seems to have died down concerning the parking situation. This conclusion is drawn from the fact that no faculty member would serve on the policy investigation committee. There was no response to a general appeal by the faculty council to all faculty members.
>
> There was still no response after personal approaches to the individual faculty members who seemed most concerned (prior to the enactment of the present temporary policy).
>
> Other than the problems which are seen as solved by the suggested revisions, the Committee thought the parking situation is flowing extremely well and no negative student reaction was perceived.

The process of solution revealed new strengths and old weaknesses.[6] Various parts of the school community were brought together to forge a solution. The forging took place via frank negotiation and ended in a compromise that was both consensual and made provision for empirical evaluation. The use of the policeman as an aid in data gathering also contrasted with the previous year's use of him stereotypically as an issuer of tickets. Finally, a summary statement of the response by users of the parking lots was undertaken, results and conclusions being brought back to the source of the solution: virtually a textbook case in problem solving.

But weaknesses also appear in this story. Paralleling the norm of consensual decision making that Sr. Claudia had enunciated and which became evident in the unanimity of the vote, was the explicitly enunciated recognition and fear not only that the administration but also the faculty would be outvoted by students if a decision came to just the vote. Crucial parts of the school community were under-represented in this representative body.

Added to the issue of sheer power of numbers was the issue of particularism vs. universalism. If particular interests of the faculty were not to be given special weight over student interests, and if decisions in the 13 were going to be based on the good of the school as a whole and on the basis of consensus, then faculty interests that actually were particularistic would have to seek some other outlet for expression. The Trinity 13 could, of course, simply deny that they existed or that they were legitimate. If particularistic interests did exist, however — and Sr. Wilma's proposal is not, as we shall see, the only evidence that they did exist — it would deny them only at substantial cost to the faculty cooperation it might later seek. At issue was the inclusion in, or exclusion from, collective problem solving of strong, particularistic interests of a key segment of the organization, the faculty, and particularly the lay faculty. Part of this particularism might be eliminated by a change of attitudes — which imposes its own demands. But part of it stemmed from the status (and power) differences between faculty and students in any educational establishment: the faculty know more of what the students are there to learn and it is the faculty's role to arrange conditions for student learning. Students are inherently subordinate in important respects to faculty. Did this status difference extend to such matters as parking? The Trinity 13, led by Sr. Claudia in this matter, said, 'No', and the negotiation that ensued produced an effective solution. But the larger issue of giving faculty status its due would return.

Finally, we see not only faculty reluctance to participate in implementing the Trinity 13's solution — no doubt for a variety of local reasons — but also a student response to that unwillingness which we shall see was characteristic: disappointment that generated an articulate complaint which, in turn, fell on deaf ears. The reluctance on the faculty's part and resulting disappointment on the students' part constituted not merely states of two separate collective minds, so to speak. Rather, these two sentiments defined a student-faculty relationship that was often distant, even alienated.

Summary

The problem-solving process engaged in by the Trinity 13 contrasted sharply with that of the previous year's Trinity council in respect to the variety of constituent realities integrated into its action, the degree of pre-discussion preparation, the openness and negotiating nature of its inter-action, the resources available to it and used by it, the degree of tested consensus reached, its capacity to collect and analyze data relevant to its implemented solution, and its articulation of results back to the council itself. These strengths were accompanied by two weaknesses also charac-teristic of the 13, namely, its uneven representativeness of various sections of the school, particularly the lay faculty, and its outright normative exclusion of particularistic interests. In the course of this particular instance of that more general improvement in process, a certain distance in working relations between students and faculty was expressed by students, ex-pressions that will be heard from the previous year's episode now to be narrated and analyzed.

Notes

1. Everyday linguistic usage in stating problems must be distinguished from the foregoing statement in the text. Graduate students often render Sr. Claudia's problem at this point in words like, 'Sr. Claudia's problem was to create a new governance'. Such a statement hides the fundamental opposition inherent in adaptational problems and gives a privileged position to goals or solutions, undervaluing the gaps, failures, losses, and threats to which the goals and solutions are a response. Adequate statement of a problem always captures an opposition, signalled by 'but' or 'on the other hand' and the like.
2. The implementation of the solution took place in the year, 02–03, the year after Susan Allan and I left Trinity. Our data gathering, however, continued. Sr. Claudia and others she recruited into her administration routinely tape recorded every meeting of each of the several councils that replaced the Trinity council during that following year of implementation. Such tape recording would be intrusive in most administrative research settings, but routine taping by us of both the Trinity council and the executive council during 01–02 and a norm of taping all administrative meetings of the religious order at the regional level, added to our absence, made such taping virtually unobtrusive. Sr. Claudia, in particular, was strongly in favor of our follow-up project, and the class coordinators were evidently comfortable with it. Each class council assigned a student to be responsible for the taping and for labeling the box, and each student performed regularly and accurately. Minutes and agenda were collected for us, along with a variety of other documents. In addition, a problem-solving group headed by Sr. Janet, who began to assume a new role at Trinity (of which more below), provided us data about some of that subsequent year's (02–03's) implementation process.
3. We did not ask Sr. Claudia her conception of governance and she never made a systematic statement of it. She made various impromptu and unfortunately unrecorded comments. At one point she distinguished 'governance' from 'adminis-tration' in terms comparable to the difference between what Etzioni (1961) would call a normative or cultural organization from an instrumental organization.
4. Sr. Claudia's awareness that attempts to coerce conformity through 'detentions' was ineffective, and her preference for persuasion was precisely parallel to Etzioni's (1961) analysis of the effective means of securing compliance in normative,

instrumental, and coercive organizations. In particular, the means appropriate to instrumental and coercive organizations (rewards and coercion), if used in a normative organization like Sr. Claudia's Trinity, contradict and subvert its own appropriate means, persuasion through the invocation of central values.

5. Complete tape samples of four meetings of each of the four class councils and of the Trinity 13 were examined for the distribution of types of problem. The types, derived from examining all of the tapes, were: (1) all-school problems — e.g., inter-class antagonism between members of the senior and sophomore classes; competition between students and faculty for desirable parking spaces; mounting garbage left in the north cafeteria; (2) communication with constituencies — passing problems or solutions up or down the line; (3) school or class 'spirit' activities — e.g., ad hoc football games, a class picnic, baby picture contest; (4) maintenance functions — e.g., scheduling elections, discussing ground rules for discussion, recruiting resources; (5) local, symbolic, and special interest — e.g., seniors' desires for expanded privileges like a smoking lounge, off-campus leave during the day, a vacation trip to Mexico or the Bahamas; and (6) other — e.g., a service project of decorating the school's nursery school, official response of sympathy and financial help to a stricken family.

Percentages of problems falling in the combined categories of spirit and symbolic-special interest for freshmen, sophomores, juniors, and seniors, respectively, were, of 23 problems considered by the first three classes, 35 per cent, 30 per cent, 35 per cent, and of the 35 problems considered by the seniors, 60 per cent. Percentages of problems in the all-school category were, respectively, 4 per cent, 39 per cent, 35 per cent, and 20 per cent. In contrast, the percentage for the four sampled meetings of the Trinity 13 falling in the spirit and special interest vs. all-school categories, respectively were, from a total of 24 problems considered, zero vs. 71 per cent.

While the 'sub-councils', as the class councils were sometimes called, paid considerable attention to all-school problems, therefore, they effectively siphoned off all of the 'spirit' and symbolic activities from the top advisory council. It should be noted that a considerable number of the all-school problems considered by the class councils were initiated by Sr. Claudia in the Trinity 13 and then referred downward for brainstorming and proposed solutions.

6. 'Strengths' and 'weaknesses' in the capacity to develop solutions that integrated diverse realities, mobilized new resources, and altered unwanted conditions. The actual problem tackled in this instance was not as demanding as some, nor as sweeping in the number of persons affected. The seniors' successful challenge of previous years' policy against senior field and vacation trips was the occasion for even more intensive preparation, case-building, and persuasion. Important to attend to in the parking illustration are the qualities of process exhibited.

Chapter 19

Sr. Claudia Confronts Her Problems With the Trinity Council

We turn now to the narrative of events that led to the changes described in the previous chapter. To recall the time frame in terms of the conflict between the two co-directors, this third episode begins on January 14, 02, just three days before Sr. Norma made known to the Trinity faculty that she would not return the following year and about six weeks after Sr. Claudia had begun to rethink administrative roles.

An Initial Schema

In a regular Friday meeting of the executive council on January 14 Sr. Claudia passed out a diagram sketching out the elements of governance she was then considering, Figure 19.1. Sr. Claudia said she had this schema 'in most sketchy fashion — as a work sheet almost', but that she was 'pushing toward this' because the following Monday she had to 'start contacting people' to fill whatever administrative positions she finally decided on. Sr. Claudia said she wanted to 'lure into the administration' the best people she possibly could for the new roles of coordinators. She was anxious to recruit people before general announcements of all new positions for the following year went out the following Monday from the regional center.

Sr. Claudia said she wanted to keep the schema open enough to avoid 'imposing ... our understanding on persons that have to ... do it for a whole year'. But without even such a sketchy schema, Sr. Claudia said, 'I don't even know how to talk to anybody when I'm trying to ask them if they'll do it. I want to have *some* consent [from Sr. Norma and Sr. Catherine] so I can say, "We think that it's going to go in this direction"'.

Reorienting the Trinity Council

Sr. Claudia explained her thinking on each item of her diagram, holding off comments and discussion until her discourse (of about twenty minutes) was

Figure 19.1   Sr. Claudia's January 14 'schema' of 'administrative responsibility'.

Director

Associate Director:	Coordinators: Senior
Public Relations	Student Affairs Junior

Sophomore
Freshman

Activities Manager	Business Manager	
Registrar	Attendance Clerk	Clerk
Assistant Registrar	Assistant Clerk	
Academic	Trinity	
Senate	Council	

finished. After extended discussion of elements of the schema, Sr. Claudia noted that Sr. Norma was scheduled to leave the meeting early and sought her help in thinking about the Trinity council. Does the Trinity council understand, as the Academic Senate does, she asked Sr. Norma, that its vote on any matter is advisory?

Her question launched Sr. Norma into the history of the Trinity council's formation, concluding her remarks with 'I think that there's people .. faculty and students, who want to be more than advisory ... So I think we have to put the cards on the table and the decision made: "This is the way it .."' Before she could finish the phrase, Sr. Claudia interrupted with her own version of what must be said to the Trinity council: 'We have to *talk* about it'. Then in a soft voice she added: 'And I don't know how you *do* that'.

✿   ✿   ✿   ✿

That Sr. Claudia should interrupt Sr. Norma on just this matter reflects one element of their conflict. Sr. Norma appeared to Sr. Claudia, and often to us from independent observations, to be more readily direct, telling, and peremptory with others than Sr. Claudia. From Sr. Claudia's perspective, Sr. Norma's disciplinary style was a 'punishment approach'. What Sr. Claudia wanted was 'a counseling approach', one in which discussion, reflection, and persuasion were the central means. Thus, just where Sr. Norma was ready to put her 'cards on the table' and tell the council members 'the way it is', Sr. Claudia was ready to engage in talk.

When she said quietly, 'I don't know how to *do* that', one must note that the 'that' could well promise to be complex and difficult. By means of talk she was faced with persuading, not forcing, faculty and students to give up a stance of decision making in favor of a stance of advising. To elicit support for a weakened power orientation on the part of those who would, to all appearances, be weakened was the task facing her. Clearly, advice-giving had to be made to seem more attractive in council members' eyes than it apparently had been.

＊　＊　＊　＊

Sr. Claudia: How do you get this started? That's my question: how you find out whether they are open to that [an advisory role] or not?

Sr. Norma: I think perhaps, maybe, inviting them to a meeting that we're having on, you know, the role of the Trinity council thus far and how it is going to look for next year with us right now ... (1/14/02: E; I, 2:600–40)

Relevance of Advice

Further discussion explored the usefulness and acceptance of advice, once given. Allan guessed that council members would discover the kind of reception their advice would have in the very process of any meeting Sr. Claudia had with them. Sr. Claudia tied acceptance of advice to its relevance and usefulness:

Sr. Claudia: ... Parents' advisory councils, I think, become essential to you or kind of non-essential, depending on the things they feed in ... But if they are generating information for you that you are really not looking for in given situations time after time ... I think of the Mothers' Club, for instance, and the things they sometimes think are issues. Probably, you know, we can go along for months without even thinking of [half laughs] needing their kind of input ... just because of what their interests are. (1/14/02: E; I, 2:650–75)

＊　＊　＊　＊

Sr. Claudia's caveats about advice are important. We see the nature of her conception of relevance: to what extent is the information being offered by the advisory group the kind of information she is looking for? The possibility that an advisory group might offer information that was surprising and not relevant to the day's agenda, but still important or even cruical for her to know, was simply not a part of her schema of 'relevance' or 'usefulness'.

255

Relevance and usefulness, thus, pertained not to the school's functioning broadly, but to Sr. Claudia's currently conscious intentions. How difficult was it for Sr. Claudia to appreciate the relevance to the school of advisory information that was not relevant to her immediate agenda, that revealed unexpected aspects of the school's functioning? An evening meeting with the Trinity council would soon present such an item, showing that these words of hers, about the essentiality or non-essentiality of an advisory group and whether its advice was what one was looking for, reflected more than merely passing thoughts.

☼　☼　☼　☼

Continuing the narrative, the rest of the executive meeting was taken up with further discussion of elements not related to the functioning of the Trinity council including, after Sr. Norma left, Sr. Claudia's 'absolute frustration' at Sr. Norma's having failed to announce to Trinity's faculty her decision not to return the following year. But Sr. Claudia's question about how to deal with the Trinity council had been answered. She would talk with them — directly as a group, not through prominent members as she had done earlier, in the first constitution episode.

Trinity Council's Evening Meeting

Having taken pains to secure Sr. Norma's approval for calling a meeting of the Trinity council, Sr. Claudia invited the members of the council to meet with her on the evening of February 2, a bitterly cold night. Only Lighthall, Louise Nolan, Sr. Norma, and Mrs. Marchand were absent. As it happened, the meeting unfolded in three parts. First, Sr. Claudia directed an exploration of how decisions were made by the executives and of the role of advice-giving in that process. Second, diverging from the issue of advisory vs. decision-making functions, a range of sentiments about student-faculty relations was articulated — sentiments not on Sr. Claudia's agenda. The third part saw Sr. Claudia redirecting attention to council-administration relations and to the council's own role in re-designing its future functioning.

Sr. Claudia opened the discussion by asking a question:

> Sr. Claudia: How do you think decisions are made for the school? ... for instance, a decision comes out over the PA ...: 'We won't accept students the following year who have not completed their work for the previous year and received credits that are required for the previous year'.... Like, how do you imagine that came about? (2/2/02: C; 1:25–38)

Eight students replied with a variety of views. Sr. Claudia punctuated their replies with questions to keep the flow of ideas coming. She then answered the question herself, the central thrust of which was that advice was taken seriously in decision making:

> Sr. Claudia: I can't remember any decision in the past three years in the area of curriculum [her own area of expertise, she said], any policy that's been set, that hasn't been recommended by the Academic Senate. And at no time in those years have we ever gone *counter* to what the Academic Senate recommended. We'd be *fools* to do it. (2/2/02: C; 1:100–115)

In response to Sr. Claudia's question whether the students would be willing to have the council take an advisory rather than decision-making role, discussion explored sentiments pro and con. Examples were: if the administration ever 'vetoed' a recommendation, that would turn the Trinity council into just another student council (Hester Dulany); the council could be advisory on some matters, and decision-making on others (Sonia Griffin); making decisions had to be considered also in light of the power to carry them out (Sr. Claudia); and one reason the council had been limited to 'trivial' content this year, like changing the dress code to include sweaters, was that it had assumed a decision-making role and not an advisory role (Mr. Sullivan). A student suggested that 'trivial' content, to the contrary, was due to do both student and faculty 'apathy' reflected in the fact that neither students nor faculty had brought important matters to the council for action.

Discussion then focused on the fact that important matters had not been brought to the council. Leonore Phelan ('Leo'), widely regarded as one of the most perceptive, judicious, and forthright student members, identified three issues that seniors had brought to her but that she, Leo, had failed to present to the council: a smoking lounge for seniors, an open campus policy, and senior independent study courses. Hester remembered a suggestion of early graduation for seniors who had the required number of credits that also had not been brought up in council.

Sr. Claudia asked Leo and Hester if they felt they could not bring these matters before the council. After Lucy Ellen Garvin gave an example of a matter being settled elsewhere even before it could be brought to the council, Leo Phelan noted an obstruction. She had brought up a discipline case in council and had been told by Sr. Norma that such matters were to be brought up in private first with Sr. Norma. She then answered Sr. Claudia's question more generally:

> Leo Phelan: The thing about independent classes is that it seems that whenever something like that comes up, the council will talk about it and talk about it and then someone will say, 'Well, we can't do anything about it without Sr. Claudia here anyway', 'we can't do anything until we hear from Sr. Norma anyway', and so that's why I just wouldn't bring it up here because none of us has the power really to do anything about it anyway.

A lively discussion followed, carried mostly by Sr. Claudia, Leo, Nora Quinn, and Hester. A central issue was whether the council had sufficient information on a whole range of matters to make decisions, countered with assertions that if the council really did represent students, faculty, and administration, why did it not have, and why could it not have, all the information necessary to make decisions? This discussion was brought to a close by elaboration of a point by Hester, that making decisions entailed 'enforcing' them as well, a power and an authority all were ready to locate in the administration alone.

At this point in the discussion, Sr. Claudia shifted attention to the way in which faculty had been involved in the council and asked their views of the council. Mr. Sullivan, Sr. Nannette Noyes, and Naomi Higgins (a faculty member of the council who uttered no more than a few words in her entire year's attendance) all indicated that the faculty had made virtually no comments to them about issues for the council or about council activities. Sr. Janet Acker's characterization of the faculty's view of the council then refocused discussion on the ability of faculty and students to work effectively together:

> Sr. Janet: The faculty ... have so many other channels [besides Trinity council] to go to that they don't have to, maybe, 'play games' — that's how they think about it [i.e., that to work through the Trinity council to achieve goals instead of going through more direct channels would be to ['play games'] — and so therefore they think, 'That's for the kids. If I want something done I go to my department chairman. I can make an appointment directly with Sr. Claudia and I will get it .. or Sr. Norma'. I don't think they even want to bother, in a sense, because the whole concept of teachers and students working together is something new.
>
> Kathy Kuhlen: I know, I wish there were some way we could just show them that, like, we are working together, we are getting things done.
>
> Beth Dolan: Well, are we?
>
> Nora Quinn: But are we?
>
> Lucy Ellen: I don't think we are! (2/2/02: C; 1:757–774)

Mr. Sullivan said he thought even some faculty members in the council, as well as many outside, did not take the council seriously and wondered how the students regarded faculty involvement. Leo Phelan said that Sr. Sabrina, with whom she had worked intensively on a school-wide discipline survey and on recommendations made to the council, was certainly involved, but added 'but I personally don't feel the faculty and students work well at all together'. Several students and Sullivan pursued this theme, enumerating three instances where all-school and council-sponsored events were only meagerly attended or not attended at all by faculty members of the council. Leo's comment was, 'You can't wipe away three things like that'.

Sr. Claudia came to faculty members' defense, pointing out that much faculty time was spent in invisible things, like meetings of the departments or of the faculty as a whole. Susan Allan interpreted the students' concerns as not 'involvement' of the faculty council members in general but a question of 'how much actual contact the students have with the faculty . . . in a personalized and direct sort of way'. A number of students agreed with Allan's interpretation, and Sr. Claudia agreed that direct social contact was different from general involvement in the school.

A bit of student-faculty confrontation was triggered by Sonia Griffin's bemoaning the absence of most of the Trinity council faculty members from the well-publicized time and place of photographing the council for the annual yearbook. Sr. Nannette Noyes excused her absence on the grounds that she didn't write it down and it completely slipped her mind. Nora Quinn replied rather characteristically for her, that 'it seems kind of funny that all sixteen kids that are on the council show up' but that only three adults were able to remember, showing in her tone of voice that she rejected forgetting as a valid assessment. After some discussion ('wrangling' might be a more accurate term) about time commitments promised the previous year, Leo Phelan said that Sr. Sabrina had commented to her that she thought some of the faculty members did not take the council seriously and added:

Leo: . . . and I've noticed that some of the faculty members don't take the students on here seriously. What I mean by that is in answering a student, um, it strikes me as being very condescending [student murmurs and light laughter]. I see nods. And I don't know how to work around that . . . I think that's really a drawback to this because I don't think we have the feeling that we can just speak . . . it's just the attitude that faculty members have.

Sr. Claudia. That what you say is 'just the word of a student'.

Leo: Yeah. It's kind of like, 'Now honey', and then they pat you on the head you know, 'you'll understand — a couple of years from now'. (2/2/02: C; 2:188–208)

Further discussion raised issues of power differences among students, faculty, and administration, and feelings of intimidation by students in particular during council meetings.

Sr. Claudia: I think I heard in the background a kind of insecurity . . . I don't think you can just overlook it, but I don't think you can solve it either. You're *elected* [laughs]. You know, I mean it's kind of accidental grouping . . . If you allow yourself to be voted

259

for, then you're, you know, taking the chance that you'll be elected . . . And so, you know, the chemistry of this group will be different next year. And so you'll have another whole hassle. And if everything depends on how well you get along *personally* with everyone on the coun . . I'd be afraid to say, you know, that the success of [laughs lightly], you know, or partial success of a group . . . would depend on the chemistry of the group to such an extent . . . Could I come back to one thing, in terms of the administration again? (2/2/02: C; 2:358–373)

    ❖   ❖   ❖   ❖

Both student and faculty members raised, clarified, and documented a number of related problems, all related to student-faculty working relations. Sr. Claudia categorized these student-faculty relations as one might do, quickly and at the moment — especially if one were still working one's way out of an intense, debilitating *interpersonal* conflict — as matters of getting along *personally* as 'accidental', and 'chemistry of the group'.

With the benefit of time to review and think about the tape recorded discussion, we can see that Sr. Claudia coded the *inter-group* conflict within the council, student members' commitments and attitudes vs. faculty members' commitments and attitudes, as the random *interpersonal* relations that result from elections. She thus did not take in a conflict in commitments that, on logical grounds alone, was important to the functioning of the council, that would again be in evidence, would be ignored or denied, and would contribute to the demise of the multi-council, representative governing structure whose origin Sr. Claudia was now, in February, just beginning to stimulate and guide into being.

    ❖   ❖   ❖   ❖

Sr. Claudia ended the second phase of the evening meeting, discusssion of student vs. faculty members' commitments and attitudes, and initiated the third phase by calling attention to the short time and posing first some hypothetical conditions and then a question:

Sr. Claudia: . . . could I come back to one thing in terms of the administration again? Hypothesis: administration, single director, next year; a number of associate directors, number still unknown. What kind of tie-in from that kind of administration should be on the council? . . . What kind of administration input does the council most need, see? That's what I'm asking. (2/2/02: C; 2:372–385)

After considerable discussion, Hester began to summarize by stating that the council would be 'an advisory board', when Sr. Claudia interrupted. She cautioned that 'your constitution isn't drawn up' and that she had heard 'a lot of people saying they want to set policy . . . and follow through on it'. (The audio tape reveals that only a single person, Leo Phelan, had argued for a policy-making role.) She saw much more room for discussing 'what you want to do and what you'll take responsibility for doing'.

Sr. Claudia urged members not to wait until her own administrative reorganization was completed but to get right to work. She outlined some issues to be faced:

> Sr. Claudia: Is this the size that's needed? . . . Have you got the most involvement from students this way? . . . Is this the way to get faculty involvement? If this is, then okay, then why don't you recommend it for next year. I think that's what you were talking about in terms of a constitution. That's what a constitution does . . . You describe what you are . . . who composes it, what your relationship with other bodies in the school would be, what your committees are, when you meet, that sort of thing . . . I'd hope you wouldn't just put in writing what's happened this year. I hope you put in writing what you wish would be, what you realistically think could be . . . Really go ahead on that. (2/2/02: C; 2:484–500)

Following these suggestions, Sr. Claudia said repeatedly that she was putting pressure on them: 'I don't think you can diddle with this thing any longer, in terms of what it's going to be like. It's February. We're in third quarter'. Discussion turned to the specifics of next meetings, to parts of the task of writing goals, to deciding the advisory-decision making issue, and the like, with a number of specific suggestions from Susan Allan and Sr. Claudia about using small discussion groups. Sr. Claudia's closing emphasis was time pressure:

> Sr. Claudia: I'd like to say thanks for your openness of discussions, for your coming out on a night like this . . . And I really do . . . want to put you under pressure . . . You know, not in a week or something like that, but I mean really getting to work on it . . . And I would like very much to hear a progress report . . . If you've had a good meeting with a group, to just stop in and say some of the things that came from it. (2/2/02: C; 2:616–630)

After answering a question verifying that planning was to be oriented to the future, not the past, Sr. Claudia summarized the point to be kept in mind. In so doing, she expressed a crucial ambivalence about the council that was still to be resolved. What was needed, she said, was an answer to the question, 'What would be most *effective* as a student .. as a school government thing?'

Summary

Two variables affecting the integration of organizational realities into action are brought into view. We see Sr. Claudia addressing her problem of the council's functioning by communicating directly with it as a body: her communication *aim* is not peripheral or off-center (as it was in the first episode), but appropriate. A second variable is psychological: the problem originator's orientation to advice and complaints. In the evening meeting with the Trinity council, Sr. Claudia successfully pursues her own agenda but was also confronted with complaints about the working relations between student and faculty members of the council. As related as this matter was to Sr. Claudia's overall agenda, she did not synthesize these complaints as an organizational problem. The students' realities regarding their problem, directly expressed to her, did not register with her, while her solution-oriented communications did register with them: council members (possibly excepting Leo Phelan) were ready to see an advisory role as possible and appropriate, given their sense of the council's ineffectiveness that year in a decision-making role. This one-sidedness of success in pursuing an immediate agenda is nothing new: organization members often succeed in downward communication where they fail in upward communication. What is new is that Sr. Claudia had earlier described her own selective outlook toward others' advice in terms precisely parallel to her own behavior in this segment. Others' advice, she said, could be so necessary or so unnecessary, *depending on its relevance to one's own agenda* — quintessential localism. The students' complaints, too, were locally framed by them, not as a solution, however, but *as a problem*. While communications couched in terms of problems should ordinarily have greater problem-inducing impact in daily organizational commerce than those couched in terms of solutions (on grounds elaborated in the course of this episode), Sr. Claudia synthesized their inter-role problem as an inter-personal problem, a problem of 'chemistry' between persons who happened to be elected, thus discounting its importance.

Chapter 20

A Vacation Request Upsets Sr. Claudia

An important glimpse of Sr. Claudia's communication with the Trinity council was offered in the previous chapter. The present chapter provides a glimpse of communication between the faculty at large and the executive council. Featured are a member of the lay faculty and Sr. Claudia, with Sr. Catherine as intermediary message-carrier.

While the particular give-and-take of an interchange is important to examine in understanding communication flow and blockages, just as important is the quality of *relationship* between the communicating parties. If the relationship is one of mutual trust, respect, and affirmation, then communication can be open even in the face of momentary conflict of interests. If the relationship is that of strangers, then caution, tentativeness, and protectiveness will generally characterize communication until the relationship crystallizes in a positve or negative direction. If the relationship that has been built up previously is one of mutual mistrust, disrespect, and hostility, then communicative content and process will tend strongly to follow suit. This chapter throws light on the relationship between Sr. Claudia and the faculty.

Fairly early in the Fall, Allan had remarked to the executives that there seemed no way for faculty members to bring an agenda item of concern to the executive council as a group. Time and place of the executive meetings were not announced and no mechanism existed for communication to the executive council *per se*. Realizing this, the executives immediately tried to remedy what they regarded as an oversight by placing a notice in the faculty lounge and on the faculty bulletin board stating how faculty members could bring items for discussion at the Friday executive meetings. No one responded to that notice until the morning of February 4, the morning of an executive meeting. So far as we know, no one used that means of communicating with the executive council thereafter.

The executive meeting on February 4,02 made only passing reference to Sr. Claudia's meeting with the Trinity council the previous Wednesday. It dealt with nuts-and-bolts problems of administration — e.g., forms for contracts for the sisters (an innovation). After Sr. Claudia had finished reporting on her items, Sr. Catherine brought up what she regarded substantively as just another administrative matter, but one with special procedural significance to her: the first response from any faculty member to the executives' Fall invitation for communications from the faculty to the executive council as an entity.

> Sr. Catherine: This was brought to me by Carrie Fox, saying that the faculty representatives sent her in to put it on our agenda this morning ... she said Easter vacation begins March 30 and ends on the sixth — which [would bring everyone back to school for] Thursday and Friday, the sixth and seventh of April. And the question was, could it be considered to be Monday, April 10? Why had we brought them back the Thursday and Friday ..?
> Sr. Claudia: We had to have the *days* of *school*!
> Sr. Catherine [continuing]: .. and asked if it could be considered, ah, if we could just ..
> Sr. Claudia [interrupting, with sarcasm]: The other thing is that we could bring them back Wednesday, and have Wednesday, Thursday, and Friday if they feel there's no point in having two days of school.
> Sr. Catherine: Then that's the reply, the 'count' [i.e., the number of school days required by the state]. There's no way we could adjust ..
> Sr. Claudia: The count. We have to. Unless they want to go later in June. And we can't *get* them here ... (2/4/02: E; 1:519–530)

Sr. Claudia pursued which and how many faculty Carrie Fox was representing in a way that led Sr. Catherine to 'accept responsibility' for the communication, explaining that Mrs. Fox had been at a lunch table when someone had claimed that there was no way a faculty member could 'get anything to the executive council'. In response to this reported assertion, Sr. Claudia said, in a high pitched voice, apparently exasperated: 'That was *posted*'. She said she might consider it seriously if 'sixty or seventy members were interested in prolonging the school year to have two extra days at Easter'. Sr. Catherine said she had asked Mrs. Fox about the request and had been informed that 'several of us were taking trips'.

> Sr. Claudia: I hate to get uptight about this thing but I feel myself [separates her words] so uptight about, you know, three or four faculty members wanting a change in calendar .. you know, *she* was *on* the faculty last year, and could [have] indicate[d] this. Other people outvoted her ... and then to want to change the calendar *now* for the Easter recess, in terms of her trip and a couple of other people's trip .. do you understand what I mean?
> ...
> Sr. Catherine: I'm kind of pleased, though, that it would come in.

I think we can give a very logical explanation ... and I kind of welcome the opportunity to say, 'Okay, we considered it and you had voted on it'. We have a very .. I don't think uptight explanation for saying ..

Sr. Claudia [interrupting]: I'm not uptight about the explanations. I'm uptight about somebody coming in February to make a basic change in school calendar that would touch parents and students and an entire faculty ... I feel it *irresponsible* this time of year. So I'm uptight about that ... (2/4/02: E; 1:566–587)

Allan explored with Sr. Claudia how aware or unaware faculty members might be of the constraint of state requirements. Sr. Catherine remembered that Sr. Christina, who had been at the lunch table during the discussion of the request, had also been unaware of the executives' posted notice on the faculty bulletin board. Sr. Claudia replied, 'Christina worked for two months on Academic Senate setting up this, see? So, you know, do you see why I get uptight? [with rising pitch] I just think they're *unreal*. [Sighs in exclamation] God!'

Part of the ensuing discussion was precipitated by a question from Sr. Claudia to Sr. Catherine about why Carrie Fox had not brought up her question at the recent faculty meeting, where the 'action line' procedure (described below) had been used to convey and assess consensus on a great variety of problems. Sr. Claudia, responding to her own question said, *sotto voce*, 'They blow my mind'. Later, after indicating that faculty members who simply could not be present for the two-day week might send a substitute teacher, Sr. Claudia reviewed aloud grounds for believing that faculty members should have more sense than to ask questions like Carrie Fox's:

Sr. Claudia: And we talked about it at length at Academic Senate, in terms of giving them an extra day there [during Easter recess]. Now they're saying, 'As long as you gave us the extra day, give us two more'. So they sound like students! .... We spent an awful lot of time working on that calendar for this year ... You work on a calendar for the coming year. You don't work on it and revise it constantly through the school year ... because we publish it and parents see it and count on it. (2/4/02: E; 1:630–650)

Allan inquired how it might be that the Academic Senate could have a long discussion of something and the faculty at large still not be aware of the difficulties and issues underlying the discussion. This led to a discussion of the responsibilities of department chairs to communicate to their department members. Sr. Claudia expressed pessimism and helplessness:

Sr. Claudia: Communication by word of mouth is ineffective because it keeps being said in different ways, you know. You have 15 department chairmen and so 15 different messages get sent. So that's bad. Announcements they don't listen to. Written bulletins quite evidently are not being used. Posting notices doesn't work. How else do you communicate? Body language, I suppose.

Allan: Have you ever considered sending up a flare? [all laugh] ...

Sr. Claudia: That whole communication thing has me uptight, as you can tell. I think they're children. And they're being paid for it ... (2/4/02: E; 1:780–792)

Sr. Claudia related another incident that revealed what she referred to as the faculty's 'unreal' attitudes and conceptions. At the recent faculty meeting an 'action line' format had been used. It employed small group discussions from which reporters from each group would summarize for the entire faculty the problems or suggestions identified by that group. Each reported problem was publicly assigned its number in sequence and everyone present marked a personal rating of that item on a scale from very important to unimportant or even inappropriate. One of the suggestions was that all notices for a given day be put in faculty mailboxes the previous night so they would be available first thing in the morning. She finished her story by asking: '*Who* is here at night? Who do they *think* is going to *do* this? ... The *unreality* in terms of ... [trails off]'

Allan suggested that in some respects, perhaps, the students were more aware of administrative realities than were faculty members. In the exchange, Sr. Claudia said that what was important to students was often not important to her. Harkening back to Hester's and Leo's comments about an open campus policy, senior smoking lounge, and other matters of interest to seniors that were mentioned at the Wednesday night meeting with the Trinity council, Sr. Claudia concluded, 'When I heard the things that were important to them, you know, I understood that those were, like, things I didn't even want in my life'.

٭   ٭   ٭   ٭

Mrs. Fox's request could have been handled by Sr. Claudia straightforwardly, if all that it depended on were numerous and sufficient reasons to simply deny the request. But the request was not made into a problem of filling a gap in one or more faculty members' understanding. It was turned, rather, into a problem of personal and professional *adequacy*. The mere asking of the question was taken, first, as something to become 'uptight' about, which I translate to mean anxious and indignant. Here was a move, in Sr. Claudia's eyes, to abrogate a carefully worked out agreement among the faculty for the evident comfort and convenience of a few. Even to make such a request, given the earlier process of voting, the lack of extra 'snow' days, and effects on others who came to count on the calendar, was not merely a slip of memory or momentary thoughtlessness. It was irresponsible. Sr. Claudia's problem quickly became generalized, moreover, to the whole faculty ('they blow my mind'). Her problem regarding the faculty's personal or professional inadequacy led her to name-calling: 'I just think they're *unreal*,' 'they sound like *students*,' 'I think they're *children*'.

The relative ease with which Sr. Claudia could, in this period and in the context of the faculty's organizational functioning at least, be brought to categorize the faculty so sweepingly and with such denigration reflects simply that kind of relationship: one where the social and psychological distance between them could transform a narrowly focused faculty request, seeking added convenience and comfort without regard to organizational ramifications, into a threat which called out anxiety and anger manifest (behind closed doors) in terms like 'irresponsible', 'childish', and 'unreal'. Everything Sr. Claudia said on such an occasion about the factors that made the requested change unworkable might be completely correct in factual content. But the thoughts and emotions thus expressed reflected a relationship with the faculty in which any sympathy for faculty realities or sense that there might be legitimate, adult problems behind their childish-seeming request were readily, and on occasions like Mrs. Fox's request, completely pre-empted by a need to maintain an order of her own definition. Or, to put the matter more succinctly, her relationship with the faculty in this period was shaky enough that a request for an unworkable change could send her into an angry, defensive tizzy.

Was the vulnerability of her relationship due to her own, personal insecurity (a word she used to describe herself retrospectively later in the year) brought on by her conflict with Sr. Norma and lack of support felt from the regional administrators? Or was it due to the fact that Sr. Claudia had few informal social contacts with lay faculty members and had an office physically far removed from faculty comings and goings? Sr. Catherine would later describe Trinity's front office as a 'buffer' between the school's workaday world and Sr. Claudia's office down in the south wing. Or was her defensiveness on this occasion triggered by the particular content: a request to abrogate a carefully worked out prior agreement in order to satisfy personal comfort of a small number irrespective of its impact on the rest of the educational enterprise? All three of these were no doubt at work, converging to turn the year's one communication from faculty members to the executive council into a few minutes of revealing expression of threat and defense. The relationship between the faculty and the executive council as a formal entity, and more particularly between the faculty and Sr. Claudia, was distant and rendered communication within that relationship vulnerable to the kind of emotional transformation we see in this instance.

Chapter 21

Council Restructuring Begins

The Trinity council's first response, on February 8, to Sr. Claudia's evening meeting dealt with important substance, but devoted most of its time identifying issues and organizing a group structure for subsequent discussions.[1] Sr. Claudia and Lighthall arrived after the meeting had started, missing a presentation by Mr. Sullivan of some ideas he and Sr. Claudia had talked about some months previously. The most important substantive discussion of the meeting was under way.

Council Planning

What Kind of Advisory Relation?

The issue was whether the council's advice to the executive council should be merely reactive, responding to matters sent to it by the administration, or proactive (my terms, not theirs), initiating its own advice. Miss Nolan, Hester, and Lucy Ellen Garvin argued the proactive side, while Mr. Sullivan argued the reactive position.

> Mr. Sullivan: There are many things that can be handled very quickly and very fairly over an administrator's desk. If the situation arises in which the administrator feels the advice of a larger group is necessary, then that administrator can take it to that larger group ... Then only things an administrator is really honestly interested in hearing a reaction about come to the council.
>
> Hester: What if the students are honestly interested in letting an administrator know something that the administrator is not necessarily .. Oh! [turning to Sr. Claudia] I don't mean to unconsciously point over there, either [joking and laughing is heard]. No. What if the students are interested in letting the

administrator know something that the administrator is not necessarily aware of?

          ❁   ❁   ❁   ❁

For advice to be relevant only to the local realities of the administrators is not necessarily, as Hester was quick to point out, to be relevant to all important parts of the organization, some of which 'the administrator is not necessarily aware of'. Also noteworthy is that once again faculty realities in the council's advisory process were being ignored. It was the students, not the faculty, who were being considered as bringing something to the attention of the administrators via the council.

Hester's question pressed for a source of advice other than problems locally synthesized by the executives. Theirs was the perennial claim of the less powerful in any organizational hierarchy. Their claim is that upward communication is every bit as essential as downward, that initiative for disclosing problems must lie wherever problems arise in the system, not merely at the top. It is a claim, in other words, that once again asserts that many matters of general significance to the organization *become noticed only locally and must be communicated from that locale to other locales.* The experience with the change of the dress code to include sweaters was a case in point. The executives and the faculty who were members of the Trinity council considered the 'sweaters issue' to have been 'trivial'. In their local realities it was trivial; in the freshmen girls' realities, who could not wear sweaters and who sat in sometimes cold and draughty classrooms, it was not.

          ❁   ❁   ❁   ❁

Returning to the narrative, extended discussion explored the origins of advice, the routes by which matters for advice might come to the council for advice, and mechanisms for the council to decide in each given case, the route that would be used. Sullivan suggested that such routing decisions be made by the 'impartial chairman' of the council. Then he realized that Lighthall had come in after the meeting had started and had not heard the ideas he and Sr. Claudia had talked over some months earlier. Mr. Sullivan reviewed these ideas — revealing once again his informal role as sounding board and private conferee with Sr. Claudia in matters relating to the council. They had imagined together a council made up of eight students, four faculty members, and an administrator 'and then an impartial person, whether it be an administrator or a faculty member . . ., as the chairman'.

Further discussion of the powers of the impartial chairman and of who might be considered impartial led Lighthall to comment that this kind of issue was one of many like it that was better considered not by the full council as it might arise, but rather by a smaller committee to do some of the 'spade work'. Discussion then turned to arrangements for future discussions.

Planning Groups

Hester enunciated members' agreement to break up into small groups to plan in parallel. Mr. Sullivan called for a statement, beforehand, of what the groups would discuss. Seven topics can be identified in the ensuing discussion (but were not enumerated or summarized in the meeting) to be addressed by each small group:

1. The most effective number of council members.
2. 'Areas of consideration' or competency: which of the two functions, decision making or advice, would be appropriate for each kind of issue considered by the council?
3. Mr. Sullivan's (and Sr. Claudia's) 'plan', including the impartial chairman.
4. The possibility of grade- or class-councils (suggested by Lighthall).
5. Rules by which a matter would be considered 'mandatory' for the council to address.
6. The routing of issues, i.e., administration first, council first, or council sub-committees first.
7. The setting of priorities among agenda items — by urgency or by importance.

Attention soon turned to the task of dividing into small work groups. Hester summarized the groups' charge: each was to come up with its own plan for the council for the following year. One person would act as secretary of each group and each secretary would attend a meeting Thursday the following week to 'synthesize' the plans into a single set of recommendations. Chairs scraped, names went up. The names of those absent were allocated to groups with fewest signatures. Meeting times of each group were negotiated among its members. When all but a few had left the room, Lucy Ellen asked Sr. Claudia if she was going to be in on the small group planning.

> Sr. Claudia: I'm going to come for that final thing [the synthesizing meeting]. Maybe I'll bring something. How about that?
> Lucy Ellen: Why don't you come to this one [indicating her own group, listed on the chalkboard]?
> Sr. Claudia: Because I don't want to ever .. I don't want to influence any one of these. Because I want them to be free. But suppose I put in an idea .. Sr. Catherine and I can get together the same time you people are and try to work out a plan. We'll

bring in a sixth and toss it into the pot on an equal basis with everyone else's. (2/8/02: C; 1:888–895)

o   o   o   o

Division of the council into five, and with Sr. Claudia's group six, working groups, each working on a plan of the Trinity council's structure and functioning, produced a structure of participation that achieved several things. First, it multiplied by six the number of social units that could express local problems with the council and solutions for them. Second, it provided another set of opportunities for students and faculty to establish close working relations, relations of the kind a number of students had complained were lacking. And third, it created a participatory context in which the executives' own planning for the council, and particularly Sr. Claudia's planning, became legitimated as a parallel group effort rather than merely as the top-down voice of administration. It might also, of course, allow the sixth, more powerful group to preempt other groups' plans even while participating as an 'equal' group. Whatever any group suggested, it would be received by others who had worked over some of the same ground and who were primed to take in what others would suggest.

o   o   o   o

The 'Sixth Group' Plans

The executive meeting on February 11 was again devoted to restructuring of governance for the following year. Sr. Claudia had agreed that Sr. Norma would not attend because it had become too painful for Sr. Norma to participate in planning Trintiy's next year. An intern in the social psychological specialist program from the University of Chicago, Franklin Patrick ('Pat'), joined Lighthall, Sr. Catherine, and Sr. Claudia. Pat had been assigned to the Academic Senate and was helping it organize an 'action line', a communication format (described above, page 266, and of which more, below) to increase direct communication from the faculty as a whole group to the administration. The executive meeting explored three aspects of governance, only the last two of which will concern us here:

1. Administrative reorganization — the executive council and other administrative roles.
2. Trinity council structure and the expansion of councils as a means of coordinating, hearing from, and communicating to identifiable constituencies of the school.
3. Administrative linkage to the councils.

In addition, three rather more specific, focal problems or fears of Sr.

Claudia's came into view and were attended to: student class officers as roles that did not fit into Sr. Claudia's conception of effective governance; the danger of too much parental influence over a private school; and the 'action line' as a form of communication from the faculty.

A Pre-Meeting Discussion.

Lighthall arrived on February 11 as usual well before time to hear the morning announcements, about 9:05. He dropped in on Sr. Claudia, who waxed enthusiastic about Olympic ski jumping she had seen on television. She was fascinated by 'the absolute discipline' of the ski jumpers, 'the mastery thing'. She ticked off the topics and 'loose ends' she wanted to take up in the morning's meeting, saying that she 'kept coming back to the Trinity council in terms of . . . tying it in' to the administration and the rest of the school. The idea of having separate class councils 'really appealed' to her.

She thought of these class 'mini-councils' as doing much of the work of clarifying issues prior to their consideration by the Trinity council. Student members of the 'central' Trinity council could be elected by the mini-council of each class. Those class councils would, she thought, be composed of representatives from each of the class's approximately fifteen home-rooms. With the new role of class coordinator and perhaps one other teacher, that would bring the number of members of each class council to seventeen, 'a large group'. Each of these mini-councils would have an agenda committee to ensure preparation that had been lacking in the Trinity council. She and Lighthall discussed ways of selecting fewer representatives from the class at large and the desirability of some continuity of membership from year to year.

Thinking out loud, Lighthall drew four circles on the chalkboard that Sr. Claudia had ordered for the meeting, writing the numeral eight in each circle, reflecting their discussion that somewhere nearer eight than seventeen would be a more effective size for the class councils. A fifth, empty circle, represented the central, all-school council. Sr. Claudia agreed that two representatives from each class council would be better than one, and thought two administrators and two teachers selected from the faculty at large would also be suitable representatives, creating a central council of eight student members and four adult members, not an unwieldy size. Lighthall commented that the 'synthesis committee will be a constitution writing committee'.

In reference to the central, all-school council, Sr. Claudia said what she would 'love to do' was 'not to have a popular election' of students, but to have the very best students selected by the class councils for positions on the central council. Another advantage of the separate class councils, Lighthall said, was that they could take care of all the problems or even decisions that pertained only to the separate classes themselves (e.g., sophomore class dance) and not bore the central council with discussions of those class-specific matters. The four class councils would also, Lighthall said, multiply by four the amount of input to the executive council, to which Sr. Claudia replied, 'And the other way around, too'.

The meeting lasted three hours, going well beyond the usual noon luncheon adjournment. Sr. Claudia reported 'quite a bit of thought' about the tasks and general functions of various roles, including the new 'administrator-counselors' (eventually called 'class coordinators'). Discussion of how the class coordinators might and might not be the ones to link the executive council to the Trinity council led to agreement that it was best if the director herself be the administrative link to the Trinity council.

'A Different Kind of Council'.

The composition of the executive group was still an open question. Franklin Patrick raised a question about function that crystallized the ideas of distinct constituencies and their representation:

> Patrick: What is the function of the [Trinity] council? ... Somehow or other the council, the Academic Senate, the executive [council] have to have some kind of cohesion between the three of them. The only way I can see that, of course, is that people who are actually on the executive [council]be on the [Trinity] council and the Academic Senate at the same time.
>
> Lighthall: You bring up another good point, Pat, and that is that maybe a member of the Academic Senate in addition to yourself [Sr. Claudia] might be a member on the council.
>
> Sr. Claudia: See, like Sabrina is now — accidentally.
>
> Lighthall: Just happens to be that way.
>
> Patrick: That has to be built in. Academic Senate membership also has a seat on the council, the student body has a seat on the council, teachers have representatives on the council, executive board [sic] has representatives on the council.
>
> Sr. Claudia; That's good.
>
> Lighthall: That's excellent.
>
> Patrick: But the council becomes, then, instead of just a student council thing . .
>
> Sr. Claudia: Should have parents on it.
>
> Patrick [agreeing enthusiastically]: Parents on it!
>
> Lighthall: You said it!
>
> Patrick: I mean, really!
>
> Sr. Claudia: Good point. That's a different kind of a council!
>
> (2/11/02: E; I, 2:2–20)

'*Avoiding Trivia; Attending to Substance.*

Sr. Claudia complained that Trinity council had not contributed to a curriculum revision effort she had initiated with the Academic Senate. While members of the Academic Senate, she said, were defending their excessive course requirements (in her eyes), some sophomore students would come into her office and complain legitimately (she thought) about the excessive load. She asked in frustration why excessive curricular demands could not come up in Trinity council discussions: 'We've got statistics now ... ten seniors had failures, eight juniors had failures, *eighty-one* sophomores, ... and twenty-three freshmen'. She said, 'We can't wait for 14 year-olds to generate those problems ... We haven't been asking the right questions of the council ... You know, like, what have I ever sent to their agenda?' She and Lighthall speculated enthusiastically about how the 'administrator-counselors' might help their respective class councils bring problems up for discussion and avoid concentrating on 'trivia'. Sr. Claudia reminded that it was the five council groups, not the executives, that had been charged to prepare a plan for the following year's council structure, but that 'this is one of the ideas that we can suggest to them'.

'Listening to it,' Sr. Claudia said, 'it appeals to me tremendously ... but I have a feeling it won't appeal to the students ... As soon as we say, "parents on it", ... that's the one I think they will resist.'

> Sr. Claudia: They wanted student government .... And they want at-large elections, they want a popularity contest ... Hester Dulany .. Boy! I remember last year the kinds of arguments that went into that; she was the hardest to sell even in terms of having faculty on it .... (2/11/02: E; I, 2:346–376)

⚬　　⚬　　⚬　　⚬

The 'sixth group', which Sr. Claudia had said would put its ideas 'into the pot' along with the other five, had generated a differentiated council structure based, not on concepts of school administration, but on ideas about societal governance: a system of councils, each representing a major constituency, each sending its representatives, in turn, to a central representative council. The central, Trinity council would offer the executive council advice, to be sure, but advice that would (1) have been purged of the merely parochial concerns of local constituencies, (2) have been prepared and clarified by local council deliberations, (3) have been guided, in the case of each student council, by a member of the administration, and therefore, (4) would be of such a nature as to render the executives 'fools' not to give it weight.

We learn that the executives had had to 'sell' the Trinity council to the students the year before, and that it had been a difficult task of persuasion.

Now they would again be selling a more complex council structure — to the students. No resistance was seen coming from the faculty, who were not even mentioned in this connection.

✿   ✿   ✿   ✿

One idea led to another, and Lighthall and Patrick became caught up in the new structuring. Patrick chalked in the number of representatives from each constituency to its respective council.[2] Sr. Claudia responded to the chalkboard notations: 'I looked up at this and my feeling for it was Claudia sitting on top of [laughs] a whole can of worms [laughs again]'.

Discussion turned to the composition of the executive council, and the chalkboard again registered ideas. Sr. Catherine suggested that the new structure being planned took over any purposes served by class officers. Lighthall was suddenly struck by their omission from the scheme: 'Are those done away with? ... Holy mackerel!' Sr. Claudia saw them as redundant with the planned council structure. She suggested how the idea of class officers and council representatives might be combined to gain acceptance:

> Sr. Claudia: You can call them [i.e., class council members] class officers if it helps them: these eight people, in a way, are class officers ... Then you don't have just some representatives of one clique that set up activities [e.g., dances, benefits, jean days] ... And I think you're pretty bound to cross the lines of just the popular students.
> Lighthall: So the proposal is: do away with these. (2/11/02: E; I, 2: 735–745)

Sr. Claudia's opposition to the concept and role of class officers would be expressed again — in response to students' repeated (but not unanimous) expressions of commitment to having their own class officers, justified by the need to have 'figureheads', the need for 'leaders' to 'look up to', the need for a 'clique' of 'popular' girls to set up class activities.

Subsequent discussion of this 'sixth group' revealed its shifting attention among items sketched on the chalkboard. How members of the *parent* council might be selected led to expressions by both Sr. Catherine and Sr. Claudia of worries about parental 'take-over' of the school. The two executives talked about ways to gain the advantages of a parent council — to help them, for example, discuss salary, tuition level, and discipline issues — while still not giving up executive power to such a group.

Lighthall expressed enthusiasm for the action-line format of communication between the faculty and the administration. This process of dividing the assembled faculty into small groups to identify important issues and problems for consideration Lighthall called 'our mobile trouble-shooting mechanism'. The action line had previously communicated some proposals, like after-school mailbox deliveries to the faculty for early-morning availability, that Sr. Claudia felt were 'irresponsible'. Her almost *sotto voce* reaction to the action-line format was, 'May we all live through it!', a remark unnoticed by Lighthall at the time. Sr. Claudia said it had been a 'rich' meeting and promised to report these ideas to the 'synthesizing' meeting, a meeting she agreed to have tape recorded.

◦   ◦   ◦   ◦

Two different reactions to the possibilities of being influenced by the realities of others can be seen in the foregoing. Sr. Claudia and Sr. Catherine both wanted more contact with parents, but on matters of salary, levels of tuition, and discipline, not on basic matters of personnel appointments. They wanted to steer a mid-course in this matter. Regarding the open communications from the faculty afforded by the action-line format, Sr. Claudia was less inclusive, most leery. While she did not say so, it is not irrelevant to point out that the spontaneity of the action-line format ran counter to repeated expressions by Sr. Claudia in favor of groups' being 'prepared' in their discussions and for issues having been 'winnowed'. Preparation and winnowing of issues are carried out in small groups, not large assemblies, and maximize rational argument and order while minimizing heterogeneity, unpredictability, and emotionality.

Summary

This chapter's narrative reveals localism in new ways. First, Hester and others in the council address localism explicitly as an *issue*. Opposing Mr. Sullivan's view of advice-when-asked-for, Hester asks, 'What if the students are interested in letting the administration know something that the administration is not necessarily aware of ?' The issue was not resolved, but the discussion adds validity to our inclusion as a variable the orientation of the problem originator, and more generally, of protagonists, to advice and complaints. At issue is openness or closedness to unanticipated organizational realities. A second glimpse of localism came in Sr. Claudia's comment about the action-line format of communication. That open-ended format is precisely designed to open channels of communication upward without reference to any agenda except that of the complainant. Her comment was, 'May we all live through it'. That format minimized relevance of 'advice' to a superordinate's agenda, maximizing its relevance to others' agendas. Finally, in the executive planning session, Sr. Claudia's own values, emphasizing competence, rationality, and preparedness, led her to exclude as valueless elections based on 'popularity', which served what students voiced as the need for 'figureheads' who could be 'looked up to'. The 'sixth group's' local values did not include this student outlook, one that would be expressed repeatedly, would be the focus of manipulation attempts, and would finally be contested outright by vote.

Notes

1. Sr. Claudia attended but Sr. Norma did not, a presence and an absence, respectively, that held true for most of the remaining council discussions.
2. Lighthall and Sr. Claudia had had a conversation about the possibility of one of the nuns, Sr. Janet, receiving training at the university toward the possibility of developing a role at Trinity of 'organizational consultant'. He thought Sr. Janet might become a 'facilitator' of the Trinity council, and chalked this label on the chalkboard. For an account of Sr. Janet's successful development of her role as an internal organizational consultant the following year (in contrast to 21 other much less successful attempts), see Lighthall and Braun (1976).

Chapter 22

The 'Synthesizing' Meeting

Around the time that Sr. Claudia's 'sixth group' was planning the future of the Trinity council, five other groups of Trinity council members were also discussing the council's future. We have no recording of those discussions, as we have of the executive group, but some aspects of their meetings are evident from members' comments in the 'synthesizing' meeting. The five student secretaries of these planning groups met with Sr. Claudia from 3 pm until a little after 4 pm on February 17. Sr. Claudia said she would report last, and the girls reported the results of their respective groups in the order presented in Table 22.1. The meeting unfolded in three clearly discernable sections. First, each student reported what she remembered of her group's recommendations. This took about 15 minutes. Then Sr. Claudia took about ten minutes to do the same for her 'sixth' group, using a diagram she had extracted from the previous executive meeting as a guide for her remarks. The remaining forty minutes were taken up with questions and conflicting opinions about, and elaborations of, Sr. Claudia's plan.

The Five Planning Groups

Composition

The groups' student-faculty ratios varied from 1:4 to 4:1, but the reporting secretary for each group was a student. The composition of each group, identified by the name of its reporting secretary, is presented in Table 22.1.

Note that while the faculty members who were from the religious order distributed themselves over four of the groups, the four women who were lay teachers all signed up for the same group, a group no nun joined. Most (57 per cent) of the faculty were lay members, of whom 92 per cent were women. Thus, Sonia's quartet of faculty led the same kinds of lay lives as the majority of the faculty, lives not totally committed to the school as an

Table 22.1.   The Composition of Trinity Council's Five Sub-groups for Planning its Future.

1. Beth Dolan's group[a]	2. Donna Laughton's group	3. Ellie Sanford's group
Nora Quinn	Dale Devlin	Laura Hanrahan
Kathy Kuhlen	Sr. Janet Acker	Mary Donnelly
Fran Novak	Joan Noonan	Roz Donahue
Sr. Sabrina	Pam Roe	(Sr. Norma)

4. Leo Phelan's group	5. Sonia Griffin's group
Sr. Nannette	Miss Nolan
Mr. Sullivan	Mrs. Marchand
Lucy Ellen Garvin	Miss Higgins
Hester Dulany	Miss Cohler

a — Beth Dolan's group met four times, Donna Laughton's met once, Ellie Sanford's once (but without Sr. Norma), and Leo Phelan's at least once, perhaps twice. Sonia Griffin's faculty 'group' never met as a group; Sonia spoke with each member briefly.

apostolic mission but, rather, having family, social, and leisure commitments quite different from those of the nuns.

        ✿   ✿   ✿   ✿

Four Dimensions of the Groups' Planning

Rather than narrate the details of each student's report, it seems useful to summarize all five of them in terms of four dimensions of the groups' discussions: (1) proper function of the council, (2) technical roles, (3) class officers, and (4) size and composition.

1.   Proper functioning.   All but Beth Dolan's group conceived the future Trinity council to be advisory in all but a few areas of activity — the function finally adopted.

2.   Technical roles.   Two groups, Donna Laughton's and Leo Phelan's, recommended that both the chair of the council and its secretary be chosen on the basis of expertise, rather than general vote, and that neither be voting members — staff roles also finally adopted.

3.   Class officers.   The question whether separate class officers, as positions in addition to council members, should be retained was treated by all groups except Sonia Griffin's 'group', whose members were all faculty members except Sonia. Sonia's faculty group never did meet; Sonia approached each of them individually. Two of these four groups, Beth Dolan's and Leo Phelan's, favored outright retention of separate class officers (though Leo herself did not). Ellie Sanford's group, made up of two freshmen and two other sophomores (with Sr. Norma as nominal member only), split along class lines, the freshmen favoring retention, the sophomores favoring Trinity council members being also class officers. Donna Laughton's group favored this same position. The division among the group plans reflected divided sentiments in the larger student body.

The question of 'class officers' seems at first trivial, not worth tracking in a narrative like this. But its insistent reappearance as an issue warrants attention. The matter is complicated, but a brief word here is in order. Beneath the surface of discussion of whether class officers should be eliminated was, I believe, an unspoken conflict over whether purely instrumental functions ('getting things done') were to be served or whether expressive, symbolic functions, too, were important. The symbolic functions were those of modeling, of 'figurehead', of a 'leader' who could be 'looked up to'. At issue, latently, were the psychological functions of identity and identification and the social function of class cohort solidarity. Sr. Claudia saw only instrumental values. Some students could see both instrumental and expressive-symbolic values, but had difficulty articulating and defending the latter.

4. Size and composition. Beth's and Donna's group both recommended two representatives from each of the two 'underclassman' classes, three representatives from the junior and senior classes, four faculty representatives and Sr. Claudia from the administration, totalling 15. No plan for membership went beyond a total of 16, ten fewer than the then current Trinity council, except the freshmen girls in Ellie Sanford's group, who felt 23 were needed: four from each class and seven faculty. Leo's group recommended 13 members: two from each class, four faculty, and Sr. Claudia. Testimony collected by Sonia from her group members was similar: two or three students from each class plus four faculty members.

Sonia's conversations with her lay faculty members revealed sentiments quite in keeping with the fact that they had never met as a group, sentiments of a major constituent's (the lay faculty's) organizational reality regarding the future council's composition and functioning. Sonia reported that her faculty members felt it was not important for faculty to be involved in the council: 'the faculty themselves wonder why they should be included on a student government'. They had referred, she said, to the 'amount of student policies that were made that really didn't involve the faculty that much'. Leo countered that that might have been true that year, but that this planning was for the following year.

Other members of the synthesizing meeting reacted quickly:

Donna Laughton: Without us they're nothing and without them we're nothing.
Sr. Claudia: . . . no matter what problem is being discussed, it

> seems to me that both groups are involved in it, you know, intrinsically.
>
> Sonia Griffin: Well, this was just one idea that came up.
>
> Sr. Claudia: Okay. If that's how they feel, I think we ought to hear about it [laughter among the others].
>
> Unidentified: We may not *like* it, but .. [laughter]
>
> Sr. Claudia: We'll get *mad* at it .. [more laughter] (2/17/02: Syn; 1:127–145)

✿   ✿   ✿   ✿

The planning for the council the following year had now involved faculty, students, and administration. Even at this first, synthesizing, meeting clear evidence was present that, with regard to both participation and substantive sentiment, realities of lay faculty members were in conflict with those of Sr. Claudia and the student reporters: the lay faculty neither wanted to participate in the planning group for which they had chalked their names nor saw future faculty participation in the 'student government' itself as important.

The response of the synthesizing group was not to seek more information about the faculty to explore that antagonism further. Rather, it was to indicate how out of date the faculty's perspective was (Leo's comment about this year's events not bearing on next year's planning) and to deny any separateness of faculty from the students and council by affirming their interdependence (Donna and Sr. Claudia). Leo, Donna, and Sr. Claudia were arguing, to themselves, how the faculty were simply wrong in thinking and feeling this way. Sonia, now under the pressure of this synthesizing group and no longer in the presence of faculty, defended herself by minimizing this strong, explicit, operating reality of her lay faculty members as 'just one idea that came up'. Having been minimized, it could now be laughed at as an object of strange otherness, as something not to be liked, as something to get '*mad* at'. In this brief interchange we see how a reality different from the group's is received, transformed into an error, and rejected as unimportant rather than integrated for subsequent action.[1]

The Sixth Plan

Sr. Claudia explained that the reason she had not joined one of the five groups was that she did not want her views deferred to: 'I felt it was unfair to a committee to be in there pushing'. Instead, she said, the next executive committee meeting was devoted to 'dreaming up this structure'. As she passed out a diagram, she said, 'It's *very* different from what the present one is'.

As Sr. Claudia handed out her diagrams, she explained that the new 'solution' addressed 'the fact that there are not enough students *directly involved* in council work; I don't mean committees, I mean directly involved in it'. The various councils of her plan were a way to have 'everybody in the whole school community' 'belonging' to some council. She figured about eight members to each council, she said, but added 'we didn't even talk about how many people on those'. She ignored or suppressed the explicit discussion of numbers in the previous Friday's executive meeting (in order to make the plan seem less fixed, more open to change?). Elections would be within classes, 'not all the sophomores electing the seniors'. Each advisory council, she said, would have the goal of 'problem sensing', a goal opposite from one where an administrator would say, 'Consider this and give your opinion'. Problems would be identified, that is, at the 'grass roots' (Sr. Claudia's words), and to the extent possible also solved at that level, she explained.

Sr. Claudia went on to explain that the Trinity council membership would be indirectly elected by the other councils: two from each class council, one from the faculty council, two parents, and one each from the executive council and academic senate. She joked about calling the Trinity council the 'lucky thirteen', and explained council functioning with enthusiasm:

> Sr. Claudia: What they [the thirteen members of the proposed Trinity council] do is bring in what's already been winnowed out ... The freshmen say, you know, 'We've got to have this problem solved someplace'. They've taken care of a lot of other stuff and they've set some activities for themselves ... so the Trinity council doesn't have to do that [i.e., the class councils have local decision-making power on matters of purely class concern]. But they bring things as freshmen see as a problem ... What they couldn't handle in their council, they bring before the Trinity council. (2/17/02: Syn; 1:200–218)

Sr. Claudia went on to explain the new roles of 'counselor-administrator', and the place of these new roles in her conception of how discipline ought to be handled at Trinity. The counselor-administrator for each class-year would address her own class's discipline through face-to-face duscussions with misbehaving students in which the student would be confronted. Sr. Claudia gave an example:

> Sr. Claudia: Instead of saying, 'Ha! Detention!', [the counselor-administrator (later known as 'coordinator')] says, you know, 'Okay, this is what you did today and three days ago you did the same crazy thing. How come? Why are you doing this'. And then they kind of dicker it out, between. Okay then if the girl comes in again ... like for the third time ... the administrator [note the

change in title] says, you know, 'Three times is the charm'. At
this point maybe there would be some kind of detention ...
[The counselor-administrator of a given class-year] really belongs to the students; she doesn't belong to the administration.
(2/17/02: Syn; 1:218–240)

Leo, Sonia, Ellie, and Sr. Claudia herself expressed enthusiasm for the
enlarged council concept. Sr. Claudia was excited about the 'two advantages' of 'communication upward and downward' which she considered
'darned important'. Ellie responded: 'We don't communicate in this council
with the school at all'. Sr. Claudia waxed enthusiastic about getting 'that
whole bunch of people working with you so that you've got a kind of built-in
involvement'. One could still have a good discussion, she said, with a group
of 13. Pointing to the class councils on the diagram she said, 'Here's where
the action's going to be. The fights are going to be here, the real hassling out
of problems. The emotion can be here, see. And then you come with your
arguments to this one, see [laughs lightly, pointing to the Trinity council on
the diagram]. You know, you bring your big guns here'.

       ✿   ✿   ✿   ✿

Sr. Claudia's description of the division of labor, here, between the local
councils and the Trinity council makes clear her desire to maximize the ratio
of rational, disciplined, prepared thought to 'fights', 'hassling', and 'emotion' in the new Trinity council, the council where she herself would come
in contact with the local problems. She wanted the new Trinity council to be
reserved for the 'big guns', i.e., the well-prepared, rational arguments,
'winnowed out' from the implied chaff of fights, hassling, and emotion, and
from the purely local, class activities that she wanted handled locally.

       ✿   ✿   ✿   ✿

Ellie: I love it.
Sonia: Oh yeah!
Donna Laughton: I have a question. Oh group, I have a question.

Implication: Eliminate Class Officers

With Donna's question, the group began to explore implications of Sr.
Claudia's plan, the third phase of the meeting. Just before leaving the
meeting, Donna broached the question of class officers: were the two
representatives to the Trinity council to be the president and vice president
of the class? Leo Phelan opposed class officers. Sr. Claudia said, 'We felt
very strongly about titles'. (Her 'we' should more accurately be read 'I'.)
The girls began to talk 'over' each other, and transcription of the debate

became impossible as it became increasingly heated. One theme centered on whether the popularly elected class officers became 'caught' in their own 'images', leading Ellie to exclaim that the offiers did not 'do anything' but were 'looked up to' because of being president and vice president. Beth asked, 'Is that wrong?'

After some interchange, Sr. Claudia suggested that the students 'think of' council members 'as officers'. Leo elaborated on how students thought about the class offices:

> Leo Phelan: When you're an officer, it's prestige. You know, you've reached the peak, type of thing. And I think it's hard to overcome. It's always been there that .. I mean that's sort of like the culmination [laughs lightly] of your, ah, political career here ... A lot of kids don't want the opportunity of being an officer taken away from them. (2/17/02: Syn; 1:431–436)

Beth then disclosed, for the first time, that her group had agreed that class offices should be continued, as she said, 'for purposes of responsibility and organization and .. ' She was cut off:

> Leo: Responsibility for what?
> Ellie: Organization I can see ..
> Beth [with higher pitch and more volume]: To get things done. Organization to follow up ..
> Leo: *What* things?
> Beth [with still higher pitch and markedly greater volume]: Leo you can't say there's nothing to do! You're saying that senior class president ...
> Leo: Beth! Don't *yell* at me.(2/17/02: Syn; 1:437–441)

Beth calmed down. Leo conceded that some activities were carried out by officers but considered them insignificant. Sr. Claudia supported Leo's position. Leo argued that whatever the officers did could be done by the councils, to which Beth again tried to emphasize the need for 'leaders'. Sr. Claudia and Leo opposed 'titles'. Sr. Claudia urged that respect for leadership positions was 'earned'. Sr. Claudia meant by 'earned' productive, instrumental actions, not some fashionable 'popular' image or demeanor. She saw the indirect election of representatives to the new Trinity council as a means of producing effective student leaders, which she called 'officers': 'And boy! You get good officers that way'. The local class councils, knowing well the strengths and weaknesses of their members, would elect only the best: 'This way, you're not going to have the inarticulate ones ... Do you see how well prepared they'd come to a meeting, too?'

❂   ❂   ❂   ❂

Clearly Sr. Claudia was committed to her plan, not merely 'playing' with it speculatively. She was selling it to these leaders. Sr. Claudia's enthusiastic selling was matched by her listeners' eager buying. These buyers, further-more, were among the most influential student members of the Trinity council, having emerged from their groups largely as Sr. Claudia imagined leaders would emerge from the proposed class councils to the new Trinity council.

※　※　※　※

Discussion moved from communication between the proposed councils and class members to the disillusioning experience of students that year with the Trinity council. The students expressed disappointment at the Trinity council's impotence in changing policy. Sr. Claudia pointed out some ways in which, as she said, 'it's not the neat thing to make policy that kids may think it is' and went on to clarify that the benefits of the proposed scheme were in the cooperation involved:

> Sr. Claudia: ... this way, it makes the policy making much nicer because .. in terms of the fact then that I've got a whole group of people making it with me ... Legally, I'll be making it. But ·actually this group .. you know, would I want to say to all this group, 'I veto it'?
> Leo: You'd alienate all your support. (2/17/02: Syn; 1:649–675)

Leo turned discussion to the faculty's probable reaction to it. Using a metaphor from child growth and development, Sr. Claudia said she thought the faculty 'ought to grow out of' its reluctance to bring up important matters in the presence of students, but that the new structure provided a council for their own voice. Leo and Sonia expressed satisfaction with 'the plan' and Beth bemoaned the fact that her group had met four times and thought their ideas would be much better than the other groups' ideas but that in comparison with this plan, theirs was nothing.[2] The group talked about how continuity might be 'built in' (Sr. Claudia's words) from year to year and how 'this plan' might be presented to the whole council, how other members might be approached to secure their understanding, acceptance, and elaboration of 'this plan'. In the course of this discussion, which brought the meeting to an end, Ellie Sanford asked if it would be all right to talk with 'kids outside of council'. Sr. Claudia voiced approval, and Ellie explained:

> Ellie: 'Cause I brought up this thing about what the freshmen were saying about no class officers, and they said, 'Don't do that, Ellie. It will look like the council kids just want everything for themselves' [laughter]. (2/17/02: Syn; 1:830–833)

The topic of class officers came up the next day, at the regular Friday executive meeting. Sr. Claudia summarized the 'synthesizing' meeting for the most part accurately and rather completely, as judged by the contents of the tape recording. She became less accurate about the meeting on the matter of class officers, where she tended to assimilate others' views to her own:

> Sr. Claudia: The first concern [expressed the previous day about the 'plan'] was, 'Where's the president and the vice president?' Titles. And I would say, of the six of us there, five people, including myself, immediately said, 'There's one thing we don't want and that's titles'. . . . It seems to me that for one student in a school this large to think of herself or to have students think of her as being somehow the school leader is a . . an old fashioned concept. (2/18/02: E; 1:67–104)

Eleven days later the Trinity council met to consider the 'synthesis' produced by Sr. Claudia and the five students on February 17.

Summary

This chapter's narrative reveals the functioning and effects once again of linearity in sequential participation: re-emergence of the whispering parlor game effect. The lay teachers convey their view to Sonia Griffin opposing faculty membership in a future Trinity council. She brings that view to the 'synthesizing' meeting, without any lay faculty present. That group receives her information, discounts or opposes it, and she acquiesces. There being no lay faculty member present to defend and explain that view, it succumbs to the realities that members can represent and explain, namely their own. Thus later realities replace earlier ones rather than becoming integrated with them.

This chapter's narrative also reveals more detail about Sr. Claudia's orientation to unsolicited information from advice givers. In her characterizations of the benefits of the council advisory system, 'feeding in' to the Trinity 13, she emphasizes preparedness and the fact that the 'fights' and 'hassles' will be at the level of the local councils and only the 'big guns', the well prepared arguments, would come to the Trinity 13. Thus, *if* unsolicited advice or *if* unanticipated complaints came up the line to the 13, they would be prepared, non-emotional, rational. Her orientation to emotionality, then, seems to be related to her aversion to advice that is 'unnecessary' or irrelevant to her own agenda. With the gain in preparedness and rationality, however, comes the loss of direct contact with the parties making the complaint. And with that interposition of 'rationality' between the complainant and the Trinity 13 would come greater vulnerability to the effects of linearity, exactly as had happened with the lay faculty and Sonia Griffin's report to the 'synthesizing' committee. Distance from emotionality may bring distance from local realities and a reduced capacity to explore them.

Finally, the narrative shows how a specific kind of commitment on the part of students, a particular local reality vis à vis 'leaders', continues to be discounted on grounds that these leaders fail to accomplish much, that is, on instrumental grounds. This despite Leo's specific testimony that 'it's hard to overcome. It's always been there . .', that election to class offices is 'the culmination' of a girl's 'political career here', and that 'a lot of kids don't want the opportunity of being an officer taken away from them'. The students' *symbolic* commitments become discounted on *instrumental* grounds.

Notes

1. Irving Janis and his colleagues (Janis, 1972; Janis and Mann, 1977) point to such 'groupthink' or 'concurrence-seeking tendencies' as detrimental to effective decision making. True enough. But this is not merely a psychological, cognitive 'failure' or 'misperception' or 'misjudgment'. The very structure of six planning groups allowed for heterogeneous views. The group dominated by faculty membership, Sonia's, did, in fact, correctly *'perceive', express, and record* (in Sonia's memory) a part of the organization's reality with respect to future council functioning. The weakness in the reality-integrating process was not cognitive, it was communicative. It was not excessive and narrowing solidarity on the part of the synthesizing group but insufficient cross-group communication, an insufficiency of communication by proxy (Sonia) rather than by direct, face-to-face interchange, interchange in which the 'synthesizers'' objections could be actively countered rather than allowed to remain untouched in their localism.

   What appears here, in this synthesizing group, as 'groupthink' and classical concurrence-seeking tendencies can, in the next phase of the larger process, be broken through, reversed, with a new integration. As is dramatically evident in Sonia's own case, what can happen in one social setting, Sonia's successive contacts with faculty, hearing expressions of apathy, can be reversed a few days later in another social setting, Sonia with the synthesizing group, diminishing the prominence of the faculty's low commitment ('just one idea that came up'). That reversal, too, could have been reversed. Regarding this particular 'synthesizing' meeting at this juncture in the process of problem solving, we must give due weight to Janis' emphasis on concurrence seeking: from its first mention this meeting was called the 'synthesizing' meeting — not a 'brainstorming' meeting or a meeting to 'explore the different groups' views', for example. Yet with a wider perspective, encompassing the whole problem-solving process, not merely particular decisions within it, organizations are, indeed, established to develop working concurrences in order to accumulate some coherent effect. Thus, concurrence seeking is *not generally* detrimental, but rather essential, to effective problem solving. What is central to effective organizations regarding a certain matter, X, then, is not concurrence- or difference-seeking regarding X, but both of these in the service of integrating the only reality an organization ever has regarding any X, the pluralistically and locally synthesized realities regarding X that are dispersed among its constituencies. And that integration depends every bit as much on reality *conveyance* as it does on reality *decoding*.

2. Beth's feelings of having put in so much work only to have it swamped by Sr. Claudia's better plan was similar to sentiments expressed at various times by faculty members. One member characterized Sr. Claudia's mind as 'multi-simultaneous',

meaning both that she could keep multiple aspects of a problem or situation in mind simultaneously and that her thoughts about matters apparently arose simultaneous with the matters themselves. These were sentiments of being faced with *overwhelming competence*, a competence that often had the effect of saying to others working with Sr. Claudia, 'Sr. Claudia has matters well in hand, so well in fact, that your efforts are not really needed and won't yield solutions as effective as hers'. While in many respects Sr. Claudia's solutions were often more thoroughly thought through than those proposed by others, Sr. Claudia could not, by herself, imagine or represent all organizational realities relevant to a problem or solution. Lay teachers' realities regarding council participation, for example, operate in lay teachers, not religious teachers, and tend to be expressed, if at all, only by lay teachers. But lay teachers and others, seeing a proposal of Sr. Claudia's as extremely well thought out and defended, could easily withdraw from exploring it, thus allowing its unexposed exclusions of their own realities to remain. Then, only after protracted implementataion of the proposal would those excluded realities become exposed and, as in the case of this third episode, contribute to the implemented solution's local, ad hoc, and piecemeal dismantling.

Chapter 23

Trinity Council Addresses the 'Synthesis'

On February 29 the Trinity council considered the 'synthesis'. Segments of a solution to Sr. Claudia's problem of governance had emerged, had begun to be transformed, and had begun also to spread outward, recruiting participants, some enthusiastic, some doubtful. In what follows, we again see unfold theoretically and practically important variations in the expression and integration of organizational realities with respect to an organizational problem. The present chapter reveals the particular localism of various groups implicated in Sr. Claudia's problem of governance.[1]

¤   ¤   ¤   ¤

The Trinity council's two-hour meeting on February 29 devoted most of its discussion to functions of representation, constituencies to be represented, and roles and election procedures through which representation would be effected. Hester Dulany had taken the unusual step of circulating an agenda (Figure 23.1) more than a week in advance, expecting a report from someone in the synthesizing group. Hester had assumed that someone from the group of six 'synthesizers' would come prepared to report on the synthesis. None of the girls from the 'synthesizing' meeting had been appointed to prepare a report and none had prepared. Sr. Claudia had come prepared with the diagrams of the proposed council structure she had prepared for the 'synthesizing' meeting.

Leadership: Functions and Structures

Ellie Sanford ended the 53-second silence of members' studying the diagram by urging that the question of officers on the councils ought to be discussed, that a number of girls had told her that there should be officers on each council, to which Leo Phelan responded, 'Why?'.

Local Realities, Local Adaptations

Figure 23.1.   Facsimile of the agenda of the February 29, 02 Trinity council meeting.

TRINITY COUNCIL MEETING

BLUE ROOM

Tuesday, Feb. 29, 02   3:00 pm

I.   Opening

II.   Brief presentation of Council plan; six committee representatives

III. Discussion — vote on plan

IV. Enumerate fine points of plan:

    A.   Number of people on Councils
    B.   Qualifications of candidates?
    C.   When to elect Councils (April, May, September)
    D.   Duties of representatives
    E.   Miscellaneous

V.   Appoint of [sic] committee to:

    A. Write down and organize results and decisions of IV discussion
    B. Determine method of presenting idea to students
    C. Decide method and calendar for elections
    Other? Committee is preferably volunteer.

> Ellie: Mainly for leadership . . . Some reasons given were, like, the Fall dance: who's going to do that? Will the 16 or 24 of them [eight members indicated on the diagram for each class council] get together, you know — like, sophomores, juniors, seniors — will they all get together and do that? Stuff like that. (2/29/02: C; 1:50–55)

✿   ✿   ✿   ✿

Embedded in Ellie's and Leo's interchanges were several of the issues that subsequent discussion explored. Instead of providing extended quotes of the often shifting discussion, I will lay out the structure of issues and provide illustrative quotes of the arguments. This brief interchange between Ellie and Leo raised, for example, the issue of function, though that term was not used. Were representatives to plan activities? Or were they, as Sr. Claudia had explained in the 'synthesizing' meeting, to sense and help solve important problems? Or would they do both? Ellie and Leo were also raising the issue of particular positions or offices — or, as Sr. Claudia often referred to it, the issue of 'titles', the particular organizational

292

structures in which functions would be located and through which they would be implemented. A third issue, more subtly embedded in Ellie's answer, was the issue of constituency. On whose behalf would representatives act: for a local constituency, like a class, or for the whole school? Should there be leaders of only local constituencies (again, this term was not used) or only of the whole school, or possibly of both?

Examining the meeting's discussion reveals references to four functions the new Trinity council might serve and five possible structures for serving them. While not all permutations of these functions and structures were discussed, most were noted.

Functions

1. Activity Leadership: 'Spirit'. Students and adults at Trinity often referred to 'school spirit' and 'class spirit' — e.g., 'the sophomores this year don't have much class spirit' and 'the reason you want football games with [rival school] is to build school spirit'. Extra-currricular activities of all kinds added to school spirit, and it was the job of officers to select and organize activities that would call out widespread and enthusiastic response of the kind meant by 'school spirit'. A 'big turnout' was evidence one had succeeded in promoting class or school spirit, the noisier and more hilarious the more successful. Building spirit by concocting and effectively executing activities, expecially class activities, bears an obvious resemblance to the kind of rituals Durkheim (1965) and others have observed to revivify an emotionally intense sense of solidarity with one's group. Such solidarity can make important contributions to adolesents' development of a sense of identity (e.g., Erikson, 1959, pp. 102–161), and is closely connected to images and opportunities of leadership.

2. Symbolic Leadership: Figurehead, Heroine Function. As we shall see, girls made reference to 'looking up to' class leaders who had been elected in class-wide or school-wide elections. Incumbents in such positions served as models of style and demeanor, supporting a sense of identity among the girls, an ideal or heroine image that served the further function of promoting solidarity among class members.

3. Representative Governance. Opposed to symbolic leadership was the image, held most clearly by Sr. Claudia, Hester Dulany, Leo Phelan, Nora Quinn, and Ellie Sanford, of the effective leader in the instrumental sense, willing and competent to face problems, who would identify important things the school or class needed to accomplish and set about accomplishing them.

4. Communicative Linkage Among Groups. Sr. Claudia and Sr. Sabrina made a number of comments about needs for groups (e.g., parents, students, administration, homerooms — again omitting the faculty) to communicate regularly with each other.

Structures

1. Role of Class Officer. In years past only the senior class had had class officers, elected in the junior year. They were elected, however, by the entire student body, not by their own class alone. With the creation of the Trinity council in 01 came a parallel move for class officers for each class, also elected by the entire student body. Their functions were consciously to promote 'spirit' for their class, in the form of dances, football games, benefits, jean days, and the like. Much less consciously, but not entirely unconsciously either, they also embodied the visible, shared ideals of the student body regarding a 'class leader'.

2. Directly Elected Trinity Council Representatives. Student and faculty representatives for the first Trinity council had been elected directly, at large, students electing students and faculty electing faculty. Their role as representatives had remained ambiguous and was discussed integrally with issues of structure: was it to address matters of school-wide governance or of concern to their constituency (instrumental functions), or was it to oversee school-wide 'spirit' activities (expressive functions)?

3. Proposed Representatives for the Council in 02–03. These would be indirectly elected by 'sub-council' membership, each one representing a council rather than an entire constituency (e.g. the sophomore class or the faculty at large). Again, both 'spirit' and governance functions were discussed.

4. Indirectly Elected Class Officers. A combination of #1 and #3, above.

5. Directly Elected Representatives to Local Councils. Discussion attempted to clarify the relations among the parents' council, the proposed class council, and the faculty council, on the one hand, and the central council, on the other.

Discussion Process

The following summary and excerpts convey the tenor and style of the discussion.

Sr. Janet distinguished the symbolic function of class officers from the instrumental function:

... it's good to have visible leaders, you know, people you can see
... and that's different from aspirations about getting things done.

Nora Quinn countered that visible class officers were needed for 'getting things done' because with a group of representatives, no one (like the class president) would be responsible. Each one could say to herself 'somebody else do it'.

> Lucy Ellen Garvin: I agree with what Sr. Janet said. I think the people have to see a visible student body leader, someone for the whole entire school, not just from the class.

> Ellie Sanford: Well, what I heard in the [synthesizing] meeting, and I agree with it, is that the eight people, say, that are elected to freshman council could better handle the problems of the freshman class than a body of 25 people ... What do you need someone to represent the whole school for? (2/29/02: C; 1:88–95)

Kathy Kuhlen said in frustration that every time the subject of officers came up the same arguments were 'brought forward: responsibility, leadership, even symbolism. I think the school needs it. Everybody says figureheads are bad, but I don't think so'. Ellie said she didn't know whether she favored class officers or council officers, but one thing she was sure of:

> Ellie: You're saying you need someone to represent the school ... to see one leader. Well, fine. But then you've got freshmen electing some junior that they don't even know. I think school-wide elections are a farce. (2/29/02: C; 1:125–130)

Vigorous discussion invoked analogies with structures of federal and state government: Point (Miss Nolan): We don't elect representatives from California, but from Indiana. Counterpoint (Hester Dulany): But you do vote for the president of the United States. Rejoinder (Leo Phelan): But we don't vote for speaker of the House of Representatives. Sr. Janet saw the possibility of combining the representative function with the heroine or modeling function. With the right type of publicity, she thought, the two representatives from each class to the Trinity council could be 'the symbols' or 'the heroes'. The idea of construing local council representatives as the visible leaders, the 'figureheads' — as a way of avoiding school-wide 'popularity' elections — was to reappear later in a more vigorous and manipulative form.

Beth Dolan called for a vote on the issue of class officers. Sr. Claudia intervened to stave off the vote. She asked that they 'talk about the theory of the thing itself, the whole thing' and pointed out some unaddressed issues: 'why you felt the Trinity council this year was not functioning to the fullest extent of its potential' and 'you thought there were lots of girls in each year who are uninvolved, that the faculty was uninvolved ...' She said, 'I don't know that you involve more people by setting up figureheads

...' and urged, 'think of the theory of the thing ...: what would be the best way to get more people involved?' Sr. Claudia was attempting to shift attention to the third and fourth functions, to governance, problem solving, and linkage, and away from both the symbolic function of 'figureheads' and issues of level of constituency and 'titles'. 'The' theory, of course, was the instrumental theory of governance that had been worked out in her executive meetings in which the idea of class officers had been explicitly ruled out.

Hester was against 'figureheads', but her autobiographical explanation was a clearer elucidation than any other comment or event of the power of the adolescent 'leader' in serving functions of identification and identity and, thus, group solidarity:

> Hester: When I was a freshman I used to look at the student council officers and think, 'Oh, wow, They are cool'. And I ... would often see, how does she wear her hair? That's how I should wear my hair to be cool [laughter]. How do they walk down the hall? That's how I'm supposed to walk.
>
> That's not what a leader should be and that's how it's been associated with, as a figurehead. Freshmen and sophomores have looked up to the ... quote 'student council' officers .. They've put them on pedestals. I ... remember once I saw a student council officer smoke and I was absolutely horrified.... No one person should be put up to be like this ... (2/29/02: C; 1:220–240)

Once again a vote on 'the plan' was urged. Sr. Claudia again tried to keep discussion open by asking Hester, 'Are they accepting a parent council?' Hester's reply to Sr. Claudia, an unusual assertion of her powers as presiding officer in view of the deference she and her classmates regularly showed most adults, was, 'There's no more discussion. We're voting on it now'. Amidst a jumble of voices Sr. Claudia's emerged: '... a parent council. We've never had one', which pulled Hester up short. Sr. Claudia said she hated 'to have you just jump to a decision on something that hasn't been considered', that they could do it if they wanted but it would be 'irresponsible'. Discussion turned forthwith to the parent council's functions.

After some parliamentary confusion about a vote on cloture vs. a vote on a substantive motion to approve the idea of a parent council, it was approved. Beth Dolan brought that discussion to a close by moving to 'accept the plan that Sr. Claudia presented'. It passed, fifteen to one, Nora Quinn opposing.

✿   ✿   ✿   ✿

Several comments are in order about the meeting's discussion. First, most of it was carried by students. Second, by far the most intense interaction was over the retention or elimination of class officers — the symbolic function. Discussion of instrumental functions of governance was shorter and less intense. Third, it was Sr. Claudia, with occasional assists from Miss Nolan, Hester, or Sr. Sabrina, who argued for the functions of governance — advice, decision making, problem sensing and solving. From our vantage point as analysts these years later a certain pattern of localism is discernable: the students were most involved with the symbolic function; Sr. Claudia was most involved with the instrumental functions of governance; and the faculty were mostly uninvolved.

Each participant tended to argue for or against some single structure or function or structure-function combination. It is clear that no participant was aware of anything like the discussion's functional-structural dimensionality I have described above. Nor was anyone trying openly to identify such dimensions. Each was claiming the importance of a small part of the larger picture, the small part most prominent in her local reality of ideas, commitments and priorities. The council, like most other organizational discussions, exhibited what we might call an exclusionary reduction of dimensionality in its discussion. Not only was one's own reality pressed forward (even by the faculty, in its mostly uninvolved silence), but it tended also to be pressed in exclusionary, either-or fashion. Sr. Claudia, for example, supported problem-sensing representatives as opposed to, and instead of, class officers. Arguments tended to be for A and against B, rather than for accommodating pluralism. Each one's local reality tended to be urged as *the* reality rather than as one important reality to be accommodated with others. Each participant seemed unwilling to attend to the other's different claim, each wanting the other to attend to her own — a mutuality of non-reciprocity, a reciprocated exclusion of 'other'.

Substantively, three realities vis à vis the problem of governance were expressed. First, certain members, most notably Sr. Claudia, were against direct, school-wide elections of students as 'popularity contests'. They saw no symbolic value of 'figureheads' or 'heroes'; rather, they were committed exclusively to an instrumental role of representatives, a role of actually doing things for the school and their local constituencies. Second, a number of students felt deeply that they needed leaders they could look up to, leaders who, frankly, did serve as 'figureheads', as symbols of their ideals. Finally, a reality of the lay faculty regarding governance was expressed, one with deep roots. It was expressed, however, not in the usual language but as virtual absence. While physically present, the faculty expressed no views of their own about the new plan. Further, the issues that were considered were issues of either the students or the administration, not the faculty. While the first two realities were expressed and debated consciously, the faculty reality found voice only behaviorally and remained unnoticed by others.

❀   ❀   ❀   ❀

After approving 'the plan' in general terms, the council spent most of the remaining twenty minutes of its meeting discussing and clarifying Sr. Claudia's new role of counselor-administrator: How was this different from each class's advisor, would they have a vote on their respective class councils, and so on. A vote was taken generally approving the idea of the counselor-administrator, though no motion had been stated. A few minutes later a similar vote was taken on the general approval that all class councils have the same number of members, no motion having been stated and no calls being made for abstentions or nays. People had been drifting out. A quorum count revealed only fifteen present, one fewer than a quorum. The next meeting was set for two days later. Sr. Claudia asked all to think about the next agenda items (see Fig. 23.1), qualifications of candidates, election times, and duties of representatives. Sr. Janet urged members to consider ways minorites in the school might be represented in the council structure, an issue that was to bloom fully later.

Post Mortem

Because we wanted to have at least one Trinity council meeting on videotape, and because scheduling permitted, this meeting was videotaped. To exploit the occasion more fully, Lighthall asked Sr. Claudia, Hester, and Lucy Ellen to join him in a post-meeting discussion of the meeting itself. Sr. Claudia expressed dissatisfaction with the absence of planning for the meeting, and Hester focused on the group's passivity: 'We liked it [the plan]; we accepted it'. Lucy Ellen said she had never seen the diagram of the new council structure before the meeting. Sr. Claudia admitted disappointment at what she regarded as the lack of preparation of the other five groups at the 'synthesizing' meeting earlier:

> Sr. Claudia: ... there was no other plan, as such, presented. There were some reactions to the present structure ... but there was no overall Trinity council plan submitted by any other group, see. And that was one of the reasons that the committees were to meet. (2/29/02: C; 2:69–73)

✿   ✿   ✿   ✿

Sr. Claudia ignored or was unaware of the greater resources available to her group than the other five planning groups. She apparently forgot the special influence in her group's planning of Franklin Patrick's conception of *equally represented constituencies*, a conception new enough to have provoked her to exclaim, 'That's a different kind of a council!' Beth Dolan, earlier, had despaired at the inadequacy of her group's efforts in contrast with Sr. Claudia's. Now we see Sr. Claudia, too, making a depreciating comparison of her group's product with those of the other groups. Her plan's complexity and relative comprehensiveness could appear, by contrast with the others, to be totally sufficient. The contrast obscured flaws in the far better plan.

¤   ¤   ¤   ¤

The Faculty and Accountability

After further discussion, Hester prompted a comment by Sr. Claudia by complaining that the faculty seemed extremely uninterested in developing plans for the council. Sr. Claudia speculated that 'the pressure will be greater next year' on any faculty member who is absent from a Trinity council meeting: The 'minutes out in peoples' mailboxes' would show 'this council not represented'. She hoped 'that a kind of accountability would grow up within the council itself'. She elaborated, using the sophomore council as her example:

> Sr. Claudia: Let's say that from the sophomore council next year neither of the sophomore members who are on the council show up. I would think that those eight [sic: six other] people in the sophomore council would call the two to accountability for it . . . . And maybe that would be something . . . in our description — that each of the councils calls the Trinity council representatives to accountability for participative presence . . . (2/29/02: C; 2: 210–220)

¤   ¤   ¤   ¤

'Accountability' and 'participative presence' were important terms in Sr. Claudia's lexicon, referring to values that had been underscored by her experience with Sr. Norma that year. They were deeply felt by her. And, like deep values for all of us, they acted as orienting lenses through which Sr. Claudia viewed the rest of her world. The faculty's non-involvement in the Trinity council was seen, not as reflecting a different, legitimate reality of its own, but as an absence of accountability. Sr. Claudia believed that the 'pressure' of accountability the following year was 'built into' (a frequent phrase of hers) the system of council representation. The new governance would in this way, by its structure, correct the faculty's non-involvement.

Sr. Claudia was well aware at this point, then, that faculty non-involvement could threaten the success of the system of governance. It was a shortcoming that the new structure itself would help them 'grow out of'. Their relative lack of investment was not regarded as a response to a different reality, but a lack of response, one that could be called forth.

Summary

Once again we see the insistent expression on the part of antagonists who wish to preserve a traditional form of leadership against protagonists' pressure for change. Hester provided details from her own experience as a freshman to make plain the nature of symbolic leadership — and then argued that that kind of leadership was invalid. The discussion of symbolic vs. instrumental leadership reflected the parties' orientations to each other's quite different realities: an either-or framing of the possibilities pre-empted completely a both-and framing. Each one's local conception was argued for, each other's local conception was argued against — a reciprocal exclusion of 'other'. Another characterization of the faculty as uninterested in the council, conveyed by a student, was again discounted by the problem originator: that would tend to be different, Sr. Claudia argued, under the new system of council. The faculty's *lack* of interest could be corrected by *adding* the new structure. The presence of good reasons behind that lack was evidently not contemplated, much less explored — 'good reasons' referring to the faculty's different problems and priorities.

Notes

1. Sr. Claudia's administrative life was one of multiple problems. Just as a rope has many strands, spiralling around a center — any one strand spiralling up to the top surface of the rope and then down again toward the bottom surface, and then eventually up to the top again — so an administrative life is made up of many problem-solving strands any one of which appears at the top for a bit and then is replaced by another, with many problem-solving transformations continuing but only a few visible on the top surface at any given time. But unlike the strands of a rope, which add strength to each other, the multiple problems and transformations of administrative life often draw energy and resources away from each other. Six other problems operated simultaneously in Sr. Claudia's end-of-February reality — besides her problem of conflict with Sr. Norma, traced in Part III. Each received some attention in the executive meeting of February 25, which was silent about governance for the following year.
    1. Relief vs. Racial Justice. Sr. Claudia had referred the names of about 100 girls rejected from Trinity's applicant pool to another, somewhat less prestigious religious high school, the Muenster school. Brother Pious, from the regional archdiocese, believed that if these 100 girls, almost all of whom were from white, well-educated, middle-class families, were allowed to compete in the (test-score regulated) competition with the regular applicant pool of Muenster, which was made up of girls from black, relatively poorly educated, blue-collar families, they would crowd out a large number of black girls who ordinarily would be admitted to Muenster. Sr. Claudia now had to deal with both Brother Pious and the angry parents of the rejected girls.
    2. Class Scheduling. Scheduling Trinity's large number of students into classes for the Fall each year took more than a month of steady work on Sr. Claudia's part.
    3. Increased Regularization: Contracts for Nuns. Misunderstandings with nuns

working in various capacities at Trinity led Sr. Claudia to prepare explicit contract forms for which she wanted advice from her co-executives.

4. A Personnel Decision. Two lay teachers and a nun, whose positions called for them to work together, had presented many complaints about each other's work since the beginning of the school year. Sr. Claudia sought help in the executive meeting to clarify possible causes and feasible remedies.

5. Summer School. Details of summer school had to be dealt with, making possible summertime use of the large auditorium and theatre facilities of the school.

6. Smoking. Student smoking in nooks and crannies of the school had become frequent and uncontrolled.

Sr. Claudia had to allocate resources across a wide front, causing relatively thin allocations to any one problem, leaving resources too weakened to solve complex problems effectively. Rationality and effectiveness, thus, must be assessed in the context of all current problems and allocations to ongoing solutions, not just one problem.

Chapter 24

Representation, Resistance, and the Issue of Going Public

A quick succession of three meetings of the council, on March 2, 7, and 9, followed fairly closely the agenda presented in the February 29 meeting (Fig. 23.1), dealing with the 'fine points' of the plan. The present chapter examines how these meetings confronted and extended Sr. Claudia's plan of governance, beginning with the issues of what sub-group's realities would be expressed in the councils, how strongly they would be expressed, and in what mode they would be expressed, and ending on March 9 by confronting the issues of whether and when the new plan would be taken to the wider community for its modifications or approval.

Whose Voices Heard, Whose Leaders Visible?

The council's first action on March 2, following a chorus of 'seconds' to a motion by Miss Nolan, was to abolish the positions of class officers — positions unsuccessfully defended as 'figureheads', 'heroes' (never 'heroines'), and 'one person to look up to'. Commitment nevertheless remained strong among many students to maintaining visible peer models. We see in this debate two modes of representation being put forward: verbal discussion, a mode of discourse, on the one hand, and prominent visual presence of role models, a mode of observable leading presence, on the other.

The question of minority representation was raised regarding black students and 'those radical kids' (sometimes referred to in private as 'the rat pack'), students associated with the recently formed Concerned Committee for Conscientious Change. Dicussion switched back and forth between two means of including minority voices: (1) election of class representatives from minorities and (2) a minority council, organized separately, having representatives elected by each minority constituency. A suggestion that a separate council be established for black students drew a chorus of 'no, no's'. It was objected that if black students had a separate council, every minority group would want one. Hester, opting for the individual minority representative (#1, above), said that a black student would probably be elected to the council next year, as one black student had failed by only one vote the previous year. Leo, opting for organized minority constituencies, suggested a separate, single council of clubs, representing organized minority groups, such as the Concerned Committee for Conscientious Change, the honor society, and the Black Student Union, with one representative to the Trinity council. Neiter of these suggestions was put into a motion or was voted on.

◦   ◦   ◦   ◦

Council members, principally the students, were addressing, in their own terms, how various local groups, with their own local realities regarding a wide range of issues, might be integrated regularly into the governing structure so that their realities would regularly be available for integration into collective actions. No mention had yet been made of the faculty as a constituency whose realities vis à vis governance would, in most matters, be crucial.

◦   ◦   ◦   ◦

Hester stated what she regarded as 'the' problem: 'What we started out with, our initial problem, was how to most totally involve the minorities or represent all factions of the school'. Discussion led the council to adopt officially the following purpose: 'We are searching for minority representation and our approach is geared towards all factions of the school represented'. Hester's phrase, 'all factions of the school', was taken by all to mean 'all factions in the student body'.

After discussion of sizes of each council proposed by Mr. Sullivan, and Nora Quinn's suggestion of smaller class councils for freshmen and sophomores than for juniors and seniors, Hester declared, 'We already passed a motion that the members were going to be equal', a statement that set off considerable debate over whether such a motion was ever put or voted on. A certain recurrent confusion in the council arose once more, a characteristic that shaped members' attitudes about changing or even participating in the council:

> Hester: We already passed a motion that the numbers [on each of the new councils] were going to be equal, at our last . .
> Nora Quinn: We did?
> Hester: Yes . . . Lucy Ellen, do you have it in the minutes?
> Voices: It was. It was passed.
> Lucy Ellen: That was not a motion. It was a suggestion by Leo Phelan. She said, 'I would like to suggest . .'

Leo: But we voted on it.

Hester: We voted on it and it was passed.

Lucy Ellen: No, that's not true.

Hester: Lucy Ellen, wait. Maybe my line is wrong, but I wrote down what we voted on ... and equal .. wait. Does anyone remember voting on it?

Leo: Yeah. I made a motion, I remember.

Hester: Okay, everyone remembers voting on it, so ..

Nora: When was this? [voices: Tuesday] Was this past 4:30?

Voices: No.

Nora: My mind's going.

Recordings indicate that no formal motion had been made or voted on, but a suggestion had been made by Leo and Hester had called for a show of hands — without calling for abstentions or opposing votes.

A motion carried, with only Nora Quinn opposing, that set the class councils each at eight, the faculty council at four. The size of the other councils was left to be settled either later or by their own constituencies. The March 2 meeting ended with a decision to hold council meetings twice a week until work on the plan was finished.

✧   ✧   ✧   ✧

A look at the functioning of individual council meetings would show, meeting after meeting, repeated instances of parliamentary confusion, extended struggle of the group to recall what it had voted on, and the like. Within the time frame of single meetings, therefore, the council would on several criteria be judged disorganized, wasteful of members' energies, and ineffective. In a larger time frame, however, the accomplishments that were buried amidst the confusions of given meetings added up, collective memories were retrieved, and systematic work did accumulate. Somewhat like the child learning to walk, whose hundreds of stumbles become unimportant in relation to the eventual accomplishment of walking, the council's actions did accumulate into a new governance with higher levels of effectiveness.

✧   ✧   ✧   ✧

Qualifications and Resistance

After a relatively brief and inconclusive council discussion, on March 7, of qualifications of *student* candidates for election as representatives (discussion of qualifications for faculty would come later), attention turned to how the two representatives from each class council to the central, Trinity council would be elected. Again student feelings were voiced about having a visible 'hero' or 'figurehead'. Sr. Sabrina, Nora Quinn, Sr. Claudia, and Sr. Janet — an influential foursome — opposed these class officer positions. Donna Laughton sensed a we-they disparity: 'We're deciding that they need eight people, but ... maybe the class needs one person to look up to'. Sr. Claudia sought a compromise, suggesting that each class might elect a person with chairmanship skills to preside over meetings but who would not vote: 'She would not be one of the eight. She would be a facilitator .... And it would give you a chance to have another student on each of the councils'.

The motion eventually passed, however, was more in line with Sr. Claudia's original plan than with her current compromise: class council representatives to Trinity council would be elected from within each class council and each class council would be chaired by its class's new administrator-counselor. The motion passed without a call by Hester for nays or abstentions.

Discussion was amoeba-like, now moving off in this direction, carrying its body with it, now in another, yet all the while covering ground. Lucy Ellen's summary of 'duties' that the group had identified after considerable discussion was the only instance of such a summary in council discussions that we can identify:

> Lucy Ellen: I just wanted to repeat all these duties that we have so that people know, so there's not as much repetition as there's been ..
>
> > take care of social activities,
> > be a problem-sensing group,
> > be aware of minority group feelings,
> > act as a grievance board for the individual,
> > provide for the leadership in the problem-solving,
> > set up the necessary committees for carrying out the functions of the council,
> > must have meetings before and after Trinity council meeting,
> > must be willing to contribute to the activities of Trinity council through representation,
> > and must be ... a communicator between council and the students.

Lucy Ellen accepted a revision from Miss Nolan of the third of these duties: 'seek out and represent minority group feelings'. A vote was immediately called to establish these duties officially and passed unanimously.

The group returned to qualifications of student candidates for election. Leo Phelan, supported by Sr. Norma in a rare appearance, favored requiring parental approval to run for election but vigorously opposed the idea of faculty approval for a student's candidacy. Something of the character of Leo's opposition can be conveyed by indicating the members who directed comments to her or who interpreted her words:

Mrs. Marchand (ten responses)
Miss Cohler (six responses)
Miss Nolan (six responses)
Sr. Claudia (seven responses)
Nora Quinn (three responses)
Sr. Janet (two responses)

About two thirds through Leo's defense of the position that anyone who has parental permission to run should be allowed to run, without any further endorsements or screening, Leo expressed very briefly the commitment behind her resistance and then gave up her fight:

> Leo: I don't know. I just . . If you want minority representation on these councils, well I just . . Forget it. Take the vote.

Sr. Janet drew Leo out further: 'In order for me to vote . . . I don't want to delay things, but I think I'd have to know what Leo's worried about'. Leo explained that she was worried about the girls like those she knew in her own senior class, girls she felt ought to be represented on the council, who would interpret requirements of signed recommendations from faculty members as 'asking permission to run' for office, girls Leo could not 'ever, picture them running around getting recommendations'.

Leo defended against renewed criticism of such a *laissez faire* position with variations on the theme of 'I think you should make the field as open and varied as you can'. Sr. Claudia offered what she regarded as a compromise: a normal procedure where recommendations were delivered to a board that would verify compliance, but also openness to the possibility that a candidate would present herself before the board and explain why she thought the recommendations were not necessary.

> Sr. Claudia: Like, when the nominations committee would meet, perhaps then they could discuss this with her as to why she saw this and her name could go or maybe wouldn't go on [Leo: Right] depending on that screening procedure.
> Leo (acquiescing): Yeah.
> Lighthall: Can I ask a question?[1] First of all, I'd like to make a comment. Leo, I think your . . your representation of your view has been terribly effective and has squeezed all kinds of hidden meanings from this group in a way that pretty rarely happens. I think you should be commended. [members applaud spontaneously] But the second . . a question I had was do you think a screening board would have more of a dampening effect than the other [than the blanket requirement for candidates to have a minimum number of recommendations]? That's, you know, that's a possibility.
> Hester: Did we even say that there has to be a screening board? . . . She used the word, 'screening board'. Does that mean

personal interview where we . . . personally say, 'You're okay to
run'? . . . .

Leo: I don't know. I just sort of think this whole issue of the
screening board is . . I know I need a lot of time to think about it.
'Cause that question Mr. Lighthall brought up. I mean, I don't
know if I could talk about it now.

❖   ❖   ❖   ❖

So, bolstered by Lighthall and Hester, Leo reversed her acquiescence and
Sr. Claudia's compromise dropped out of sight, to be replaced by another.
The council would soon again support the idea of a screening board.

❖   ❖   ❖   ❖

Hester mentioned adjournment. Nora's suggestion that they vote on 'the
recommendation thing before we leave' met with strong 'No's' from Leo
and another student. The meeting broke up with Hester's admonitions to
'think about it some more', and a resolution was indeed reached in the
meeting two days hence.

Three major issues were expressed in the extended portion of the
meeting of March 9 devoted to governance, all of them directly related to
the inclusion or exclusion of classes of persons in the formation of policy: (1)
whether all (student) candidates would be required to submit recommendations or 'testimonials' to some sort of screening board; (2) whether and
how faculty as well as students should be 'screened' for suitability for
council candidacy; and (3) whether the new plan for the council should be
shared with the rest of the school before it was further developed or only
after it had been completely developed by the council.

Nominating Procedures

Lucy Ellen Garvin reminded the council that 'the question hasn't even been
settled if we're going to have qualifications or not'. Sr. Claudia then offered
a new solution, addressed directly to Leo's worry about barriers to
inclusiveness. In place of any special nomination procedures preceding
elections, Sr. Claudia proposed a double-election in which an open
'nomination election' would precede a second, 'run-off' election of some
twenty-five persons 'screened' by the first election. Sr. Claudia stipulated
only that the duties and functions of representatives be widely circulated
before the first election and that parental permissions, which no one had
objected to, be obtained before the first election. After initial expressions of
approval, Nora Quinn, who also approved, suggested inserting between the

two elections required discussions between nominees and members of the Trinity council. Leo agreed.

Mrs. Marchand eventually offered a seven-step elaboration of Sr. Claudia's modified proposal, moving Nora's discussions earlier in the sequence of steps:

1. 'General explanatory sessions for anyone interested' in running for election.
2. Self-nominations.
3. Presentation of lists of self-nominees to each class.
4. Class elections to 'pare the list down to sixteen'.
5. The sixteen then each would present four recommendations of themselves to 'the board'.
6. Board verification that recommendations have been submitted.
7. Final election of eight representatives from the sixteen for each class.

A lengthy argument ensued about whether the powers of the board should be decided before or after voting on Mrs. Marchand's proposal. A motion for Mrs. Marchand's seven-step procedure passed, including the requirement that students gather testimonials from four persons they had consulted with, all of whom, in principle, might oppose the student's running without invalidating her nomination.

The issue of eligibility requirements for *faculty* was broached by Kathy Kuhlen, who asked if students would be called on to give testimonials for teachers. Miss Cohler and Mr. Sullivan replied that testimonials for teachers would be sought only from peers and 'authorities'. The argument that followed bore on the question whether students or department chairs understood enough to judge whether a teacher might be ready to commit the time necessary for adequate council representation. It also provides another revealing glimpse of the relationship between students and faculty generally. Finally, the argument illustrates the transformation of an openating reality (Miss Cohler's) via communication of discrepant realities (students').

> Lucy Ellen: Miss Cohler, did you just say you saw no need for a faculty member to get a testimonial from a student?
> Miss Cohler: We're faculty representatives. We're to represent the faculty. I'm not representing the student. Why should a student have to testify that he thinks I'm representative? I don't think
>
> . .
>
> Voices: No. No, but . . We're not talking about . . [jumble of voices]
> Miss Cohler: [inaudible] . . or whether I should or not. Okay, well, why is it important whether *you* think I should? I think it's

important that the group I'm representing .. [a shrill cacophony
of voices drowns her sentence out]

Ellie Sanford: ... [inaudible] what kind of teacher you were.

Miss Cohler: Can you .. my whole purpose in the authority thing
[her suggestion that students obtain two testimonials from
'authorities'] .. Okay. The teachers are your authorities. My
whole thing was .. your primary purpose in being here is
academic — schoolwork. My primary purpose is being here is
teaching. My authority figures know how well I'm teaching.

Ellie: So do your students.

Sonia Griffin: So do we. [laughter]

Miss Cohler: The authority bases part of their evaluation of me as a
teach .. They consider you in evaluating me, I mean that's ..
[laughter]

Sonia: Miss Cohler, you know what I think? I think that what
comes up [in a student's testimonial conversation with a teacher]
is whether or not a teacher teaches well and looks like she's
always unprepared and never has time for it. If the student says,
'Do you really think you'd have time for that? You know. You
come to class unprepared and just give us studies all the time'.
That type of thing, you know?

Miss Cohler: Don't you think ... the department chairman would
know that?

Voices: No.

Sonia: No. [loud jumble of voices]

Miss Cohler: I'm amazed!

Sonia: Students would know whether or not a teacher has enough
time or .. or responsibility to run.

Miss Cohler: Wow! [jumble of voices]

Mrs. Marchand: Would you honestly tell a teacher .. [engages]
Sonia in argument whether students would be so openly critical]

Hester: Lucy Ellen.

Lucy Ellen: I really, really think it's necessary that there is student
recommendations .. [Miss Nolan: Not recommendations.] ..
Okay, talk-to, student talk-to, because the faculty member and
the students are supposedly going to work together — like we
were going to here. [Laughter mounts to a crescendo as the
meaning of her verb tense sinks in.]

Miss Cohler: You've got a point, Lucy Ellen.

Lucy Ellen: It just doesn't work! [more laughter] I hate to be so
blunt as to say that, but it's true.

Miss Cohler: No. That's interesting. No. You know I .. I at this
point withdraw my argument. I can see the validity, then, of
student testimony. I .. I'm amazed, though, at some of what
you say ... I was always under the impression if the students felt

the teacher was doing a terrible job, then they complained and it
got back to the department chairman ...
Voices: But see, kids never .. Uhn Uhn. They complain to their
friends and that's it. [laughter] (3/9/02: C; I, 1:705–750)

It was presently voted that teachers would be required to secure
testimonials from two students, one peer, and one authority, with a single
election to select the faculty council.

✿   ✿   ✿   ✿

Here we see not only student sentiments about student-faculty relations,
but also an illustration of how differing organizational realities are distributed among persons, roles, and levels of the organization. As such, these
realities are not available in one location or to any one person, role, or level
except as they become located, expressed, and integrated via communication. Here, a teacher, Miss Cohler, becomes newly aware of students'
realities regarding teachers, aware too that some student realities do not
become conveyed to department chairs as she had assumed.

Of immediate importance in the process of creating this new governance is the fact that in the foregoing interchanges the faculty, for the first
time, were the subject of council deliberation and discussion as a functioning part. The single qualification discussed was the faculty's available time
and commitment for council work. Lack of faculty commitment and
participation had been noted in the February evening meeting of the
council. Discussion of faculty qualifications, furthermore, was immediately
placed in the context of the working relations between the faculty and
student members of the council during the current year, relations that had
disappointed many of the student members. Here were a few more straws
in the wind indicating that the faculty had not been well integrated into
council functioning, indications whose substance or implications were not
pursued by the council even though Lucy Ellen's cleverly phrased comment
provided a fleeting opportunity to do so.

✿   ✿   ✿   ✿

Going Public with the Plan

Hester raised questions of whether and when the rest of the school would
have an opportunity to voice their reactions to the plan. Was the council
ready to go public with its plan? Mr. Sullivan wanted to wait until the
council had 'the whole thing formulated'. Hester countered by quoting an
argument of a student, ending with the student's question, 'Don't you want
our reaction now, when you could change it?' Members took sides in the

succeeding discussion: should the plan be opened up for wider discussion — again, among students — opening it to possibly radical change, or should discussion be confined to the council until it could produce a whole plan? Sonia Griffin favored members' conferring others individually 'now'. Sr. Sabrina urged, 'If you do that, keep it in the form of discussion and not go out and say, "This is what we've done so far". It's .. again, it sounds like we've already decided upon something . . .' Susan Allan replied, laughing, 'Except that you have', to which Sr. Sabrina agreed, but emphasized that the girls' get reactions' rather than report 'so strongly' what had been passed by the council.

✿   ✿   ✿   ✿

Sr. Sabrina's advice to those who would convey the council's actions to others outside the council, and Sue Allan's brief challenge, opened a theme that would re-appear: 'Convey what the council has done in terms that will be acceptable, that will arouse least resistance from outside the council, that will portray it as most open to further influence from those outside the council'. Sr. Sabrina was the first but not the last to urge members to soften their assertions about what the council had 'decided'.

✿   ✿   ✿   ✿

After Hester reminded of the need for a committee of some kind to draw together all the actions and ideas expressed about the plan so far, Sr. Claudia expressed oblique but unmistakable opposition to legitimating change in the plan from wider discussions with students:

> Sr. Claudia: . . . Even in terms of time, you know, how much more time do you want to spend on just the design itself? . . . We all represent [the school's large 'student' body].[2] To go back to them and now say, 'This is the way it is. How do you like it?' or 'What would you suggest?' and so forth, and then bring all those [ideas] back in again? [That] is what I thought had happened, you know, weeks ago, with that group of six, you know, that came together with their ideas of what to do. I'm just asking the question in terms of the time involved . . .
>
> Lucy Ellen: I think that that's a very good point because . . . if kids go out and bring this stuff out, . . . things we have already voted on — you have to think of it like that — if the kids don't like it, are we going to change it? . . .
>
> Sr. Claudia: You could do it once a month. See, I really think you could go back again to another group . . . (3/9/02: C; I, 1:925–950)

The meeting adjourned with Hester indicating that she and Lucy Ellen would pull together all the minutes of the last several meetings for distribution at the next meeting.

Summary

The narrative reveals a number of struggles of the 'otherness' of local realities to be heard. Leo Phelan's resistance to procedures that would screen out some minority groups among students was an attempt to keep open future possibilities for including otherness.The students' frank discussion with Miss Cohler directly expressed their realities regarding who knows and who does not know teachers' capacities for taking on council responsibilities. Their persistence led to success in penetrating her quite different reality: they knew, she learned to her surprise, more than she about whether students or department chairs understood teachers' capacities to work effectively with students on the Trinity council. Discussion of whether to 'go public' with the new council plan before it was finished was a debate, in effect, over whether antagonists' realities would be heard before or only after protagonists had finished the plan. How open was the council to antagonists' influence? We also hear expressed once again the students' problem of frustrating working relations with faculty members, a problem that remained unaddressed. A theme is discernable: how may local organizational realities, different from those that dominate, be heard and integrated into organizational life?

Notes

1. I had observed Leo's resistance with astonishment. Sustained opposition was almost non-existent in the council, and rare in the school — particularly between a lone student against an array of peers and adults. I was impressed, too, at the number and variety of justifications for screening procedures and recommendations which her stubborn position had forced into expression. I was surprised and dismayed when Leo acquiesced in Sr. Claudia's assumption of a screening board and I interpreted it as a capitulation. For all of these reasons, and because my own values agreed with Leo's own position favoring heterogeneity among constituencies to be represented, I was pulled into the substantive discussion. While I rarely expressed myself spontaneously in the Trinity council's ongoing discussion, I did so on this occasion, quite as I might were I an active consultant only, and not also observing for research purposes. The consultant part of the researcher-consultant role, while providing the kind of legitimation for the researcher that extended presence and intimate access demand, can also, as it did here, create unnecessary intrusion into on-going process.
2. Sr. Claudia specified the size of the student body, a number we delete to help protect anonymity. She made no reference to communications with, or changes in the plan emanating from, the faculty.

Chapter 25

Council Planning: Problems and Process

Council Planning: Three Problems

Between the March 9 and the March 14 meetings of the council, three problems were synthesized concerning the council's on-going planning process. Each problem generated action, relevant to and rational within its own local realities, that impinged, in varying degrees, on the council's on-going process. First, Lighthall and Allan, assuming temporarily a more active consultative oulook vis à vis the council's functioning, were worried lest the cumbersome processes of the council, acting as a total group of twenty-five, prevent effective planning for the following year. Second, Sr. Claudia worried that the council would be too slow to meet her own scheduling needs. Finally, Lois Chapman, a student not a member of the council but concerned with student participation in the revamping of the council, felt the council was moving too rapidly on its own.

Lighthall and Allan: A Changed Council Structure to Improve Functioning
We had observed, since early on, that the council had repeatedly attempted to carry on discussions neither prepared nor followed up by a small group's capacity to search, sift, and synthesize. To fulfill our initial promise to the council to help improve its functioning we decided to suggest the council form a permanent steering committee to explore and prepare issues more effectively for the council at large. Sometime between March 9 and 14 we developed an addendum to the written agenda for the council's March 14 meeting (Fig. 25.1).

Sr. Claudia: A Speedier Council — Or Less Dependence Upon It   About a half hour before the council's meeting on March 14 Sr. Claudia and Lighthall talked briefly about the impending meeting and their respective agendas for it. Sr. Claudia made clear to Lighthall that, as a field note records, she intended 'to move ahead with parent and faculty group representation', that is, establishing parent and faculty councils, even if the

Figure 25.1.   Facsimile of the added agenda prepared by Lighthall and Allan for distribution at the 3/14/02 Trinity council meeting.

Trinity Council Meeting 3/14/02

I.   A problem: Discussions and decisions seem to take place only in the Council itself. There seem to be no systematic deliberations outside of council. There seems to be no structure for issue identification, for intensive deliberation, or for narrowing possibilities so that meaningful choices can be made by council.

II.   Two alternatives.
    A.   Continue to have council meet as a whole and work as it has,
    B.   Develop a structure for dealing with next year's communication-recommendation arrangements which would:
        1.   Concentrate energy in a small, committed group.
        2.   Identify pressing and long-term issues and make recommendations either (a) on their resolution or (b) on the means by which they might be resolved.
        3.   Narrow possible choices among governmental arrangements for next year down to choices among pairs and trios of arrangements so that council's discussion could be focused and could deal with issues already laid out by the small ad hoc steering committee.
        4.   Fill the leadership void that seems to exist.
        5.   Still leave council an influencing role by (a) voting on steering committee's members and (b) voting on steering committee's alternatives and recommendations.

III.   Recommendations: establish II, B, a steering committee on problem-sensing and communication structures (and procedures)
    A.   With the above functions
    B.   With the following composition:
        1.   Two students
        2.   One or two faculty members
        3.   Sister Claudia
        4.   Mr. Lighthall and Mrs. Allan

Trinity council was unable to do so. The parent council would be her responsibility, with the help of Sr. Catherine, to recruit and to provide with adequate direction. The faculty council, too, would have to be legitimated and implemented by her, and she wanted to do just that: it would take time to persuade the best people (often the busiest) to make that commitment. Sr. Claudia, therefore, wanted either speed from the council or independence to act on these matters at her own speed.

Lois Chapman: Less Speed, More Inclusion   Lois Chapman, whom Lighthall did not know, appeared at his elbow as he looked at a hallway display of photographs. A field note captures the interchange:

Contact #131, 3/14/02 (w.t. 8:30 AM, 3/15/02). Lois Chapman, eyes red from crying, caught up with me in the south bldg. hallway, just as I was looking at the display of pictures . . . .

Lois was upset because she had heard from Leo [Phelan] that the council was discussing procedures for 'running the school' next year and she had not known about it. I took her crying seriously and we found our way into Claudia's now empty office where Mrs. Wagner said we could talk for a few minutes.

Lois was upset that the council was discussing and voting on changes in structure without the knowledge of the student body. She was upset about being excluded, but also about the seclusion and secrecy (my words, not hers) of the discussions about matters of such great importance. She said that others had said that the council meetings were open, but how, she asked me, could she attend meetings if the time and place weren't announced? I asked her if they weren't announced by way of the minutes, which were posted, I thought [incorrectly as it turned out: Lucy Ellen's writing of the minutes was tardy by a number of meetings]. She said that, well, that was perhaps true, but how many people read the minutes? . . .

Last year Lois was, as she explained it, active in mounting an opposition to the rule that no one could run for council who did not have a 2.5 average or better (4 being equivalent to A). She complained of the student apathy — only 8 students had bothered to return questionnaires about how they felt about the 2.5 ruling. She was encouraged by others not to give up but to keep working this year. She got on the election committee [a sub-committee of the Trinity council] this year just because of its presumed role in deciding qualifications. They had influenced eligibility qualifications for class officer elections, she said. But now, with the most crucial kind of election, she had been told by Leo Phelan that the council had considered it so important, that it and not the election committee would decide qualifications.

Now the point had been already reached, she said, where voting was about to take place on these qualifications and she had not had a chance to even know about the discussions . . . She had calmed down more by the end of our approximately 15 min. talk and said she would be coming along to the council meeting in a few minutes. She did attend and did speak . . .

✿   ✿   ✿   ✿

In these three examples of local realities, visible in some detail and before their actual expression in the council, we can see how three very idiosyncratic commitments and outlooks each can have common relevance for the major problem undergoing transformation: a *common* goal of an effectively functioning council contradicted in three *different* ways by three *separate* perceptions of its ineffective current functioning. Three sub-problems had been synthesized locally and each originator was about to express her or his problem in action that required the assistance of the council.

Going Public vs. Staying Private

This section's narrative illustrates some of those progressively strong protective tendencies protagonists develop in solving their problems that were described in detail in Chapter 17 (Fig. 17.1 and p. 219 ff). There, recall, we spelled out seven progressively strong reality-excluding tendencies of organizational action that seem to develop in episodes of organizational problem-solving: protagonists increase their commitment to, and protection of accomplished transformations of their problem and increasingly resist the integration of realities not already integrated into their solutions and plans. Taken together, these progressions point to what we might call a principle of *cumulative commitment and exclusion*. Baldly stated it is this: a solution is maximally open to the influence of organizational realities early in the process of problem transformation, closest to the confusion and problem phases of a problem-solving episode. A solution is least open to accommodating realities late in the process. In other words, those constituent realities expressed close to the problem's emergence (see Fig. 17.1) hold a privileged position; those expressed only close to the solution's implementation are received by participants with prejudice and integrated into ongoing action least completely. The narrative of this chapter bears on this principle directly.[1]

¤ ¤ ¤ ¤

Sr. Claudia opened substantive discussion in the council meeting with a statement that she was under pressure of time to form the parent and faculty councils. She asked whether the council planned to take prompt action on them. But Dale Devlin had been disturbed by too much speed on the council's part:

> Dale Devlin: ... I think we have to get what their [the wider student body's] ideas are now before we ... finalize everything because what if people didn't like it [the plan]? ... we have to be ready for their thoughts.... we're kind of closing ourselves off and giving off superior airs about, like, the experience ... but I really think we have to go back and talk to these kids and get their ideas ...
> Sr. Sabrina: Dale, ... you said yourself you don't know if going back is going to change very much. I wonder if you're not talking about .. rather than getting feedback in order to re-change what we've already changed, isn't that another bag that we're talking about, getting reactions? ... Can't we keep on going back for changes as we're going along? ...
>   See, we're to a certain point now. Now just because everybody doesn't agree with that, does that mean we have to ... refine

and refine and refine until we come up with something that's acceptable? . . . with the pressure of time and so forth do we have to wait until that ideal?

Dale: Well, I think we should have done it before . . . and that we should maybe stop right now and do it this week and present whatever we have, you know, before we go on. Just to get, you know, reaction . . . just to get it, whether we're going to act upon it or not . . .

Sr. Sabrina: . . . We can do that, but does that mean we stop all activity? (3/14/02: C; 1:5–40)

$\circ \quad \circ \quad \circ \quad \circ$

Sr. Sabrina's 'we're to a certain point now', and her further argument expressed nicely the principle of cumulative commitment and exclusion: after a certain point participants want to protect the solution that those involved *thus far* have produced. She was saying that that point had been reached even though 'everybody doesn't agree'. One important question is: 'Just *when* is the point reached in an *effective* problem-solving effort that a solution should be protected from further change?' The answer implied by the social constructivist conception of organizational reality espoused in this book — where organizational realities (a) operating in its members are (b) dispersed through the organization, and (c) divided between 'constituents' and 'non-constituents' as earlier defined — is that reality inclusion can effectively cease when all constituent organizational realities have been integrated into on-going organizational action. A fuller answer would address how such constituent realities can be identified.[2] For now, it is sufficient to note that a major constituent in this problem we are following was that of the lay faculty and that repeated indications of resistance from its members, already noted at several points in the narrative, were either not coded by Sr. Claudia and others or were rejected or denied outright.

$\circ \quad \circ \quad \circ \quad \circ$

Sr. Claudia repeated her concerns about whether the council felt it could act on the parent and faculty councils, indicating that if the council was not prepared to move ahead she was pressed by time to do so. Donna Laughton urged the council to proceed on the assumption that it had the trust of the student body. Hester received permission for Lois Chapman to comment. After Lois explained that she had followed the council closely but that 'it didn't dawn on' her that a new structure of governance was being discussed, Hester agreed, and indicated that the work of the council would be impeded if the homeroom representatives attended and actively participated:

Hester: . . . we say these meetings are open, but nobody wants . .

> I mean ... if people came, we can't ... at all get work done at
> this type of meeting ... So we say they're open but kind of
> meaning subconsciously we don't really want too many people to
> show up because we know that the suggestions shouldn't be
> coming in now at a meeting like this. So it's our fault. I know if I
> ... wasn't involved in Trinity council I probably would have no
> idea what was going on in the meetings. (3/14/02: C; 1:105–115)

❖   ❖   ❖   ❖

A solution is constructed out of the realities of the participants. That group
working on a solution at any given moment has two major tasks, it seems, if
it is to be effective: recruiting relevant realities to integrate into a solution
and forging an integration of the realities it has gathered. In gross
requirements the process of social or organizational change is often
implicitly assumed to resemble an individual's securing of nourishment:
food must be found and ingested, and then digested. Lois Chapman
complained, in effect, that students could not bring their desires and
observations (nutritive substance, realities) to the council if they did not
know it was developing new forms of collective life — i.e., in terms of the
ingestion-digestion metaphor, they would not feed it (give their views) if
they did not know it was hungry and eating (formulating a new structure of
governance). Hester, on the other hand, was explaining the council's
inherent difficulties of integrating (digesting) diverse realities already
expressed while simultaneously being called on to take in new realities
(ingestion). Using the ingestion-digestion metaphor, the council could
either ingest or digest, but not both simultaneously — at least in Hester's
view. The council had favored digestion of locally available views over the
gathering of wider views, wider views that Lois was ready to assert were
necessary for the right kind of sustenance and growth.

❖   ❖   ❖   ❖

Sr. Claudia made it clear that if the council found it necessary to 'go back
and start from scratch' by seeking input from the student body, that was all
right, but that she was constrained by deadlines to proceed with the parent
and faculty councils. The choice between forging ahead within the council
and obtaining wider participation was further debated, with Lois Chapman
articulating the strength of the council's tendency toward growing commitment and exclusion:

> Leo Phelan: ... now, in midstream, we are shifting directions and
> talking about going back to the students. And I think we have set
> upon a course of action. We should follow through and then
> present it to the students.
> Hester: Even if .. follow it through even if all along there are

students coming up to us saying, 'We don't know what's going on; we want to know what's going on'?

Dale: Yeah!

Leo: Hester, how can we answer them when it's not . . I don't think you should present something to them that's half formed. [Voices: But then . .]

Lois Chapman: But then if it's formed already, you will have the problem that the student council ran into last year . . [Leo: I don't think so.] . . that it'll be done. And nothing can be, you know, changed.

Leo: But, see, that would not mean . . I don't . . You're already assuming that simply . . . after we consolidate everything and present it to the students that'll be it. Whereas . . [Lois: You people already . .] . . I personally think there could be room for amendment. The point is, what could be gained by this?

Lois: You see, already . . . five weeks you've spent on this? And *already you're reluctant to change* [emphasis added]. You know, I'm not suggesting that it's a good idea to, but can you imagine if you plan the whole thing and people suggest change, how you'd feel then?

Leo: No. You . . I think you misinterpreted what I said. I'm not reluctant to change. But I don't like this . . I don't like the reasons for the change. If you can understand that.

Lois: You don't like the students to be informed about the process of reaching your decisions on the structure for next year?

Leo: No. No that's not . . No. I think . . I'm all in favor of, you know, now . . yeah, all right, getting more student input whatever way you want to work it. But I cannot see dropping this arrangement. I feel it's very good. (3/14/02: C; 1:150–170)

A discussion of whether the council's planning at this stage was 'half formed' or 'half baked' or 'halfway through', became a shouting match between Leo and Hester: were they ready to explain to others the 'particulars' of the plan? Lois Chapman interrupted with a suggestion that the council hold a 'forum' to say to the student body, 'This is what we've come up with so far. What do you think? Do you think we should do more? Do you have any good ideas?' She advised that the council 'tell them it's a half-baked idea', that they admit they 'don't know particulars', asking the students for 'suggestions about particulars'.

Lucy Ellen moved formally that 'each group' set up a forum 'that will be informative and that will present what we have so far and ask for ideas and suggestions'. Sr. Claudia said she thought the council did not have 'the time constraint' that she had and asked, 'Do you understand why I will just go ahead in terms of the parents?' Discussion turned to details of implementing forums, including an impassioned plea from Dale Devlin that the forums not hold up continued work on the plan. Louise Nolan, impatient at the slow pace of the council's discussion, delivered herself of a long, repetitious soliloquy about how repetitious the council's discussion had been, including at times her own, and ended with a plea to vote on the matter. Lucy Ellen's motion passed 14–4, after which she restated the motion, adding 'that each representative group go back to the group which she or he represents and present the basic structure'. After some discussion about the logistics of holding assemblies, Lighthall asked to make a brief presentation.

Lighthall's and Allan's Proposal

Lighthall enumerated some difficulties of the council's discussion process: the large group tended 'to try to do work of a small group in a large group'; its discussions had 'no preparation' and there was 'no focusing of issues'. He then passed out the added agenda (Fig. 25.1) and turned to the contents of the sheet:

> Lighthall: So if you agree that that's a problem, if that's also a problem that you see, then I would offer alternative B.... The thought I had, briefly, under B, is that you need a small steering committee to do the between-meeting work, to formulate the issues, to bring them before the larger group, and to conduct discussion on them — make sure that discussion stays on the issues. (3/14/02: C; 1:420–430)

Lighthall asked that discussion begin with the problem itself and asked that discussion be limited to ten minutes, the proposal to be voted on only at the following meeting. Subsequent discussion mixed approval with considerations of detail, but also noted that this proposal had itself taken time away from the council's regular work. Discussion of how members of the steering committee might be chosen ended with a call by Lucy Ellen to accept the proposal followed by Lighthall's explanation that it needed between-meeting thought before a vote.

Back to the Forums

Sr. Claudia said the forums should be held during the regular school day, so people would take them seriously, and that the presentations should be made by people who understood the plan and who had prepared for such a presentation. She reminded, 'You know your rhetoric well enough to know that the way something is presented will determine to a large extent whether it's accepted'.

322

❀   ❀   ❀   ❀

Two points: first, discussion of obtaining 'input' from outside the council was aimed at student input, not faculty input, and the forums would be organized for each student class. The lay faculty's realities continued to be excluded from the new structure of governance. Second, Sr. Claudia's reminder about rhetoric clearly showed that she regarded the forums as devices of persuasion, not of further 'input' to the council. It was the students who would accommodate to the plan, not the plan to (students') realities.

❀   ❀   ❀   ❀

Subsequent council discussion voted into existence a forum committee to plan the presentations to be made to the student body. The committee was to be made up of volunteers, with its chair elected from its members. Sr. Sabrina suggested functions and powers of the committee that in effect combined and extended those envisioned by Lighthall and Allan in their 'steering committee' with the immediate substantive planning of the forums.

> Sr. Sabrina: I would like to see that small group make some decisions, give us some direction, and call a meeting of the council when they feel they've got something to give us to do. (3/14/02: C; 1:805–810)

While no vote was taken, it happened that the 'forum committee' did take on the functions Sr. Sabrina suggested.

Sr. Claudia made it clear to the council that she would not wait for a final approval of the plan, but would set in motion the formation of parent and faculty councils. While there is no evidence that she ever met with the faculty as a whole in forming its council, she may well have spoken to individual faculty members. As it happened, the faculty's own initiatives were already developing a faculty organization. The council meeting adjourned after Hester repeated the decision (not voted) that volunteers would meet after adjournment in the same room. The council itself was not to meet as a group for almost a month (April 11), during which time the forums would be planned, carried out, and followed up with a report and recommendations.

Those who remained, thus constituting the full forum committee, were: Sr. Claudia, Beth Dolan, Hester Dulany, Sr. Janet, Joan Noonan, Sr. Sabrina, and Ellie Sanford — with a notable absence of any lay faculty members. They set the first meeting for two days hence. That two-hour meeting, at which neither Lighthall nor Allan was present, was tape recorded. By the time they met, Sr. Claudia had made arrangements to extend the normally 15-minute homeroom period to 25 minutes on March 22 for assemblies ('forums') for each of the school's four classes.

❖ ❖ ❖ ❖

Two points are worth noting. First, that no lay faculty member volunteered for the forum committee constitutes a variant of the 'progression of contacts' described in Chapter 17 (progression #4, p. 218 ff). Only nuns, sharing Sr. Claudia's experience of a celibate residential community, volunteered for this committee.[3] By Hester's unwitting call for volunteers, only those faculty strongly committed to community and shared governance — as distinct from a school and its administration — were recruited. Thus, the very group, the lay faculty, was further excluded from planning whose realities vis à vis shared power and school governance were both resistant and crucial to the plan's effective functioning.

The second point concerns Sr. Claudia's choice of a single homeroom period for the class forums. Selection of a single homeroom period was an important choice from available alternatives, which included after-school discussions and homeroom periods on successive days. First, it would ensure that all students were involved, not merely those interested or who had nothing more pressing to do. Second, it forced presentations of council members to focus on only essentials of the plan developed thus far, given the limitations of time. Third, it ensured, intentionally or unintentionally, that students' reactions and collective discussion of them would be limited. Fourth and most important, the choice of class assemblies during the single homeroom period stamped the whole effort, once again, as oriented to students, not faculty.

❖ ❖ ❖ ❖

The Forum Committee's Process

Discussion in the forum committee meeting on the sixteenth was devoted almost entirely to seven topics, each topic being a vehicle for accomplishing seven organizational functions.

Seven Functions: More Local Adaptations

1. Logistics. A place had to be selected large enough for each class and yet with suitable wiring for a public address system. Floor microphones would be needed; attendance had to be taken; everyone at the forums would have to have a diagram of the proposed council structure — these items received the group's attention first. Schedules, persons, resources, and material were coordinated into a plan for class assemblies, a familiar form of downward (stage to audience) communication that needed modification to accommodate both downward and upward communication.

2. *Dangers to be avoided.* Two major fears were expressed and dealt with. Hester feared a widely varying set of presentations which would prevent the plan from being 'truly communicated'. Sr. Claudia's fear was that someone who opposed the plan might be chosen to make a class's forum presentation. One important function being served was dealing with this committed group's fears and problems — of preserving the collectively produced plan *as this committee interpreted it*:

> Hester: I know there's still twenty-five different interpretations of what this thing is. . . . I'm scared of four different ideas [in the four class forums] of this plan going through. I think we better decide who's going to speak and who's going . . and how it's going to be done if we want it to be truly communicated.
>
> Beth Dolan: Would it be better to you know, make up one plan and have each kid just take it?
>
> Sr. Claudia: Yeah. I think that would be good.
>
> Beth: A fact sheet.
>
> Sr. Janet: A diagram.
>
> Hester: We have to make sure that person understands it, though. I have someone in my mind right now that I know has a completely different idea of this . . . Say, if we had Sr. Nannette talking to a group of people, you know? I mean of the faculty. Her idea of this plan is probably not what is . . what it was even meant to be, maybe . . . with different questions starting, different answers coming from different people.
>
> Sr. Claudia: Yeah. I think that's the danger. Also, I think the danger that I've heard in discussions . . I have the sense that *some people don't even like the plan very much.* Well . . . *if they don't, I don't think they ought to say anything* [emphasis added] . . . The idea is to give information. The idea isn't to say this is good or this is bad. The idea is to say, 'This is what we've passed'. And so I . . I'm kind of concerned about that, because I think the way it's presented the first time is going to have ripples all next year! [laughs] . . .
>
> Sr. Sabrina: Well, can we assume that the people here are going to be the presenters, or is this too much of a presumption?
>
> Sr. Claudia: I don't think it would be.
>
> Sr. Sabrina: Okay, well . . . if we get this so-called fact sheet down, and we kind of have a general consensus on this is the way it's going to be, then couldn't it be your job [addressing the students] between now and Wednesday to get together with

> other council members and, you know, say, 'This is the way I
> feel', and then see how they react to it and *make sure that they
> are on the same wave length* [emphasis added], huh?
> Sr. Janet: Do you want to do it? Do all of you?
> Sr. Claudia: Are you willing to do that?
> Ellie and another voice: Yeah. (3/16/02: FC; I, 1:230–260)

❖ ❖ ❖ ❖

Here we see a growing commitment in the small group to homogeneous
solidarity regarding 'the plan' — a decidedly transformed representation of
the *varied* realities operating in the council as a whole. Indeed, the small
group acknowledges and even identifies variations in council realities
regarding the plan. Instead of conveying the council's *varied* set of realities,
the committee dealt with the only reality locally accessible to it by virtue of
its members, in this case a narrowed subset of the council's realities. By
calling for only 'volunteers', a particular set of realities had thereby been
selected: the realities of the committed.[4] They were now handling their
fears about varied interpretations of the plan by settling on a single diagram
and by choosing themselves as its interpreters. The council's transformations of Sr. Claudia's problem (and others') vis à vis the council was not
being simply *conveyed* via forums. Rather, the transforming process itself
continued in the hands of this committee. For example, only those who
agreed with the plan were proposed (by Sr. Claudia) as legitimate
interpreters of it — all in the name of neutral, non-evaluative conveying of
'information'.

❖ ❖ ❖ ❖

3. Functions of the councils and responsibilities of council members.
Right after that interchange about the dangers of misrepresentation — an
ironic interchange, in view of what was to come — the group turned to the
hand-out sheet itself. Besides the diagram of the structure of councils and
the numbers of representatives, what should go on the sheet? Council
functions would be important, they agreed. A final list of nine items was
settled on, a list mixing the functions of the councils with responsibilities of
their individual members:

1. To be a problem-sensing group.
2. To provide for the leadership in problem solving and provide
    committees for carrying on business of the class.
3. To seek out and represent minority opinion.
4. To contribute representation to the Trinity 13 [the next year's
    Trinity council].
5. To be involved in and support Trinity 13 activities.

6. To act as communicator between Trinity 13 and the entire class.
7. To have meetings before and after Trinity 13 meetings.
8. To act as a grievance board for groups and individuals.
9. To take care of social activities. (3/16/02: FC; I, 1:480–525)

❂   ❂   ❂   ❂

These functions, taken largely from their review and re-wording of Lucy Ellen's minutes, were to be carried out by the four class councils. In listing them for presentation, the forum committee itself was carrying on its own function in a problem-solving process of conveying virtually intact that part of the collective product, the plan, that did not violate its own shared local realities.

❂   ❂   ❂   ❂

4. Reasons to justify the reorganization. Claudia noted that an important omission from the minutes was any explanation of the need for a reorganized council in the first place. It was 'important for the girls to hear that', she said. Her explanation emphasized, again, content that would appeal to, or at least not alienate, the students:

> Sr. Claudia: . . . the reason *we* came up with a different structure, you know, the group that presented this plan, was what we had been hearing. . . . We were reacting to the things that we had heard the council members say . . . like, you would always say, 'Well, we didn't work out this year because . . or 'The kids are saying that we're not effective'. So we were reacting to what you saw of yourselves, *not what we thought of you* [emphasis added]. Do you see what I mean?
>
> And what we thought immediately was that the . . . students weren't enough involved and that the faculty wasn't enough involved. . . . That was the biggest thing that came through all the way along. And so, the first thing, then, that we tried to build in was how to get more people involved. And so we did it by setting up individual councils. (3/16/04: FC; I, 1:685–720)

❂   ❂   ❂   ❂

Two comments are in order. First, Sr. Claudia obscured the executive council's strong role in originating the plan in response to concerns raised there, realities not felt or voiced by members of the Trinity council, realities, indeed, which she took pains to explain to the council itself that cold evening meeting in February, about advisory vs. decision-making functions of the Trinity council. She denied both the originating reality, dissatisfactions with the council's decision-making stance, and the originating locale of that reality, herself and the executive committee. She substituted instead a different problem, lack of student and faculty involvement, portrayed as coming from a different locale, the council's students themselves. The plan was thus portrayed as merely solving the council's problems of 'involvement' by including greater numbers of students. To explain the plan's origins authentically, however, as they can be seen from the narrative to have emerged, would have, in Sr. Claudia's eyes, jeopardized the plan's acceptability to students. The plan would then have been seen as coming from 'authorities' and it would have been seen as limiting the council's powers to merely giving 'advice'. We begin to have evidence, here, of the third (most extreme) form of protection identified in Chapter 17 (p. 220 ff), where the effort goes beyond 'selling' the solution to manipulating the antagonists to whom it is to be sold.

Second, in terms of numbers alone, the plan as then developed, called for a faculty council of four members, just half the number on the current Trinity council. Further, the number of faculty representatives to the new 'Trinity 13' would be only 2, reducing their relative command of votes on that body from approximately one third to fewer than one sixth. By the criterion of either numbers or proportions, the faculty would be the losers in this new scheme. But the argument Sr. Claudia was making was to the students and for a student audience, not for faculty. This undermining of faculty voting power in the new scheme did not seem at the time very significant to us because the then current Trinity council had not divided along faculty-student lines in its voting. It also, however, had never taken up an issue important primarily to its faculty members (e.g., teaching duties or salary).

o   o   o   o

The question of class officers came up again, touching off a new round of reinterpreting realities observable in the council's previous action, transforming them into a plan calculated to be more acceptable to the student body.

5. *Class officers.* The minutes of the council's March 2 meeting described the council's action to abolish class officers in these words:

> The opening discussion of this meeting was about the idea of class officers for the year, 02–03. Miss Nolan made the motion that class officers be eliminated for the year 02–03 (motion carried).

Referring explicitly to the minutes, Sr. Claudia said, 'I think it would be terrible to say what it says here: "... class officers be eliminated"'. This set off a group effort, guided principally by the three Sisters, to reconcile two irreconcilable realities. On the one hand was the observable reality of the language of the minutes and of the recorded, observed fact that the council had voted to eliminate class officers. On the other hand was the group's awareness of many students' commitments to having class officers and the group's fears that students would reject any proposal that baldly eliminated officers. They set about protecting the council's decision to eliminate class officers while simultaneously making the plan palatable.

❂   ❂   ❂   ❂

One organizationl function the group was serving here was conflict management, conflict between themselves and that part of the student body committed to officers — one set of antagonists. The committee's means were camouflage and verbal equivocation and an attempt to orient or directly manipulate students' realities in response to the new structure. Their mode of conflict management, thus, was exclusionary.

❂   ❂   ❂   ❂

The re-naming process by which the 'terrible' was transformed into the acceptable is instructive:

> Sr. Sabrina: They're [the class officers are] just being transferred to another place [i.e., from 'class officers' to 'representatives of the class councils'].
>
> Ellie: More like a union between council reps and class officers. [Hester: Yeah.]
>
> Sr. Claudia: Yeah. That's a good thing . . [Sr. Sabrina: That's a good idea.] . . then instead of having two groups [class officers and class representatives to council], sometimes even working in conflict, that there be the one group called 'freshman council', 'sophomore council'. What about that? And then you don't have to say anything about officers.
>
> Ellie: You could say that they're being united with the council reps. If that's all right. Or don't you want the class officers . . [chuckles]
>
> Sr. Claudia [interrupting]: I don't want the idea of class officers in there. That's out, see?
>
> Sr. Sabrina: . . . we're not . . just . . like we said, you know, eliminating the officers; we're just transferring the idea of the officers as a combination of them . . [Sr Claudia: And the whole task of them.] . . yeah, so that they're included — and not destroying their image.
>
> Sr. Claudia: Yeah. That's good. Combining tasks and . .
>
> Sr. Janet: Would you say, like, the leadership in past years has been in two ways: through the homeroom representatives and through the class officers. And now, to organize that better,

we're taking their tasks and combining them, you know . .

Sr. Claudia [finishing Sr. Janet's sentence]: . . into a council . . . .
And then someone will say, 'When you said that, did you mean
that there aren't going to be class officers?' And then the answer
is: . .

Sr. Sabrina [indicating how one answers Sr. Claudia's question
without actually saying, 'No. They are eliminated.']: You shake
your head [laughs lightly].

Sr. Claudia [continuing, answering her own question]: . . Well,
specifically, the answer might be yes, but in reality there are the
class officers because [Ellie: Yeah.] the representatives in the
council are your leaders. . . .

Sr. Janet: You keep changing it to 'leaders' as much as you can, you
know, and *making them think they're really talking about
leaders* [emphasis added].

Sr. Claudia: Yeah. [Sr. Claudia and Sr. Sabrina laugh lightly.]
(3/16/02: FC; I, 2:4–18)

In later discussion all agreed that forum presenters should not 'evade'
student questions or become 'defensive'. They decided to include a 'tear-
off' sheet as part of the material to be passed out, to enable anyone unable
to speak at the forums to write their comments. Hester summarized what
her own response to questions would be: 'You're not going to have officers.
Okay. We're going to have *leadership*'. After discussion of some difficulties
with class officers in the past, the group rehearsed how negative reactions
to the proposed plan might be handled. Sr. Claudia assumed a coaching
role:

Sr. Claudia: . . . don't let yourself say, 'No, no. That's not what we
meant', or something. Say, 'The way we discussed it . .

Ellie: 'The idea behind that was . .' [laughs lightly]

Sr. Claudia [continuing her sentence]: . . was this'. But the kid has
had a chance to say her . . so she doesn't get a put-down.

Hester: The reasoning. Right. Not . . [jumble of voices] . . . .
Remember all your lessons in rhetoric.

Sr. Claudia: Right! [pronounced Riiight] (3/16/02: FC; I,
2:100–105)

6. *Testimonials, 'authorities', and the 'screening board'.* The group
reviewed Lucy Ellen's minutes further, coming to the section on nomination procedures. Sr. Claudia thought the word, 'authority', mentioned
under 'testimonials', raised a 'tender' issue. She asked, 'Do we have to say
"authority"?' She argued that since she and other administrators and
counselors were faculty members, the term, 'faculty', covered all relevant
authorities. The requirement of testimonials was therefore considered to

read that students were to have two testimonials from faculty members (in addition to two from peers and parental permission) — with no mention of 'authorities'.

Hester drew attention to the screening board whose functions Sr. Claudia explained as being 'just to see that a girl has two faculty, two peer, one parental'. To Beth's query, 'That's the only . .?', Sr. Claudia replied, 'That's it'. There was no further discussion of how the screening board would deal with students who had failed to obtain the stated number of testimonials or of any nomination procedures for faculty members. When Ellie suggested, 'Maybe we shouldn't include anything about the board in this', Sr. Claudia agreed and added, 'because we really haven't discussed it'.[5]

If the board wasn't to be mentioned, how would the question be answered, someone asked, about who would receive and read the testimonials? Sr. Claudia said it would be proper to answer, 'We'll tell you later'. When a matter was in question, she said, the best policy was to be honest: 'You know, let's be honest'.

Hester expressed some discomfort at this process of redacting the council minutes for presentations at the forums:

Hester [in a very soft voice]: We're taking out part of the thing we voted on, then, as procedure [i.e., the screening board].
Beth: No. We're just going to tell them that.
Sr. Sabrina: No we're not.
Hester: Well, I mean . . I agree. I just wonder . .
Beth: Oh, it's okay. We just haven't told them yet. We'll tell them, you know, . . [inaudible as Sr. Claudia speaks]
Sr. Claudia: You can do that for a right reason, Hester, in terms of the fact that *you don't want to bog down* [emphasis added] and get all the questions caught up with something you haven't even been able to discuss yet, rather than, you know . . 'cause you only have fifteen minutes.
Hester: And that's where we'd run into misinterpretations and everything.
Sr. Janet: Or, at the end of all this, after you read this, say that we know we have to construct some group that's going to organize and run this, you know, and if you have any suggestions about that . .
Sr. Claudia [finishing Sr. Janet's sentence]: . . write it down on your sheet. (3/16/02: FC; I, 2:145–150)

❋   ❋   ❋   ❋

Sr. Claudia had become the guiding hand — sometimes the commanding voice — in this group. She was the one who explained the origin of the plan — the only one in a position to do so — and she put her own stamp on that explanation. She spearheaded the move to assimilate the class officers into the category of 'leaders', and stamped out any mention of class officers in the planned presentations ('That's out, see?'). She actively coached the manner of handling questions. She laid the groundwork for skirting the 'tender' issue of 'authorities' and for deferring answers to questions about the screening board. In terms of the seventh progression noted in Chapter 17 (p. 219 ff), Sr. Claudia had thus far completely avoided the fairly general tendency in organizational problem solving to delegate successive subordinate tasks to others, thus setting up a linear, non-looped structure of sequential contacts over the course of an episode. To the contrary, she had been forcefully present to express and clarify her realities and to guide action — down to the very details of who should say what in explaining the plan. If she had been forced to take a 'hands off' approach in her first attempt, traced in the first constitution episode, where she worked around the edges of the council but not with the council as a body, in her renewed attempt after January 14, she was definitely a 'hands-on' participant — not only in council deliberations but also, now, the dominant force in the smaller forum committee, the committee to prepare the council's product (in acceptable form) for public presentation.

Sr. Claudia's offer of 'a right reason' for eliminating the screening board from forum presentations reflected her commitment to a persuasive promotion of the plan. The right reason was to maintain the plan's speed of development and installation. Going before an audience without preparing a full explanation beforehand, with known answers, would slow the progress of the plan; it would 'bog down'. The plan had become its own justification.

✿ ✿ ✿ ✿

7. *The 'steering committee' and the forum committee's future.* Having addressed the essentials of the forum presentations and of the manner of handling questions, the group turned briefly to its own future and functions. Did they constitute the 'steering committee' that Lighthall and Allan had proposed? Sr. Claudia and Hester thought not, that this group was only an ad hoc committee to plan the forums. They discussed the possibility of making recommendations to the council for the prompt election of a steering committee for the rest of the year, but left the matter inconclusive.

The committee reviewed the tasks each person or sub-group would carry out and adjourned after setting their next meeting for the day after the class forums, March 23, at which time they would pull together all the suggestions from the tear-off sheets and make recommendations to the council.

Summary

This narrative segment begins with three local problems and their local solutions regarding council planning. Sr. Claudia is committed to her plan and does not want to be held back by the council's slower pace in setting in motion the parent council. Lois Chapman, suddenly realizing what the council is up to, wants the council to slow down long enough to obtain and consider the views of the student body, so far virtually excluded. Lighthall and Allan, concerned with the plodding discussion process of the council as a whole, propose a smaller steering committee to prepare issues and keep discussion focused. Sr. Claudia establishes her freedom to proceed at her own pace; the proposal by Lighthall and Allan at most reinforces a process routine at such junctures; and the newly arrived outsider, Lois Chapman, has a major impact by arguing for including a wider sampling of views.

Lois Chapman's arguments triggered elements of the process toward protagonist closure and protection referred to in analyses of the second episode. Sr. Claudia reminded council members about the role of rhetoric in determining whether a plan is 'accepted'. She called attention to the danger of having someone present the plan who did not 'like the plan very much'. The narrative and analysis showed a re-naming process by which the forum committee sought to camouflage aspects of the plan that students would, they imagined, find unpalatable. 'Authorities' became 'faculty' and 'class officers' and 'representatives' became combined as 'leaders'. Sr. Sabrina rationalized that 'we're not ... eliminating the officers; we're just transferring the idea of the officers as a combination of them'. And Sr. Janet summed up the effort: 'You keep changing it to "leaders" as much as you can, you know, and making them think they're really talking about leaders'.

The protagonists had become committed sufficiently to protect their solution by manipulation — omission, equivocation, and re-naming. They worked to sell the newly packaged plan in a way to block off, not elicit, antagonists' realities regarding the actual plan that the council had approved. The forum committee's actions constituted their own solution to the problem of being open while being closed; of gathering reactions to a plan while seeking acceptance of a more palatable transformation of it; of including antagonists' realities while excluding them. Nevertheless, an opening was also built in for antagonists' expressions: tear-off sheets were provided for written comments.

Notes

1. A similar idea underlies Bass's (1974) discussion of two contrasting modes of collaboration between social scientists and practitioners, two ways of developing innovations between academics and managers.

2. For a fuller discussion of identifying constituencies of problems, see Part V, p. 385 ff.
3. Even if the lay faculty had volunteered, however, there is no assurance that lay faculty resistance to working faculty issues through the planned system of governance would have been expressed. After all, the dominant frame of reference in setting up the forum committee had been, and was to continue to be, communication with students, not the faculty.
4. Janis' conception of 'groupthink' (Janis, 1972; Janis and Mann, 1977) is entirely relevant here, but the qualifications I made earlier (see p. 282, 288 ff) also apply.
5. This assertion was literally contradicted by recorded discussion of the previous week's council meetings — although a *decision* about the powers of the screening board had been left up in the air by the council.

Chapter 26

Forums, A Report, Final Council Action, and the Faculty Organizes

On March 22 the forums were held for each class year. The seniors were relatively satisfied with their meeting with their class, but most agreed that the juniors who had presented the council plan became overly defensive with their peers. The freshmen were sufficiently dissatisfied with their presentations that they held another day of after school communications with their class mates. A significant product of the forums were the 'tear-off sheets' at the bottom of the diagram of the multi-council structure that had been handed out. The forum planning committee met the very next day[1] to review each class's reactions on the tear-off sheets.[2] On March 29 the committee met for the last time and completed its discussion of five questions in sufficient detail for Hester and Sr. Claudia to present a written report of recommendations to the council.

1. What shape would the parent council and faculty council take, and how would they be established?
2. What functions would the councils finally serve?
3. How would the conflicting aims be met of recruiting candidates *qualified* to represent their constituencies (championed by Sr. Claudia and favored by most council members) and yet recruiting also students who would not be candidates if they were required to obtain *permission* of someone other than a parent (championed by Leo Phelan)?
4. What scheduled sequence of events would actually implement recruitment of candidates and elections to form the councils?
5. How would the question of class officers finally be resolved?

The council met twice more, on April 11 and 14, to consider and vote on the forum committee's recommendations. Consider first the recommendations addressed on April 11.

The Forum Planning Committee's Final Report

Would the council itself undertake to shape the parent and faculty councils as it had shaped the class councils and the Trinity 13? The planning committee (consisting still of Sister Claudia, Sister Janet, Ellie Sanford, Sister Sabrina, Hester Dulany, Beth Dolan, and Joan Noonan) recommended that the *parent council* send two representatives to the Trinity 13 and that its membership be chosen according to procedures worked out by Sr. Catherine (as Director of Public Relations) and the parents. The committee recommended one representative to the 13 from the *faculty council* and that the faculty form its own council. The issue of council functions was handled by setting the functions of the central council, the Trinity 13, omitting the details that Sr. Claudia had already described in her letter to parents (see note 1). It recommended that the *Trinity 13* be a synthesizing group which: (a) *recommends policy* [emphasis added]; (b) suggests problem areas for full school-community consideration; (c) initiates activities it perceives as being beneficial to the entire school-community; (d) consists of representatives who share as a common goal in meeting together the honest effort to *represent their own faction's point of view* [emphasis added] and to work together weighing alternatives in order to arrive at a resolution which seems to be most beneficial to the school-community; and (e) assists individual councils in their activities.

In a convoluted clause emphasizing solidarity of community ('share as a common goal', 'meeting together', 'work together', 'most beneficial to the school-community'), we find the phrase, 'represent their own faction's point of view'. This seems quite a dilution of the item earlier listed by the forum committee as 'to seek out and represent minority opinion'. Had Leo Phelan's stubborn opposition been for naught?

Earlier, Sr. Claudia had responded to Leo Phelan's resistance to qualifications for nominees by proposing a two-stage election procedure, the first election would produce 'nominees', the second, 'run-off' election would elect representatives. The first election would require no testimonials or recommendations whatever — just the capacity to become elected. That proposal provided Leo with a virtually complete solution. The forum committee recommended election procedures that in effect strengthened this solution while also strengthening recruitment of qualified (student) candidates. Note that in the proposed calendar of election procedures (Fig. 26.1) three, not two, separate elections appear. On April 25 freshmen, sophomore, and junior classes would hold elections from nominations (including self-nominations) submitted on April 21. This first election would create a slate of candidates whose nomination was confirmed by at least two votes. These candidates might well number more than sixteen, so the second election on May 2 would select the sixteen receiving the most votes within each class. On May 10 eight of these sixteen would be selected by the final election.

Figure 26.1   Details of the nomination and election procedures recommended by the forum planning committee.

Proposal

We propose that the following calendar be followed for election procedures:

April 19 — Leadership day [Note: These dates were actually pushed back one or two days.]
   a) Finished product of Council presented
   b) Information needed to run presented
April 20 — After-school explanatory session to interested candidates
April 21 — Candidates submit names to Council mailbox or Council Room
April 25 — Individual class run-off elections
April 28 — [Election Committee, below] meets candidates, receives testimonials
May 1 — Lists of candidates posted
May 2 — Class run-off elections for sixteen candidates [Election Committee] meets with candidates
May 4 to May 9 — Candidates meet with students, question and answer period
May 9 — PA announcements [regarding election details]
May 10 — Final election

Proposal

The Forum Committee proposes that an Election Committee [called 'screening board' in earlier council discussions] be formed at the [Trinity council] meeting of 4/11/02 with the following duties:

1. Conducts mechanics of election
2. Discuss testimonials with and advise candidates (suggesting nominee talk to guidance counselor), and composed of the following people: Four seniors presently on Council, Sr. Janet, Sr. Katherine Parnell [new co-ordinator for the next year's freshmen], and Miss Carey [new coordinator for the next year's juniors]. Additions?

But the schedule of election events not only was more open; it also strengthened requirements that student candidates obtain advice. First, it began the election with a day set aside to raise both student and faculty awareness of leadership issues: what ideas of 'representing' did participants have? What commitments were necessary for effective council participation? What kinds of issues should the councils deal with? This day was not just for candidates but for the whole school. Plenary sessions for describing the new council structure were mixed with small discussion groups. The faculty, too, had their meetings, devoted to the relation between the faculty council and the newly formed Faculty Forum (of which more below). Then on April 28 student candidates would present their 'testimonials' (not recommendations) to the election committee, successor to the 'screening board' of earlier council discussions, and would receive advice from that committee. They would be advised (not required) to talk

337

with their counselor, who could help evaluate the compatibility between their course load and council responsibilities. Finally, from May 4 to 9 was set aside as the period candidates would be available after school to talk to their constituents. Student testimony in June revealed that the election campaigning by students in this period was more intense than it had been for at least four years, and that members of some minorities absent from candidacy in earlier years stood for election this year — and were defeated. In sum, Leo Phelan's earlier resistance had kept the process open to all students for initial entry into candidacy, and Sr. Claudia's interests in increasing student competence and commitment also became built into the election calendar.

Returns of the tear-off sheets revealed that only members of the junior class cared much about class officers[3] and that of the fewer than 25 per cent of their returns that mentioned class officers, 46 favored and 36 rejected the retention of class officers. This split in sentiment was sufficient to call for new procedures to settle the matter. The forum committee offered three options to settle the now narrowed issue of senior class officers:

ISSUE: Senior Class Officers — OPTIONS OPEN TO COUNCIL:

1. Take an educated vote of entire Junior Class, after explanatory visits to homerooms have been made
2. Base our decision on the results of the assembly handouts [i.e., use the 46 to 36 ratio in favor]
3. Make judgment for class as representatives

FORUM COMMITTEE PROPOSAL: Should council choose option #1, we recommend that if the juniors vote affirmatively for Senior Class Officers, then these officers be considered a separate entity from the Council.

While the council approved straightforwardly the previous recommendations (with slight modifications in the calendar of election events), here it was faced with a choice. As it happened, members were not prepared to reconfirm their previous action to abolish class officers. But they were also not about to establish them, either. Discussion on April 14 centered on the 'educated vote'. Hester favored taking the junior class's vote on Leadership Day, when all the issues were fresh in mind. Opposition came from those who favored rejecting class officer positions: time was needed to make conditions right for a favorable vote.

Lucy Ellen Garvin, who at that point favored eliminating class officers, said that elections had to be 'prepared', not just 'held'. Beth Dolan and Nora Quinn joined Lucy Ellen in arguing against Hester. Lucy Ellen summed up most succinctly the point her trio was trying to make: 'You get real hot at the meeting when you're all together' — 'real hot' being translated as defensive about giving up the senior class officers. Nora Quinn elaborated:

338

Nora: When you're in a huge group like that, they're going to be, like, . . . 'Let's band together', like how they always say, 'safety in numbers?' That's what they're going to think of. Really. I think if you give them .. at least give them that night, and maybe the next morning in the homeroom. There's not quite as many people and it's a little more calm. (4/14/02; C; I, 1:160–170)

    ✿   ✿   ✿   ✿

The trio's fear was that the referendum would approve class officers if it were held when the juniors were 'hot' and 'all together' as a class. Just as the forum committee had tried to present the plan in a way most likely to win approval, this trio of strong supporters (from the junior class) of the council's position of eliminating officers was trying to manipulate conditions favoring a vote rejecting senior class officers. As it happened they succeeded in obtaining a more extended 'cooling down' period than one day.

    ✿   ✿   ✿   ✿

A meeting of the junior class on Leadership Day was largely devoted to pro and con arguments about eliminating senior class officers. Reaction from members was, as Lucy Ellen would have said, 'hot'. Four days later the juniors voted to eliminate senior class officers. Seventy-one per cent of the class favored abolishing the positions. The council never did discuss, however, questions of informing the faculty of the council plan or of obtaining reactions of faculty to it, much less issues of recruiting and electing faculty representatives.

With the council's April 14 approval of the election events, a solution was at hand to Sr. Claudia's problem complex regarding the functions and functioning of the Trinity council. Parents had been recruited to consult with all but one academic department, and these parent consultants were to be one of the groups from which representatives to the parent council would be selected. The faculty had met by themselves and had expressed sentiments in favor of a 'faculty forum' in which they might bring up problems of work load and other matters related to duties and expectations. How this fits into the independently developed council structure is told next.

Emergent Organization: The Faculty Forum

While the Trinity council was at work on its own future, the faculty had begun discussions of their own needs. Both through an 'action line' format (see p. 266, 277), where small discussion groups of faculty reported lists of concerns to assembled members, and in a regularly scheduled faculty meeting, faculty sentiment had been crystallizing toward the formation of a regular faculty group for discussing problems shared by faculty members. An all-day, regularly scheduled faculty meeting (a Faculty Day) had been held on March 3. Small-group discussions had dealt with matters that had emerged from a previous action line.

Sr. Claudia earlier had gotten wind of informal meetings of some lay faculty members — held at a nearby restaurant and bar. She was disturbed that she had set aside a whole Faculty Day (March 3) to allow faculty issues to surface while one of the issues, salary, had not even come up in the action line. Informal discussions at a bar, she felt, should not be allowed to undermine or pre-empt full discussions of the whole faculty on Faculty Day. She approached Lighthall with the question of how to ensure that the faculty's real issues were in fact discussed on Faculty Day. Lighthall suggested that they set aside, in addition to one table for each topic identified in the action line, a table labeled 'other', where anyone interested in some other topic could go for the small group discussion.

Some fifteen faculty members, predominantly lay faculty, showed up at the 'other' table, later joined by Sr. Claudia. A number of those at that table had become increasingly dissatisfied with aspects of faculty-administration relations — with the way interpersonal conflicts of members with department heads had been allowed to fester despite Sr. Claudia's alleged awareness of them, with uncertainty in the interpretation of appropriate extra-curricular loads, etc. Discussion at that table was sharply critical, and guardedly critical after Sr. Claudia arrived. One suggestion made that particularly bothered Sr. Claudia was that because the religious faculty and the lay faculty had different needs and commitments it might be wise to have an opportunity for them to meet separately to discuss their separate problems. A more general suggestion was made that the faculty, as a whole, did need some structure for its own meetings to air concerns.

A field note written by Lighthall about informal lunchtime conversations with and among faculty members on Faculty Day provides a glimpse at some faculty fears about approaching Sr. Claudia alone, face to face:

> ... The third contact [of three reported in the field note] involved myself, Sue [Allan], and four faculty members — three nuns and Laura Dudley. There was a good deal of discussion of Claudia's style of thought and communication. Two phrases were used by Laura to describe Claudia's highly prepared and almost overwhelmingly competent style of thought: 1) 'panoramic' as contrasted to 'linear' and 2) 'multi-simultaneous'. Claudia's mode of interacting with others was described as being so quick thinking that others who were not so fast on their feet were made to feel inadequate ... (Bk. V, p. 50e)

Three days after the Faculty Day the faculty received invitations to attend a 'Faculty Forum' after the close of school. The source of the invitation was evidently a small group of lay faculty. A considerable crowd showed up. Lighthall and Allan were absent, but Franklin Patrick ('Pat'), an intern who had been helping the faculty with its action line, was present and obtained permission to tape record the meeting openly. Peter Harris, a lay faculty member, chaired the meeting. He began by explaining, and handing out diagrams of, the new Trinity council structure, pointing out the provision in it for a faculty council. He suggested that the faculty council might and might not be identical with a faculty forum. He said Sr. Claudia had given him the diagrams that morning — probably those she used in the 'synthesizing' meeting with the five students on February 17. He reported that Sr. Claudia had thought the faculty council might take the place of the faculty forum. This meeting on March 6 can be summarized by quoting statements of the forum's purpose and of issues it might deal with.

Early on, the forum was described as having two broad functions, one of which was bilateral meetings between faculty representatives and the administration. The description given of the Faculty Forum was 'a faculty group that would come together and try to represent the concerns of the faculty to the administration and also kind of a sounding area where people can bring their ideas and their complaints'. Another person added the qualification that these meetings were to be just among the faculty, without students. Another responded to Peter Harris' reference to the faculty council in Sr. Claudia's diagram as having a voting representative in the Trinity 13: 'The purpose is not to get votes, but a line of communication between the faculty directly to the administration . . . Those aren't voting kinds of issues. Those are talk-out kinds of issues'.

✿   ✿   ✿   ✿

The theme here, clearly, was 'direct' communication with the administration on a strictly bilateral basis. We see here a commitment, not to representative governance on an equal footing with other 'constituencies', but to dealing with 'talk-out kinds of issues' between the faculty and the administration. What were those issues?

✿   ✿   ✿   ✿

One teacher cited a need for a forum to 'compare your teaching situation with others'. If you don't know, you may think you are getting a bad deal . . .' Another who had come in late wondered: 'if the word "forum" is being used delicately to really mean "union". Is this the dirty word that no one wants to say?' Mr. Harris replied that there was a broad spectrum of possibilities. Another member declared that a forum would not take up individual teachers' problems but only those *shared* by the faculty. No one voiced a reaction, positively or negatively, to the question about the union.

The question arose whether the group favored some kind of forum for the remaining four months. Mr. Harris asked for a show of hands and concluded that there was support for a forum to be organized now. As to issues, one person identified four kinds that needed voicing: 'questions of policy, of atmosphere, of attitude, and of inter-departmental communication'. No specifics were asked or given. One person pointed out that a forum might well serve the administration's purpose as well as the faculty's. The administration might want to know, she said by way of example, why so many faculty members were doing something, or failing to do something, why they could not 'follow the rule'? Sr. Norma supported her, saying that administrators often needed to know how many faculty felt a particular way about something: [as an administrator] 'you won't know it unless you have a representative like from the faculty forum to tell you that'.

One member struck a responsive chord in many when she raised the question of how appropriate some administrative expectations were of teachers. She spoke of some faculty members extending themselves well beyond the limits of the contract. This kind of extra commitment on the part of some had the effect, she thought, of setting up expectations that *all* teachers should demonstrate such extra commitment. Many faculty members, she said, had family and extra job commitments, commitments that prevented them from extending themselves beyond the contract (which included extra-curricular duties and other non-teaching obligations). Most of those who extended themselves, she pointed out, did not share those family and job commitments. She asked whether refusal to extend oneself as far as the most deeply committed members extended themselves might become 'material' to be used to pressure a person to leave Trinity or to be used as criteria against them because they were not supporting the institution. That kind of issue could, she said, be aired in a forum.

✥ ✥ ✥ ✥

It was not explicitly said by this person, but the implicit distinction that divided faculty with families and outside jobs from those with neither families nor outside jobs was the lay-religious distinction. Those whose commitment extended well beyond the contract, one might say the devoted, were the religious. Would their devotion be the criterion of normal adequacy? Here was a reality operating locally in lay faculty members that (a) had to be expressed in somewhat oblique terms, so as not to offend, and (b) was directly related to another basic difference in the realities of lay and religious faculty, namely salary: lay teachers negotiated salary on bases quite different from those used by nuns under a vow of poverty.

✥ ✥ ✥ ✥

A member summarized: there was enough consensus to show that there were, indeed, issues needing to be aired. She asked what next steps might be, and made reference to the kind of structure a forum should have. After a suggestion that a 'core' group was needed for continuity and for any face-to-face discussions with the administration, a vote was taken on the degree of support for having a core group of about five members to plan and sustain the forum. It passed. Volunteers for core membership were to put their names in Mr. Harris' mail box for an election two weeks hence, March 20.

The next faculty discussion took place as part of Leadership Day (actually taking place on April 20). The only information we have came through Sr. Claudia, who reported on the discussion in a mood of pessimism and suppressed hostility. The faculty met as a group, separate from students but with Sr. Claudia in attendance, after the formation of the Faculty Forum Core group. Leadership Day, recall, had been set aside, free from classes, to focus attention on the responsibilities of council membership, on the qualities of leadership needed, and the like. The faculty were presented with the council's 'finished plan'. Faculty discussion groups were guided by open-ended questionnaire stems like, 'Some faculty members probably hesitate to nominate themselves for Faculty Council because . . .' and 'Faculty members would be more involved in Trinity Council concerns if . . .' Another asked why a faculty member would, and would not, be interested in serving on the new faculty council and the Trinity 13. Faculty were asked to discuss the relationship between the recently organized faculty forum and the proposed faculty council, and the number of members appropriate for a faculty council.

What had dismayed Sr. Claudia in the discussion was faculty members' objections to bringing up anything important to them in a broadly representative group like the proposed 13. Some reportedly felt discussion of faculty concerns in the presence of parents and students would be inhibiting. Others looked upon any such representative group as a barrier to direct contact with Sr. Claudia, or with the executives as a group. It was that direct contact, they felt, not buffered by a representative group, that would lead to stable, straightforward ironing out of important matters. If the decision-making power lay with the executives and Sr. Claudia, they felt, discussions in any lesser body would be a waste of time.

✿   ✿   ✿   ✿

These sentiments had been expressed twice before to Sr. Claudia. Sr. Janet had represented faculty sentiments vis à vis the Trinity council in the evening meeting on February 2 (see p. 256 ff) and Sonia Griffin had conveyed similar sentiments from her uninvolved group of faculty on February 17 in the 'synthesizing' meeting. The second of these occasions prompted Sr. Claudia to say, first, that both the students and faculty were 'intrinsically' involved, and second, that if the faculty felt that way, she and the others should hear about it and added: 'We'll get *mad* at it (emphasis in her original tone). Her prediction of anger could not have been more accurate. But her claim of 'intrinsic' involvement of both students and faculty was valid only from her perspective of representative governance of a school-community, not from the perspective of lay faculty, whose realities regarding 'direct' communication she was now hearing for the first time directly from them.

⚬   ⚬   ⚬   ⚬

Sr. Claudia, in her own controlled way, was incensed. She regarded these expressions of the faculty's, statements of the need to communicate directly with Sr. Claudia without intermediaries, as a throw-back to the old days in the religious order when everyone was simply told what they would do, where 'participation' or 'input' from subordinates could be disregarded and was ordinarily not sought. The faculty seemed to her to be pushing to by-pass representative discussions and to want to deal only with the single authority at the top.

The push for a direct bilateral relation between the faculty and Sr. Claudia (who negotiated all faculty contracts) was coming from the lay faculty, a group that had never experienced the old kind of authoritarian administrative order that her religious order had so recently thrown off. In the lay teachers' realities, constrained heavily by the occupational and professional culture most familiar to them, teachers' contracts, for example, were negotiated with school administrators pure and simple, without participation by parents or students. For them, the faculty's relation to a school's administration was part of a culture of labor-management relations, not part of a community's governance. They were teachers in a school, not constituencies in a representative government. Neither she nor we could see this all then and so were unaware of the fact that the conflict she felt stemmed from a conflict in *constructions of social order*. She was developing a new, more fully participative governance; the lay faculty was developing a new, more fully organized channel of communication to those responsible for setting the conditions of work. It was the contrast between the governance of a society and the administration of a private school.

⚬   ⚬   ⚬   ⚬

Sr. Claudia explained, in the executive meeting on April 21, that confrontation of different groups' issues was important. She gave the example of faculty salaries. It was essential that the salary question go to the Trinity 13, she said, because it was closely tied to the tuition bill for each student, and students and parents would have strong views on that question. In bilateral negotiations between the faculty and the executives or with the director, Sr. Claudia explained to us (but not, so far as we can tell, to any faculty group), no such confrontation between issues of salary and issues of tuition costs would be possible. The faculty's insistence, the previous day, on protecting their issues from discussion by representatives of other 'constituencies', led Sr. Claudia to a momentarily global pessimism. She exposed a gloomy and at points derogatory view of the past performance of students and faculty in the current year's Trinity council:

> Sr. Claudia: Curricular change has never originated from our students. Our students are interested in an extra day off or wearing a sweater .. a different sweater ... and our faculty, do you see, is interested in having a bed [requested by someone for the smaller of two faculty lounges] and having another place to hang wraps, and so forth. Those are the issues that have come up ... — unless the issue is raised in ... a faculty meeting, where I say, 'How do you feel about ..?' Then the feelings come out. (4/21/02: E; 1:188–193)

She wondered if 'the whole thing from December' was 'an exercise in futility', questioning whether, with the faculty's reticence in bringing up their own important issues for discussion with anyone but the director, all those attempts since December to get 'feed in' had been a waste of her time and everyone else's: 'To what end, all this energy?' Her outlook, for the moment, was bleak.

Lighhall asked her if she felt the whole process of building a new council structure was something she had merely gone along with or whether it was 'something that you have actively owned and produced?' She replied that she actively owned and had produced it, all right, but her question was, 'How eager am I to drag behind me [deleted number] students and [deleted number] faculty members? Not only how reluctant [note the shift from 'eager' to 'reluctant'], but how able am I to do it?' It was a prophetic question.

As discussion turned to other matters, Sr. Claudia took a somewhat broader perspective, while still keeping her worry in focus:

> Sr. Claudia: Don't misunderstand me .... I got the feeling from the faculty that they liked it ['the new form of government'] very much .... I got the idea, though, that, you know, the big hassle was going to be between remaining 'The Faculty', without having to go before students or parents or anybody else, and being a faculty that was involved. (4/21/02: E; 1:766–780)

The best available summary of faculty realities regarding the new structure is provided by a single-page, unsigned bulletin from the 'Faculty Forum Core group' (see Fig. 26.2). That group met after Leadership Day as well as participating in it, and synthesized their views of faculty sentiment on a number of issues posed during Leadership Day.

        ✧   ✧   ✧   ✧

Figure 26.2.   The Faculty Forum Core group's memorandum to the faculty.

The following are notes from the Faculty Forum Core group's meeting. We submit them to you so you can think about them and discuss them before Wednesday's [May 3] Faculty Forum meeting.

The reports from the group discussions indicate that most people would like nine members on the Faculty Council.

Proposed Election Schedule

May 3 Faculty Forum — Discussion will clarify roles of Faculty Forum and Faculty Council next year.
May 5 Self-nominations due.
May 10 Informal meeting with nominees.
May 16 VOTE Polls will open early.

The nine candidates with the highest number of votes will be considered elected.

On the question of whether or not to have two separate Faculty groups — the Faculty Forum and the Faculty Council — or one group — the Faculty Council, there was a wide divergence of opinion. The chief reason in favor of two separate groups is that *faculty members do not want faculty business aired before the students in Trinity 13* [emphasis added]. Many mentioned that the Faculty Council would be sufficient provided that it would have direct access to the administration whenever this was deemed necessary. Another suggestion is to make the Faculty Forum a part of the Faculty Council.

One solution might be to begin the year with one group, the Faculty Council, which would have direct access to the administration for any matters that it could not settle alone and that did not involve students or parents. If, during the year, the Faculty Council found that it had too much work or the faculty found that they wanted the Faculty Forum, the group could be formed when the need was felt.

Concerning the list of duties [the nine listed on pages 327, with 'the class' modified to read 'its constituency'], no additions were suggested. It would seem that because this is the list of duties for all Councils, we could not delete those which do not seem to be applicable to our Council. Since this plan has not yet been in operation, it would seem hard to be more specific about the duties.

The 'big hassle' that Sr. Claudia feared, the faculty's ambivalence about going along with council participation vs. desiring direct, bilateral access to Sr. Claudia, was also clearly articulated in the Faculty Forum Core group's own memorandum to the faculty. The Trinity council itself never addressed this 'hassle'.

Summary

The final phases of implementing the council structure reveal: the protagonists' commitment to the plan to the point of further manipulatory

346

planning; organizing by the faculty, whose constituent realities had been ignored or excluded; and the precise constituent realities that had been excluded from all of the planning, a victim of the protagonists' cumulative closure and commitment. In keeping with Lucy Ellen Garvin's comment that elections must be 'prepared', not just 'held', a cooling off period was scheduled between the junior class's plenary discussion of the issue of senior class officers and their vote to decide the issue. The faculty organized for its own purposes, which it explored in meetings of its own. Faced with the council structure, it was a matter of almost indifference whether to retain the Faculty Forum or to merge the Forum with the Faculty Council. Of central importance to the faculty, however, were two kinds of independence. It retained the right to 'have direct access to the administration' concerning faculty business and to re-establish the Faculty Forum separate from the Faculty Council if the council got bogged down in work or if 'the need was felt'. Their retention of a direct, bi-lateral channel to the administration asserted the particularistic view Sr. Wilma Tisch was to argue the following year, regarding reserved parking spaces for faculty, and revealed an underlying organizational reality shared by the faculty that had never been addressed in the Trinity council's or executive group's planning processes. That was the view that evaluations and expectations of teachers by administrators were matters to be talked out between those two parties alone, that this was a matter of negotiation in the context of contracts, not a matter of representative government to be decided by vote or by consensus. The root framework of thinking was not the governance of a community or societal government through representation of constituencies, but labor-management negotiation of contracts and grievances. Neither the root framework nor the power of bi-lateral initiatives from faculty to administration had ever been explored, much less integrated in the planning process. This faculty outlook and commitment to a bi-lateral channel was left to work its influence outside and independent of the solution of Sr. Claudia's problem of governance. That solution process had excluded more than brief mention of the faculty's reality until two weeks *after* the solution had been completed. It was not that faculty members themselves had been excluded from the process, nor even that this very reality, that the faculty needed no Trinity council since it had direct access to the administration, had not been voiced. Sr. Janet did voice it in the initial, evening meeting with Sr. Claudia. But this reality local to the faculty remained local, unintegrated, precisely because *it was irrelevant to faculty members for them to press a body irrelevant to them, the Trinity council, to take this reality into account.* They were perfectly able on their own, supported by the tradition of bi-lateral negotiations between teachers and administrators, to insist that they retain that power of initiative and that bi-lateral channel. To confront, explore, and integrate this reality into planning would have had to be initiated and pursued by the protagonists, not the antagonists, since the protagonists depended more on the antagonists in this matter than vice versa. It was Sr. Claudia and the protagonists who were trying, unwittingly, to change the frame of thought, to shift from the tradition of teacher-administration negotiations to the quite different tradition of constituent representation and participative governance.

One resistance to closure and to exclusion, a relatively minor one, did make its mark. While most council members had readily agreed with Sr. Claudia's values of responsible membership and preparedness, Leo Phelan's persistent resistance, aided by Sr. Janet and Lighthall, was sufficient to establish open nominations of students, subject only to parental permission and 'testimonials'.

We turn now to the final chapter in this story.

Notes

1. This same day Sr. Claudia sent a report to parents, part of which described the new structure and functions of the councils:

   The Trinity Council is presently being re-structured to allow for greater representation and wider involvement during the school year 02–03.

   'Trinity 13' will be composed of elected representatives from each of the seven Councils which make up the constituency of the school community. One member of the Executive Council will also function on Trinity 13.

   The Councils take as [a] major goal a *problem-sensing* role at their specific grass-roots level. Each of these councils elects its representatives for Trinity Council — a synthesizing group which recommends policy, suggests problem areas for full school community consideration, plans projects, assists individual councils in their activities.

   Freshman, Sophomore, Junior, Senior, and Faculty Councils would be composed of members elected by their respective constituency. These Councils would organize appropriate and needed committees.

   Parent Council would be composed of departmental consultants, representatives of Mothers' club, and parent advisors to administration. The Parent Council will elect two representatives to the 'Trinity 13' — this representation will assist us in obtaining the parent viewpoint as issues surface.

   [At this point a diagram of the council structure was included.]

   Two prime advantages of this plan:

   1. Many more persons involved in decision making and problem sensing; yet, groups for basic discussion small enough to be viable.
   2. Communication lines upward and downward are built into the plan.

2. Allan and Lighthall were both out of town during the last two weeks of March and from March 30 to April 6 Trinity was closed for vacation. No tape recordings were made of the single remaining forum planning committee meeting or of any conferences between Sr. Claudia and Hester as Hester was writing the committee's report. While the April 14 meeting was taped, the rest of these meetings are represented in our data only through documents, interviews, and references made by participants to this period in later recorded meetings.

3. Except for the current year, the only class that had elected class officers had been the senior class.

Chapter 27

Coda: The Decline of School 'Governance'; The Return to School Administration

Vatican II had decreed that power in religious communities should be shared more evenly to enliven and enrich apostolic participation. Sr. Claudia believed the implications of sharing power extended to education in the wider democratic society: young women had to *learn* effective participation in decision making as part of their own enriched development. That meant much more responsibility for decisions must be transferred to girls as they went through secondary school, responsibility that entailed their making mistakes and their facing the consequences. Vatican II's pronouncements had just as much to say to education, therefore, as to community, Sr. Claudia felt. Just as important for Sr. Claudia was the *acceptance* of decisions by those who participated in the decision making. It was a vision of community, education, and decision making that produced a new governance for Trinity, a governance that achieved many of its objectives with respect to participation, linkage, and effectiveness, as we traced in Chapter 18.

Three years after a power-sharing structure of governance had been achieved, however, it had virtually disappeared from Trinity.[1] While our gathering of episodic data had ceased, documents and interviews provide a clear picture of the basic skeleton of changes. In brief, school-community governance was replaced by school administration. Concepts of the religious order relevant to community, participation, and sharing of power yielded to concepts relevant to traditional schooling in the secular culture — to student government as a source of 'spirit' activities and of visible leadership positions valued on applications for admission to colleges. Governance also gave way to organized labor-management relations and negotiations. Consider first the changes and then speculation about causes.

The Directorship

Sr. Claudia expressed deep satisfaction to the other members of the Trinity 13 at the end of the 03 school year. Certain improvements were needed, but the council system was serving its purposes well. But in May of that year, Sr. Claudia was elected to the religious order's Regional Administration. Sr. Sabrina was appointed as Acting Director for 03–04, and as Director in 04–05 and for some years thereafter. Sr. Claudia's solution of her problems of an acceptable, productive social order in the school-community were bequeathed to Sr. Sabrina, and Sr. Sabrina was, of course, a different person from Sr. Claudia. Sr. Sabrina's only experience in school administration had been to head Trinity's department of guidance and counseling. While Sr. Claudia was recognized as having expertise in curriculum and curriculum development — she was Trinity's Director of Curriculum as well as Director of the school — Sr. Sabrina professed no such special competence. And while Sr. Claudia had been heavily involved in the changes in governance of her religious order, Sr. Sabrina had been much less involved and held few of Sr. Claudia's images of the school as a community in need of participative governance.

In short, Sr. Sabrina's problems were not Sr. Claudia's. So Sr. Claudia's solutions as director were not solutions for Sr. Sabrina in that same office. Sr. Sabrina's problems generally (we know few details) were those of keeping head above water during that first year, and of managing conflicts that arose between the Academic Senate and the Executives.

Executive Council

During 02–03, the only year of Sr. Claudia's participation in the new council structure, the executive council had the following composition:

Sr. Claudia, Director
Sr. Catherine, Associate Director
Sr. Patricia Johnson, Senior Coordinator
Miss Irma Carey, Junior Coordinator
Sr. Mary Ann Cross, S.I.C., Sophomore Coordinator
Sr. Katherine Parnell, Freshman Coordinator

Only Sr. Claudia and Sr. Catherine had participated in the 01–02 development of the new structure of governance, since the others had not been at Trinity or had been on the faculty but uninvolved (Miss Carey). During 02–03 the class coordinators became, in varying degrees, confused about their role in the executive council. Were they to actively engage in policy formation and decision making or were they merely being informed by Sr. Claudia about present and past policies? Were their questions and amendments expected by Sr. Claudia? These questions were gradually clarified, but the coordinators found that their roles had far more to do with the details of discipline than they had expected, and they occasionally met separately to take care of those matters. They were also all new to administration at the secondary level and to their roles, roles Sr. Claudia had conceived of, while Sr. Claudia had been in the Trinity administration for four years. It was reasonable for Sr. Claudia to be relatively dominant, therefore, diminishing their roles in making policy and decisions.[2]

Sr. Sabrina's first year reversed this relative imbalance in experience: the four coordinators were now the chief source of experience for Sr. Sabrina in how matters might be handled. In Sr. Sabrina's first year, therefore, new patterns of participation in policy developed, where the director was relatively less dominant and where the idea of sharing power among students, faculty, and parents was correspondingly less dominant. The inversion of power between the new Director and her four, now experienced coordinators became manifest in another way.

Sr. Sabrina presided over the academic senate; she was not its curricular leader as Sr. Claudia had been as Director of Curriculum (a position vacant the first year of Sr. Sabrina's directorship, subsequently assumed by Sr. Pat Johnson). Thus, when the academic senate (the chairs of departments) passed a new schedule of examinations, Sr. Sabrina brought it back to the executive council for discussion and decision. Sr. Claudia previously had represented the executives in the academic senate and, on matters of curriculum, made the executive decisions in interaction with the senate. When decisions came out of the academic senate under Sr. Claudia, therefore, they were decisions, not advice, and were communicated as information to the executive meetings, not ordinarily as matters for discussion and decision. Under Sr. Sabrina the executives, not any other body or persons, made decisions. On the occasion of this new examination schedule the executives took issue with it substantively. Sr. Sabrina was not in a position of strong advocacy, either within the executives as a first-year, 'acting' incumbent or from the point of view of curricular expertise, and the executives ended up reversing the senate's 'decision'. With this emergence of the executives' power in academic matters, and the relegating of the senate to advice giving, came struggle between the coordinators on the one hand and the chairs of departments making up the senate on the other, a struggle that Sr. Sabrina now had to face and manage.

The Trinity 13

Sr. Claudia had said that advice from groups like the academic senate or the Trinity council was such that only 'fools' would ignore it. To the co-ordinators, the full representativeness of the Trinity 13 did, indeed, make its advice extremely authoritative. But what kind of role did that imply for the executives? If the executives had the final decision-making power, which in their view it had, then why was such a widely representative group like the 13 needed? After Sr. Claudia had departed the executives had no strong answer.

The particularistic interests of the faculty members, which Sr. Wilma

Tisch shared and expressed in arguments about solutions to the parking problem (see p. 247 ff), ran directly contrary to the norm for everyone to 'face the music' on an equal footing. Faculty members felt their claims regarding working conditions took precedence over students' claims regarding conditions of school attendance. With Sr. Claudia's departure, Sr. Sabrina was faced with either holding to that egalitarian norm or to fall back on voting. But the administration and faculty were both outvoted by the students on the Trinity 13. Not having integrated faculty members' conceptions of their role and status as in important regards special and prior to students' status, the Trinity 13's functioning depended on an authoritative (not necessarily authoritarian) leader's strong commitment to the idea of equal claims of constituencies — that is, a strong commitment to the idea of school-community *governance*. Sr. Sabrina's commitments to a more democratic governing of the school were simply swamped by her commitment to surviving as a novice administering a large school.

In addition to weakened support for the Trinity 13 due to the new persons who made up the executive, and partly because of it, the 13's own functioning became weakened. Sr. Sabrina felt early on that too much time was taken with little return by the Trinity 13. Her move to cut meetings for the 13 to only once a month, less than half the frequency used by Sr. Claudia, met with little resistance. But one meeting a month was insufficient for the Trinity council to keep up with the pace of that year's decisions, and of the events it was supposedly dealing with. Toward the end of the first year as acting director, Sr. Sabrina made the generally supported decision to discontinue the Trinity 13.

Parent Council

With the withering away of the Trinity 13, the parents' council (rarely active in its advice-giving through the 13) had no body through which to advise. It reverted to the previous model of the Mother's Club, with a twist: it became a Father's Club. Sometime during Sr. Sabrina's first two years, a poignant need arose as the result of a student's father's death: the estate left insufficient funds to support the girl's continued education at Trinity. The Father's Club formed its central agenda around this particular event: it would raise funds to pay for insurance that would allow any Trinity girl whose father died to pay for the remaining tuition through her graduation. The club also became, as Sr. Pat Johnson put it, the occasion for periodic 'poker smokers'.

Faculty Council

Faculty council representatives to the Trinity 13 were supported, recall, only so far as purely faculty matters were not under consideration. The

'Faculty Forum Core' group foreshadowed the kind of particularistic interests to which Sr. Wilma gave voice in the Trinity 13's solving of the parking problem (Chapter 18): the lay faculty, who were more active in the faculty council than the religious faculty, felt they needed a channel for strictly bi-lateral discussions with those empowered to make decisions. The demise of the Trinity 13, therefore, was no obstacle to this commitment to bi-lateral communication.

The faculty council members' commitment to bi-lateral communication was actually fed by Sr. Claudia herself in the first year of the faculty council. When the matter of salary increments came up, Sr. Claudia sent her proposals not to the Trinity 13, but to the faculty council. She asked the faculty council to canvass the faculty and make a choice among three ways of allocating the 5.5 per cent salary increment. If it were to choose the option she preferred, a merit pay arrangement, then it (not the Trinity 13) should form a committee to work out the criteria and procedures for distributing the money according to merit. The faculty council, thus, survived with its central role being bi-lateral communication with the executives on matters of particularistic interest. It took its emergent role of collective bargaining so militantly one year, indeed, as to embarrass many faculty members. The faculty elected a rather less strident set of representatives subsequently. The faculty council remains the *de facto* collective bargaining agent for Trinity faculty — though it is not unionized and has not moved overtly toward the strike as a bargaining maneuver.

Class Councils

With the demise of the Trinity 13, the class councils had no agency to provide downward input of school-wide problems. They became wholly occupied with local 'class spirit' activities. A consensus developed that the class councils became too isolated from each other and not enough interested in 'school spirit'. After two or three years, the class councils were abandoned. The irony of the form that emerged to take their place can be appreciated only in light of Trinity's brief history.

In the years before we came to Trinity, students participated in school government by the traditional means, for both state and private schools, of a student council. The year before our arrival, Sr. Claudia, Sr. Norma, and the other two members of the executive team decided that a more meaningful form of government was needed, one including faculty. So the Trinity council was formed whose operation we have viewed through the lenses of Sr. Claudia's problem vis à vis governance. That gave rise, in turn, to the more fully representative council structure examined in the preceding chapters of Part IV, eventuating in the Trinity 13. With the appointment of Sr. Sabrina and in the context of the relatively new group of executives (except Sr. Catherine, whose role was always centered on publications, publicity, and public relations), commitment to participative governance waned, the council structure collapsed, and now a new form was needed for student participation in school government. The form chosen brought the history full circle: a large student council. Not only did the student council contain eight students from each class, but it came full circle in another respect. It made a place for 'figureheads', 'heroines', and 'leaders to look up to': students were once again elected at large for president, vice-president, secretary, and treasurer. The 36-member student council was supervised by one faculty member, one who was not a class coordinator (a role which was retained) and thus who had no membership on executive council.

The lay faculty, whose realities regarding governance vs. administration were most persistently excluded from the formation of the new council structure, currently, after many years, enjoy the strong survival of their structure, the faculty council. The lay faculty leadership had, after all, developed their own 'forum' from within their own ranks as a response to their own local problems. The keystone of the representative council structure, to which the faculty council was to offer advice, faltered in its second year and then died. The repeatedly rebuffed minority of students who favored class officers and who, in the 'end' were voted down, saw their cause rise again like the phoenix to re-establish those offices.

o   o   o   o

What would account for the rather prompt replacement of governance by more traditional forms of administration? Two strong possibilities are contained in the question itself: 'prompt' and 'traditional'. Consider tradition first. The culture of schooling — public and private — represents a complex tangle of shared expectations about who properly does what, in short, about forms of participation in the enterprise of schooling. The widespread and dominant forms of such participation do not come from the governance of societies, from representative democracy as a means of ordering political participation in the social order. Nor do they come from the governing structures of religious institutions. They come from the division of labor in schooling — where students do not make decisions, or give 'input', they study; where teachers do not participate as representatives of a constituency in governance structures but as professional employees in the accomplishment of tasks and in negotiations about their work and compensation; and where administrators do not share power by means of consensus seeking or voting councils to sense and solve joint problems and to receive council advice so much as they use power to pursue fairly standard institutional goals and to enforce fairly standard rules, and seek advice, when they do so, from individuals and ad hoc committees.

These cultural forms of participation were, in effect, precisely what Sr. Claudia was challenging, were precisely the difference between traditional 'administration' and school-community governance. She was attempting to infuse the culture of schooling with the culture of community in the image of Vatican II. That is the kind of project that always faces daunting odds. And the issue in attempting such a project was precisely intuited by Sr. Claudia at the end when she wondered, 'How eager am I to drag behind me [all those] students and [all those] faculty members? Not only how reluctant, but how able am I to do it?' The issue, in short, is whether the project has support that is diffused. Culture, it seems, cannot be intentionally 'dragged' in some direction. If 'drag' is the appropriate verb in a given situation, as it was with Sr. Claudia's image of governance, then we know the culture in question is already resistant, already going in another direction. Does that mean that we, knowing that, should avoid intentional attempts at cultural transformation? Doesn't each such failed attempt provide the culture with one more resource to transform itself? I would say yes, it does. But it is also well for those who engage in such projects to know consciously what they are up to, that they are in the realm of cultural change, not mere organizational change.

A second force to account for the demise of governance is suggested by its very promptness. The promptness of the change reflected the replacement of one person by another as the school leader. That change is packed with many dimensions: experience, confidence, skill, concepts, values, and with all these, problems that the leader synthesizes. The school's leader has enormous influence over what problems will and will not be synthesized and therefore what adaptations will and will not be forged or continued. Since the person is the agency for synthesizing problems and the leading person is the agency for synthesizing leading problems, that person becomes theoretically and practically focal in understanding organizational problems and processes.

Sr. Claudia's vision of the school as a community was a vision whose viability was conditional: it depended on the kinds of commitments, concepts, and skills which she possessed but which her successor did not. It is possible that Sr. Claudia could have made it work, that she could have accommodated the lay faculty's bilateral needs, as she had begun to do in regard to salary issues, within the council system itself.[3] But her commitments, skills, and vision — her reality regarding education and community — were hers. As universalistic as they might seem, they were nonetheless socially and organizationally local. Her concept and structures of governance were local adaptations — as was the reversion to the standard student council and class offices at the hands of Sr. Sabrina.

Summary

After two years the council system of representative governance, and the concepts and commitments behind it, all but disappeared from Trinity. Sr. Claudia's adaptation via 'governance', the faculty's resistance to being reduced to the status of a constituency in the council system of governance, and Sr. Sabrina's undoing of that system in favor of more standard school structure and administration all support the same conclusion: organizational adaptations will be as local — or as integrative — as the constituent realities that generate and guide them. More particularly if problems are the centers of energy and guidance within realities, then *organizational adaptations will be as local or as integrative as the problems that generate and guide them.*

Notes

1. For an account of another, more sweeping attempt to innovate at the school building level which also disappeared quickly, see Smith and Keith (1971). For a re-interpretation of Smith and Keith's study in terms of the pragmatic constructivist perspective of this book, see Lighthall (1973). For commentary on both Smith and Keith (1971) and my re-interpretation, see Fullan (1982). Smith, Kleine, Prunty and Dwyer (1987) re-visited the site of the original innovation fifteen years later.
2. In their self-evaluation as a group, in the spring of 03, the executives discussed the coordinators' relatively lower participation in executive meetings in contrast to Sr. Claudia's relatively heavy participation (see Lighthall, 1978).
3. One tendency observed in Sr. Claudia in the course of this episode that casts some doubt on whether Sr. Claudia could have accommodated lay faculty demands was her construing of requests from the lay faculty with which she disagreed strongly as 'childish' or as something 'they should grow out of'. Such construing may have been mostly a function of the emotional overload she experienced in this period with her mother's illness and Sr. Norma's withdrawal. Sr. Claudia's career in the years since Trinity suggests, from a distance and without episodic data, an increased reliance on building on others' already operating realities.

Chapter 28

Five Variables Synthesized

From the first constitution episode we culled seven variables that appeared important in determining that episode's ineffectiveness (see Table 5.1). Of these, six were seen again in the episode of conflict between the co-directors, an episode with mixed effectiveness. From that second episode, fifteen new variables were identified at four levels of social complexity (Table 17.1) — twice the number of variables in the first episode, along with new differentiations of complexity. Would the third episode again require that many more new variables to account for its effectiveness? Would each new episode require mostly its own, idiosyncratic variables and levels to account for its effectiveness? If so, the prospects for generalization would seem dim. The first task of this chapter is to answer three questions about idiosyncracy and generalization. How many new variables did the third episode yield? How many of these pertained only to the third episode, not to the other two? How many from the first two episodes again were in clear evidence in the third episode? After answering these questions, the full set of variables will be shown to cluster in five groups, five more general variables. Finally, I will consider the relative theoretical importance of the five variables.

Two New Variables

Analysis of the narrative of Part IV yielded only two new variables comparable to the earlier ones. One of these two was in evidence in the third episode only. Of the twenty-two variables accumulated from the three episodes, eleven were in clear evidence in all three. Three more variables were evident in two of the three episodes. Three successive cullings, then, captured both idiosyncracy and generality in the variables, a good sign: generalization seems possible. What were the two new variables from the third episode?

Protagonist's Orientation to Advice/Complaints/Requests

Sr. Claudia wanted 'input' and 'feed-in' from other segments of the school community. She went to extraordinary efforts to develop a system of advisory councils. She was committed, thus, to being open to advice. But Sr. Claudia saw advisory councils 'essential to you or kind of non-essential, depending on the things they feed in' — non-essential referring to advice that one was 'really not looking for in given situations time after time'. Advice had to be relevant to the immediate problems one was trying to solve. Further, advice had to be 'prepared', with issues that had been 'winnowed', if the advice were to be really useful. When members of an advisory group provided 'feed-in' that was not on Sr. Claudia's problem agenda, as the students did in her evening meeting with the council (pp. 256 ff), she could regard those matters as 'things I didn't even want in my life'. The 'action line' format, that allowed the open expression of problems by the faculty, caused Sr. Claudia to sigh, 'may we all live through it'. If the 'feed-in' was in the nature of complaints that she immediately felt unreasonable and that created difficulties for her, Sr. Claudia could be closed and sometimes indignantly derogatory (Chapter 20) rather than exploring the others' realities. About such unsought 'inputs', then, Sr. Claudia was ambivalent, mixing a kind of ideological egalitarianism of representative governance, emphasizing *competent and relevant* advice, with a certain ego-centric insensitivity to causes behind others' complaints, requests, or unwanted advice. Protagonists' orientations to unsought advice, complaints, or requests appears as a variable for the first time in this third episode. It is a close cousin to the first variable of Tables 5.1 and 17.1, the problem originator's inclusive vs. exclusionary synthesis of her own problem. They differ in what the others provide the protagonist as problematic. In the case of advice, complaints, and requests, the content is communicated verbally and intentionally to the protagonist. In the other case, others' *actions* to solve their *own* problems come to the protagonist's attention and are synthesized by the protagonist as a problem without regard for any problem behind the others' actions — as with Sr. Claudia's response to Trinity council's parking solution in the first episode.

Power-Dependence and Status Relations Among the Problem Originator and Constituents

In the first constitution episode Sr. Claudia was stymied — unable to do more than work at the periphery of the Trinity council, through individual members. She was dependent on Sr. Norma, since the council was Sr. Norma's bailiwick. But she could not depend on Sr. Norma to represent executive interests in the council. In the second episode, she could and did work directly to bring her antagonist into direct confrontation with her problem. She became less dependent, more powerful, by enlisting the aid of superordinate authorities.[1] Her efforts achieved mixed success, but she was far more empowered in relation to Sr. Norma than she had been in the first constitution episode. While no parties in that second episode achieved a fully satisfying solution to their respective problems, all achieved some success. Power-dependency and status were honored on all sides, if not fully on any side. In the third episode Sr. Claudia was clearly dominant.

Sr. Claudia was influential at each juncture of the second constitution episode, and her influence accumulated — even if it was never complete. Partly as a result, her own solution, developed out of the executive meetings, advanced in comparative dominance to the 'synthesis' meeting, from there to the Trinity council, thence to the forum committee, to the forums, back again to the council, and finally to the Faculty Forum. Her dominance, especially evident in the forum committee's preparation for the forums, dictated a close fit between the solution and her problem, but a poor fit between the solution and the lay faculty's problems — and an even poorer fit with Sr. Sabrina's problems. At various junctures Sr. Claudia was aware of her dominant influence and sought to soften its strength — e.g., by not joining one of the five parallel planning groups of the council and by reporting last in the synthesis committee. But these were attempts to soften influence only within certain narrow bounds: her commitments were strong and her will could be iron. Her program of 'built-in' participation did not weaken her image of governance or her attempts to realize it. But her steadfast — one is tempted to say unrelenting — attempts to realize participative governance did weaken her realization of it.

By being so steadily dominant an influence, by excluding so completely the realities of the lay faculty and those of a more moderately committed and a more moderately powerful successor, she rendered her solution effective for her own tenure as director but not for a successor. The very nature of governance requires the support of the governed — a principle she knew well and actually articulated, a principle she, and we, were unable to see applied with increasing and finally full force to the lay faculty and to her successor. None of us thought of a successor, thought of institutionalizing governance with an eye to the *person of the governor*. So, for Sr. Claudia, success in this third episode was virtually complete — but short lived. Her dim awareness of the limiting effects of her own dominant power in the episode was poignantly expressed: was it all, she wondered, 'an exercise in futility? To what end, all this energy?'

If the three episodes suggest a lesson, then, about power-dependence and status relations among the problem originator and the other constituents it is this: interdependence of functions to be performed by different segments of the organization must be matched by a sharing of power-dependence among the constituent parties — *in synthesizing a shared problem and in devising the solution to be implemented*. In the first episode, Sr. Norma's power was dominant, combining her legitimate power of position with her private move to become independent. As co-director, Sr. Claudia was dependent: Trinity council was Sr. Norma's domain. Having to influence the council through others only, their realities could easily supplant Sr. Claudia's, and each others', in a succession of non-cumulative efforts. In the third episode, if the solution were to be carried out only by Sr. Claudia or were not dependent on a successor's holding similar skills, commitments, and experience, then Sr. Claudia's dominance in the process may be considered more adaptive. It looks as though she herself might have been able to accommodate her lay faculty's long excluded realities through minor adaptations of governance. But if the solution is to weather succession, and therefore depends on more widely shared realities and skills, then dominance of the degree Sr. Claudia enjoyed renders the solution vulnerable, makes success turn on the chief protagonist's person. In that case, the degree of adaptiveness of the solution is measured by the duration of the dominant protagonist's incumbency. For Sr. Claudia it was one school year.

A Synthesis: Five Variables

One advantage of a large number of relatively specific variables is precisely their capacity to focus attention, to limit the scope of inquiry or intervention. So a listing of twenty-one variables across four levels of social complexity, as in Table 17.1, is useful. A disadvantage is that, taken together, they diffuse attention and obscure differences in relative power and comprehensiveness. In an effort like this one wants both specificity of focus and comprehensiveness. My solution to this problem is to group twenty of the 'old' variables of Table 17.1 and the two new ones, above, into five coherent sets.[2] Each 'old' variable now becomes a component of a more comprehensive, more abstract variable. Table 28.1 lists the twenty-two component variables under each of the five major variables to which they contribute. Some commentary on each of the five major variables is in order, after which I shall consider their relative importance.

I. Individuals' Orientations to Others' Realities

Three variables contribute to this predominantly *psychological* variable. The focus here is on participants in whom the focal problem is induced, the protagonists. Are they receptive to others' problems to the extent of formulating their own problems *in reciprocity with* the others, to the extent of exploring the problems behind others' complaints in the course of solving the focal problem, and to the extent of not avoiding emotional expressions of others, expressions that signal intensity of immediate problems? In short, do protagonists *take in others' realities*, particularly antagonists' realities, as the protagonists synthesize and solve their own problems? To the extent that they do, they maximize chances for working exchanges with others, exchanges that create bonds, accumulate common experiences of support and collaboration. To the extent they do not, they support independent, not interdependent action, and promote a climate of alienation.

II. Communicativeness of Interactions

Given the pluralism and localism of organizational realities, to induce — I am tempted to say transduce — a problem across its constituents implies that nothing short of a *problem-specific community* must emerge, a community whose local problems share a common problem which serves as a pragmatic *conscience composante collective* (to borrow from Durkheim) that animates and guides collective action toward solutions, plans, and implementations. Such emergent, pragmatic communities — pragmatic in that they arise and disappear on the basis of getting something done together — require above all effective communication. Effective in this context, as throughout this book, means expression and exploration of local realities relevant to some originator's problem such that implicated members see a clear relation between their local realities and that problem (or a shared transformation if it). Once those relations are seen, as they were by those students leaders who attended both Sr. Claudia's evening February meeting of the council and the 'synthesizing' meeting (in that case between their own dissatisfactions with the council and Sr. Claudia's 'plan') then a problem-centered community may, or may not, emerge. If problems are not only mutually understood but also mutually induced, then that community will have become established.[3]

If communication is a necessary but not sufficient condition for emergent, problem-specific community-within-organization, what qualities of communicative attempts, of interchanges, are important? We have culled five components of communicativeness from the episodes (Table 28.1). First, do participants direct what is important to say about a given problem (or solution, plan, etc.) to persons or groups centrally, or only peripherally implicated? Relevant realities can be expressed to irrelevant parties, i.e., to non-constituents of the problem, a malfunction if non-constituents completely displace constituents as recipients of those realities.[4] Second, realities can be fully and authentically expressed and explored, or they can be withheld, obscured, or distorted. Third, we obscure problematic realities when we express only transformations of problems — e.g., solutions, plans — de-contextualized from their originating problems. Either of these kinds of obscuring invites local participants to construe their own local problems as the reason for the solution or plan, and to proceed, as Mr. Sullivan did on December 7 regarding the constitution, unwittingly to subvert the original problem-solving effort.

Talbe 28.1.   Synthesis: Five Major Variables Hypothesized to Account for the Effectiveness of Organizational Problem Solving

Component Variable	Major Variable (page reference in the narrative)

I.   INDIVIDUALS' ORIENTATIONS TO OTHERS' REALITIES

1. Problem synthesis by the problem originator: inclusive-cooperative vs. exclusionary-defensive (II:[a] 50, 53; III: 109–10, 166–67; IV: 248, 265, 340, 346).
2. Participants' orientations to emotionality and expression of conflict: expressive-confrontive-inclusive vs. suppressive-defensive-denying-exclusionary. (III: 127, 130, 133, 155, 187–88).
3. [b]Problem originator's and other protagonists' orientation to advice and complaints — i.e., to expressions of constituent realities not their own: open, ambivalent, closed (IV: 255, 259–60, 265, 269, 277, 283, 318–21).

II.   COMMUNICATIVENESS OF INTERACTIONS

1. Aim and level of intervention: centered; addressed to relevant persons and relevant positions (i.e., constituents) vs. off-center; addressed to non-constituent persons or positions. (II: 50, 53, 54; III: 109, 146; IV: 255, 256, 344).
2. Expression and exploration (vs. denial, withholding, obscuring) of relevant organizational realities. (II: 54, 59–60, 64–5; III: chapters 11 and 12 and pp. 109–10, 126, 149, 153–55, 177; IV: 285, 296, 310, 312, 325–26, 329–31, 336, 340–41, 341–45).
3. Expression and exploration of *relatively untransformed* (vs. only transformed) organizational realities. (II: 55, 64–5; III: 110, 135, 146, 164, 174; IV: chapter 26 and pp.).
4. Scope of unit's explicit formal or informal agenda: inclusion and communication (vs. exclusion and non-communication) of work related interpersonal problems. (III: IV:).
5. Contact: fleeting, single, and unplanned vs. extended, multiple, and planned. (II: 50, 54–5; III: 109–10, 117–18, 185; IV: chapters 20, 22 and 26 and pp. 256 ff, 272 ff, 291 ff, 304 ff, 324ff).

III.   RELATIONS AMONG CONSTITUENTS

1. inclusionary vs. exclusionary *relationships*: trust/congeniality vs. mistrust/antagonism. (III: 104–5, 112, 118, 147, 161, 171–72, 176, 183, 187; IV: chapter 20 and pp. 340–42, 346).
2. Mode of dividing labor: reliance on static categories and agreements vs. regular communication to review interdependent plans and effects. (II: 50; III: 129, 165, 167; IV: chapter 22).
3. [b]Formal and informal power/status relations among problem originator and other constituents — direction and magnitude of differences among protagonists, among antagonists, and between protagonists and antagonists. (II:[c] 59–60; III: 162, 186–87; IV: 249–50, 258, 259–60, 271, 286).
4. Between-constituent (between-person, -role, or -group) and between-level relationships/linkages: number, regularity, and communicativeness (vs. exclusionary defensiveness) of contacts. (II: 50; III: chapter 11 and pp. 112, 121, 156, 185, 187; IV: 248–49, 259, 281–82, 340–41, 342, 343).
5. Distribution among episodic participants of motivational investment in the focal problem: the invested vs. the uninvested and the rejecting — motivation-based relationships. (II: 50, 74; III: chapter 11 and pp. 121, 127, 133–35, 137–8, 164; IV: chapters 22, 24, and 25, and pp. 398, 340).

Talbe 28.1. (continued)

Component Variable	Major Variable (page reference in the narrative)

IV. SEQUENTIAL STRUCTURE AND FUNCTIONING OF PARTICIPATIONS

1. Linear vs. looped structure and functioning. (II: Part II and pp. 54–5, 64, 66, 68, 71–2; III: chapter 11 and pp. 118–19, 126, 130; IV: chapters 22 and 26 and pp. 247, 269, 272, 279 ff, 303, 323, 340).
2. Protagonists' action in the period of asymmetrical awareness: transformation of the problem toward action *before* antagonists first enter the problem-solving process — time, number of pre-antagonist contacts, amount of transformation accomplished toward implementation. (III: 104–5, 114; IV: chapters 19-25 and pp. 317, 329–30).
3. Mode of conflict management after first inclusion of antagonists: inclusionary vs. exclusionary. (II: 50; III: chapters 11 and 12 and pp. 118–19, 138, 153–4, 156–57, 183; IV: chapter 26, and pp. 247, 341–42, 346).
4. Strength of resources and mobilization to mitigate or reverse exclusion of constituent realities: (a) to what extent were exclusions of constituent realities expressly opposed or otherwise interrupted and (b) how successful was the opposition (or interruption) in securing integration of previously excluded constituent realities? (II: 64–5, 68; III: chapters 11 and 14; pp. 119, 126, 132, 164, 167, 171, 176; IV: 256 ff, 306 ff, 318 ff, 318, 321, 325, 336, 338).

V. THIRD-PARTY OPTIONS

1. Extent of third-party participation. (III: chapters 11–13, and pp. 104–5, 131–33, 133–35, 138, 162).
2. Third-party recruitment and legitimation: unilateral/partial vs. bilateral/full. (III: 104, 135, 139).
3. Third party's response to received legitmation: passive, acquiescing vs. actively testing and establishing legitimation. (III: chapter 12 and p. 168).
4. Third party role: mediation vs. arbitration. (III: 186, 187).
5. Extent of support and resources for arbitrator role: participants' sense of shared crisis and arbitrator's powers of surveillance and enforcement (III: chapters 14 and 15, and p. 215).

a. The first page references, following the first variable, II: 50, 53 refer to pages 50 and 53 in Part II of the book. Variables associated with entire chapters appear cumulatively across numerous acts and communications in the narrative, and are only partially captured in small segments of it indicated by page references. Variables found in one episode that also appeared to be of extremely limited generality or durability (e.g., the appearance of a particular reality distortion in a problem originator, as Sr. Claudia's construing of Hester as 'them' in Part II) were not included in this table.
b. These two variables were suggested by analysis of the third episode of Part IV.
c. Where appropriate, variables first noticed in analyzing later episodes (Parts III or IV) are retrospectively identified in passages where they appear in earlier episodes (Parts II or III).

Fourth, it is important whether the content of communication can include, or must exclude, realities regarding working relationships. Work in any organization always involves working with others, which implies communication. Can problems of communication themselves be included in communications, or are they ruled out by implicit taboos or fears? It is the question whether the scope of a group's agenda includes its own problem-solving and communicating difficulties, problems in their own right. Finally, how frequently, how long in each instance, and how planfully do episodic participants have contact? Short, few, and unplanned contacts, even between friendly parties disposed to be fully open to each others' realities, are insufficient to accommodate expressions and explorations of an important range of realities. The most important problems are often those requiring the most emotional work, the most time to express and explore. An office, committee or department whose formal or informal meetings cannot last more than a half hour every two weeks may easily be *ipso facto* closed off from organizational realities that seriously threaten its functioning. This question takes on special force regarding contacts between a problem's protagonists and antagonists.

III. Quality of Relations Among Constituents

At the time an organizational problem first is synthesized by an originator, a set of relations has already been built up between the originator and constituents, among the constituents, and among the organizational units — committees, departments, administrative teams, councils, etc. — of which constituents are members. These relations facilitate or impede the communication of problems, solutions, and plans; they facilitate or impede, therefore, collaborative, cumulative action. They constitute the network structure through which transformations of that problem must take place. If the problem constituents are lay teachers, religious teachers, students, and executives, then communication related to the problem must go on such that the constituent realities local to these four groups become integrated into action on the problem in question. Since realities of problems, commitments, and priorities are always in important degrees local, communication *by* these parties *to* these parties, directly or indirectly, must take place for successful integration of organizational realities. But interactions between, say, lay teachers and executives are stamped indelibly with the *relation* between them that obtains with respect to the problem at the time the originator's problem is synthesized. A working relation, like the one between Sr. Jeanine and Sr. Georgette, promotes fluid exchange of realities and reciprocal influence. A mistrustful relation, as between Sr. Claudia and Sr. Norma regarding accountability, or between Sr. Claudia and the wider student body regarding the plan of governance, promotes the withholding and distorting of organizational realities. Ambivalent and stranger relations, too, put their limits on the fullness and authenticity of communication that can go on between the parties so related.

Participants who rely heavily on static categories and agreements regarding what they may legitimately care about and collaborate on — categories of 'areas', 'columns', or bailiwicks of authority — are parties trusting categories, agreements, *and stability of local realities* more than a working relation with their co-workers. They are parties whose strict maintenance of boundaries denies their interdependence with those in other bailiwicks. The mode of dividing up labor used by the Trinity executives — conceived as legitimate also by Sr. Jeanine — reflects a working relation that jointly supported barriers to communication. The distribution of power-dependence and status among constituents reflects a certain kind of relationship among them, as does the number, regularity, and communicativeness of their interactions over the course of an episode (quite beyond the qualities of interaction characterizing participants at the episode's outset). And the distribution of motivational investment of participants over the course of the episode also is an index of their relations with each other with respect to that focal problem or its transformations. Motivational investment is generally visible to participants themselves at each point in the unfolding process — e.g., enthusiasm of the synthesizing group, apathy of certain faculty, continued involvement of Sr. Claudia in council development as compared, for example, with members of the lay faculty. It tells the analyst where the energy is and is not, and implies a relation (not necessarily conscious) among the invested, among the non-invested, and between them.

IV. Sequential Structure and Functioning of Participation

In adaptations it is not only what people do in an adaptation, but when, that counts. Four component variables specify sequential, cumulative, and reversing aspects of any adaptation. First, as we saw in the first constitution episode, a predominantly linear structure of participations, one with few or non-correcting loops, can easily lead to a mere succession of local reactions to local realities, without integration of them and without cumulative action. The structure that involves early participants only early, middle participants only in the middle of the episode, and late participants only late promotes the whispering parlor game effect, where each successive participant re-contextualizes earlier information in terms of merely local frames of reference and commitments, each setting a new direction with its new content. Loops in the sequential structure are important: later participants who also participated early can represent those early realities in the later process, thus correcting any linear obscuring or distortion of earlier realities. But if such loops exist in an episode's sequential structure, how corrective were they actually? Sr. Norma, the originator of the idea of a constitution as a way of holdng the Trinity council to an advisory function, never introduced that purpose in her later council discussion of Mr. Sullivan's quite opposed conception of a constitution. The council, and Sullivan, were thus kept in the dark about those opposed conceptions of the functions of a constitution. It is a familiar division of labor to induce such linear structures by separating 'planners' from 'implementers', where few or only weak interactions occur between the two, leading to subversion of continuity and the triumph of the local — the local, like Miss Nolan's, that happens to participate last.

The second component brings the sequential participation of protagonists into relation to that of antagonists: how much transformation of a problem has been accomplished before any antagonist enters the problem-solving process? This is an expansion of the question of asymmetrical awareness and the unilateral action of the first-aware party to protagonists and antagonists in general. The lay faculty's realities were in important regards antagonistic to Sr. Claudia's concept of governance, which included particularly their opposition to multilateral discussions of questions of salary and work assignments. Entering only later in the process of problem-solving, only during the phase of implementation, they had only limited options for integrating their different realities. Earlier participation would have allowed fuller confrontation of the issues of bilateral vs. multilateral communication and agreements and of school administration vs. representative governance.

The third component variable raises the more general question of the mode of conflict management throughout the episode, whether it was primarily inclusive or primarily exclusionary. Even beyond the period of asymmetric awareness or of the first exclusion of antagonists from the process (whether intended or not), over what segments of the process after antagonists were *first* included were they *subsequently* included? Further, to what extent did 'inclusion' of antagonists inform them of relevant details known by protagonists?

Finally, an important component in sequence is the strength of the episode's resources for mitigating or reversing exclusion of constituent realities — the potency of antagonists and their recruits to break through the prevailing exclusionary protagonist outlook and to inject it with heretofore excluded organizational realities. One looks for the number and strength of the Lois Chapmans, who call for 'going public' before the plan is finished; for Leo Phelans who persist and gradually recruit support for minority participation; for the intervention of superordinates like Sr. Jeanine and Sr. Georgette, who are able to arrange more fully exploring considerations of opposed realities; for junior class promoters of senior class officers, who persist in articulating realities rejected by protagonists until they get a full confrontation of the issue by all concerned — irrespective of the outcome. If exclusions in any process are normal, and I think they are, the capacity of a problem-solving effort to reverse them, to bring inclusion by secondary and tertiary routes, will determine its reality-integrating strength.[5] To stumble in one's infancy is no tragedy, so long as one learns to walk. But one dare not delay appropriate growth too long. The longer a constituent reality is excluded, it seems, the tougher it is to reverse the exclusion in a way that effectively integrates that reality.

V. Third-Party Options

Protagonists and antagonists always have the possibility of obtaining help from third parties. The component variables are those already discussed in reference to Table 17.1. It remains only to say that some form of crisis needs to be reached by a protagonist before giving up control over problem-solving. That is, the originator and other protagonists must, in their own estimates, no longer be able by themselves to solve the problem to the point where they are ready to relinquish substantial measures of control to others, who may extract concessions from both protagonists and antagonists. A sense of crisis, thus, is the fulcral condition and, as the second component variable specifies, it is important whether that crisis is sensed only by the protagonists or is shared also by antagonists. From there, questions ensue about active third-party efforts to spread legitimacy, choices between mediation and arbitration, and resources to support any arbitrated settlements, questions dealt with in Chapter 17.

Relative Importance

Which of the major variables are most important? Important for what purpose? If we are empirical researchers perhaps we want to lay our hands on those few major variables that promise to explain most (variability in) problem-solving effectiveness. In that case, we eliminate what seem to be the most restricted variables until we have a few left, being necessarily the most comprehensive, or least limited. So, set aside as rather too specialized and crisis oriented the third-party choices, variable V. That variable promises to be very useful but only when third parties are recruited. Then set aside variable II, communicativeness of interactions, on the grounds that any given interaction, as effective or ineffective as it may be, can be reversed by interactions that come later. Interactions are brief and unstable — too limited in the time dimension. That leaves us with three major variables, orientations to others' realities, relations among constituents, and sequential structure and functioning of participations.

Individuals' orientations to others' realities brings into focus *psychological* functioning. On that ground it might be dismissed as subordinate to structural factors at a higher level of social complexity, e.g., relations among constituents. But under conditions of change and uncertainty, precisely the conditions of disturbances and problems, the systematic impact of structure is likely to be mitigated if not vitiated by the needs of individuals to look after their own personal adaptive niche and to fashion locally fitting adaptations. How participants in an episode take in or reject each others' realities, therefore, should account for a good measure of their success or failure in releasing from each other the motivational and intellectual resources necessary to solve their problems effectively. It is a psychological variable, but it operates in the aggregate, across participants, and involves a judgment about how much exchange of problems or reciprocal openness to the causes behind complaints or emotionality is evident across an episode's problem-solving process. Are participants generally responsive to unexpected complaints or emotionality regarding organizational functioning, generally ambivalent, or generally unresponsive? Or is there a clear pattern, like protagonists having one orientation and antagonists having the opposite? This dimension of collective psychology probably has a strong impact on problem-solving effectiveness. Indeed, I dare say that with relatively little sampling of episodes across roles and levels, knowing participants' aggregate orientations in the three ways specified by the three component variables might tell us a great deal about the whole organization's ethos regarding individuality vs. reciprocity and mutuality and might account for a good deal of variance in the effectiveness of the organization as a whole.

As to the relations among constituents, being relatively more stable than interactions and yet impinging on communicativeness, they promise more durable explanation of problem-solving effectiveness than the second major variable. Relations in networks of linkages are also fewer than interactions, so provide more focus and more possibilities for seeing big patterns. Further, relations among constituents (i.e., relations with respect to problematic content) tell us where power concentrations and differences lie, and so indicate whose realities are likely to be sought and heard, and whose not. Finally, relations as here conceived in terms of five component variables are also defined at the motivational level. Relations among constituents (and among groups of which constituents are members) tell us who is, and who is not, likely to be invested in the problem and its solutions. Knowing relations among constituents and implicated structures in these several dimensions, therefore, puts one in possession of substantial explanatory power *provided* one is trying to explain short-term influence and brief adaptation — like Sr. Claudia's in the second constitution episode.

If one is trying to account for adaptational effectiveness that goes beyond and is not dependent on the personal qualities of the problem originator, however, then not immediate influence in an episode but participants' collective capacity to integrate diverse organizational realities is at issue. And that brings us to the third of the three variables I think are most powerful, the sequential structure and functioning of participations. Knowing the sequential structure of participations adds an inclusionary-exclusionary dynamic to one's knowledge: the presence or absence of functioning (or non-functioning) loops, the tendency across the episode's action to focus on problems or, in contrast, on solutions, the general inclusionary or exclusionary character of the way protagonists and antagonists address each other, and the resources available for corrective infusion of excluded organizational realities. If I had to choose among these three major variables (I, III and IV) to account for adaptational effectiveness, I'd put my bets on I, aggregate psychological orientations, and IV, the sequential structure and functioning of participations.

Are any of these variables new? Communicative interactions and relations (II and III) are classic variables. The first is old in its emphasis on openness and 'empathy' but offers a focus on emotionality and on a new concept of 'problem'. Inclusion of third-party options takes an old concept, third-party facilitator, and brings it into the organization's hierarchy in a way that allows for asymmetry in legitimation and choice among three options: coalition, arbitration, and mediation. The fourth major variable, structure and functioning of sequential participations, is new. It brings into view a new kind of structure — the *structure of sequence*. It brings into view behaviors which establish certain decisions, policies, or solutions *and subsequent behaviors which undo* those decisions, policies, or solutions. It brings into view pressures to undo and resistances to undoing. In short, the fourth major variable allows us to focus on degrees and kinds of cumulativity and reversibility by which we can examine the forces that support and undermine the stability or robustness of decisions, policies, and solutions. It raises, as the timeless structural variable does not, issues of redundancy, correction, recovery, and subversion and reminds us in a tangible way, by virtue of being an explicit variable, that organizational life is as much change as it is stability, that every stability came into being through a process of cumulative change that resisted reversal. We need to study the supports for cumulativity, reversal, and resistance to reversal. It is only with such variables as the fourth major variable, not through variables like structures, that we capture and begin to comprehend the dynamics of stability and change.

Time Frame and Reversibility in Organizational Action

The very reversibility that is so evident in problem-solving episodes, however, poses an important methodological and theoretical issue. Part III presented in some detail the history and analysis of a single, abortive problem-solving episode. It has certain whole-like qualities that recommend it as an entity. People become involved in an action and drop out, one by one, leaving none but the initiator of the action who still wants the matter settled. We could have ended our data gathering there and chalked up one wasteful organized action. But in Part III another episode of a rather different kind of problem, an interpersonal conflict overlapping chronologically with the first problem, shows how one factor (the limit of Sr. Claudia's legitimate authority) contributing to the ineffectiveness of the problem-solving in Part II was changed; and in Part IV the problem ineffectively solved in Part II becomes, in a subsequent time period, assimilated into a larger set of changes and, in that context, becomes solved much more effectively. That is, with the expansion of time frame, an unmitigated failure becomes mitigated, reversed in a number of dimensions.

Yet the story unfolds further. In a still more extended time frame of four years, the solution successfully found in one year and effectively implemented the next year becomes largely dismantled, reverting to conditions prior to the first year. Thus, a half year's failure was reversed by a solution in the second half of the year and an implementation of that solution the following year. That reversal, in turn, was itself reversed.

Depending on which time frame we might have chosen we would have revealed very different phenomena. Or to put the matter another way, the interpretation of the phenomena in the period t to t + 1 is substantially altered by the addition of data in the period from t + 1 to t + 2. A phenomenon of one kind turns, with new information, into a phenomenon of a different kind. Then further, the interpretation of events from t to t + 2 is substantially, or even radically, altered by gathering data in a following period, t + 2 to t + 3. Any generalization about data from the one time frame is seriously altered by data from an expanded time frame. The time frame of an apparent phenomenon itself provides a seriously limited basis for interpreting that phenomenon. More time is needed. But how much more? Can we achieve any stability in our characterizations of events without going beyond their own duration in gathering data? Can we achieve stability of generalization even with such expanded time frames?

I try to show, through the narrative data, that the problem of time frame is solvable, at least in part, by using the *cultural categories of the actors being studied* rather than the categories forced by the investigator's own sub-culture of formal theory and discipline, i.e., by integrating the participants' culture regarding time frames into a study's design. The cultural unit in case of Trinity is the school year. It was around the school year that Sr. Claudia, Sr. Norma, and the Trinity council planned. To account for these participants' actions, data should be gathered in the specific sub-cultural categories and units of time that dominate these participants' own thinking. The study of local adaptation in schools would be the study of problem-solving episodes, therefore, within the time frames of school years. Similarly, the study of local adaptation in a manufacturing concern would focus on problem-solving episodes in the context of the fiscal quarter or year. In neither case would a three- or six-week study be appropriate because the action of those being studied would be guided by larger time units, units that would allow end-of-quarter or year-end reversals of decisions, policies, or solutions arrived at in those three- or six-week periods. Finally, the minimal test of the stability of a given adaptation in a setting whose major time unit was the school year would be two years — the first within which the adaptation takes place and the second to see if it were robust enough to be carried into the succeeding unit of time. In the present case, we see Sr. Claudia's adaptation of governance robust enough to survive and be implemented for one year, but to come apart at the boundary of another cultural unit: directorship — the duration under a particular leader's leadership.

With a change in leader, however, often come changes in problems; and with changed problems, changes in solutions. Stable solutions for one leader will be stable for the next only to the extent that the two have similar skills, have similar conceptions of the stage of development and needs of the organization, and in general that they have synthesized similar realities with respect to themselves and the organization.

Notes

1. In terms of Emerson's (1962) four basic modes of power equalization, Sr. Claudia addressed Sr. Norma's intransigence by Emerson's operation number four, forming a coalition with the regional administrators. When she did not prevail against Sr. Norma's further withdrawal, Sr. Claudia employed Emerson's first operation, a shift in her own expectations to 'zilch'. Sr. Norma, in the first instance, was employing Emerson's first operation, withdrawal of motivational investment in goals mediated by the religious order, and then also in goals mediated by Sr. Claudia.
2. The fifteenth variable of Table 17.1, Extent of mutual induction of problems and constituent realities by protagonists and antagonists, was deleted in this final culling because it seemed too global to be useful, a description not of an 'independent' variable so much as a dependent, criterion variable.
3. Alternatively, such an action community may emerge around only a specific combination of problem plus person, where the problem's importance depends on the originator's personal qualities. An example of perhaps the weakest form of such an action community was Miss Nolan's and Joan Noonan's attempt to follow Mr. Sullivan, who seemed to Miss Nolan at the time to know what he was talking about but where Miss Nolan ended feeling 'duped'. A much stronger form, of course, is the action community Sr. Claudia generated in the third episode.
4. James Coleman (1987, pp. 182–188) provides good examples of the benefits of communicating with antagonists directly only after communicating with both non-constituents and co-protagonists, the latter communications promoting what Coleman calls 'functional community' in the context of conflict management.
5. My emphasis on communication and the inclusion and integration of local realities is not to be confused with some global commitment on my part to organizational 'democracy' or egalitarian organizational politics or consensus. I agree, for example, with much of Gomberg's (1970) criticisms of the Harwood experiment reported by Coch and French (1948), reinterpreting 'participation' in decision making as 'manipulation' and co-optation. Integration of Sr. Norma's commitment to the *status quo* regarding her position at Trinity, or of Sr. Claudia's commitment to be freed from dependency on Sr. Norma was accomplished by a decision from above. But it was weakened not by Sr. Norma's non-participation — she did participate — but by

the exclusion of her salient realities, among others, from the decision. Participation does not guarantee reality integration. In the case of co-optation, participation is often a way of pre-empting reality integration (see Lighthall, 1989, for perspectives on participation).

Part V
Conclusion

Chapter 29

Contributions to Data, Theory, Method, and Practice

This book has focused on people in an organization trying to get things done together. It presents as its window the problem-solving episode, a unitizing of data capturing local adaptation. The unit has its roots in a commitment to understanding those thousands of monthly (weekly?) adjustments organizations make to their internal and external environments. The episode provides a focus on action that moves from felt difficulty to organizational change. Three exemplars were narrated and examined with respect to factors affecting how participants succeed or fail in integrating organizational realities into their collective action. Five major variables, each consisting of specific contributing variables, were extracted from the three episodes. The project as a whole seeks to contribute in four ways to examined knowledge: data, theory, method, and practice.

Data

The most important contribution of this book, perhaps, are its three episodes of problem-solving. I believe they are the first narratives of organizational problem-solving that trace problems from their origins, psychologically, through solution implementation. They capture sequence, cumulativity, the truncation or abortion of cumulative coherence, and reversals. Quite aside from my own theoretical orientations, they can be read and used by others from other theoretical perspectives for what they reveal about sequence, cumulativity, and complex interactions.

The second way that these episodes contribute is as data about the person, their single originator, Sr. Claudia. We get a glimpse of one administrative personality in the context of serious, consequential organizational problem solving. While the book focuses on organizational processes primarily, because its three problems all originate as Sr. Claudia's problems, we are given a window into on person's cognitive, emotional, and social functioning as she synthesizes and solves her problems. We see her response to emotionality, her preparedness, her commitment to the principle of shared power and her ambivalence about, and conditions placed upon, allowing others to influence the shape and direction of solutions. But if we see the person, Sr. Claudia, we see her in this particular year of troubles — with a colleague who absented herself at a time when Sr. Claudia had to cope with the terminal course of her mother's cancer and then the fashioning of a new school governance. The person, whole, came into view only in interaction with these special conditions. Yet it was clearly Sr. Claudia's personal commitments and vision that led to the representative council structure. The narratives, then, constitute the first contribution of this book to social and organizational psychology and to social science more generally.

Theory

The concepts, orientations, analyses, and variables of this study make a number of contributions to a theory of organized, adaptive action.

1. Organizational Adaptation

Organizational adaptation is active because organizational reality is active. When individuals or groups adapt they do not merely fit into an environment. They create new environments, both inwardly and outwardly. Individuals do not just take in reality. They synthesize perceptions with the reality they have already composed and tested, including their very subjective fears and hopes, thereby creating modified realities day by day, week by week. Adaptation with respect to an organization or its units refers to reciprocal, multilateral accommodations among those parts whose stable functioning is construed by some member(s) to be threatened or disrupted by a sensed condition. These accommodations either maintain a direction or pattern of functioning or adopt a new, more valued, less wasteful or disruptive pattern or direction. The Blessed Sisters of Trinity forged an adaptation when they reconstituted their whole pattern of governance and decision making in keeping with Vatican II and with the accumulated changes in society and church that brought about Vatican II.

While it is useful to have a general conception of adaptation (singular, in the abstract), events and processes at that level are so complex as to be literally unmanaged: they happen, growing out of multiple intentions and smaller adaptations (plural and concrete).[1] To study an organization's generalized adaptation is to study its history. To study an organization's adaptations, plural and concrete, is to study a chain of unfolding transformations of an organizational problem in the context of purposes and reasons (explained and attributed) and of perceptions of surrounding conditions. The problem-solving episode is one of conceivably many units with definable beginning and end points, though I think so far the only such unit, by which one can capture and analyze concrete, intentional organizational adaptations. Specific, concrete attempts to forge adaptations can result, as we see in the first constitution episode, in almost complete failure, judged on the five criteria employed in this study.

2. Criteria of Effectiveness

The conceptual tangles in the literature on organizational effectiveness are legion (Cameron and Whetten, 1983). The five criteria employed in the present study were criteria, not of organizational effectiveness, however, but of problem-solving effectiveness, a far more restricted focus. They constitute a contribution in the spirit recommended by Goodman, Atkin, and Schoorman (1983), to forego global studies in favor of 'microstudies', but they also retain the possibility of usefulness across episodes and organizations.[2] The first two criteria, involving satisfaction of participants, have been widely used. Investigators have also differentiated among participants, using satisfaction of the most powerful group as the criterion of effectiveness, for example — a criterion that would be supported only in the short run by the results of the second constitutional episode. Distinguishing between the problem originator's satisfaction and other participants' satisfaction is one way of capturing the differences between protagonists and antagonists, a distinction ignored in the literature on over-all organizational effectiveness. The remaining three criteria address the episode's mobilized capacity to effect observable change in conditions (judged problematic by the originator and protagonists), to effect change in constituents' operating realities (their confusion or cross-purposes leading to wasted resources), and increase or maintain resources available to the organization. Each of these criteria is independently assessable, allowing mixed kinds of effectiveness. Further, analysis at individual, dyadic, and group levels is possible for each of the criteria, capturing more of the actual complexity of outcomes. While differentiated, these criteria are sufficiently contentless to be generalizable across different kinds of organizations.

3. 'Existential' Reality vs. Operating Realities

The book attempts to focus attention on the social psychological sources and directions of energy in an organization. One of its contributions is a seating of realities and problems in the domain of ongoing psychological functioning rather than in the objective world of the organization 'out there'. It contributes to the field of work generally known as 'symbolic interactionism' in two ways. First, it presents and uses analytically a distinction between 'existential' reality and operating reality, between the single reality of 'the' world or universe 'out there', on the one hand, and multiple, *synthesized* realities on the other, realities to which humans actually respond, which command their resources. These are realities construed, created, constructed, realities 'in here', including not only *assessments* of reality 'out there', but also *expectations* about that reality; including not only *memories* of events 'out there', but also *hopes for* events to come; including not only *predictions* about the world, but also *fears and doubts* about the world and about oneself. Illustrated in use, in sum, is a distinction between a single reality that can be argued or proved to *exist* and multiple realities created locally by each person which instigate and guide *response*.

An organization's buildings, machines, furniture, book value, and cash reserves, in this perspective, constitute mere artifacts, by-products of its core functioning. The core of an organization's energies and direction lies at any given time in its adapting, interdependent members — in their collective, cumulative minding: their motivation, intelligence, judgment, values, and goals. The only reality *accessible* to an organization is through its members' mindings, the realities to which they actually are responding. The only energizing goals are those to which its members are actually committed, not those written down in by-laws or speeches. Members' mindings with respect to any given matter are varied, not uniform. And the variability is related to each member's adaptation to her or his construed circumstance.

Reality is too gross an abstraction for analytical purposes except to refer to the sum total of an organization's or sub-unit's realities with respect to some matter. An organization's *accessible realities regarding any given matter* are plural and diffused across the organization's levels, roles, and members. The daily challenge to any organization's central mission or purpose is to *integrate* its diverse, local realities into collective action while at the same time preserving both its division of labor and its separately adapting persons.

The second contribution to symbolic interactionist scholarship is to rescue Mead's and Dewey's conceptions of *adaptation* from the oblivion suffered so far in symbolic interactionist studies. Goffman (1959, 1967), for example, took from Mead (1938) the concepts of role and generalized other and created an almost full-blown dramaturgical perspective in sociology. But he ignored Mead's *act* (Mead, 1938), at the center of which lies a concept of adaptation owing much to Darwin. And symbolic interactionists have been deafeningly silent on Dewey's (1938) conceptions of inquiry and problem. I bring problem and act together, parallel to stimulus and response. An organizational problem is synthesized as a condition of operating reality, of mental conflict; an act responds to that condition and brings the actor into social engagement in an unfolding context of individual and interdependent adaptation in the organization.

The individualistic localism of operating realities is suggested not by the symbolic interactionist tradition but from the earlier writings of William James (1890) and from a different stream of thought altogether, of which Martin Buber (1965) and Mikail Bakhtin (1981; Gunn, 1979; Holquist, 1986) are the central figures — particularly Buber, with his concepts of distance and relation and of the 'elemental otherness of the other'. These diverse streams of thought become integrated in conceptions of multiple realities, problem, organizational problem, and problem-solving episode.

4. Problem, Organizational Problem, and Episode

Part of the book's attempt to focus organizational behavior psychologically is to synthesize the conceptual work of Mead (1938) and Dewey (1938) with Festinger's (1957) concept of 'dissonance', thus introducing two new units by which to analyze organizational functioning: a psychological unit, the problem, initiating and contained within a social psychological unit, the problem-solving episode. Part of this contribution has been to elaborate the distinction between 'problem' as it was conceptualized by virtually all cognitive and educational psychologists, on the one hand, and the emergent, psychologically functional concept parts of which Dewey, Mead, and Festinger each described. Another part of the book's contribution has been the attempt to seat this adaptational concept of problem within a larger context of minding, a context not so concerned with cognitive processes, which occupy so much of current psychological research, as with cognitive contents. While 'operating realities' can theoretically be infinitely varied in content, and while *kinds* of content are relatively limited, one *form or pattern* of contents appears as energizing, directing, and universal: the opposition between two contents of operating reality, each of which is invested in commitment, a problem.

   This synthetic, content-specific but form-general element of operating reality has great analytical advantages over the analytical units more familiar to cognitive and social psychologists. Understanding people's attempts to get things done with others in organizations — and very often in initial or continuing opposition to others — is not well served by examining their actions through the atomized units so widespread in experimental social psychology — attributions, attitudes, instances of obedience or conformity, and the like — or through short-term Goffmanian 'encounters' or Skinnerian behavioral 'repertoires'. Adaptation, a cumulative process, involves all of these relatively small categories of behavior and is not visible through any one of them. The adaptational conception of problem is more suited, having an opposition of contents and a tendency toward resolution within it. But 'problem', left unqualified, has no necessary connection to an organization; this book focuses on organizational problems: where at least one of the incompatible elements of a person's operating reality is identified by a participant as a condition in the organization beyond that person's own powers to change, where he or she is dependent on others' acquiescence or cooperation.

Yet even the concept of 'organizational problem' is insufficient to encompass adaptive action within an organization. Such adaptation implies interaction among interdependent parties, each with their own realities and adaptational agendas. The unit of analysis that captured the struggles of multiple parties, at various levels and in various roles, to solve any given organizational problem is the problem-solving episode.

Problems — those confusion-reducing, energy-mobilizing and action-directing oppositions of minding — are usefully conceived as the starting point of adaptive organizational action. Problems are unique in their capacity to capture simultaneously both (1) a person's values and (2) the person's perceptions and construings of his or her world, while at the same time (3) being flexibly able to capture *any* two opposed commitments: e.g., two opposed emotions, an emotion and a value, two opposed perceptions. But no matter how flexible 'problem' is with respect to content, it always captures those centers of motivation we call commitments or investments. In this view, unless an aspect of the organization becomes synthesized in this form, or some transformation of it like solution or plan, that aspect is not responded to, does not enter the stream of organizational action. For the organization or its members, that aspect simply does not exist. A problem operating in some member, thus, is the necessary but far from sufficient condition for any aspect of an organization to be allocated any resource for change. For such sufficiency, a problem must come to be shared by its *constituents*.

5. Dispersed, Differentiated, Local Realities

Problems of any consequence to a person involve elements of that person's commitments. Since our commitments tend, even within organizations, to be personal and to have idiosyncratic roots, meanings, and intensities, our organizational problems tend also to reflect those personal and idiosyncratic qualities, to be stamped with our localism. A second source of localism in organizational problems is our special organizational role and position. Supervisors not only 'see things' differently from workers and higher management, they also want and fear things differently. Since every role in every organization is established and maintained with respect to its limited set of functions, its specialized contribution to the whole organization (e.g., for students in school it is studying and learning), each role carries with it, as Berger and Luckmann (1967, pp. 138–139) have well illustrated, its own family of perceptions, norms, and role-specific problems. These, as well as each person's own personal problems of living, command each person's resources.

That first source of localism, the person's sense of self, self adequacy, and identity, will ordinarily set limits on energies and attention devoted to any problem arising out of immediate organizational work, as they did with Sr. Norma. Personal problems may pre-empt resources typically devoted to organizational work. To Berger and Luckmann's secondary socialization into a role and primary socialization by the family we must add the individual's unique realities, which are often all the more demanding because their uniqueness, or perceived uniqueness, blocks them from expression to others. Am I getting what I uniquely deserve from this organization? Sr. Norma felt she had gotten a raw deal; Sr. Claudia felt betrayed by the failure of the regional administrators to appoint her as Acting Director, as they had indicated; Miss Nolan felt duped by Sullivan. The realities that actually occupy one in an organization, then, are local and often uniquely personal even when they do refer to effects the organization is having on one.

'Local and often uniquely personal' implies substantial *autonomous* preoccupation in a *logically interdependent* set of work relations. Members' *logically functional* interdependence with respect to the overarching purpose of the organization must not be confused with members' social *psychological* interdependence. Persons who occupy interdependent roles seek adaptations consonant not merely with organizational purposes, but also, and with more focal force, consonant with their own persons and lives. At the level of concrete organizational adaptations, the combination of local realities of organizational situation, autonomous problems of person, and interdependent functions of role creates an ineluctable tension: the local and unique have their demands, with their own answering routines and mobilizings of energy, but the superordinate organization of roles, norms, and obligations has its demands too — and often sufficient energy and other resources are lacking to do them both justice. In a pinch, the local, situational, and personal wins at the level of behavior — a particular bias in the satisficing that Simon (1979) describes. And if the local tends to win, so much the worse for organizational solidarity and effectiveness.

6. *Local Solidarity*

Because organizational problems usually involve different roles and levels of authority, problem-solving action implicates cross-role and cross-level solidarity and alienation. The degree of solidarity depends on the degree of cross-role and cross-level integration of realities and, specifically, problems. The study of organizational problem-solving becomes, willy nilly, the study of emergent, problem- related, organizational solidarity among participants. The most important solidarity one can achieve, movtivationally, social psychologically, and adaptively, is with the constituents of one's most important problems, those on whose cooperation one depends to help solve those important problems. Solidarity with others comes from common, supportive attempts to forge important adaptations. Solidarity with others is promoted when one's own problems are synthesized by, or induced in, others, thus bringing them into possession of some of one's own important realities. From a motivational and social psychological viewpoint, *problems are the chief if not sole vehicle for solidarity of intentional effort*. Sr. Claudia worries about the students' accepting an advisory role for the Trinity council. When she succeeds in inducing in most of them her problem of a council making decisions beyond its power to enforce them, she transcends their localism and builds solidarity of effort between them and herself: now her problem is theirs. But when she offers Sr. Norma a solution without also expressing and inducing in Sr. Norma her problem, Sr. Norma resists. Again, when Sr. Claudia does not explore students' expressions of problems — their attempts to add a sweater to the uniform or their complaints about student faculty relations — she forgoes solidarity with them in their struggle.

But solidarity of any duration is a two-way street. One can synthesize others' problems as one's own for just so long before one expects reciprocation and, failing to obtain it, diminishes support for (and soldidarity with) the other. The roles and positions of any organization are locally interdependent by virtue of its logical division of labor — a means-ends logic guided and made coherent by the overall purpose of the organization. Thus, normal commerce between roles or levels is based on logical interdependence between them. That interdependence is honored and promoted when members performing different functions address each others' organizational problems. It is denied and undermined when such parties ignore each others' organizational problems for very long. When one shares one's organizational problem with other members, one acknowledges, and shares, one's dependency regarding this problem. Since dependency is the obverse of power, by sharing with others one's problems and thus one's dependency in some matter, one affirms the others' power in that matter.

7. Constituent Realities and Influential Realities

Are all local realities equally important to the effectiveness of an adaptation? Is there no hierarchy of relevance or of status or of power that limits the number of member realities necessary to integrate into organizational action? As we see in the second constitution episode, where Sr. Claudia was in many ways recurrently dominant, power is not perfectly correlated with the integration of realities into concerted action. *Dominant power can be, and often is, the very condition to block the integration of constituent realities*. Local adaptations have a limited set of purposes, arising out of concrete maladaptations, or threats of maladaptation, sufficient to mobilize a defense. The specificity of each occasion for an adaptation, along with the specificity of functions divided among roles in an organization, set limits on who, in any given problem, would be affected by, or whose cooperation would be required to implement, a solution and whose local realities, therefore, are required to be integrated into any effective solution. These are the *constituent realities of a problem*. In each specific adaptation, therefore, the realities of only a specific set of roles or persons are implicated.

8. *Problems vs. Solutions and Plans*

Problems stir new vigilance, new awarenesses, new action. Solutions and plans, in contrast, do not originate new vigilance, awareness, or action. They *are* new in each case, but they do not originate newness, innovation, adaptation. Rather, they embody settled issues; they relieve tension; they guide action originating in problems; they become precedents and routines, even traditions. Solutions and plans, as transformations of problems, can easily become progressively remote from their originating problems. In the course of organizational problem-solving, a strong collective tendency is to focus attention and communication on only the current transformational state of the problem, progressively displacing earlier origins and trans- formations, dealing with ever more subordinate problems of planning and implementation. This tendency to move away from problem to solution, away from solution to plan, and away from plan to implementation, reversible but nonetheless strong, moves participants in episodes away from the psychological conditions necessary for *a cumulative and integra- tive* mobilization of participants' energies, attention, thought, and imagin- ation. Our resources are allocated by us to our problems, not to other people's or to an organization's solutions — unless we see others' solutions as solutions to our own problems as well.

For Sr. Claudia to promote an adaptation with respect to Sr. Norma's absences, Sr. Norma's cooperative action is implicated and so too, there- fore, is her operating reality regarding Sr. Claudia's communications to her. Since Sr. Norma's action will be responsive to Sr. Norma's problems and to Sr. Norma's solutions in Sr. Norma's priorities, it is Sr. Norma's reality into which must be induced Sr. Claudia's *problem*, not her solution, if Sr. Claudia is to secure Sr. Norma's cooperative action on Sr. Claudia's problem. Sr. Claudia's brief communication with Sr. Norma, however, evidently put more emphasis on Sr. Claudia's solution than on her problem, a solution that in no way fitted any problem operating in Sr. Norma. Sr. Claudia communicated her *transformation* of her problem more vividly and completely, evidently, than her problem itself. A defensive reaction resulted, as it must if the recipient is to attend to her own adaptations.

It is at just this point that the problem-solving theory proposed here departs markedly from most administrative practice and a good deal of theory. It follows that if Sr. Claudia wants Sr. Norma to work on Sr. Claudia's problem, she must induce *her problem* in Sr. Norma. Does it not also follow, therefore, that if she wants Sr. Norma to work on her solution, she must induce in Sr. Norma *her solution*? No, it does not also follow — not according to the ideas of Dewey, Mead, Festinger, and Buber that I am drawing on, nor on empirical observations like those reported in this book. Attempting to induce solutions in another party secures their cooperation only when the solutions in question promise to solve problems *already operating* in the other party, either the originator's identical problem or complementary ones. Thus, if one of Sr. Norma's problems were a commitment to find more time away from Trinity for herself, on the one hand, and feeling obligated but reluctant to spend time at Trinity in her job, on the other hand, Sr. Claudia's offer to find a substitute would solve Sr. Norma's problem. But among Sr. Norma's commitments was public fulfillment of her year as co-director, without change in status. Sr. Claudia's solution did not fit any of Sr. Norma's problems.

The fact that people often do cooperate in offered solutions is commonly mistaken as support for the assumption that simple induction of solutions is straightforwardly possible. Under that mistaken assumption, it appears only efficient to describe in detail to others one's solutions and plans, and as only inefficient to go into the 'background' of problematic origins. But the theory of adaptation proposed here would argue that problems are not background, psychologically. Problems are foreground and pre-emptive. They are the origins of energy for action, and they determine when action will shift from one direction to another. In this view, the most efficient thing one can do in securing others' committed cooperation is to *avoid* solutions or plans until after one's problem has been induced in those whose cooperation is desired. Such problem induction is the most direct result — never the guaranteed result — of communicating in descriptive detail, by narrative, the events one has experienced which prompted the problem. By focusing on one's problem, in the first-person singular, one takes the most direct route to mobilizing the other's energies because such a focus establishes an environment in which the other can also express his or her problems and can, in any event, reveal his or her reality with respect to one's own problem. One works on others' proposals, solutions, plans to the precise extent that they seem to accord, and continue to accord with one's own problems.

Problem induction has ramifications for community or solidarity. By inducing her problem in the regional administrators but not in Sr. Norma, Sr. Claudia achieved a certain kind of community with them, namely a coalition — an exclusionary community with respect to Sr. Norma. Induction of problems, if not multilateral among constituents, will create a partial community, an in-group and an out-group, an exclusion. And once a constituent person or unit becomes an excluded member, realities are the more resistant to expression: each side tends then to respond with exclusionary communication, avoiding communication about problems and focusing instead on solutions and plans, and on prescriptions for the other's behavior. Since, as a species it seems, we are not wired to do for very long what we are merely told, from the outside, but only what will solve problems internally synthesized, such tellings become, not guides for action, but elements of reactive problems.

Well, must *all* constituent realities be integrated into a solution for it to be effective? Wrong question. As soon as we speak of integrating realities into a *solution* we have forgone further transformation of the problem, and it is problems that release, organize, and guide resources. Not: 'We have to solve the problem of your absences, Norma'. But rather (making some assumptions for illustration): 'We have to solve my problem of your absences and your problem of lower commitment and withdrawal while still keeping you publicly installed as Co-Director and still allowing me a free hand to plan for the following year'. So rephrase the question: must we include all constituent realities into *problem-solving action*, starting with problem, for it to be effective? The full, theoretical answer is yes. For maximum effectiveness all constituent realities must be integrated into problem and problem-solving action. But theoretical considerations need not be black and white. Satisficing is a widespread mode (Simon, 1979), and need not succumb to mere localism. In that case some distinctions among constituents can be made.

A useful generalization can be made that sufficient, not complete, integration of organizational reality would be accomplished by integrating the local realities of constituent members who were *active or influential* with respect to the full group of constituents. That would include first, all persons with official status or position holding legitimate authority over a given solution. (Constituents, remember, are relative to solutions, since different solutions will implicate different persons, roles and levels of authority.) Thus, Sr. Jeanine and Sr. Georgette were important and influential, not just constituents, with respect to solutions to Sr. Claudia's problem regarding Sr. Norma's absences. Beyond this, all members holding informal positions of status or influence regarding given solutions would be implicated. If there had been a person, for example, trusted by both Sr. Claudia and Sr. Norma but not a member of the regional administration, and thus in a position to influence a mutual accommodation, that person (both his or her realities and his or her participation in interchanges) would have warranted inclusion in the problem-solving process. Third, any constituents who have organized around issues implicated in a solution — as workers organize in unions with respect to wages or as members of the junior class favoring senior class officers might have been organized, but were not — would be possessed of influence that could affect reality integration and therefore relevant to be included in forging the adaptation. Persons holding any combination of those positions of influence, of course, would be even more powerful in effecting integrations of constituent realities. Finally, because having high status and being organized shape realities often different in important respects from the realities of the average, unorganized constituent, on whom the work of solution implementation falls, integration of the realities of some of the unorganized, uninfluential constituents would seem to increase degrees and probabilities of effectiveness. Criteria are available, then, for distinguishing between more and less influential constituent realities to be integrated: on the grounds that they, themselves, can facilitate or impede the process, not of domination, but of integration — including most especially influence to transform local problems into translocal, multilateral problems.

9. Protagonists and Antagonists, Problems and Conflict

Given the local commitments that develop from members' personal lives and specialized roles, when one member synthesizes a problem about some aspect of the organization, it will frequently and perhaps normally be the case that the very conditions which that member finds problematic other members will value or depend on for their normal or convenient functioning in their roles. Sr. Claudia found objectionable the council's action on parking violations, but the council members viewed their action as only the normal extension of other decision making they had done, normal extensions, too, of routinized parking regulations and punishments to prevent damage to valued property. The council found objectionable certain parking patterns created by drivers who, on their part, were merely coping in normal ways with limited parking spaces. This book's data and analyses suggest, therefore, that organizational problems *frequently or normally, imply a conflict of interests between two problem-specific subgroups: protagonists and antagonists.* Clarification of that implication of problem-solving in the organizational context is one contribution of this study.

The link between problem and conflict implies, further, that organizational problem-solving theory may benefit by incorporating into its often cognitively oriented concepts the social dimension of interpersonal and intergroup conflict. Two current limitations on this potentially happy alliance are that the great body of conflict theory (a) refers to dyadic relations and interactions and (b) is built on experimental investigations, where subjects' own commitments are minimal and brief, where consequentiality to them is usually nil, where organizational context is lacking, and where both experimental parties (if there are two parties) are simultaneously aware of the experimental conflict, thus eliminating any period of asymmetric awareness. Clearly, we need more studies of problem solving, and therefore conflict management, in on-going organizations. One of the methodological contributions of this study, described below, involves inherent barriers to any study of exclusionary conflict management.

Another contribution this study makes is to the study of the origins of organizational conflict. I can find no studies and no theoretical pieces in the literature on asymmetric origins of symmetric conflict. Since the overwhelmingly dominant mode of studying conflict is experimental, and since experiments use tasks in which both parties immediately see, and indeed are explicitly informed about, the inherent conflict, it is not surprising that only symmetric concepts of conflict prevail. Most of the conflicts that my students describe in their papers and class discussions about ongoing organizations, however, have asymmetric origins, so Sr. Claudia's and Sr. Norma's was not atypical. Since not many inclusionary managements of conflict appear in students' papers (or in the literature) I cannot report any observed covariation between mode of problem solving (inclusionary vs. exclusionary) in the period of asymmetric awareness and mode thereafter. Nevertheless, I would guess that, other things being equal, the mode chosen by the first aware party would be the mode of the entire conflict management. In actual, as contrasted with experimental, conflicts in organizations, then, incipient conflict can be investigated as one party's problem of conflict before it reaches full, symmetric conflict. In that period of asymmetry, one crucial question is, 'What kind of environment of conflict management is the first party creating for the second party?'

Finally, the present study suggests differentiation of modes of managing conflicts beyond the two widely recognized, 'cooperative' (or 'co-ordinative' (Pruitt, 1982)) and 'competitive'. A few important distinctions suggested by the conflict episode produce no fewer than six strategies or modes of action open to persons facing a problem of conflict. A first distinction is between an orientation away from the other party and an orientation toward the other party. Sr. Norma's orientation was away from the sisterhood, Trinity, and Sr. Claudia: she sought independence. Independence seeking is a mode of conflict management quite different from either exclusionary or inclusionary struggles. It seeks to eliminate the fundamental precondition of conflict, interdependence. In inclusionary and exclusionary modes of conflict management, in contrast, both parties intend to continue as members in the organization, thus continuing to be interdependent in their work. While Sr. Norma's seeking independence was exclusionary, an inclusionary mode is entirely conceivable, where the withdrawing member reports to those affected by her withdrawal the fact that she wants to leave and wants to work out jointly the smoothest departure possible. The other basic orientation, toward a continued but altered relation with the other party, implicitly acknowledges dependence on the other party. The first distinction, then, is between leaving the relationship and staying in the relationship, between seeking independence and acknowledging dependence. While Sr. Norma sought independence in an exclusionary mode, Sr. Claudia assumed interdependence, acknowledging her own dependence on Sr. Norma: thus, two parties can assume asymmetric orientations toward one another. But probably not for long. It would not be long before the dependent party, assuming interdependence,

Table 29.1. Six Modes or Strategies of Solving Problems of Conflict

	Oriented Away From The Other: Seeking Independence	Oriented Toward The Other: Affirming Dependence	
		Seeking 3rd Party Help Yes	No
INCLUSIONARY	Open, Joint Smoothing Of The Exit	3rd Party Intervention	Cooperative Conflict Management
EXCLUSIONARY	Closed, Private Arranging Of The Exit	Coalition Formation	Exclusionary Conflict Management

would realize she could expect 'zilch' from the other party, and assume a symmetrical orientation of independence by no longer depending on the other, thus dissolving the relationship completely.

Within the dependent orientation, cutting across both inclusionary and exclusionary modes of dependence, is another distinction: between those struggling parties who are willing, or feel forced, to give substantial influence (or total control) to a third party and those who struggle on by themselves, without third-party intervention. The parties can be inclusive or exclusionary, either in their seeking third party assistance or in working through the conflict on their own.

Exclusionary seeking of third-party help, Sr. Claudia's major mode, reduces to coalition formation.[3] Once again, as it happened with the two co-directors, help-seeking can be asymmetrical. Implied by these distinctions, then, are six, not two, modes or strategies of solving problems of conflict, six choices open to each party, as depicted in Table 29.1. Since each is a strategy of solving a problem of conflict and therefore characterizes possibilities for the individual (not the dyad), each strategy or mode is open to each party. Twenty-one combinations of these individual modes are therefore theoretically possible[4] — leaving plenty of room for asymmetry between the parties. While asymmetries tend to become symmetrical, as between Sr. Claudia's dependent mode and Sr. Norma's independence seeking, the actions taken by each until symmetry is reached generally have cognitive and motivational consequences for the party made to feel stupid, foolish, or duped by being dependent in the face of the other's independence, by staying in the relationship when the other had already left.

10. Processes Within Structures

Change processes take place *within stable structures*. Define 'process' as change that cumulates systematically into a coherent product via a series of transformations of a problem. This book has focused on adaptational processes in a school, with other schools and other organizations in mind, processes that lead to concrete adaptations via problem-solving episodes. The processes are given different names depending on the level of social complexity addressed: problem synthesis, dyadic communication, conflict management. But each transforming process takes place within a surrounding structure that is less changing. Problem synthesis arises within a relatively stable set of commitments — values and goals in a more stable set of beliefs, a personality, and a career. Perceptions form within a more stable role within an organization. Communication arises within a more stable relationship or network of relationships, and within a stable set of roles. Conflict management arises also within a network of more stable relationships, and these in a more stable hierarchical structure of authority. Each process is nested within an environing, constraining structure, and that structure, in turn, possesses its own more stable structure. More generally, while everything is changing, the change we focus on proceeds within, and takes shape from, lesser change around it — and holds more rapidly changing parts within itself. Since process is always dependent on its immediate, more structured context, it is important to allow both process and structure into one's data and theory.

In the naturalistic setting it is difficult to keep both process and structure from one's data if one uses organizational problems as one's starting point and problem-solving episodes as one's unit. Sr. Norma's administrative behavior at Trinity takes place within, is constrained by, and is understood in terms of, her changed relationship to her religious order: a weakened and ambivalent performance grows out of a weakened and ambivalent relationship. Sr. Claudia communicates with Sr. Norma immediately after November 2 within a temporarily changed relationship between herself and Sr. Norma, and returns to avoidance and strained communication as the forces driving the 'old' relationship once again take hold. Again, Sr. Claudia's problem of governance at Trinity is synthesized within images formed while helping develop the form she regards as better, less 'old fashioned', for her religious order. She wants to 'share power' at Trinity, just as her religious order developed a governance of sharing power. The structural change in the superordinate organization virtually gives birth to smaller change within Trinity. Each emergent change is understood not merely in terms of its own indigenous properties, but in terms that include first- and second-order relations between it and more slowly changing structures immediately and then next encompassing it. One can never fully understand anything; there are always contexts beyond ones included. But to ignore all context is to ignore a crucial and defining property of adaptation.[5]

11. Communication

One contribution I hope this study makes is to focus attention in communication studies away from *message content* as the criterion of adequacy and to focus instead on the *constituent realities* of communicating members. In countless experiments by social psychologists communication has been taken as adequate when the receiving party can substantially reproduce the contents of messages received. In the context of organizational functioning, however, that criterion is insufficient and misleading. Sr. Claudia might well be able to reproduce what Sr. Norma *said* to her on this or that occasion, but if Sr. Norma withheld her actual intentions, do we want to conclude that communication was adequate? More generally, if a subordinate lies to a superordinate and the superordinate is able to repeat the content of the lie word for word, has communication been adequate? Certainly not. If two parties are undertaking a task or function in which their labor has been divided but do not speak to each other, is this non-speaking, this absent of messages sent and received, simply not a phenomenon of communication? No, it is a communicative phenomenon, a failure to communicate. But on what criterion, if not messages, will we justify the inclusion of lies and the absence of messages as failures of communication?

My answer in the data and analyses of this book is that communication has to do with community and communality and that a fundamental, psychological base for these is *the expression and exploration, not of messages, but of realities*, the realities giving rise to message sending or message withholding. Consider first message sending and then withholding. On any occasion when a person approaches another with a message, verbal or non-verbal, written or spoken, this person has a purpose and further, she is solving some problem. The criterion of the degree to which communication has taken place, from the perspective of multiple organizational realities, is the degree to which the party approached, after the message has been sent, is able to reproduce, not the 'sender's' message, but the sender's *operating reality with respect to the sender's problem and her transformation of it*. If the receiving party understands — not necessarily agrees with, but understands — the sender's problem and her transformations, the receiver has one half of the basis for community in that problem-solving enterprise. The other half is the extent to which the receiver's relevant realities come to be understood by the sender. Organizational communication, like organizational adaptations, has to do with organizational realities, particularly organizational problems.

In the case of avoidance by two interdependent parties, as Sr. Claudia and Sr. Norma were by virtue of their co-director roles, a refusal to talk on the telephone (Sr. Norma) or refusal to face the other's emotional outbursts (Sr. Claudia) are highly significant communicative phenomena. The warrant for judging these absences of message sending as communicatively significant is the parties' interdependent relation in the division of organizational functions. As soon as that interdependence is eliminated, so too is the warrant for judging the absence of exchanged messages as communicatively significant: they no longer are expected by superiors or peers to perform complementary functions, to be part of that sub-organizational community we call 'role set'. Communication, then, has much less to do with messages than with community and interdependence, each of which is reflected in the sharing or non-sharing of problems, solutions, plans, and action. A move of Sr. Claudia to communicate with Mr. Sullivan is a part of Sr. Claudia's problem solving. Its adequacy as communication should be assessed according to degrees of conveyance to Sullivan of the organizational realities impelling her move. That is necessary because otherwise he cannot share in her problem-solving but will be left to his own projections of what her problem must be. We have seen where that can lead. It led, in the first constitution episode, to neither organization nor community but rather to a kind of autistic guessing game, to a succession of pre-empting problems each with diminished commitment and, in the end, to feelings of being 'duped'. Realities, not messages, are criterial; message contents are themselves the subject of analysis with respect to realities conveyed or distorted or withheld.

12. *Sequentiality, Cumulativity, Reversibility*

One resource available to problem solvers in the ongoing world not available for study in the experimental setting is time. There are many other resources, of course, but time opens the door to all of them. An organizational problem by definition must involve at least two persons, but most involve a number of persons and often different roles and levels in the organization. For transformations to proceed across persons, roles, and levels takes time, and with time comes sequentiality and the possibility of cumulativity and reversibility.

The question of sequentiality has to do with what tends to happen early in a problem-solving episode and what tends to happen late, the question of those seven overlapping progressions described earlier (pp. 213 ff). It matters not only what a participant contributes, but also when and how long. If one's participation is early rather than late, solutions are not then so settled, expectations not so firm: there is room for change. One's local realities can more easily be accommodated. Not so, for late participation. Therefore, timing in the sequence is important — especially since those with positional power tend often to be early participants and those depended on for implementing tend to be late, a built-in structural bias that does not correspond with the distribution of constituent realities.

Clearly the longer one participates over the course of an episode, the greater one's chances of influencing accommodations of one's local realities in organizational planning and action. But that also brings increased chances that the planning and action will fit one's own local realities too well: so well that planning and action integrate only one's own realities and do not accommodate the realities of others on whom action depends. Cumulativity of action depends, it seems, on cumulative integrations of local constituent realities, but increased tendencies of closure and of excluding late-arriving realities implies that all constituent realities, certainly all powerful ones, be expressed in the early, middle, and late phases of an episode. Mr. Sullivan's reversal of Sr. Claudia's intentions, in his conception of the nature and purpose of a constitution, showed what can happen if a problem can reach expression only early and not also late, irrespective of the positional power of the problem originator.

Having said that, it must be recognized also that the abortive effort that resulted from Sullivan's reversal (contributed to perhaps importantly by Sr. Claudia herself), was itself reversed. Reversal possibilities are brought with time, as time brought Sr. Claudia opportunities to transform her conflict with Sr. Norma and restructure her relation with the Trinity council — transformations which opened the way for her to approach the council directly as a body, rather than through individuals. Part of any adaptation are possibilities, seized or forgone, for reversing the effects of particular segments, particular communications. A cabinet maker once told me that the mark of a master craftsman was not how well he could design or execute a set of plans, but how well he could compensate for his mistakes — a distinctly adaptational view. I hope this book prompts the study of reversals in problem-solving processes, both those, like Sullivan's, that lead to non-cumulative, abortive adaptations and those, like Sr. Claudia's second constitution effort, that reverse abortive reversals and lead to greater cumulative effort. Indeed, reversals may be closer to the heart of adaptation than anything else. Witness the reversal of Sr. Claudia's cumulative and effective effort two years after she left Trinity. Many, but not all, of the effects of Vatican II have also been reversed under subsequent popes. The narratives and analyses of these three episodes lead me to conclude, then, that three fundamental dimensions of any local adaptation are sequentiality, cumulativity, and reversibility. These dimensions only show up in units which, like the problem-solving episode, transpire over *reality-transforming time*.

13.   Rationality, Adaptation, and the Garbage Can

March and his associates (Cohen, March, and Olsen, 1972; March and Olsen, 1979) mount arguments against calculable rationality as a sufficient basis for understanding organizational decision making. They see much ambiguity and discontinuity in organizational behavior and wish to make a place for it in organizational theory. They do so by means of a metaphor, by now widely cited: the garbage can. Organizational decisions, like the

Trinity council's writing a constitution for itself, arise like the contents of a garbage can: the residues of many independent 'streams' of activity come together in more or less random order. The lines of activity are not individual, but collective. March and his associates posit four 'relatively independent streams' of events in any organization: problems, solutions, participants, and choice opportunities. Problems, they argue, do not move relentlessly or even rationally toward solution; available solutions are often not adopted — indeed seem substituted from quite unrelated domains; choice opportunities appear unpredictably and often remain unimplemented; and participants flow in and out of decision making in unpredictable ways. It would seem that their characterization might fit the Trinity council, for example. Certainly the first constitution episode was the occasion for successive substitutions of unrelated solutions.

It would take me too far afield to undertake here a thorough critique of March and associates' concepts, argument, and data. It is sufficient to focus on two of their concepts, intentionality and problems, and on some qualities of their data. First, they treat intentionality as if it were somehow observable in the logic of 'the' problem that organizational participants are trying to solve. They conceive of problem, then, as 'out there' in the organization and observable in any given situation. As the data of each of the episodes of the present book clearly reveal, the problems that different participants are working on in any given interactive situation vary. (To call them 'decision situations' already imbues them prematurely with coherence and rationality.) Their intentions, consequently, also vary. Since March and his associates do not gather the kind of data presented here, they cannot be confronted with the variability of problems, and therefore of relevant solutions, from participant to participant. These investigators are left free, therefore, to deduce 'the' problem 'the' group is working on. Their reliance on retrospective testimony and documents prevents their gathering contemporaneous interpretations from their participants of the participants' own behaviors and intentions, those that might account for their shifts in behavior. That lack of data at the social psychological level, the level of multiple interpretation and intentionality, in their various case studies leaves March and associates free, also, to show how solutions and choices — which do not fit 'the' problem they (not their participants) have decided that the group is working on — have only random relations with that problem.

The random relations among problems, solutions, participants, and choice opportunities are indeed qualities of the collective events March and his associates have selected for study. But those events are far from the only ones actually going on from the participants' viewpoints. The qualities of randomness, ambiguity, and predictability that appear in the data of March and his associates occur, rather, as qualities necessary to any analysis that posits singularity where there is plurality. They are in much the same position as the two-dimensional protagonist of Abbott's (1952 [1884]) classic fable, *Flatland*, who is at a loss to explain the appearance in two dimensions of the three-dimensional sphere. Their data (see especially March and Olsen, 1979, Chapters 15 and 16) show loose connections with the singular problem they, as investigators, have decided to focus on as the common intentions of their participants. But episodic data of the kind we have gathered, and that March and associates did not gather, show not loose connections with a single problem, but tight connections with multiple problems. Sr. Norma's solution of a constitution is adopted by Sr. Claudia because they do share the same problem. But Mr. Sullivan's entirely different problem produces an entirely different interpretation of the function of a constitution. He is loosely coupled with Sr. Claudia's problem but tightly coupled with his own. The constitution, as 'solution', does not exist out here in the world as a solution to a problem. Nor, indeed, did its prototype, the American Constitution, constitute a single solution. The garbage can metaphor suggests a randomness that fits the data only if the data themselves are deprived of the contemporaneous, problematic realities that operate in the participants as the action unfolds.

When we begin to include such subjective realities, as the narratives of this book do, we see that each participant is rational in terms of her or his own reality, but that realities differ — not only across persons but also within persons across situations. Given Mr. Sullivan's problem that the council might lose its continuity, his construing of a constitution and of the minutes as a relevant resource is rational. Given Miss Nolan's different problems, her 'failure' to 'implement' the council's choice is also rational. And given Sr. Claudia's original problem, its initial connection to the writing of a constitution, and the changes in her reality from November 2 to the end of January, her further pursuit of a new constitution that de-emphasized writing and made no reference to the council's action on Mr. Sullivan's motion on December 7 is also entirely rational. Each was trying to solve her or his own problem at a given time. With plurality of realities, and in particular, plurality of problems, the need for a garbage can metaphor disappears. A more apt metaphor, perhaps, would be ethnic cuisines and menus, offering clusters of related choice, with great variability. But that metaphor, like the garbage can, ignores the fact that organizations are themselves coherent solutions and that their parts have a logic of inter-relation built into them: roles are not random — we do not find bank teller roles in schools or demolition experts as regular parts of libraries or universities.

The data of problem-solving episodes and the concept of operating realities go much further than March and his associates' data and conceptions do to support their basic quarrel with calculable rationality as a model for organizational behavior. There is no single calculable rationality; but only multiple calculations, based on quite idiosyncratic values, changing situations, and changing construings of situations: where Sr. Claudia wants drastic change in the Trinity council, Mr. Sullivan wants continuity; where the new council structure is rational within Sr. Claudia's conception of 'governance', it is wasteful and irrational within Sr. Sabrina's conception of school 'administration'. Given a shared commitment to make the organization work more or less effectively, individual rationality of most members dictates that no one's individual reality be taken by them as the basis for rational calculation. Rather, rational selection (not choice, which denotes a person's cognitive decision) emerges from *social processes* which no individual participant can calculate — but which nevertheless are not random. Patterns of reality inclusion and exclusion have patterned, not random, consequences. In sum, the narratives and analyses we have presented clarify how March and his associates' refutation of calculable rationality can be strengthened while also providing a basis for refuting the garbage can metaphor they offer as an alternative model.

14. *Innovation Adoption and Implementation Theory*

A large body of literature, much dealing with planned change in schools, has grown up around the concepts of innovation and implementation. Briefly, observations and theory focus on the 'adoption' by a school system or other organization (the 'target' or 'receiver') of some innovation developed elsewhere, by persons other than members of the target or receiving organization, where the innovation is to be implemented. These studies deal with coherent systems of procedures or curriculum materials, large 'packaged' programs designed not to be sampled, cafeteria style, according to the varied tastes of members of the receiving organization, but adopted whole, as a way of thinking or of teaching or of managing. These studies identify variables which account for the adoption or rejection of the innovation, the degree to which it is implemented as originally conceived and structured by the innovators, and the like. The most frequent finding is the transformation of the 'innovation' to meet the local 'situation' by the 'implementers'. Three weaknesses characterize such studies, from the viewpoint of multiple, local realities and adaptations.

First, the pre-packaged innovation is taken as the criterion of success. If it is adopted and used unchanged it is counted a success. Unexamined in these studies is the more basic relation between originating problems and the innovation itself. A perfect implementation of a packaged innovation that was only a poor solution to its originating problem would be a failure, not a success. The origins of innovations themselves are not examined. From the point of view of problem-solving episodes, theories of adoption and implementation of innovations study only the last parts of a more complete process of change, the very parts in which, if the implementation is to remain intact, there are fewest degrees of freedom for integrating local realities. A second weakness is that the day-by-day processes are ignored by which members of the receiving organization absorb the impact of the outside innovation through their own, daily and weekly processes of adaptation to local problems. Third, while organizational problem-solving is a fact of daily life in any school, no studies have been undertaken to examine, and no theories developed to account for, the mutual impact of that daily, local process of adaptation and the 'implementation' process of adopting one of these pre-packaged, imported innovations, like the 'new math' or 'mastery learning'. In sum, the studies are not fine-grained enough to trace local adaptations within the receiving organization nor coarse-grained enough to include both the problematic origins of the innovation and its post-implementation fate. It is a mistake to focus on 'the innovation' as the criterion of anything, a mistake comparable to using the message as a criterion for communication adequacy. An innovation — like the new math curriculum or management by objectives or quality work circles — is a solution to some person's or group's problem, usually remote from the intended site of adoption, and is a window neither to the originating problem nor to the quotidian problems and problem-solving processes through which it must pass at the target site in order to be integrated into local realities and action. Such innovations arise from realities remote from their intended sites and it is not surprising that they typically succumb to local, site-specific values, skills, norms and resources.

It might be argued that Sr. Claudia's concept of governance was just such an innovation, derived from Vatican II and her religious order, remote from Trinity. Partly yes, and partly no. Its origin was exogenous, but not so remote. Sr. Claudia herself had participated importantly at the regional and national levels in developing it and she was its chief guide throughout the second constitutional episode — hardly the kind of linkage one sees in the innovation adoption studies. But more important, the council system itself grew gradually out of the local site — from student council to student-faculty council to council system — with the council's active participation in developing the innovation itself. Still, the most glaring misfit of the council schema was between the underlying idea of governance of a society, which the religious order did constitute and which called for a new openness and sharing of power, on the one hand, and the administration of a school, on the other, not a self-contained, relatively homogeneous society calling for representation but a mixed membership more than a half of which conceived of themselves as professional *employees*. So a misfitting idea was imported as an important concept of an innovative solution. Yet, arguing again the other side, the concept was 'imported' by an indigenous member, not merely 'exported' from an outside source to Trinity. Furthermore, it was imported by the indigenous member whose role it was (and was accepted to be) to fashion the school's administration. Being thus imported by the very person who would adapt it to local circumstance, it was stamped with a substantial degree of localism and, fitting important local realities, the schema functioned remarkably well during the first year of its implementation. The Trinity study, in sum, presents three instances of a complete problem-solving process at the local level of a school, from originating problem through implementation. In that regard it stands in contrast to the large number of studies of the 'implementation' process and offers theoretical and empirical possibilities that go beyond that kind of study (e.g., Corbett, Dawson, and Firestone, 1984; Huberman and Miles, 1984; Pressman and Wildavsky, 1979; and see Fullan, 1982).

Method

The method we fashioned was admittedly crude — a 'first draft'. But even in its crudeness I can identify several ways I think it contributes to the study of organizational processes.

1. A Diachronic Dimension

The method contributes a diachronic dimension to ethnography of organizations. Ethnographic studies of organizations or organizational change generally examine chronic, stable forces — either stable structural characteristics or constraints or causes producing organizational changes. Occasionally ethnographies capture sequence in their data and analyses (e.g., Smith and Keith, 1971, and Smith, Kleine, Prunty, and Dwyer, 1987). But no ethnography I know of captures cumulative sequence in repeatable units of data; none examines possible regularities in cumulative or reversing sequences across analytical units. The very choice of subject matter, adaptation, requires careful preservation of actions *in their sequence* because the processes of change, more than stable forces and structures, are center stage.

Having committed to a diachronic ethnography, a problem of written form resulted directly, and had to be solved. Aside from narrative histories, which focus on influential leaders at the level of polities, the social sciences offered no prototypes for capturing sequential narratives at the level of purposeful, social psychological action. One early attempt, a long, coherent narrative of an entire episode followed by analyses of it, drew reactions from a number of colleagues at various universities clearly indicating that analysis of social psychological and organizational dynamics had to be intimately connected to, thus closely following, sections of narrative in which specific dynamics were unfolding or visible. Since the research enterprise was not merely historical, but also explanatory, a search for variables was entailed. Once identified, the problem had to be solved of how to make the connections clear in readers' minds between narrated actions and underlying hypothesized variables. Comments about narrative content that addressed explanatory issues had to proceed side by side, almost in step, with the narratives. The solution resulted in a new form of research report, the kind presented in Parts II, III, and IV: one that (a) included narration, (b) provided frequent, interspersed analytical commentary, (c) synthesized analyses into hypothesized variables, and (d) accumulated tables of variables, referenced to text, across episodes of different substantive content.

2. *Intimate Contact with Settings of Power and Consequence*

The method contributes a coherent means of achieving what Lofland (1976) calls 'intimate familiarity' in 'settings of power and consequence'. The combination of researcher-consultant role and the central concept of adaptation allows a method peculiarly suited to the study of the action of the powerful within organizations. Lofland (1976) identifies shortcomings of current sociological research to which the substance and method of this book are a partial response. He argues that 'it is rare for a social scientist to have much qualitative intimate familiarity and acquaintance with the kind of social life he is considered to be expert about', and points to a 'massive drift towards' the use of 'remote devices' like questionnaires, interviews, and 'experimental contrivances' as 'substitutes for' direct, intimate familiarity with social or organizational phenomena (Lofland, 1976, p. 12). The most immediate cause of this remote approach by so many social scientists, Lofland argues, is the ready availability of research methods that allow remoteness — these laboratory, questionnaire, and interview 'substitutes'. But beyond these, he notes a special gap in even those investigations which have made intimate contact with their chosen phenomena:

> ... the intimate access [that has been achieved] by social scientists is remarkably skewed toward underling and leisure settings of American society such as poor people, motorcyclists, religious extremists, social workers (and lower public workers of many kinds), patients in mental hospitals, police patrolmen, and assembly-line workers. These are the sorts of people who (a) do not have the power to say no, (b) are so discredited they no longer care who knows what, (c) are participants in an open, leisure setting from which no one is excluded anyway, or (d) are energetically proselytizing and put up with a variety of characters in the course of this quest ... Settings of power and consequence have none of these features, are anathema to many social scientists, hence are not much studied ... (Lofland, 1976, p. 20)

As a result, Lofland sees an 'eerie equilibrium' having developed 'between what social scientists find, how they find it ..., and smooth relations with the host society' (p. 20). The research-consultation regarding problem-solving is peculiarly responsive to the conditions of social science Lofland describes. It is the powerful in organizations whose roles legitimately call for them to (1) initiate research about organizational processes, most especially their own, (2) seek consultation to improve organizational processes, or (3) solve organizational problems. As to intimacy, the combination of research-consultation and its focus on organizational problems immediately enters the domain of daily, intimate thought and action about organizational conditions and changes. The method's distinctive exchange between investigator and host organization — an exchange of consultation for intimate access — provides new kinds of data and a distinctive relationship with powerful persons in the host organization.[6]

But besides being fitted to the role, authority, and needs of powerful persons in organizations, the research consultation's flexibility opens further possibilities for studying power more generally. While the Trinity study focuses only on problems synthesized by the school's most powerful member, and therefore studies what might be called the 'downward' solution of organizational problems, the method allows choice of problem originators from any sector and any level of authority in organizations. We thus can study problem solving comparatively — from the top down, from the bottom up (e.g., of students with problems of school policy or workers vis à vis management policy) and from the ranks of mid-level members (e.g., assistant principals, assistant superintendents, middle managers) undertaking efforts downward, upward, and laterally.[7]

3. New Possibilities for Theory Integration

The method contributes new possibilities for theory integration. Because the problem-solving episode includes such a wide range of social psychological and organizational phenomena, it allows the confrontation of quite disparate and otherwise independent domains of theory within a single unit of data. The three episodes of the present study, for example, brought together Deweyan conceptions of problem-solving, emphasizing the individual's relationship with the existential world, with Festinger's conception of dissonance, emphasizing the individual's inner, motivational commitment to cognitive coherence. By bringing Dewey and Festinger face to face in the context of energizing problems, we see simultaneously the weakness of Dewey's de-emphasis of 'subjectivistic psychology' and 'merely "mental" processes' (1938, p. 106) and the one-sidedness of Festinger's (1957) attention to merely cognitive processes, excluding socially collaborative processes, as the means of reducing dissonance.

The method also contributes links among different *levels* of analysis. This method of studying organizational problem solving within multiple realities at the individual level allows a link between micro-analysis (individual, psychological) and macro-analysis (collective), or rather, between micro-analysis and *meso*-analysis (purposive and cumulative collective action). A psychologically grounded unit of cognition and motivation, problem, is connected to organizational conditions and leads to purposeful, collective action across roles and levels of authority. Specifically, the multi-person, multi-level unit of the problem-solving episode promotes a link between problem-solving theory (already integrating Festinger and Dewey) and theories of conflict management. Theories of individual behavior thus become linked with theories of dyadic, intergroup, and inter-level interaction.

4.   The Relationship Between Investigators and Participants

The method illuminates the relationship between investigators and partici-pants — in ways played down in more remote, seemingly more 'objective' research approaches. While in their research-consultation roles as members of their selected committees (e.g., Trinity council and executive council), the investigators intervene into problems peripheral to the ones they are studying or at a level, like occasional semantic clarifications or illuminating a member's role, that has only short-term effects. In this way, the investigators come into the data and come under the direct scrutiny of those who read the investigators' research report. A report like this gives readers a more authentic account of the place of the investigators in the collection of data and of their relationships with episodic participants. The researcher-consultants' degree of role engagement with the groups and persons whose processes are being studied subjects the researcher-consultants, however, to the dynamics of the organization's own internal antagonisms and congenialities.

In particular, the researcher-consultants become assimilated into stable triadic relations among persons and groups in the host organization.[8] Unless special steps are taken — as we did not take at Trinity — researcher-consultants' access to data about *any exclusionarily managed conflict* becomes immediately limited by the contours of those triadic relations. For example, if Sr. Claudia and Sr. Norma have become antagonistic by the time investigators, Lighthall and Allan, come on the scene, then for both of the co-directors to regard Lighthall and Allan as friendly would be to generate what balance theorists call an 'unbalanced triad'. Each of the co-directors, saying to themselves, in effect, 'a friend of my antagonistic co-director is my friend', would balk. Being friendly to persons who are also friendly with one's antagonist is ordinarily unsettling: if Peter is friendly with a Paul whom I mistrust, why should I trust Peter? But for one of the co-directors to regard Lighthall and Allan positively and the other to regard them negatively would generate a balanced triad. 'Balanced' in the sense that from each party's perspective the relations with the other two parties would satisfy four stark rules:

1.   A friend of my friend is probably my friend.
2.   A friend of my enemy is my enemy.

3. An enemy of my friend is my enemy.
4. An enemy of my enemy may be my friend.

To the extent that these rules characterize social relationships, and they did tend to account rather simply and neatly for the network of relations among the co-directors and others, a research-consultation team would become 'friendly' with some organization members (e.g., Sr. Claudia and Sr. Catherine and their supporters) and 'enemies' or 'strangers' with others (e.g., Sr. Norma and her supporters). That is, researcher-consultants attempting to make an 'entry' into the organization to study its processes would be constrained by, and assimilated into an already prevailing structure of congenialities and antagonisms — unless they took conscious steps to counteract that assimilation. Had we been aware then, as the experience has taught us to be now, that when researchers approach such organizations they do not form relationships with members singly, but with members as parts of larger nets of relationships; that we were approaching and becoming related to patterns of relationship already stable among members — that awareness might have led us to a relatively simple solution. In order for outsiders like us to form positive bonds with parties who themselves are antagonistic, we might well separate and become attached to those parties and detached from each other. Thus, Susan Allan and I would have become researcher-consultants separately to the co-directors — or perhaps at first merely researchers interested in the co-directors' respective roles, organizational tasks, and problems — while having virtually no interaction with each other at Trinity itself. Creating, thus, separate and independent worlds with our respective antagonists, we each would not be perceptively linked with the other, unbalancing, member of the triad. That would solve the problem we did not solve, of wanting data from both sides of an exclusionary conflict.

While the research-consultation can bring a certain intimacy of contact with some members, therefore, it will tend to render inaccessible other members whose conflict with those members is being managed by them in an exclusionary manner. The Sr. Norma's, being in exclusionary conflict with the Sr. Claudia's, will be inaccessible from more than remote data gathering unless the research-consultation team *differentiates itself into quite separate parts.* After completing all data gathering, the research-consultation team could integrate their respective observations and interpretations. If they then carried out a post-research consultation, based on full data and on positive relationships on both sides of an exclusionary conflict, their consultation would also be much more informed, and potentially more informative to the participants, than had they had access to only one of the conflicting parties.

That researchers may become thus assimilated into an organization's antagonistic relations does put up barriers to full data collection — barriers not easily and perhaps never completely overcome. But one considerable and substantial gain, from this very vulnerability of the research-consultation, is that balanced, stable congenialities and antagonisms become tangibly impressed upon the researcher-consultants and thus etched in relief in their episodic data. Since these very patterns of antagonism and congeniality impinge importantly on adaptational processes, as the relationships among Sr. Claudia, Sr. Catherine, and Sr. Norma did upon Sr. Claudia's solving of her problems of governance, their special and additional impingement on researcher-consultants is anything but merely an extraneous nuisance. While posing a threat to full data gathering, this power of the organization to assimilate the researcher-consultants asymmetrically into its triadic relations becomes positively informative. More generally, the research-consultation forces into the open, by its continuing intimacy with participants' ongoing interchanges, the important and all too often hidden relationship between the researchers and the participants.

5. Generalizability

The method offers a certain generalizability of findings. Given the local historical uniquenesses of any episode and the personal stamp of the problem originator upon it, what warrant has one for claiming any generalizability for findings based on this kind of unit? The only justifiable claim is that a certain generality is plausible; support for a stronger argument depends on repeated patterns found empirically in other organizations. Why is it plausible to expect similar patterns from other organizations?

First, each episode from Trinity involved many persons, not just a few. Some random variability is reduced by the participation of many varied personalities in a given result. But all of these episodes were originated by a problem synthesized by the same person. Does that person's unique qualities nullify any generalization? A second source of the plausibility of generalization is the limited number of options (at a certain level of conceptualization) open to any administrator in Sr. Claudia's position. For example, faced with a conflict with another member of her or his organization, an administrator can shorten as much as possible or lengthen the period of asymmetric awareness, thus becoming inclusive or exclusionary in managing the conflict. At the level of including or excluding problem-relevant realities, much generalizability is possible, since the full range of inclusion-exclusion, as a generalized dimension of organizational behavior, is open to any administrator in any conflict. A third source of plausibility for the possibility of generalizing these results is the variability of content, persons, and conditions across the three episodes included here. While they are all from Trinity, and all originate in problems synthesized by the same powerful person, they do involve influential behavior of many different actors in different contexts. A fourth reason to expect some generality is that the component variables identified in the first two episodes were sufficient, with only a few additions, to accommodate the actions in the third — suggesting that each new episode will not bring its own set of variables, but will be largely understandable in terms of those already available. A fifth source of plausibility is informal and impressionistic: students and colleagues who read or hear versions of these three episodes tend to see immediately and to narrate parallel episodes in their own experience, both in schools and other public and private organizations. Students, further, are able to identify and evaluate problem-solving episodes in their extended papers with the same criteria as those used in this book, and to carry out analyses successfully, if not without struggle. Findings of these students' analyses are in keeping with, and extend, those of this study. As with all other empirical inquiries, however, the extent to which the method and substantive findings are generalizable rests with future studies.

6. Four Possibilities in Unique Combination

The episodic unit, finally, provides participant-observation four possibilities in unique combination: great generality of substantive content; diachronic analysis of events over extended time; conceptual focus; and evaluation of effectiveness. First, problems can have limitless content. Second, problem-solving episodes capture events not only chronologically ordered, and planned so results of one event constitute the raw materials for the next, but also extended in time sufficiently to reveal their resistance to reversal. Third, far from being aimlessly empirical, the multiplicity of realities in the context of an organization designed for *cumulative* action focuses attention and analysis on inclusion, exclusion, and integration of problem-relevant realities. Finally, since problem 'solution' is defined independent of normative criteria of goodness of solution — a solution can both qualify as a solution and be ineffective on all criteria — the method accommodates both scientific and evaluative (normative) interests.

Practice

Shift now from the researcher's perspective to that of the organizational participant. Consider members or managers of organizations who want to solve an organizational problem. What practical, if tentative advice do the foregoing narratives and analyses suggest to, say, Sr. Claudia as our client? We can think in two ways. The first attends to the five major variables, the second to general theory — on the grounds that it is *practical* to attend to practitioners' theories. I now address Sr. Claudia directly. Thinking first, now, of the five major variables, to which of them should you, Sr. Claudia, allocate your resources in order to make your current problem-solving most effective? Here, considerations of remoteness or closeness of control become relevant. For example, the relations among a problem's constituents (variable II) that exist at the moment you become aware of a problem are already stabilized. They are not quickly changed; you are 'stuck' with whatever levels of trust or mistrust have developed among the constituents and implicated structures, at least initially. Your own synthesis of your problems, however, and your orientations to others' realities generally, can come under your direct control, both immediately and as you participate in subsequent phases of your problem-solving. If you are oriented to take in others' local realities as you proceed — as in significant ways you were not in these episodes — you may make immediate and continuing inroads on inclusion-exclusion. So variables that are relatively unimportant for research purposes may be far more important to you, at your daily work in your organization, because of their accessibility to your control. It may therefore be more important for you to attend to the more numerous and detailed contributing variables than to the five major variables. Contributing variables more amenable to your own immediate control, are the following seven. Most of them are obvious, perhaps, but they can be easily overlooked or evaded under the pressure of deadlines.

1. Orientation to Others' Realities

I have already urged you to be open to others' local realities as you proceed in your problem-solving. More focally, your being attentive to the *problems* of those you enlist in your own problem-solving will help you in two crucial ways. First, you cannot initially know the local realities of your school faculties. Given that the leaders and faculties of the larger system you now are dealing with have their own local realities they are struggling with, the most effective and economical way you can come to understand those realities is by means of their problems. Not a laundry list of 'problems' in the everyday language usage; but problems in the sense I propose, of incompatible realities. You learn these, often, not by asking about 'problems', but by inquiring about the unstated problems behind their proposals, their statements of the form, 'What our school (department) really needs is X'. The X is a solution to some unstated problem; you will learn about their realities not by pursuing their X, but by pursuing *their problems* for which X was their (sometimes ill-considered, often misfitting) solution.

The second way you can help your own problem-solving efforts by actively integrating others' realities has to do with your *dependence on others' resources* to carry out any solution to an organizational problem. If you solve only your own problem, without integrating their problem into yours, you will have your own resources to do so, but not theirs. Thus, you will be alone. More often than not you will also be alone *against* the others on whom you must depend. Their resources are tied up in solving their own problems. When you are working not merely on your own local ('administrative') problems but on problems into which the problems of those whom you depend on have been integrated, you have their perceptions, experience, ideas, and intelligence working also on your problems. It is enlightened self-interest to be translocal in your synthesis of problems. It is also good for the organization.

2. Aim and Level of Intervention

Take care that your own and others' problems are communicated to persons and organizational units *directly implicated in your problem* — as you were prevented from doing in the first constitution episode but did immediately in the second. Direct approaches may come after some lateral, peripheral communication to get a better grasp of realities, but direct approaches must eventually be made.

3. Expressing and Exploring, Rather Than Withholding or Obscuring Realities

Your own normal mode of communication may well be beyond your awareness, but you can see indirectness and vagueness in others' communications and help them put their realities into words ('I'm not clear about what you're arguing for or against', or 'What, exactly, is the problem that needs solving?'). Caution: take care to regard others' initial expressions of their problems not as definitive but as groping approximations, approximations for which the others need time and support to recast before they expose the underlying realities to which the others are responding. This caution applies with special force in any setting in which the status or power of the communicating parties is unequal. It applies in general to the extent that the local realities of the parties regarding the matter at hand are different.

4. Solutions vs. Problems vs. Process

Consider, first, solutions vs. problems. Expressing the *problem* you are struggling with, including perhaps your preferred solution, is easy to forego under pressure of time — especially as you reach the stage of planning or undertaking implementations. But remaining silent about your problem in favor of describing and explaining your new plan invites transformations of your plan by others who, not hearing your problem but seeking meaning, will explain to themselves the problem lying behind your plan, drawing on their own local realities, realities which, like Mr. Sullivan's and Miss Nolan's, are more than likely quite discrepant from yours, leading them off in quite different directions in the name of your own solution! Personal experience leads me to recommend, too, Sr. Claudia, that you describe your problem not abstractly, but in a narrative, detailing simply the march of events that made you aware of your problem. The discipline of narrative also will force you to focus concretely. If experience is any guide, narrative has other advantages over abstract descriptions: it drives its point, your problem, with a story whose several unfolding details are each connected, each associated with your own experience; drawing others into your own local experience, it transcends their localism; and it is more easily remembered, thus adding longevity to your communication.[9] One apparent liability of narrating problematic events is only apparent: it brings others intimately into your own organizational life, allowing them to see things that actually happen to you and values you actually hold, goals you actually pursue. This may seem too revealing, but it is not personal; it is organizational, and your narrative is from the standpoint of anyone in your position, in your role, with legitimate values and aspirations.

Consider, now, problems vs. process. To attend to either solutions or problems is to attend to substantive *content*. It is easy to become tied to the contents of one's problems or solutions and to ignore the larger problem-solving *process* of including or excluding constituent antagonists. Reality integration gives no privileged position to any content. Rather, it depends on the process of contacting, eliciting, and accommodating constituent contents of operating realities. So, while attending to the contents of problems, do so with a sense that they are always subject to wider (constituent) realities, and support a process of discovering and incorporating those realities. By being proactively open to others' constituent realities you also establish yourself as an environment for them that promotes their being open to others' (and your) realities. A strong reality-integrating process is always more effectively adaptive than any given solution to a problem, however cogent or perfect that solution may seem to you.

5. Contact

You may easily overlook the undermining effects of brief or infrequent communications about your problems and, again under pressure, you may often settle for the fleeting comment at lunch rather than the visit to the office with time set aside. If your own or others' problems are important to solve they are important to be given scheduled time, sufficient time, and repeated time for expression and exploration. (Given your steadfast persistence in all three of these episodes, Sr. Claudia, offering this advice to you is carrying coals to Newcastle. But the point is general, and applies with special force to those whose status and power are subordinate.)

6. Linear vs. Looped Structure

Ordinarily each time a problem or its solution comes up for consideration it does so in the context of different competing problems and realities, with different persons present. Witness the change of context for the constitution from the executives to the December 7 meeting, or the changed context of the second constitution development from the Trinity council to the forum planning committee. A different constellation of persons and roles brings a different constellation of realities. Therefore, a problem integrated at one point in its transformation can be buried or emasculated at another point: if you want to ensure that your problem is considered cumulatively, and integrated with varying local realities, you must be on hand to re-explain and to consider necessary transformations that fit both your reality and the new realities. Provide loops and make sure they function to integrate your realities (which may also have changed since you first expressed your problem) with those of others: participate early, middle, and late and be open to integrating into your problem and solution others' realities that you thus encounter.

As you contemplate a given organizational problem and its possible solutions, think of yourself as being in a bubble, just big enough for you and your desk, a bubble that reminds you that in solving your problem you must depend on others, in their bubbles, to allow and to implement your solution. Remember that life in their bubble is just as demanding and absorbing to them, just as real, just as varied and boring as yours is to you and therefore that your solution may well seem as foreign to them as theirs sometimes does to you. Most importantly, when you contemplate a solution that requires their cooperation, whether you think it would be naturally forthcoming or not, it is well that you bring them into your problem early in your thinking, even when you have not thought it all out and think the matter quite unsettled. Doing that early, brings others into your bubble, a bubble that for a time belongs to you and them together. Exploring the problems they have with respect to various solutions of your problem (and vice versa), you come to know the local problems they are dealing with that are likely to compete with yours for their energies (and vice versa). When all constituents of a problem become aware of each other's problems in the solving of that problem, the reality that logically requires integrating for solving that problem well can at least have the opportunity to be integrated, an opportunity for creating working community.

7. Inclusionary vs. Exclusionary Conflict Management

Our culture, particularly our religious tradition, does not emphasize conflict of interests as a normal part of life — certainly not as a productive resource. But consider: if others' local realities are different from yours — and as you gain more positional authority the differences will increase — then the problems you synthesize also become more remote from theirs, as do your solutions and plans. Mere mundane problem-solving, therefore, brings you into conflict with others' realities, and them into conflict with yours. Straightforwardly implied, then, is that conflict is as mundane as is problem-solving in organizations.

Since your own and others' problems will ordinarily have antagonists, you know from the outset that as soon as you are aware of a problem — not a condition 'out there', remember, but an incompatibility in your own minding about out there, including *what you hope for* and therefore wholly accessible to your own knowledge — you also are aware that someone's (or some committee's) accustomed functioning will have to change if your problem is to be solved and the solution implemented. Knowing that virtually every problem will constitute also a conflict, you can begin immediately to create either an exclusionary environment for them or an inclusive one by making a choice. Either start solving it among your friends (or your department, your level of authority, etc.), *excluding the antagonists you know won't like it* or communicate at once with those antagonists about the problem and its potential for conflict. If your solution really does depend on their cooperation, then to ask for that cooperation after they discover that you have backed them into a corner, as Sr. Norma was when she first realized that the regional administrators had mobilized to examine her performance at Trinity, is to be blinded by wish. If you are dependent at any point on others who initially resist or don't seem to hear, dependent on them for going along with your solution in some way, then at that point of your dependence they actually have power over you, like it or not. So better integrate your dependence on them into your conflict management and include them immediately, thus including, incidentally, their added intellectual resources as well, in your problem-solving. Having then started inclusively, it will be much easier to continue inclusively, thereby doing what this book's narratives argue is basic: integrating the reality that you depend on — multiple, dispersed, problem-relevant and *other* — into 'your' action.

Attention to these seven accessible component variables may not be the most practical advice, however. The second way of thinking of practical applications has more to do with theory and wisdom than with separate dimensions of action. This second kind of advice focuses on central ideas. This outlook sees the practical importance of these variables as the understanding they give all together, as a whole. The key idea running through all of these variables is the idea that *organizational* reality that is accessible to you and me (1) is multiple, not single because (2) it operates in persons, rather than existing 'out there'. Organizational realities, therefore, are (3) dispersed, not concentrated in the minds of organizational leaders; are (4) relative, not absolute, differing with each different matter — thus requiring us to speak of realities with respect to specific problems; and therefore (5) are not integrated, but require integrating action. Organizational realities (6) become integrated, not in one head, cognitively, but collectively, through induction of shared problems which, in turn, creates an emergent problem-solving community. These six characteristics of organizational realities imply a seventh: that the basic, single, bed-rock variable of effective adaptation is integration vs. exclusion of local constituent realities into problem-solving action — into problems, solutions, plans, and implementing action. Integration of local constituent realities constrains coherence, cumulativity, and effectiveness of local adaptations.

Notes

1. To say 'unmanaged' does not imply random or irrational, as argued by Cohen, March, and Olsen (1972) and March and Olsen (1979). I comment below on their 'garbage can' theory of organizational choice.
2. Cameron and Whetten's (1983) seven guidelines for assessing organizational effectiveness are also suggestive for judging problem-solving episodes, and while they were not consistently addressed in the present study, the data of each episode allow their application. Their fifth item, time frame, is addressed in the last chapter of Part IV.
3. A further distinction is omitted here, between 'inside', positionally powerful third parties, like the regional administrators, and 'outside' third parties, like the federal mediators in labor-management disputes. That distinction is important, but since most conflicts in most organizations are solved from within, this restricted focus is useful.
4. Twenty-one rather than thirty-six, because only the diagonal and one set of off-diagonal cells in the six-by-six matrix are needed to characterize the possibilities. Table 29.1 is deceptively simple on two other counts. First, within the two cells of third-party involvement, the third parties themselves face the four strategic choices enumerated in the last four variables of Table 28.1 and, if more than one individual is recruited as a third party, as was the case with Sr. Jeanine and Sr. Georgette, they, too, may come into conflict among themselves, with their own twenty-one modes. Sr. Jeanine and Sr. Georgette did find themselves in conflict (see Chapter 12), but managed it cooperatively. On the other hand, when confronted with the fruits of their resolved conflict, the items of their settlement, and with the realization that an open, cooperative meeting among them and the two co-directors might lead Sr. Claudia to reject it impulsively, they managed their imagined conflict with Sr. Claudia exclusionarily, meeting with the two co-directors separately so they might 'cajole' Sr. Claudia.
5. It is useful to compare the foregoing idea of embeddedness of process within structure to Morton Deutsch's 'crude law of social relations' (Deutsch, 1973, p. 365): 'the characteristic processes and effects elicited by a given type of social relationship (cooperative or competitive) tend also to elicit that type of social relationship'. A circular, self-perpetuating structure and process is posited. The present study suggests some conditions under which this generalization would break down — not contradicting the 'law' but making it more useful by suggesting limits. First, the 'relationship' of Deutsch's law is dyadic and isolated from both a formal organization and an informal network of relations, thus ruling out resources organizations and networks provide for mitigating or reversing either inclusionary or exclusionary modes. One of those resources are third parties which, though

recruited in an exclusionary mode (as a coalition), have the power and choice to become inclusionary, as in some respects Sr. Georgette and Sr. Jeanine did become. Second, Deutsch's law ignores the possibility of independence-seeking and dissolving the relationship, as Sr. Norma was intent upon doing, thus breaking the perpetuation of competitive processes. It is only the minority of divorced couples, for example, that continue the exclusionary struggles characteristic of their married life. Most enter other, far more cooperative relationships. Sr. Claudia and Sr. Norma, for many years now, have had interchanges on professional issues marked by easy and open exchange, and none of the exclusionary struggle of the period we were at Trinity. An amendment to Deutsch's law, therefore might be: '. . . unless interventions from higher in the organization or elsewhere in the network of relations introduces a contrary strategy and unless either party decides to leave this relationship'.

Dean Pruitt (personal communication) suggests another amendment. He points out that labor and management disputes often escalate until both parties become 'scared' of future consequences of the path they are on. At some point, fear often takes over and brings the parties to the bargaining table for serious negotiation, with or without a third party. So the endless competitive spiral implied by Deutsch does have reversing possibilities, recognized and used in organizational and international conflicts. Still, Deutsch's crude law is a useful reminder that *unless* specific conditions are met, exclusionary (or inclusionary) modes, once established, will perpetuate themselves, to the detriment (or benefit) of both the individuals and their organizations.

6. This distinctive exchange also created special difficulties, as we have seen — difficulties of relationship, of data contamination and process disruption. The method builds on an important distinction between domains sensitive and insensitive to the power of a research-consultation to distort the normal processes being investigated. A distinction is made between observer effects (and absences of effect) at the level of particular acts during the time of their occurrence, and removed from the contents of problems being researched, on one hand, and effects at the level of cumulative problem solving and conflict management, over the duration of the whole problem transformation, on the other. This is a distinction between short-term isolated effects, separate from problems studied, on one hand, and long-term, cumulative effects upon problems studied, on the other.

    The method allows for consultation, during the period studied, concerning short-term problems whose specific content is remote from problem solving episodes then currently being studied. After the episodic data are gathered, consultation can be carried out regarding those very central episodes, or other matters, in which the more pervasive and cumulative problem-solving processes can be addressed. Interventions of rather different scope and impact, thus, can be carried out both during and after data gathering without jeopardizing the aims of research. The research part of the research-consultation exchange gains intimacy from the developing consultative relationship; and consultation gains empirical substance from the research.

7. We can also study organizational problem solving initiated by, and central to the interests of, members of particular professional groups — e.g., teachers, counselors, school social workers. In short, the method allows study of how any class of organization members moves its problems from the psychological level of problem through levels and roles of the organization.

8. Stable in this context meaning already 'balanced' in the sense of Heider (1958), Cartwright and Harary (1956), and Davis (1963).

9. Schank (1989) theorizes that narratives are more durable in memory than arguments presenting the logical 'points' or lessons of the narratives. Schank (personal

communication) also would argue on logical grounds that narratives would be more persuasive, would more easily induce action, than presentations setting forth the logical points or implicit arguments of the narratives. He reasons that the narrative's advantage over logical argument in inducing sympathetic action in a person is that the narrative gives the person the concrete data from which to draw his or her own conclusions.

Appendices

Appendix I

Dimensions of Operating Reality

Contents[a]

Directions and Standards

Goals, intentions, desires, wants, wishes
Values, beliefs

Constraints

Assessments and assumptions about:

    commitments, contracts, role, promises
    objective reality: impediments, resources; causes, effects; past, present, future conditions
    others' operating realities

        definite persons
        indefinite persons: 'they', 'the group'
    present task, role, or contract requirements

Monitorings, Evaluations

Assessments and assumptions about:

    contents of reality as positive-negative, liked-disliked
    current success-failure: outcomes less than, equal to, or more than expected, sought, or valued

[a] Contents or patterns of contents may be conscious or unconscious, and will be accompanied by varying degrees and kinds of emotional arousal.

Monitorings, Evaluations (continued)

personal skills, flaws, resources: less than, equal to, or more than requirements of present task or imminent task, role, commitment, or contract

importance of present task, role, contract, or commitment in relation to resource and energy demands or level of current success-failure

personal consequences: outcomes in relation to
Directions and Standards

opportunities relevant to fulfilling goals, values, commitments

Patterns of the Foregoing Contents

Resource-Mobilizing Patterns

Confusion, disorientation
Incompatible contents: problems (violated expectations, conflicts, 'dissonance')

Resource-Immobilizing Patterns

Ambivalence
Overload: multiple competing priorities

Appendix II

Organized Interventions Carried Out by Lighthall and Allan at Trinity

---

1. A two-hour workshop on November 23, 01 with Trinity council members. Sr. Catherine and one or two other faculty members attended (neither Sr. Norma nor Sr. Claudia attended), with mostly students. Eleven concerns about council functioning were identified and prioritized: most prominent was, 'Why are so many disenchanted with the council?' After some discussion, lengthy attention was given to students' concerns with the powers of 'the administration', chiefly Sr. Norma, to determine the council's direction. Then Allan, Patrick, and Lighthall presented a panel discussion of how successful council members were, or were not, in expressing concerns in the meeting that some had expressed earlier in the council office or elsewhere.

2. A two-hour workshop on November 30, 01 with Trinity council, attended by most students and faculty, including Sr. Norma. A segment of an earlier council meeting, discussing with the senior class officers their powers, was passed out and the tape played. After members noted their thoughts and feelings as they remembered experiencing them at the time, a compilation of each member's own comments at the meeting was given each member. The question then discussed in groups of four or five was the extent to which members had, indeed, been able to express relevant thoughts at the time. Open interviews with each group about their findings and conclusions provided details that were then discussed in the open council meeting.

3. An hour and a half workshop on January 11, 02 focused on 'problem analysis'. Paired members filled out sheets analyzing the goals, barriers, hoped-for-solutions, and problem 'locations' implicit in segments of two earlier Trinity council meetings, one referring to the writing of a constitution, the other to clarifying the powers of senior class officers. Discussion centered on the extent to which the Trinity council tended to be 'problem oriented' in its discussions or 'solution oriented'.

    The workshop ended with preparations for its next meeting. Brief written descriptions were offered and explained of several participation roles in groups like the council — e.g., 'goal identifier', 'barrier identifier', 'solution identifier', 'resister', 'passive accepter'. Members volunteered to take the various roles in the Trinity council's next meeting on January 18, 01. In that January 18 meeting no discernable effect was noticed of any role playing on the discussion process or content.

4. On May 16, 02 Allan led a two and a half hour review of an episode of problem-solving involving 43 events over the period from the spring of 01, a year earlier, to mid-April. Virtually all members were there, but Sr. Claudia, who had played an important role early in the year, was not. The episodic review traced how supervision of the school's four lunchroom periods each day became transferred by the executives from the faculty to the Trinity council, and was delegated by the council to a cafeteria committee, which consisted, in the end, of a single junior girl, Donna Laughton. Members attending the review interpreted the events and the motives behind them in lively, sometimes heated discussion, and found the workshop to be the most engaging of any.

5. In late May, 02 Lighthall met individually with Sr. Catherine and Sr. Claudia, who had expressed interest in having him comment in any way that might be helpful on their administrative actions during that year. Each of these two sessions lasted about an hour, and focused on each sister's personal style of communication and participation in the executive meetings.